MARKETING
LIFE AND HEALTH INSURANCE

Edited by
Nancy E. Strickler, FLMI

FLMI Insurance Education Program
Life Management Institute LOMA
100 Colony Square, Atlanta, Georgia 30361

The Life Office Management Association is a research and educational association of life insurance companies operating in the United States, Canada and a number of other countries. Among its activities is the sponsorship of an educational program intended primarily for home office and branch office employees of these companies.

The FLMI Insurance Education Program is comprised of two courses—Course I (Parts 1 and 2), "Fundamentals of Life Insurance," and Course II (Parts 3 through 9), "Advanced Life Insurance." Upon the completion of Course I, the student is awarded a Certificate. Upon the completion of both courses (nine parts), the student is designated a Fellow of the Life Management Institute (FLMI) and is awarded a Diploma.

ISBN 0-915322-47-1

Library of Congress Catalog Card Number: 81-83848

Printed in the United States of America

Preface

Every industry has an identity—a character or personality which serves as its mark. For some industries that identity is with research; for others, it is with manufacturing, or construction, or transportation. For the life and health insurance industry, that identity is a concern for people and for their financial security. This identification with people is inextricably linked with the marketing function of insurance companies. For marketing is the function that deals with people, the function primarily concerned with defining the public's needs, with developing products to meet those needs, and with delivering those products in an efficient manner.

The extent of life and health insurance marketing is impressive. In the United States, over 144 million persons are covered by legal reserve life insurance companies; 177 million persons are covered by private health insurance plans. In Canada, over 12 million persons own life insurance. To reach the public, insurers use a variety of distribution systems: career agents, brokers, all-lines agents, home service, and direct response. Each of these distribution systems is supported by market research, planning, organizing, and promotional activities.

This new book has been developed to serve as text material for the "Marketing Life and Health Insurance" part of the FLMI Insurance Education Program, and also to serve as a general reference within the industry. It represents the first comprehensive study of life and health insurance marketing. This book covers the vital role of marketing within the overall operations of an insurance company, the range of distribution systems, and the activities necessary to support those systems.

A project this ambitious was made possible only by the contributions of the individual authors, distinguished within the industry and academia. These authors gave their time and expertise to developing the contents of this book.

We wish to express our appreciation to Robert A. Marshall, Ph.D., CLU, Florida State University, for his guidance in developing Part III.

We would like to extend special thanks to Brian E. Wrixon, CLU, Superintendent of Agencies, Training and Development, Confederation Life Insurance Company, for his role in reviewing the entire manuscript from the standpoint of marketing in Canada; and Linda S. Benedict, Director of Marketing and Strategic Planning, Reinsurance Division, Connecticut General Life Insurance Company, for her active guidance in developing several of the chapters. We are also grateful for the contributions of Steve Cooperstein, F.S.A., Vice President, Long-Range Strategic Planning, Metropolitan Life Insurance Company; Jacquelyn E. Siminitus, Manager of Business Planning, Homeowners, Colonial Penn Insurance Company; and Tom Twaiten, CLU, Manager, Editorial Services, Agency Department, Pacific

Mutual Life Insurance Company, who gave substantial input to certain chapters.

We gratefully acknowledge the reviews of: Eric C. Bacon, FLMI, The Independent Order of Foresters; J. F. Bryan, IV, The Independent Life & Accident Insurance Company; Hugh B. Campbell, Jr., Phoenix Mutual Life Insurance Company; Charles B. Cooper, FLMI, CLU, American Income Life Insurance Company; Joe Cooper, Great American Reserve Insurance Company; Raymond Constantino, Independent Life and Accident Insurance Company; Richard C. Dole, FLMI, State Mutual Life Assurance Company; Edward A. Fish, CLU, Aetna Life Insurance Company; Ann H. Gilbert, Bankers Security Life Insurance Company; Lawrence J. Graff, INA; Matthew Greenwald, Ph.D., American Council of Life Insurance; C. J. A. Hamilton, Great-West Life Assurance Company; William M. Hamilton, CLU, FLMI, Prudential Insurance Company of America; Richard Henlotter, Metropolitan Life Insurance Company; Samuel S. Keyes, Aetna Life and Casualty; Fred G. Kirtland, CLU, Security Mutual Life Insurance Company; Paul Kormanick, J.D., CLU, Midland Mutual Life Insurance Company; Eugene S. Koster, CLU, Acacia Mutual Life Insurance Comapny; Kenneth A. LaSorella, FLMI, ASA, Sun Life Assurance Company of Canada; Warren Lutz, The Travelers Insurance Company; Ray E. Mauger, Savings Bank Life Insurance Fund (New York); Steve McHugh, National Life and Accident Insurance Company; Mike Oliver, Life Insurance Company of Georgia; James J. O'Donnell, FLMI, CLU, CPCU, State Farm Life Insurance Company; James Rice, Liberty National Life Insurance Company; Hugh K. Rickenbaker, Life Insurance Company of Georgia; Irene Schultz, The Mutual Life Insurance Company of New York; C. L. Trowbridge, Ph.D., The University of Michigan; William H. Woods, CLU, FLMI, Washington National Insurance Company; Cyrus G. Wurster, Aid Association for Lutherans; David N. Young, CLU, Aetna Life and Casualty Company.

The following organizations have also been cooperative in the development of this book: the American Council of Life Insurance (ACLI); the Canadian Life and Health Insurance Association (CLHIA); the Life Insurers Conference (LIC); and the Life Insurance Marketing and Research Association (LIMRA), who supplied us with their *Report on Distribution Systems* which was used extensively in the development of Part III.

I wish to thank several members of the LOMA staff who were invaluable in their reviews and editorial assistance: Margaret M. Walsh, Mary A. Alexander, Lynn Ganim, Harriett E. Jones, Robert G. Knowles, Judy B. Rich, and William R. Weston. For his ideas and continuing support throughout the project, I wish to express my sincere appreciation to William H. Rabel.

The authors, reviewers, and other contributors participated in developing this book as a service to the life and health insurance industry and to its public. I am grateful to each of them for their assistance.

Nancy E. Strickler, FLMI

Atlanta, Georgia

Contents

Associate Editor: Robert A. Marshall, Ph.D., CLU, Professor and Chairman of Department of Risk Management and Insurance, College of Business, Florida State University

Contributing Authors:

Bobo, Jack E., CLU, FLMI, Executive Vice President, National Association of Life Underwriters

Boeckner, R. G., FSA, FCIA, MAAA, Vice President, Director of Administration, Crown Life Insurance Company

Bubb, Harry G., CLU, President, Pacific Mutual Life Insurance Company

Dowsett, R. C., FSA, FCIA, MAAA, President, Crown Life Insurance Company

Eichhoff, Darrell D., CLU, Executive Vice President (Ret.), Metropolitan Life Insurance Company

Hetrick, David L., CLU, Senior Vice President, Bankers Life Insurance Company of Nebraska

Johnson, Richard E., Ph.D., Executive Secretary, American Risk and Insurance Association, Inc., Department of Risk Management and Insurance, The University of Georgia

Marshall, Robert A., Ph.D., CLU, Professor and Chairman of Department of Risk Management and Insurance, College of Business, Florida State University

Otis, Kenneth C., II, Executive Vice President, Colonial Penn Life Insurance Company

Palmer, Bruce A., Ph.D., CLU, Associate Professor of Insurance, Department of Insurance, Georgia State University

Pepper, Philip R., MBA, CLU, Vice President–Marketing, United States (Ret.), The Canada Life Assurance Company

Rabel, William H., Ph.D., FLMI, CLU, Vice President and Director, Life Management Institute, Life Office Management Association

Rubin, Harvey W., Ph.D., CLU, Assistant Vice President and Director of Marketing Research, Life Insurance Company of Virginia

Ruth, William J., Jr., FLMI, President, Kennesaw Life and Accident Insurance Company

Seward, Harry P., FLMI, CLU, Chairman, Bankers Life Insurance Company of Nebraska

Skipper, Harold, Jr., Ph.D., CLU, Associate Professor of Insurance, Department of Insurance, Georgia State University

Smith, C. Carney, CLU, Former President and Retired Executive Vice President, National Association of Life Underwriters

Stinton, John E., D.B.A., CLU, Professor of Insurance, College of Business Administration, University of South Carolina

Sullivan, Frank E., CLU, President, Mutual Benefit Life Insurance Company

Webb, Guy E., Jr., CLU, Senior Vice President–Marketing, Life Insurance Company of Virginia

Williams, William G., Director, Health Care Relations, Provident Mutual Life Insurance Company

PART I

INSURANCE MARKETING AND ITS ENVIRONMENT

Chapter 1

Introduction to Life and Health Insurance Marketing

C. Carney Smith, CLU
William H. Rabel, Ph.D., FLMI, CLU

The universally recognized economic law that all economic values ultimately arise out of human resources or human life values is the foundation on which the life and health insurance industry has been built.[1] The purpose of life and health insurance is to indemnify individuals, families, and firms against the financial losses that result when human resources are impaired or destroyed. This is an extremely important and noble responsibility in our society. Unfortunately, despite an apparent awareness of the value of insurance, consumers do not customarily initiate the purchase of enough insurance to meet their needs; because of this hesitance, society's need for protection against such financial loss will not be met unless insurance is actively and effectively marketed.

The goal of this book is to assist in improving the marketing process in life and health insurance companies by explaining the principles of life and health insurance marketing. The text strives to provide a bridge between the home office and field offices by explaining how they are intimately linked in the marketing function. It should also stimulate further thought about ways in which private insurance can be used to meet the economic security needs of individuals and business.

In its fullest sense, marketing is the function by which consumers' needs are determined, products and services are designed, and delivery (including sales) and support systems are activated to ensure that consumers' needs are

---

[1] See page 12 for an explanation of the human life value concept.

met at prices which are acceptable in a competitive environment. Fundamentally, marketing follows the same principles in all industries; however, these principles must be adapted to the unique circumstances of the life and health insurance industry. Over the years, many individuals both inside and outside of the industry have treated marketing as being synonymous with sales. Thus, it is important at the outset to distinguish between the two concepts. A sale is the step in which the client makes a purchase; it is the last phase in the marketing process, as well as the most visible and measurable. At the same time, the amount and quality of sales depends in many ways on the other activities that are carried out in a company. Stated another way, every element of a company's operations has a marketing dimension that influences sales.

Although marketing is an important (and, therefore serious) subject, it is far from a somber one. Many would agree that marketing is the most exciting and dynamic aspect of the life insurance business. In seeking to identify and satisfy the ever-shifting needs and desires of the public, a company must constantly review and revise its products and operations. Only by continually reevaluating its marketing process can a company hope to maintain its market position, much less enter new markets.

This book is based on the premise that marketing is an organic function that touches every unit in a life insurance company in some way. However, the book does not delve into every activity that takes place in a company, even though the authors recognize that sound operations present a favorable image and support the marketing effort in many other ways. These are indirect marketing influences and are touched only briefly here, when discussed at all. Instead, the book concentrates on those matters that are *directly* involved in the marketing function. It begins in this first chapter with an overview of (1) the role of insurance and (2) certain basic considerations in marketing it as a means for protecting human life values. The second chapter explains life and health insurance marketing functions and marketing plans. Chapters 3 and 4 provide an analysis of the environment within which life and health insurance are marketed. Subsequent chapters analyze the activities, processes, and procedures involved in activating and operating the plan. The final chapter looks at the challenges and opportunities ahead.

As a first step, a helpful perspective will be provided by reviewing the role of the three main systems that provide economic security to society. These systems, known as the "three pillars of economic security," evolved to deal with the perils of premature death, disability, old age, and unemployment that threaten an individual's earning power. These perils, and the way insurance deals with them, will be discussed after the three pillars of economic security have been described.

Three Pillars of Economic Security

In developed economies (such as the United States, Canada, Western Europe, and Japan), as well as in many less-developed countries, three basic systems have been established to deal with the economic threat of the four basic perils of premature death, disability, supperannuation (old age), and unemployment. Often referred to as the three pillars of economic security, these systems are (1) individual insurance, (2) employee benefit plans, and (3) social security (including social insurance and other income maintenance plans).

Anyone involved in the marketing of life and health insurance should understand these three systems and the ways in which they work together to provide economic security. Equally important, the **marketing manager**[2] must have a feel for ever-evolving relationships among the three pillars. These patterns and trends will have an important effect on the amount and type of insurance purchased today and in the future. Failure to develop an understanding of the three systems will result in a high level of frustration for individuals involved in the marketing process and a waste of resources as the company tries to determine its role in the marketplace as a provider of economic security.

Individual Insurance

Least complex and best understood of the three systems is individual insurance. In its simplest form, individual insurance is a voluntary agreement between a company and an individual in which the insurer promises to pay the insured, or someone designated by the insured, a predetermined amount if the peril insured against occurs. The insurer evaluates the risk and charges a premium for its guarantee of protection. In practice, the business of individual insurance is often very complex due to the nature of the risk, the peril insured against, the hazard involved, or broad societal requirements that influence the insurer–insured relationship. However, the direct relationship between the insured (or policyowner) and the insurer (the organization providing the protection) remains.

Employee Benefit Plans

A second pillar, employee benefit plans, comprises economic security plans that are provided through, and paid for fully or in part by, employers, or that arise out of the employment relationship. Here the insurer also evaluates the risk and charges a premium for its guarantee of protection, but the direct relationship is between the insurer and the employer (rather than the em-

[2] The term **marketing manager** refers to anyone involved in the marketing function who makes decisions about marketing. It does not refer to a particular position in an organization unless the context indicates that such a reference is intended.

ployee who is the insured). Typically these plans make use of the group insurance underwriting mechanism, since group insurance is a major element of employee benefit plans. The scope, depth, and flexibility of employee benefit plans has increased significantly since the first group life coverages were underwritten early in the century. Today they offer a vast array of benefits, and some experts suggest that the "cafeteria approach," in which employees can choose the combination of features that best meets their needs, may become widely used in the future.[3]

Although both individual and group insurance coverage have enjoyed favorable growth over the years, of the two, group coverage in force has grown most rapidly. Table I compares the growth of group and individual life insurance in Canada and the United States during the past half century. Throughout this period there has been a clear and unwavering trend toward group insurance as a means of providing a financial solution to problems of premature death. Although there are a few exceptions to this rule, a similar pattern is found in most countries of the world for which data are available. A sample of the experience outside Canada and the United States is found in Table II. In those countries where the growth of group insurance is not outstripping individual insurance, typically there is a strong financial incentive to purchase individual insurance—such as favorable income tax policy. In some countries the growth of the group sector is limited by the existence of broad benefits provided by government programs.

In the United States, group health insurance is even more pervasive than group life insurance. Table III shows that as early as 1950 group health benefit payments (which closely correspond to premiums) were 58% of the total health insurance payments. This contrasts with a group life premium share of 16% and 21% respectively in Canada and the United States in the same year. Because of the broad coverage provided under government plans, health insurance is much less developed in Canada and many other countries than in the United States.

Social Security

By far the fastest growing system in the post World War II era has been the third pillar, commonly known as social security. This system, in the domain of the public, rather than the private sector, is comprised of social insurance, social assistance, and public service plans. These three plans are designed to provide a basic, or threshold, level of financial security for a society and may include many types of benefits. **Social insurance plans** typically provide one

[3] "Companies Offer Benefits Cafeteria Style," *Business Week* (November 13, 1978), p. 116.

TABLE I
Individual and Group Life Insurance in Force in Canada and the United States: 1930–1979
(000,000 omitted)

Year	Canada				United States			
	Individual		Group		Individual		Group	
	Amount	% of Total	Amount	% of Total	Amount	% of Total	Amount	% of Total
1930	$ 6,010	93	$ 428	7	$ 96,539	91	$ 9,801	9
1940	6,310	90	731	10	100,212	87	14,938	13
1950	13,614	84	2,615	16	182,531	79	47,793	21
1960	32,128	69	14,739	31	381,444	68	175,903	32
1970	62,845	53	55,977	47	773,374	58	551,357	42
1980	177,915	41	253,279	59	1,760,474	53	1,579,355	47

Sources: *1980 Life Insurance Fact Bcok,* American Council of Life Insurance.
Canadian Life Insurance Facts, 1980, Canadian Life Insurance Association.

TABLE II
Share of Group Insurance in Total Life Insurance in Force in Selected Countries 1960–1976

Country	1960	1968	1976
France	54%	64%	81%
West Germany	15%	11%	11%
Great Britain	47%	44%	46%
Japan	14%	16%	37%
Mexico	13%	53%	60%
Switzerland	34%	51%	61%

Source: *Sigma,* North American Reinsurance Company, No. 3/March 1978.

TABLE III
Individual and Group Health Insurance Benefit Payments in the United States 1950–1978
(000,000 omitted)

	Individual and Family Policies		Group Policies	
Year	Amount	% of Total Payments	Amount	% of Total Payments
1950	$ 317	42	$ 438	58
1955	533	30	1,252	70
1960	719	23	2,350	77
1965	1,160	22	4,000	78
1970	1,613	18	7,476	82
1975	2,279	14	14,191	86
1978	3,484	13	22,868	87

Source: *1980–1981 Source Book of Health Insurance Data,* Health Insurance Association of America, p. 22.

or more of the following benefits: protection for survivors against premature death of the breadwinner, medical expense and disability coverage, and retirement benefits. Most authorities agree that social insurance is a social security program having the following features:

1. Compulsory coverage is required by law.
2. Allocated taxes are paid by or on behalf of the covered individual, and these contributions cover most or all of the cost of the program.

3. Benefits are paid as a matter of right—not of need.
4. Standards for determining benefit amounts and eligibility are set forth in the law.
5. Benefits are not usually related directly to contributions, emphasizing social adequacy over individual equity, and therefore may redistribute income and/or wealth.
6. There is a definite plan of financing which is designed to be adequate in the long run.
7. The program is administered or supervised by the government.
8. Coverage under the plan is not solely for government employees.

Social assistance and public service plans vary to a much greater degree than does social insurance, and benefits have included cash grants, food, housing, medical care, and a wide range of social services.

Social assistance programs, often referred to as public assistance, are social security plans with the following general features: (1) recipients of benefits must prove that the benefits are needed; (2) benefits are funded from the general fund not by taxes earmarked for that purpose; (3) benefit amounts are adjusted to meet the needs of the individual's financial situation.

Public service plans, sometimes called universal benefit programs, contain some features found in both social assistance and social insurance programs. Like the former, they provide predetermined benefits to set categories of persons (such as families with children). However, they are funded through general revenues as are public assistance plans. No effort is made to set up special taxes to guarantee the benefits.

The Role of Social Security

The fact that social security systems have attained some level of acceptance in virtually every country in the world attests to their broad appeal. The first type of social security plan to appear was social assistance, the modern versions of which have their roots in the poor laws of seventeenth century northwestern Europe. These were fostered by the economic conditions brought about by the beginnings of industrial revolution, and have been regarded by many as a public counterpart for private charity. Public service plans, which presume a need for benefits by all members of a particular group (such as families with dependent children) are financed from general revenues. They are the most recent arrival on the scene, having made their appearance primarily in the post-World War II era. Although public service plans have not generally been adopted in North America, they are well established in several developed countries, most notably in Great Britain and the Scandinavian region.

Social insurance programs, which are the foundation of the third pillar (social security) in North America, first appeared in Germany in the 1880s. They enjoyed steady growth over the years. However, like public service, these programs have achieved their greatest growth in the post-war decades. Undoubtedly the economic trauma of the 1930s provided the impetus to establish social insurance systems. However, few would disagree that the growth of such systems has been facilitated by the high degree of flexibility in the actuarial methods applied to them, as compared with those that are required for private insurance.

The private sector is charged with providing financial security through individual and group approaches for benefits above the threshold level. Some observers have been concerned that the expansion of social security programs might continue indefinitely, and ultimately squeeze out the private sector. For example, the degree to which social insurance has grown in the United States in the recent past is illustrated in Figure 1. In 1960, just over 40% of security expenditures were paid to the government. By 1970, the

FIGURE 1
Percent Distribution of Security Expenditures by Type of Recipient

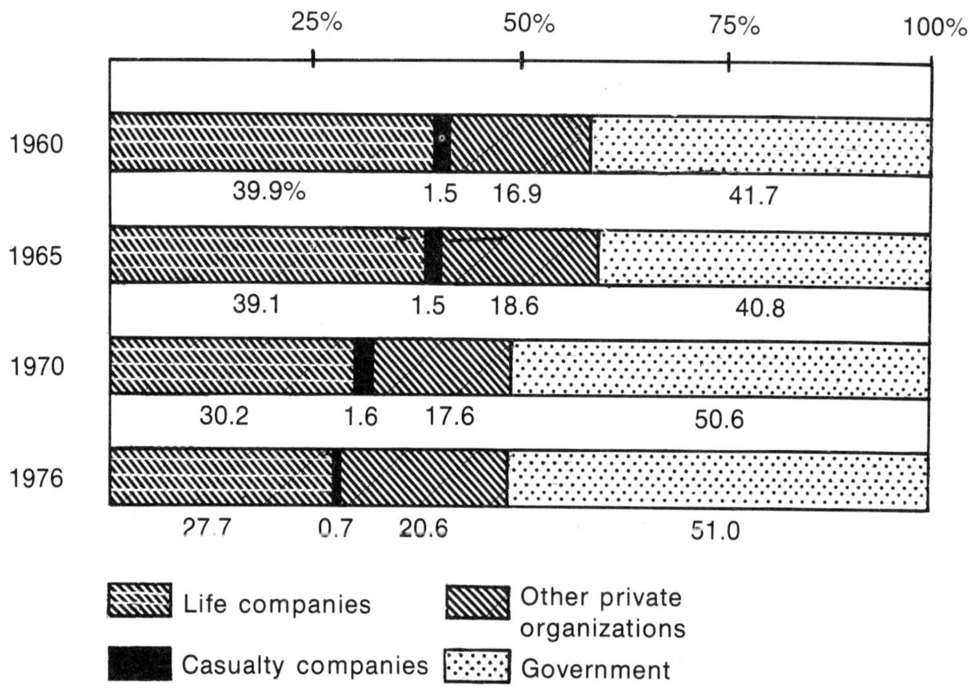

Source: *Security Expenditures in the United States: 1960–1976,* Research Report 1978-2. Life Insurance Marketing and Research Association (1978, Hartford, Connecticut), p. 13.

government commanded over 50% of the total, and its portion increased slightly through 1976. The growth of government's role is even more startling when it is recognized that as late as 1940 the government was receiving less than 10% of total security dollars.[4] However, there appears to be a general trend toward reassessing the role of the public sector, and this reassessment undoubtedly will influence the growth and development of social security systems in the years ahead.

Today, and for the foreseeable future, all planning for economic security begins with a review of benefits available under social insurance and public service plans. These benefits form the foundation upon which benefits from group and individual plans may be added as appropriate. Public assistance is not usually involved in planning, because the requirement of showing need implies that all private sources have been exhausted. It is therefore treated as a final "safety net" against economic insecurity, assuming all other public and private measures fail.

While social security systems provide a basic layer of economic security, only through private insurance plans is it possible to tailor protection plans to meet the particular needs of individuals, families, and firms. To a degree, customizing is possible through the use of private employee benefit plans, but it is through the use of individual life and health insurance and annuities that protection can be most effectively matched against potential losses from premature death, disability, and superannuation.[5] An important part of the marketing challenge is to determine the best mix of social insurance, employee benefit plans, and individual insurance in meeting consumer needs.

Marketing decisions must reflect a good understanding of the relationships among the three pillars of economic security; however, a detailed study of all the specific systems is beyond the scope of this book. This text will be concerned only with individual insurance and employee benefit plans—which together make up the private sector involvement in life and health insurance. Thus, it is important to review the consumer needs that life and health insurance are designed to meet.

Needs Met by Life and Health Insurance and Annuities

Insurance companies do not create needs in people, but simply satisfy the needs that already exist. All people face the problems of premature death, retirement, and at least a temporary disability. Individuals, families, and businesses all need protection against the loss of earning power due to the

[4] Davis W. Gregg, *Life and Health Insurance Handbook* (1973, Homewood, Illnois, Richard D. Irwin), p. 10.

[5] The first line of defense against the financial consequences of unemployment is usually a social security program. When unemployment is handled by the private sector, it usually is dealt with most effectively through non-insurance techniques. Therefore, it will not be discussed in this book.

three perils. This section will look at these needs individually in some detail, since they provide the *raison d'etre* of the insurance business.

Premature Death

Premature death affects the financial security of both families and businesses. Life insurance is bought not because some die prematurely, but because the survivors must live. Every day millions of people die without warning. They are young, old, rich, and poor, of all races, religions, and ethnic backgrounds. They will leave bills and taxes to be paid. Their dependents will need food, shelter, clothing, education, and other necessities. Even though death cannot be prevented, life insurance can protect an individual's dependents from the potential loss of income that premature death brings. It can replace the earning power of the breadwinner and sustain the quality of life that his or her dependents have known. In the absence of life insurance, many apparently well-to-do families would simply be unable to meet the need for liquidity that is imposed by taxes on the transfer of an estate from one generation to the next.

Many studies have attempted to determine the amount of life insurance needed, and two equally valid approaches have been developed. The **human life value approach,** brought into prominence by Dr. Solomon S. Huebner, capitalizes the future earnings that the breadwinner will devote to dependents if his or her working life is not cut short. Alternatively, the **needs approach** capitalizes the lump sum and income needs that survivors will face if the breadwinner dies. If both approaches are applied with full accuracy, they will yield the same amount, but in practice the needs approach is the easier of the two to use. One of its great strengths is that it lends itself to estate planning because it focuses on identifiable items which can be translated easily into financial needs.

In addition to being of great value to families, life insurance is needed by businesses.[6] A partnership (or closely held corporation) with no provision for the death of one owner, may run into significant problems when one owner dies and the deceased owner's interest in the business passes to his or her heirs.[7] Life insurance is widely used to fund agreements under which a

---

[6] For an extensive treatment of this topic, see *Business Insurance* by E. H. White and H. Chasman, 5th edition (Englewood Cliffs, N.J., Prentice-Hall, 1980).

[7] Among the problems that may arise in the absence of a properly drawn and funded buy-sell agreement are:

a. The business must be sold or liquidated (required for partnerships in many jurisdictions).
b. The surviving owner buys the business (where permissible) but must negotiate terms and raise funds in a stressful situation.

surviving owner buys the interest of one who is deceased. Thus, the heirs obtain a fair, liquid value for their interest, and the surviving business owner is free to continue the business on an unencumbered basis.

Businesses also need to be indemnified in the event that a key employee dies or becomes disabled. Many firms, especially those that are small or medium-sized, rely heavily on the contribution of one or a few persons. These key people are difficult to replace, and insurance can be purchased to cover both the potential earnings loss and the development costs for the replacement employee.

Disability

When an individual is sick or injured, health insurance provides protection against the costs associated with an accident or sickness in the form of medical expense coverage. In addition, when an individual is prevented from working because of sickness or injury, another form of health insurance, disability income insurance, protects against the subsequent loss of income. Businesses can also be affected by their employees' disabilities. Therefore, to an ever-increasing extent, business uses of health insurance are being developed to parallel the business uses of life insurance.

Originally, health insurance was pioneered by casualty insurance companies, who are still active in certain lines—particularly those lines paying fixed-sum cash benefits to persons who are hospitalized or who meet some other easily determined standard of disability. These firms, and specialty insurers that write only one or a few types of health policies, are in vigorous competition with life insurance companies that also sell medical expense and disability income plans. A variety of other plans that contain some or all of the features of insurance are also found in the health field, including Blue Cross and Blue Shield plans and health maintenance organizations (HMOs). Furthermore, insurance companies are developing their own nontraditional approaches to providing health coverage, which also modify or omit some standard features of insurance. Many of these plans will be discussed in later chapters.

Superannuation

Superannuation, or old age, is a peril in that individuals are concerned that they will not have adequate incomes throughout their retirement years.

---

c. The heirs of the deceased receive income with little contribution to (or possible negative impact on) the going concern.
d. Heirs sell the deceased's share to untested outsiders and surviving owners must work with the outsiders.
e. Survivors are "frozen out."

Individuals fear the loss of financial independence that retirement can bring and question the ability of social security to provide an adequate threshold level.

Important as planning for the peril of superannuation is today, many signs indicate that it may become even more important in the future. One significant reason is the aging of the population itself. The percentage of people over age 65 has increased continuously, and many authorities predict that the shift will continue for decades to come. Table IV shows one set of projections. The population shift will cause an increase in the ratio between retired and working members of our population, which poses many serious challenges to our society, even beyond North America. It will be interesting to observe the various approaches that are developed to provide for the retired sectors of our population.

Although a number of factors account for the growth of private pension plans, one particularly important factor in several Western countries has been a public policy that encourages private saving for retirement.[8] This has resulted in a high level of competition among financial institutions for the security dollars that flow into pension plans. Insurers face competition primarily from commercial banks. Today, life companies control about 33% of private pension funds in the United States. This is down markedly from

TABLE IV
Projections of the Population Aged 65 or Older in the United States: 1980–2050
(000 omitted)

Year	Number	% of Total Population
1980	24,927	11.22
2000	31,822	12.22
2020	45,103	15.55
2040	54,925	17.81
2050	55,493	17.58

Source: Bureau of the Census, U.S. Department of Commerce, "Estimates and Projections of the Population: 1977–2050," Current Population Reports, Series P-25, No. 704, July 1977.

[8] For an extensive treatment of factors encouraging the growth of private pensions in North America, see *Fundamentals of Private Pensions* by Dan M. McGill (Homewood, Illinois, Richard D. Irwin, 1977).

the all-time high of 48% that was theirs just after World War II. However, the percentage has remained relatively stable during the past two decades. At the same time, the proportion of persons covered by insured plans has actually increased, as is shown in Table V. The improved competitive stance is due in large part to the high level of innovation that has been achieved by insurance companies in the past two decades. Among the products which have helped life companies compete with other institutions have been separate accounts, immediate participation guarantee contracts, and a variety of individual annuity policies that combine good rates of return with a tax-sheltered investment accumulation.

Each of the three needs described above presents an opportunity for life insurance companies to serve the public well and still make a profit. These needs represent markets for billions of dollars of coverage; and, despite the current size and financial strength of the industry, many would argue that life companies have only scratched the surface of serving these needs. All of the needs not met by social security (and possibly some that are) are candidates for solutions through employee benefit plans and individual coverage. The amount of money involved is staggering.

TABLE V
Estimated Number and Proportion of Persons Covered by Insured and Uninsured Pension Plans in the United States: 1940–1975
(000 omitted)

Year	Insured Pension Plans*		Uninsured Pension Plans*		Total
	Number	% of Total	Number	% of Total	
1940	695	16	3,565	84	4,260
1945	1,470	22	5,240	78	6,710
1950	2,755	27	7,500	73	10,225
1960	5,475	24	17,540	76	23,015
1970	10,580	29	25,520	71	36,100
1975	15,190	33	30,300	67	45,490

Note: Due to statistical discrepancies, this table constitutes a broad estimate only.

* Insured pension plans are those funded with life insurance companies; uninsured plans include all others.

Source: *1980 Life Insurance Fact Book.* American Council of Life Insurance.

The Distinguishing Features of Life and Health Insurance

In order to be a successful marketer, it is important to understand the distinguishing features of life and health insurance themselves. Although there are no formulas which guarantee survival or growth for a particular life and health insurance company in a free enterprise economy, certain guidelines and principles enhance the possibility of success in marketing. These have been tested in all kinds of markets and are set forth in subsequent chapters. The techniques of life and health insurance marketing will be grasped more easily if there is an understanding of the features which distinguish them from those of other products and services.

Insurance Products are Intangibles

The intangible nature of life and health insurance products is a unique characteristic that makes them difficult to market. Unlike goods, such as automobiles, dishwashers, and clothing, insurance cannot be seen, held, heard, smelled, or tasted; it is a service, not a tangible product. True enough, it is represented by a contract, but that does no more than express the relationship between the insured and the insurer—the paper containing the contract is not the insurance *per se*. Furthermore, although insurance pays tangible dollars or other types of benefits, these are the products of the protection rather than the protection itself. The lack of physical substance means that the consumer must make a purchase solely on the basis of an appreciation of a service to be performed, and it is often hard to instill this appreciation in the public.

Payments Are Based on a Contingency

A related feature is that, since benefits are paid only on the happening of a contingency (for example, premature death), insurance may never be called upon to pay off at all. Lack of certainty about the time and (in some cases) the amount of payment makes it difficult for some people to understand the value of protection. Ironically, it is the unpredictability of loss that makes insurance such a valuable economic tool. If losses were predictable, then other risk management devices such as loss funding would be far more appropriate than insurance in most cases.

Insurance Is a Technical Service

Still another reason why life and health insurance are difficult to market is that they are rather technical and consequently are hard for the average buyer to understand. For this reason, consumer education is a very important aspect of the marketing function today. In times past, if life and health contracts contained certain safeguards protecting the public interest, this was considered by most makers of public policy to be a sufficient substitute for public understanding. Today, however, the prevalent view is that consumers should have a full understanding of the coverage they are buying. With this in mind, policy wordings have been simplified and made more readable. At the same time, underwriting and other practices have been subjected to greater public scrutiny, which gives the public an opportunity to learn more about the industry. Nevertheless, a large number of persons still consider insurance to be too complex to understand, and this attitude constitutes a barrier to the sale of coverage.

Consumers Resist Insurance Purchases

Life and health insurance represent a unique challenge to the marketing manager. Many consumers recognize that they need insurance, but do not necessarily seek to buy it. It is generally believed that insurance coverage is "sold not bought." Although there is a difference of opinion about the validity of this belief,[9] there is no question that insurance must be marketed vigorously.[10] Why is this? In part, the answer to this and related questions can be suggested by an examination of consumer attitudes toward insurance.

Procrastination

A barrier to the purchase of life insurance, as well as other products, is procrastination by potential buyers. People put off decisions, particularly those that involve a long-term commitment of money. Even when an insurance decision can be delayed no longer, it is often easier to satisfy today's wants than tomorrow's needs. Long-term economic security needs are frequently subordinated to other more immediate needs, such as a new car or better clothing.

A Mistrust of Institutions

A mistrust of institutions on the part of consumers also creates a barrier which marketing managers must overcome. The root causes of this condition may be inherent in human beings, because a healthy dose of skepticism toward institutions is found throughout history. In the case of life insurance, the agent often bears the brunt of public mistrust, because most individual insurance is sold through agents. However, any employee in policyowner service, or other areas of company operations that deal with the public, is fully aware of the anxiety most people feel towards institutions.

---

[9] "Ever since 1928 . . . , LIMRA has periodically reported that according to consumers, anywhere from 20 percent to 40 percent of all sales are buyer-initiated." (LIMRA, Memorandum concerning *Buyer-Initiated Sales and Agency System Research Report, 1979-4,* May 10, 1979).

[10] Again, it is important to distinguish between sales and marketing. See page 4.

Avoidance of Unpleasant Thoughts

A final and perhaps most important challenge to marketing managers is the psychological reservations that inhibit people from thinking about insurance and the perils that it protects against. Human beings simply do not like to think about the fact that they must die some day and should be prepared for that event. By the same token, they are made uncomfortable by the thought of being disabled, perhaps through a painful accident or lingering sickness. These and related fears can keep consumers from taking a rational approach in dealing with the perils that face them.

Differentiation in Life and Health Insurance Marketing

The features and consumer reactions described above constitute barriers to the sale of life and health insurance which the marketing manager must overcome. Still another problem is that consumers have great difficulty in distinguishing one life and health insurance company or product from another. Therefore, differentiation becomes an essential element of the marketing plan.

Differentiation is the process by which a company sets itself and/or its products apart from its competitors. In effect, a perceived difference gives consumers a reason to purchase one product over another. Differentiation is particularly important in an industry in which products are perceived by consumers as being identical, as often is the case with life and health insurance.

Because insurance is an intangible or service product, it is inseparable from the company that sells it. The perceived value of the product is much more often associated with the ability and ethics of the company than is true for many tangible products. After all, the buyer of physical goods may examine them before buying to make sure that they work at least at the time they are bought. However, no evaluation of insurance protection is possible until after it is owned, and even then, it may be years until a true evaluation can be made. Therefore, consumers tend to value that protection on the basis of company reputation and ability. This feature has an important impact on differentiation of insurance as well as on other aspects of the business such as solvency and consumer protection. Life insurance companies must develop ways to differentiate themselves and their products from their competitors if they are to grow and prosper. This can be done in several ways, each of which is closely interrelated.

Differentiation Through the Agency Force

Traditionally, life insurance companies have tried to differentiate themselves primarily on the basis of their agency force. Many companies have tried to develop an image of their agents as the most knowledgeable and dependable in the industry. One approach is for a company to develop its own awards for outstanding agents. In addition, most companies also support the all-industry activities that are designed to foster professionalism in the agency force. Among these are the National Association of Life Underwriters, The Life Underwriting Training Council, the Million Dollar Round Table, and The American College. Thus, a company may boast that its agency force contains a high proportion of CLUs (Chartered Life Underwriters).

Differentiation by Company Image

Companies try to differentiate themselves on the basis of an image of reliability and financial solidarity. Without deprecating other companies in the marketplace, each company tries to stress the high quality of service that it offers and the unquestioned soundness of its financial position.

Advertising is one means of differentiating a company's image. For many years it has played an important role in insurance marketing and it appears to be increasing as companies expand their distribution beyond the agency system.

Differentiation by Service

When a company tries to differentiate its product in the consumers' minds, it must remember that the insurance product includes a wide variety of services both before and after the sale. Obviously protection is the principal service provided, but other services may make a significant difference in the way a policyowner feels about the company and coverage. For example, in many cases the client wants counseling to fit insurance coverage into an overall financial plan. In cases such as this it may be very important for consumers to have highly professional agents who have proven their competency through education and experience, and who have pledged to give clients the same service they expect.

Other forms of service may be equally important for purposes of differentiation. For example, in the group medical expense area, claims practices are particularly critical factors. Many employers purchasing group insurance view this coverage as an important source of employee good will and insist on a very short processing time for claims.

Areas which might be of particular interest to individual policyowners would include claims, notice of upcoming options, policy loans, surrenders, and changes in ownership and beneficiary, to name just a few. Indifferent or poor service will probably lead most policyowners to believe they have purchased a "lemon." Some, however, would rather give up service if they feel that it can result in a saving of premium dollars.

Since service clearly influences the ability of a company to maintain market share and to penetrate new markets, it unquestionably is an important part of the marketing process. A decision to increase the quality of a company's policyowner service effort (or conversely to cut it) has a marketing dimension just as surely as a decision to expand the advertising budget or to change the agent compensation plan.

Differentiation by Marketing Strategy

Depending on a consumer's set of preferences, all differentiation activities influence the sense of personal satisfaction that is derived from a past or prospective purchase. A company can lower its risk when entering a market by conducting research and differentiating its product in such a way as to satisfy consumer preferences. At this point, company operating philosophy plays an important role in the decision. Some companies, for example, prefer to be involved only with products that grant very liberal benefits. Obviously, such products would be expensive relative to those with a narrower set of benefits. Some feel that insurance should not be sold without the advice and counsel of an agent. This belief influences several factors, including underwriting practices and costs. Such positions stem from basic values, and as such cannot be viewed as being right or wrong. However, these values do indicate that some markets will be open to the company while others will be closed. Products designed to emphasize specific servicсs or features, such as liberal benefits, will probably not appeal to consumers who do not place the same value on those features. Alternatively, such products may appeal to consumers but cannot be marketed at a competitive price. If the company knows this in advance, it can conserve resources and minimize frustration by avoiding the market altogether.

Differentiation by Pricing and Competition

The demand for most goods and services is **price elastic,** the term used by economists to indicate that sales increase when prices fall. Although the last word has not yet been written on the subject, it appears that there is some elasticity in the demand for life and health insurance. Thus, assuming that nothing else changes, a reduction in premium rates should result in greater sales.

A related question concerns the level of competition in life insurance markets. Most experts seem to agree that there is great competition in the field of employee benefits. However, opinion differs about the level of competition in the market for individual insurance, and particularly for certain products. For example, level premium life insurance and health insurance are frequently singled out by critics, but for somewhat different reasons. Individual health insurance is criticized because there is little standardization in the way that benefits, limitations, and exclusions are expressed in policies. Thus, a prospective purchaser cannot determine how much of a cost differential between two contracts is actually attributable to lower expense and/or profit margins, and how much is due to potential differences in benefits offered. Although the features of benefits are standardized under level premium life insurance, critics charge that the reserve which naturally develops makes it difficult to compute an approximate cost on a policy. Much debate has taken place over which cost calculation method is preferable. Until one is agreed upon, critics contend, the level of price competition will remain unacceptably low.

Defenders of the status quo assert that the large number of companies marketing life and health insurance ensures a satisfactory level of competition. When commenting on cost differences for similar policies, they argue that the methods are based on inaccurate assumptions, or that methods of calculation are selected to prove a predetermined position. One observer comments, "If companies all charged the same rates, they would be accused of collusion. Since they charge different rates, critics say there is no competition."

More will be said on the subject of competition in later chapters. It appears that this issue is one which will be a topic of debate for some years to come. It is significant, however, to recognize that regardless of the final conclusions, the fact that competition is widely discussed in and of itself is a factor which must be considered in the development of a marketing strategy.

A major function of marketing, which can be aided through differentiation, is the satisfaction of consumers' personal and social needs—to ensure that they feel that they are choosing (or have chosen) the right product at the right price and have peer approval for those choices. Both are important in life insurance marketing because the insured who is satisfied with a purchase will buy more in the future and will be a source of new clients. If a consumer is personally unhappy, or perceives that peers disapprove of a purchase, the coverage may be dropped and future sales or referrals are unlikely.

Art Versus Science

Essentially, the marketing manager who can induce a consumer to take action must first be an analyst. There are tremendous unsatisfied needs for financial security, and the first task in marketing is to analyze them. Then a product must be developed and matched with a delivery system so that it can be sold, distributed, and serviced at competitive prices. Obviously, these activities require a large amount of painstaking effort. This is the "science" in marketing. However, no matter how scientific the approach or how precise the plans, much of the success of the effort will depend on the creativity of the persons involved in the marketing process. This is the "art" in marketing, and it is essential to prolonged success.

A marketer must know the size, location, and needs of many market segments. But the analysis goes well beyond these quantitative demographics. He or she must also know, or be able to sense, prospective buyers' attitudes, values, and objectives. Thus, marketing begins with science, but will fail unless there is considerable art involved in the process as well.

This text attempts to combine both elements into a coherent whole which will benefit those people who are interested in insurance marketing. We shall deal with the major areas of marketing functions and distribution and then discuss the more specific applications of marketing techniques to insurance products. In this way we hope to identify those characteristics which are quantifiable, as well as those which are more concerned with the art of marketing.

Chapter 2

Marketing Functions in Life and Health Insurance

Harry P. Seward, FLMI, CLU
David L. Hetrick, CLU

The sale of products or services to buyers plays a vital role in every business organization. Life and health insurance companies must sell their products and services in sufficient quantities to (1) build and maintain required services, (2) deliver the promises made in their insurance contracts, (3) cover operating expenses, and (4) realize a gain from operations.

Within a company the task of marketing involves the management of all those activities needed to move the products and services most efficiently from the company where they are manufactured (produced) to the buyer who ultimately uses and benefits from them. Thus, marketing concerns itself with functions ranging from product design and development to any services provided to consumers after the sale.

Life and health insurers "manufacture" products in the form of contracts that promise to deliver dollars at future dates based upon certain contingencies. Insurers must determine the proper prices for their products and services, have adequate capital (inventory, in a sense) on hand to produce them, and distribute their products to consumers, either directly or through middlemen. Thus, life and health insurers share most of the marketing problems and challenges of other business organizations, as well as having some that are unique.

This first section of this chapter examines the specific functions involved in marketing life and health insurance. The second section describes the marketing planning process, a useful tool for coordinating and monitoring these functions.

Marketing Functions

This section introduces five generally accepted marketing functions: (1) market identification—the process of examining and selecting potential markets for company products; (2) product development—the process of creating products to meet the needs of the identified markets; (3) distribution—the process of making the products available to consumers; (4) support services—the important backup services provided by the marketing and other departments; and (5) controlling—the activities of measuring results against plans and objectives. Each function is important to the complete and smooth operation of a life and health insurance marketing operation. Three of these functions—product development, distribution, and support services—involve so many elements that they will be the subjects of later chapters. The other two functions—market identification and controlling—are the main subjects of this section.

Market Identification

One of the high priority functions in marketing is the identification of potential buyers of the company's products and services and the segregation of these people from the population as a whole. Since few, if any, life and health companies can profitably be all things to all people, it becomes necessary to determine which segments of the consumer population will be the focus of the company's marketing efforts. The first step in this identification is an analysis of consumers and their needs. Then these needs must be considered in relation to the needs of those involved in distribution, the external business environment, and the company's objectives and characteristics.

The markets available to life and health insurers are quite broad. The choices a company makes to narrow its market are vital decisions with tremendous impact on its marketing progress and financial results. A company is relatively free to choose to market its products in different countries or regions, in rural or urban areas, to people over age 50 or under age 25, to men or women, to the wealthy or the poor, to members of certain professions or occupations or organizations, to specific types or sizes of businesses, and so on. It is the task of those responsible for market planning to decide which of the many market segments that exist have the most appeal to their particular company.

Determining Consumer Needs

Within the broad available marketplace for life and health insurance products are masses of potential consumers with needs for which insurers manufacture sound and practical solutions. Some of these needs are somewhat static in nature and exist for most people most of the time. They are rather constant over time. Other needs are quite dynamic and change with an individual's life cycle, economic situation, marital status, family situation, employment, age, avocation, and life-style.

If life and health insurers are to market their products successfully, they must be sensitive to the needs that they can fulfill and they must be aware of the potential for change in those needs from time to time and from one situation to another. Through proper research, it is possible for the marketer to assess the types of needs that exist among consumers, the intensity and prevalence of those needs in the general marketplace, and the ways in which individuals prefer to deal with them. These data are important to effective marketing strategy and enable marketers to select the most attractive market segments for their companies. It is perhaps easiest, however, to group the usual approaches to market segmentation into two broad categories: objective and subjective. Each of these methods of segmentation is a means of categorizing consumers according to their actual or presumed needs.

Objective Factors

Market segmentation by such objective factors as physical and demographic characteristics is widely used by insurers. Segmentation can be based simply upon physical characteristics. For example, the marketplace can be divided by such factors as height, weight, age, sex, health. Generally, however, physical characteristics are not closely correlated with insurance needs. Thus, a marketing effort aimed simply at "women" risks failure unless it considers the differing needs of homemakers, female executives, and secretaries.

Every person in the population can be classified by his or her demographic characteristics: income, marital status, occupation, family composition, educational level, geographic location, and so forth. Demographics are more useful in segmentation by insurers than are physical characteristics. For example, people with very high incomes will almost certainly need more insurance coverage than those with low incomes. And owners of small businesses will as a group not only need more insurance than retail store clerks but also have less ready access to coverage via group insurance. The marketing manager can become familiar with demographic data through various marketing service organizations, magazines and reference books.

The demographic variable of geography is frequently used in market segmentation because it is easy to determine. In addition, many insurance companies or their distribution systems are organized by geographic location. Geographic considerations in terms of regulatory environment will frequently affect a company's marketing programs. However, geography is unreliable in determining consumer's needs. While there are certainly some differences among consumers and their needs depending on geographic location, geography is best used as a tool for determining sales force location or concentration than it is for assessing customers' needs for insurance.

Objective market segmentation can be achieved by dividing a marketplace according to certain "social" factors, or **sociographics.** These are typically combinations of physical and demographic characteristics. A common sociographic approach is that of socioeconomic groupings, which combines education, income, occupation, and perhaps age or sex. This approach would allow the marketer to differentiate, for example, between the 50-year-old executive secretary and the newly hired employee with an MBA, both of whom earn $25,000. A life cycle classification is another sociographic approach. Here, the classifications could include such categories as single adult, newly married couple, family with youngest child under twelve, empty nest, or retired couple. Life cycle categories, perhaps in combination with socioeconomic groupings, allow the insurance marketer to infer consumer needs in each category with relative accuracy.

Subjective Factors

In contrast to the objective approaches discussed above, subjective methods of segmentation attempt to determine consumer needs using factors less easily measured. Rather than using intervening variables as bases for inference, these subjective methods, generally called **psychographics,** deal with the attitudes, values, opinions, activities, and interests of the public. The measurement of these factors is considerably more difficult than objective methods of segmentation, but the data revealed are (ideally) much more valuable to the insurance marketer. Psychographics may, for example, study the variety and degree of consumers' interests in providing for their families' future financial security as a basis for distinguishing among categories of consumers. Another possible subject of psychographic study may be the degree of consumers' concerns for their own retirement preparation.

The principle of market segmentation is important because the choice of the market segment will affect the choice of the product developed, training methods, sales aids, advertising, image creation, sales planning, and location and choice of field force. Both objective and subjective methods are used to segment markets and are often combined to improve overall marketing effectiveness.

The division of the broad marketplace into manageable and meaningful segments is regarded by most companies as a necessary part of their marketing approach. They seek to focus on those segments of the market to whom they can sell their products most efficiently and profitably. The term **target marketing** is frequently used in the insurance industry to indicate market segmentation. The ability to segment carefully and analyze potential and existing markets is critical to market identification and to the development of a successful marketing plan.

The Needs of Those Distributing Life and Health Insurance

Marketing in the life and health insurance industry is complicated by the importance of the role played by those who typically distribute its products. Other industries also must sell their products both to the end user and to the intervening distributors, but their task is less complex than that of insurance marketers. Food processing firms, for example, often use independent brokers to merchandise their products to grocery stores, who in turn consummate the actual sale to the consumer. Automobile manufacturers use quasi-independent dealerships to sell and service their products. In each of these examples, the manufacturer must be concerned not only with the needs and perceptions of those who eventually buy its products but also with the needs and attitudes of those in the distribution channel.

Life and health insurers must also concern themselves with the end buyer and with those in the distribution channel, but the insurance product is so little understood or actively sought by the end consumer that insurers are almost entirely reliant on agents and brokers to reach that buyer. While consumer advertising and direct response selling produce substantial sales volumes, active selling by agents has been necessary to relate the complexities of the insurance product to each buyer's particular needs. In recognition of the agent's role, insurers must be prepared to provide their agents with support and direction.

In short, while every marketer must consider the desires of the distribution channel as well as those of the purchaser, insurance marketers are often well-advised to consider the distributors of their product (the agents) as the primary consumers. At the least, a product or strategy that has its origins in buyers' needs must be skillfully merchandised to those who will distribute it if it is ever to have the opportunity of being made available to the buyers for whom it was designed.

The External Business Environment

The life and health insurance industry must operate within the framework of its total environment. In order to identify the best markets for the company, factors such as regulation, legislation, social change, taxation and competition must be evaluated. For example, changes in social security and federal estate taxation or the enactment of national health care can create or eliminate markets overnight.

The dynamics of the environment make it necessary to attempt to forecast or predict the conditions which may exist tomorrow. The economy will change. New legislation and regulation will come about to modify certain markets. Buyer attitudes, tax laws, and birth and death rates will change. It is essential that the marketing function be sensitive to these movements and be able to identify and understand the markets of today and tomorrow.

Company Objectives and Characteristics

Along with determining the needs of consumers, a company's long and short range objectives need to be considered for the identification and targeting of market segments. A corporate goal of maximizing asset growth, for example, should suggest that the marketer concentrate on segments that prefer permanent insurance to term, whereas an objective of sales growth would suggest emphasis on high-income term buyers.

A company's existing characteristics define the framework within which it can work. Existing distribution systems, products, and outlet locations; the capital available for expansion; the nature of its present customers; the quantity and effectiveness of its human resources, and management capacity all play a part in identifying the markets best suited for the company. For example, a company with a well-established agency system that is operating effectively and profitably will probably not embark on a direct response distribution system. A company with limited capital available for expansion will not be likely to concentrate its efforts on high-cost metropolitan agency development.

Product Development

The second function for which marketing management is responsible is the process of developing or modifying products that will serve the needs of consumers, be acceptable to company operations, and fit the requirements of regulatory bodies.

Input for product development usually comes from diverse areas of the company. Actuarial, agency, legal, sales, marketing, financial, policyowner service, and underwriting areas, all have important contributions to make to the product development function. In some companies, in fact, the primary responsibility for product development may rest outside the marketing department, often in the actuarial department. Regardless of the location of direct responsibility, however, marketers must concern themselves intensively with product development: a marketing strategy that is perfect in all elements except products will suffer in the marketplace.

While Chapter 5 deals exclusively with the subject of product development, a brief discussion of the factors that affect product development is presented here. Some of these important factors are corporate objectives, consumer needs, environmental forces, and pricing.

Corporate Objectives and Consumer Needs

In determining product design the marketer must consider overall company policies on distribution, profits, dividends, pricing, reserve requirements, investments, and administrative capacity. These prevailing philosophies and corporate plans and goals will serve as a backdrop against which product ideas must be tested.

Paramount to product design is the determination and understanding of the needs of potential buyers as discussed earlier. Forecasting the parameters of those needs in the future is equally important. Products must be designed to meet both current and expected needs.

The Environment

Good product planning requires that a company try to anticipate changes in outside forces rather than simply react to events as they occur. It is important that changes in consumer needs, regulation, law, economics and social factors be monitored and considered when making product development decisions. Current inflationary pressures provide a prime example of an environmental condition creating pressure to design new products that are compatible with inflation. The ability of a company to analyze the environment and predict changes can substantially enhance the quality of results obtained from its marketing operations.

Regulation

The pressure of government regulation figures strongly on product development considerations. Not only has the government chosen to compete with private insurance companies for the public's protection dollars through social security, Medicare, National Service Life Insurance, and military benefits, but the direct regulation and taxation of the industry affect every product decision.

The states and provinces in their regulatory function are ultimately involved in every aspect of insurance: nonforfeiture laws, minimum claim ratios, reserve requirements, simplified policy language, sales forms and agent licensing requirements. Regulatory practices vary from state to state, and change is continuous. There is also federal regulation to deal with; this is especially true in Canada. Product designers must maintain a constant awareness of the impact of these regulations on their decisions.

Competition

The actions of other companies play an important role in product design since a company must usually sell in the same arena with competing companies. Product innovations, pricing and services offered by these other companies have a great impact on a company's ability to market its products. Competitive considerations, perhaps more than any other factor, have been responsible for the steadily decreasing "price per thousand" of the majority of life insurance products over the years. This pressure for lower premiums is severely felt by companies as price levels in the economy reach new inflationary highs. Lowering prices while all costs are rising requires a rather delicate trade-off, yet competition is forcing this activity.

Pricing

The products offered by life and health companies must be priced to reflect profit goals; risk factors (mortality and morbidity, interest, expenses, persistency, and taxes); competitive forces; consistency and equity to new and old policyowners; buyers' needs (demand), developmental costs; and reserves. Chapter 5 looks more closely at the aspect of life and health insurance pricing in relation to product development.

Distribution

A critical decision to be made by a life and health insurance company is the choice of a distribution system. Having identified the market segments that will be pursued and the products that are required by those segments, the marketer must then determine the system that will be used to deliver those products to the potential buyers identified. Distribution systems may, of course, be combined to enhance market penetration, i.e., reach buyers more easily and in greater numbers. Systems for distributing life and health products have evolved over the years, and several are currently in use.

Ordinary Agency

The system of distribution known as ordinary, or ordinary agency, involves the use of an agent or broker to provide the actual sales and service work for policyowners. The salesperson in this system may be either an employee of the insurer (a career agent) or an independent contractor, general agent or broker representing the company. Premiums are normally paid by the policyowner directly to the insurance company rather than to the agent.

Home Service

The home service method of life and health insurance distribution, once also called an industrial or debit operation, is characterized by the collection of premiums weekly or monthly by the company's agent at the policyowner's residence or business. The agent generally spends substantial time collecting premiums and thus has close personal contact with the policyowner.

Direct Response

Distribution of life and health insurance by direct response relies on marketing techniques whereby the company solicits applications from consumers directly through mailed promotional pieces (direct mail) or print or broadcast advertising. Thus, distribution is effected without the activities of an agent.

Brokers and All-Lines Agents

Brokers are agents who operate independently of any one life and health insurance company. A company is chosen to provide coverage for a client by a broker on the basis of that company's plan being in the best interest of the client. The all-lines (multiple line) system may be either agency or home service but the term refers specifically to companies that sell both property/casualty insurance (e.g. auto and home owners) and life and health lines. In recent years some of the industry's giant life insurance companies have expanded into multiple line operations and some large casualty carriers have greatly expanded their life and health operations.

Other Distribution Systems

Life and health insurance can also be sold by other organizations such as fraternal benefit societies and, in some states, savings banks. Coverage may be sold in other forms such as credit life or disability coverage, and travel insurance packages sometimes sold by machines in airport terminals. These non-traditional methods can be as effective as those discussed above, and they warrant the consideration of marketing planners. Later chapters in the text will discuss each of the distribution systems mentioned above in more detail.

Support Services

No matter which market segments, products, or systems of distribution are selected by a company, there will be a need for marketing support services to assist in marketing and sales operations. This function provides the support needed to reach planned sales goals, gain consumer acceptance, improve agent performance and achieve other similar goals. Sales promotion, agent activities, information services, and regulatory compliance are included in this category. A brief outline of these is included below; a more detailed discussion will be presented in a later chapter.

Promotion

A broad spectrum of activities is included in the category of sales promotion and advertising: sales material to be sent or delivered to prospective customers; direct mail literature to arouse the interest of prospective buyers; advertising developed to create a positive public image for the company or to promote specific products; public relations programs; and sales campaigns, as well as contests and conventions for agents.

Agent Activities

Marketing support services will often expand to include the functions of field training, management training, field clerical supervision, advanced underwriting, field publications, management of agent financing, production statistics, and budget control. Many companies with agency systems provide home office liaison support to field offices and agents. Such liaison promotes effective communication in both directions—from home office to field and field to home office. This service may often involve direct aid to the field offices in the form of management consultation.

Regulatory Compliance

Those in the marketing support function may be responsible for assuring that sales literature and mailings meet legal guidelines, that agents are properly licensed, and that state mandated training requirements for agents are met.

Information Services

For the successful operation of a life and health insurance company a great deal of information must be collected, evaluated, and transmitted. Facts about field activity, production, persistency, agency income, and so on, are produced by marketing support units and put in usable form for those responsible for marketing management.

Other Support Services

In some companies, additional services are considered part of marketing support services: claims, policyowner services, pension administration, policy issue, or selected actuarial functions. These are considered to be marketing activities because each department's activities involve interaction between the company and customer, and the quality of such services is reflected in the actual sales process.

Many companies have marketing research groups and sometimes consider market research a part of this support function. As research into customer needs becomes more important, however, it is likely that the marketing research function will become a separate entity comparable to marketing planning or product development.

Controlling

The control function of marketing management deals with the measurement of marketing activities and the analyses of those measures as they relate to established objectives. As in all businesses, the control function is vital to effective marketing operations in life and health companies.

Without the measurement and analysis of results it would be nearly impossible to judge the progress of an organization toward its many objectives, to spot trends in performance, or to plan corrective actions. For example, life and health insurance companies may monitor total sales, total premium, agent income, premium received versus expenses, average premium per case or per product unit, amount of insurance in force, or comparable production data by region or segment or even agent. In addition, comparisons with last year's or last month's results and with the plan can be important.

Besides evaluating production or sales data, companies monitor and control the expenses incurred in their marketing efforts. In a typical life and health company, expense items related to marketing might include commissions paid, staff costs, training costs, sales promotion costs, advertising expenses, lease fees, and equipment costs, among many others. Ratios of expense items to one another, to production figures, to personnel factors, to budget objectives or to a previous time period's expense items would be typical statistics of interest to insurance company management.

It would also be common to see persistency (the tendency of policies to remain in force), agency recruiting, agent retention, mailing costs, profitability, and company growth listed as internal control measures.

Besides the internal measures, many companies monitor market share and growth/profitability rates in comparison to their key competitors. Proper selection of control points provides the marketing staff with measurements necessary for comparisons of results to the marketing plan. Perhaps the key and overriding control tool, however, is the marketing plan, which is discussed in the next section.

The Company Marketing Plan

The marketing plan is the document that brings together a company's objectives, targeted market segments, action plans, and specific goals for each critical product or line of products. The foundation for a sound marketing operation is set in the marketing plan. It establishes the strategy that the company will employ to achieve the marketing goals set up in overall corporate long-range planning.

The marketing plan is both derived from and acts as a guide for the company's longer-range planning. It must be consistent with the company's long-term plan, but it is much more specific and action-oriented. The degree of success achieved through the marketing plan will contribute to reformulation of the company's strategic direction in later years. Careful development of the marketing plan is the critical step in successful marketing since it directs the implementation and coordination of the whole variety of marketing activities.

The Functions of a Marketing Plan

A complete marketing plan combines a number of functions. Each function is essential to contribute to the effectiveness of the overall plan. This section presents the functions of a marketing plan as (1) incorporating long-range objectives, (2) selection of markets, (3) communication of the plan, (4) coordination of functions, and (5) monitoring objectives.

Incorporating Long-Range Company Objectives

A marketing plan is the key vehicle for framing the decisions and actions that must be accomplished to achieve overall company goals and objectives. Ideally, a company mission and specific, measurable objectives, or standards of achievement, should be established before a marketing plan is written. In many cases, however, construction of a marketing plan will come first. When this happens, the marketing plan will serve to initiate corporate planning, since it will point out issues and directions that must be dealt with by senior management before the marketing plan can be completed.

The corporate mission and objectives, when they exist, will be set out in broad but measurable terms with regard to what the entire company is trying to achieve. With these long-range objectives in place, a marketing plan will then lay out the specific course of action necessary to achieve the marketing-related objectives.

Selection of Markets

A marketing plan defines those specific segments of the broad market for life and health insurance products which will be the focus of a company's marketing efforts. These segments may be broad or narrow, many or few, but defining them and focusing others' attention on them is one function of a marketing plan.

Communication of the Marketing Plan

A marketing plan contains the company's marketing philosophy, goals and strategies; these should be communicated to all functional divisions of the organization. Other departments in a life and health company must be aware of the marketing plan so that they may consider the impact this plan will have on their own planning, staffing and organizing. The underwriting department, for example, needs an estimation of the number and sizes of applications that will be flowing into its offices in the next year and in the next five years so that it can hire and train personnel to provide underwriting services under the company's definition of acceptable time and mortality standards. The policyowner service department needs similar projections as do data processing, actuarial, and administration. The marketing plan provides vital philosophy and background, as well as necessary planning data, not only for the marketing people, but also for other company departments.

Coordination of Functions

A marketing plan describes the roles of those marketing and other functions (or activities) that are important for achieving the marketing objectives and sets up a method for their coordination and successful operation. It is critical that the functions covered in the plan comprise all relevant ones, including those outside the marketing department. For example, product development efforts will necessarily involve several functional departments in addition to marketing, such as the legal department, and the marketing plan serves to announce this need for others' assistance and to obtain their commitment to action.

Selecting and Monitoring Objectives

A well-drawn marketing plan identifies specific and measurable objectives in the marketing realm which support corporate goals, specifies the action steps to be taken to achieve them, and provides a system for monitoring progress toward their realization. This task may sound simple, but in reality the translation of some of these items into measurable terms may be the toughest part of the planning process. For example, if the objective is that of offering "quality" products, then planners have the task of measuring whether the company's products meet that qualification. To do that, they must establish a set of criteria against which to measure the quality of the products and a method for making the comparison.

Developing a Marketing Plan

Many decisions and steps are involved in developing a sound and functional marketing plan. These center around the people involved, determining the starting point, the internal and external factors to be considered, the objectives to be realized, the forecasts that are needed, and the actual writing of the plan.

Who Does the Planning

By its title and nature, it should be obvious that the lead responsibility for the marketing plan rests with the marketing department. Within this department, however, the job may be assigned to any of several people, either as their sole responsibility or as an additional function. Some companies have full-time planners; others assign the task to the department head; still others simply use their most capable person, regardless of his or her customary assignment.

In any event, since the marketing plan will affect nearly every function within the company, it is wise and probably necessary to have a broad spectrum of corporate involvement, including high-level corporate participation. Many companies involve their senior executives in this process, and often send them to an off-site retreat so that total concentration can be devoted to the planning effort. In addition to this senior management involvement, it is often advisable—especially when a change in direction or tactics is indicated—to involve representatives of the field sales force.

Marketing plans generally cover the first year in some detail and the second through fifth years only in a broad sense. Plans are updated annually and published as far in advance of the beginning of the new year as necessary to be effective action guides.

Determining the Starting Point

To begin the marketing planning process, one needs to know the company mission and objectives. One must then assess the current marketing situation of the company in terms of its quantitative (sales and profits) history, people available, markets served, distribution systems used, technical and logistical support on hand, and competitive situation. There are probably as many items of information that could be studied about a company's marketing posture as there are companies, and the planners for different companies vary greatly in the extent to which they analyze their past and present positions.

Consideration of Internal and External Factors

Both internal and external factors are considerations in developing a marketing plan. Within the company, market planners need to assess their company's finances, human resources and history. It is important that the marketing managers have a firm understanding of the funds that the company will make available for investment in marketing and of the sorts of investments likely to be made. For example, a marketing plan that relies on extensive and costly television advertising will not be accepted if corporate funds are tight, or if top management does not believe that consumer advertising will be of any benefit to sales. In general, the budgeting process and expense plan are critical parts of the total marketing plan, and the planner must consider the potential on each marketing investment he or she recommends.

To plan a successful marketing effort, the planners must have a good estimate of the number, quality,and attitudes of personnel available at all levels who will contribute to achieving the goals of the marketing plan. An evaluation of group and individual skills, knowledge, and experience may be important. For example, a plan that involves penetrating new and very different markets may fail if the current field force is not comfortable in these new segments or if it has no compelling motive to expand beyond those segments where it currently derives income.

It is valuable in planning future actions to know a company's past. It may be useful to know the marketing successes and failures of the company's past, the products that have worked well or poorly, the territories that have been strong or weak, the distribution systems that have worked, and services that have been used.

Within some companies a condition of "entropy" may exist, especially if the management group has been in control for some time. This comes about as an organization finds methods that work, and, over time, rejects different methods simply because they "have never been done that way here." When entropy exists, new ideas are rarely tried since they are perceived to fall outside of the accepted ways. It is important for planners to recognize this condition and shape their plans around it.

Just as with market identification and recognition of the internal situation of the company, external factors such as the business environment, competition, and government regulation affect decisions about a market plan.

The successful planner of marketing operations will need to know the business environment where company products are to be sold. High inflation, for example, may increase consumer demand for life insurance but reduce its affordability, leading in turn to more interest in term coverage and less in permanent. Or an increase in social security or Medicare benefits may mean that some consumers no longer need private coverage. A trend towards smaller families and/or serial marriages may shift consumer needs away from traditional life coverage and towards retirement planning. Thus, it is vital to know what the climate will be for the products the company wants to sell.

Another external factor which should be investigated is the activity of competitors in the marketplace. A marketing planner needs to know as much as possible about competitors' strategies: their approaches in terms of product lines, prices, targeted segments, geographic location, and so forth. As insurance consumers become increasingly knowledgeable about their purchases, competitive analysis will become increasingly important to the marketing planner.

Before developing a marketing plan in today's world it is vital to be aware of overall regulatory impacts upon the business. Will temporary licensing of agents be abolished? What about cancer insurance, or a change in regulations affecting deposit term? Will some information sources now used for underwriting be proscribed? What effect will increased cost/benefit disclosure to consumers have? Unless the planner knows the company's entire situation and condition of the external environment, it is impossible to build a plan or road map that will move the company in the direction it wants to go in the future.

Determining Measurable Objectives

Once the corporate long-range plan has been studied in terms of its relationship to marketing functions, the marketing goals and objectives can be established. For progress to be monitored, targets of performance must be specific and measurable. Thus, the marketing plan can be used in the controlling function described earlier.

Items that are commonly measured in marketing plans include the increase in insurance in force; total premium; new premium; new customers insured; persistency; market share; product mix; agent income; average agent production; and agency commission-to-expense ratios.

While any number of measures can be chosen, it is wise to focus on one, two or three that will be the key indicators of success or failure. For example, it is often true that new premium is the critical goal that must be achieved in order to produce planned levels of total premium, new customers covered, market share, agent income, and so on. In this case, new premium should be established as the primary objective, with the others labeled as secondary.

It is critical that objectives go beyond sales or product figures to include staffing and expense goals, customer satisfaction measures, and perhaps corporate image objectives (e.g., being perceived as innovative by 75% of a designated audience). In addition, it is wise to couch objectives in terms of environmental assumptions. For example, a 10% sales growth goal may be realistic in a healthy economy but totally unachievable in a recession.

Forecasting

In addition to evaluating situations as they exist today within the company and the marketplace, it is important for a marketing plan to try to predict changes that may occur during the time span covered by the marketing plan.

Forecasting the future for a life and health company is difficult, but data trends are readily available and will help in the development of forecasts. The marketing planner should investigate trends in such variables as average policy size, price level, persistency, office costs, commission rates, family incomes, taxation, regulation, discretionary income, competition, population changes and demographics. Trends in one's own sales figures, for example, can help the marketer estimate future results if no marketing variables are changed.

Forecasts will frequently turn out to have been inaccurate, but some attempt must be made to assess the future events. Surprises often mean that the marketing plan has failed, but valuable lessons can be learned from the failures.

Drafting the Plan

Once the goals and objectives of the plan are established, the present situation determined, and a forecast of the future made, the planners are ready to begin determining the course of action that will be employed to achieve the results desired.

Forging the plan itself will be a process which will tax the creativity, and perhaps the patience, of all involved, but it must allow for maximum expression of all relevant ideas and concerns, since so much of the company's future success depends upon the outcome of this effort.

It is during the actual planning that the interaction of knowledge and creativity from the various disciplines occurs. Plans must not only allow the marketing department to be effective in reaching its stated goals but also allow the necessary interaction and coordination with other departments, particularly the sales force. Because of this interplay of various functions in constructing the marketing plan, the planner should expect to go through several versions before the plan is finalized and accepted. In fact, if the first draft survives intact, it may be more indicative of a lack of management attention or commitment than of the planner's skills.

The following sections should be included, not necessarily in this order, in a marketing plan:

1. A statement of general direction and background thought. For example, "We intend to be among the three fastest-growing life insurers, as measured by premiums received. This is necessary in order for us to achieve our goals of agent retention and return on stockholders' equity."
2. An environmental analysis. This analysis should cover both internal and external factors, review the company's history in terms of

successes and failures, and assess its current strengths and weaknesses. It should also discuss broad expectations about developments in the external environment: competition, regulation, economic forecasts, social trends, etc.

3. Specific objectives and supporting action plans together with timing. For example, "Our total premiums received will increase by 20% in the coming year, with compound annual growth in excess of 20% thereafter. To accomplish this, we will (a) introduce a new adjustable life product in January, (b) recruit 100 new agents next year, and (c) open two new field offices in the fast-growing cities of Phoenix and Dallas by the end of the year."
4. Critical assumptions. Factors which affect plan achievement can be divided into controllable and uncontrollable categories. The key uncontrollable variables and the impact of a change from expectation should be indicated. For example, "We expect real GNP growth to be 2% to 3% annually. Economic growth of less than 1% or more than 5% would cause us to revise our premium expectations significantly." Sometimes, it may also be advisable to specify the critical nature of a controllable variable: for example, "If systems or other difficulties delay the introduction of our adjustable life product, or if funds are not available for sales force merchandising and training, our premium growth objectives will not be achievable."
5. Assignment of responsibility. Designation of the units responsible for carrying out a particular assignment is crucial. This is particularly necessary when actions by other departments are required, and even within the marketing unit it may be advisable to assign plan responsibilities to specific functional areas or people.
6. An expense plan. The expense plan would cover the number and level of people within the marketing department who are required to execute the plan. It would also include discussion of exceptional and out-of-pocket costs incurred in such activities as systems development, a new training manual, or advertising.
7. A statistical exhibit. Some type of statistical exhibit is needed to show the company's recent history and the marketing plan's objectives for key quantitative measures.
8. A statement of the control process. Some type of control mechanism should be set forth. For example, "We will report quarterly on our progress against each objective and action plan, with our analyses of the reasons for any deviation and with recommendations for corrective action as required."

In addition to the above sections, it may be advisable in an attachment or separate document to lay out in considerable detail the action steps, together with timing and responsibility, for each of the more critical or complicated activities required by the marketing plan.

The plan, when finally drafted, must provide, in easily understandable form, the guidelines for the strategy to be used in achieving the marketing objectives, and the benchmark goals to assess whether or not the strategy is working. The document should provide the basics for the day-to-day management of marketing activities and act as a guide for all short-term, tactical planning.

Summary

This chapter demonstrates that the same or similar factors affect a variety of decisions that a marketing manager must make. External factors such as the economy affect broad decisions (the formulation of marketing objectives), as well as specific ones (choosing distribution systems or products to be offered).

The marketing functions in life and health insurance companies are quite interrelated. To market its products successfully, a company must be able to plan its future strategy and direction, identify its markets, develop sound products, create an effective distribution system, provide support services, and control (measure) its own growth. The planning and implementation of these functions can determine the success or failure of the entire company's operation.

The company marketing plan, although discussed last in this chapter, is the key to an organized and directed marketing operation, as well as a critical control device. It provides the strategy for all of the other marketing functions. The marketing plan serves as a road map for directing the company in achieving its goals.

Chapter 3

The Impact of Government Regulation on Insurance Marketing

Harold Skipper, Jr., Ph.D., CLU

The environment in which a business operates dictates the products and services it will offer consumers and how it will offer them. This environment has many facets, each of which deserves management's attention. Two key elements of the environment—government regulation and consumerism—are examined in this and the following chapters. Each of these elements is external to insurers and technically beyond the direct control of insurance executives.

This chapter examines the impact of traditional aspects of insurance regulation on life and health insurance marketing. The impact of consumerism on life and health insurance marketing, including contemporary governmental and insurer responses to consumer concerns, is presented in Chapter 4.

Overview of Insurance Regulation

The life insurance industry may be the most regulated in the nation. Many of the laws and regulations under which the business operates have an impact on its marketing practices. Because of this, the reader should have a general understanding of why and how the insurance business is regulated, and some knowledge of insurance regulation in the past and today.

Why Regulation?

The insurance business has long been recognized by the courts and lawmakers as "affected with the public interest." Extensive regulation flows from this public interest concept. Since they must accumulate large reserves for the future benefit of policyowners, insurers are in the nature of trustees of consumers' funds. In addition, insurance contracts are complicated; as a result, it is believed that consumers can easily be misled. The long-term nature of life insurance contracts is also said to justify this extensive regulation: the insurance company is making a commitment, the consequences of which are not perfectly predictable. These reasons are said to justify the extensive regulation to which the life and health insurance business is subjected.

Brief History of Regulation in the United States

Although the insurance business in the United States is regulated primarily by the states, as opposed to the federal government, this situation exists only with the continued concurrence of the Congress.

Early in United States history, the insurance business was considered to be local in nature, and the states naturally assumed responsibility for its regulation. Although state laws affecting the insurance business were in existence in the early 1800s, modern regulation of the life insurance business in the United States dates from 1858. In that year, Elizur Wright, an abolitionist turned "life insurance consumer crusader," was appointed to the Massachusetts Board of Insurance Commissioners. During his eight years in office, he instituted numerous sweeping changes in insurance regulation in Massachusetts and, as a result, was finally forced from office. As the "father of insurance regulation," his impact on the life insurance business was enormous.

Paul v. Virginia

Bills to establish federal regulation of the insurance business were proposed in Congress in 1866 and 1868. These efforts ended abruptly with the 1869 United States Supreme Court decision in the case of *Paul v. Virginia.*[1] This case involved an insurance agent, Samuel Paul, who would not comply with a provision in Virginia law requiring the posting of a security deposit. Paul, representing several New York insurers, challenged Virginia's right to require such a deposit, claiming, among other things, that the state had no jurisdiction in the matter since he was dealing in interstate commerce.[2] In this landmark decision, the Court held that the issuance of an insurance

[1] 8 U.S. (Wall) 168 (1869).

[2] Recall that the United States Constitution provides that the Federal government has only those powers specifically granted to it in the Constitution. All other powers vest in the states. The commerce clause of the constitution provides that "Congress shall have the power to regulate commerce . . . among the several states."

policy was not commerce but a contract of indemnity, and therefore could not be interstate commerce. Hence, insurance could not be a matter for federal regulation, in effect giving jurisdiction to the states.

The Armstrong Investigation

The life insurance business enjoyed rapid growth in the United States and Canada during the last third of the nineteenth century. However, because the quality of state insurance regulation varied considerably from state to state, many financially unsound and poorly managed insurers were permitted to operate. As a result, many companies failed, resulting in a loss of consumer confidence in the life insurance business. False and misleading advertising flourished. Many other life insurance marketing practices (rebating, misrepresentation, and twisting), which today are prohibited, were then commonplace.

These abuses created public ill-will and pressure for reform. Consequently, in 1905, the New York legislature appointed a committee to investigate these abuses. The committee and its investigation bore the name of its chairman, Senator William W. Armstrong. This committee documented numerous abusive practices existing within the life insurance industry and recommended major revisions in existing insurance laws and regulations. As a result of the Armstrong Report, the New York Insurance Code was significantly modified in 1906, with other states soon following the New York lead. The broad areas in which changes were instituted included developing restrictions as to type and quantity of certain investments (holdings in common stocks and real estate were limited), instituting expense limitations, and establishing surplus accumulation maximums.

The South-Eastern Underwriters Association Case

In 1944, the precedent set by *Paul v. Virginia* and periodically upheld in later cases came to an end in *United States v. South-Eastern Underwriters Association* (SEUA).[3] The case involved the charge by the United States Attorney General that the SEUA, a cooperative property insurance rating bureau with members from several states, restrained interstate trade through price fixing and thus violated the Sherman Antitrust Act.

In defending itself against this charge, the SEUA relied on *Paul v. Virginia,* arguing that federal laws did not apply to the business of insurance. However, in its 4 to 3 decision, the Supreme Court held that insurance

[3] 332 U.S. 533 at 533 (1944).

transactions between parties in different states were indeed interstate commerce. Therefore, the Court held that all federal laws thus applied to the insurance business.

The McCarran-Ferguson Act

The SEUA decision had the potential of causing confusion regarding the existing rate regulations. But Congress was convinced, through insurance industry arguments, that the continued regulation of the insurance business by the states was in the consumer's interest. Thus, in 1945 Congress passed a bill sponsored by the National Association of Insurance Commissioners, the McCarran-Ferguson Act, which expressed this congressional intent. The act gave the states a moratorium period of somewhat over two years during which time the federal antitrust laws (the Sherman, Clayton, and Federal Trade Commission Acts) would not apply to insurance except for those passages prohibiting boycott, coercion, and intimidation. After the moratorium period, the Sherman, Clayton, Federal Trade Commission, and Robinson-Patman Acts would apply to the extent that the states had not enacted similar laws. The moratorium period was given to allow the states enough time to strengthen weak laws and regulations in the affected areas.

Many persons within the insurance industry mistakenly believe that the McCarran-Ferguson Act represents congressional abdication of the regulation of the insurance business. Instead, the act provides that the continued regulation of the insurance business by the states is in the public interest and that no federal law enacted after June 30, 1948 (with the exceptions noted above) will apply to the business of insurance ". . . unless such act specifically relates to the business of insurance . . . ." In other words, Congress can apply whatever laws it wishes to the insurance business by the mere incorporation within the law of a reference to that effect. And, as discussed below, Congress has periodically asserted this right.

State Insurance Regulation Today

At the state level, the insurance business is regulated by the judicial, legislative, and executive branches of each state's government. The courts' role in the regulation of insurance is to resolve conflicts between insurance companies and policyowners and to serve as an arbiter when insurance companies or agents challenge laws and regulations.

Each state's legislature is responsible for enacting comprehensive laws which are designed to regulate the insurance business of that particular state. Typically each state's insurance laws (code) address the following areas:

1. Organization and operation of the state insurance department.
2. Formation and licensing of the various kinds of insurance companies.

3. Filing and approval of certain insurance rates.
4. Assurance of company financial solvency.
5. Liquidation or rehabilitation of insurers.
6. Definition of unfair trade practices and treatment of unauthorized insurers and unfair trade practices.
7. Licensing of agents and brokers.
8. Setting standards for insurance contracts.

Enforcement of the insurance laws is delegated to an administrative official of the executive branch of the government. This official usually is titled the Insurance Commissioner, although some states have other titles (e.g., Director of Insurance or Superintendent of Insurance). In most states, the commissioner is appointed by the governor, with a few states providing for an elected commissioner. Insurance commissioners have broad powers. They are responsible for enforcing the insurance laws of their state and for promulgating regulations and guidelines on such matters as solicitation, replacement, and advertising of life insurance to clarify the laws.

The National Association of Insurance Commissioners

In an attempt to promote uniformity of insurance regulation throughout the United States, state insurance regulators in 1871 formed an organization now known as the National Association of Insurance Commissioners (NAIC) to which each state commissioner belongs. The NAIC provides a forum for discussions of common regulatory problems and develops solutions to these problems in the form of "model" insurance bills and regulations. The term **model bill** refers to a proposal developed by the NAIC and presented to state legislatures in the hopes that if a state legislature adopts a law dealing with the subject matter, it will be patterned after the model bill. The "model regulations" may be promulgated by the individual state insurance regulator without legislative input. Some legislatures and commissioners enact the model bills and regulations as drafted by the NAIC, others enact modified versions, and still others take no action. Hence, results of this model approach have been inconsistent, with both successes and failures.

Insurance Regulation in Canada

The life and health insurance business and its regulation in Canada have, to a large extent, evolved much the same as in the United States. However, important differences do exist.

Canadian regulatory practices initially were far less restrictive than their United States counterparts, but this difference has narrowed in recent years. The first Canadian insurance law was a provincial act passed in 1865.

With the enactment in 1867 of the British North American Act (which serves as the constitution for Canada), several provincial life insurance laws were passed, resulting in some conflicts among provincial laws.

To secure uniformity in provincial law, the Association of Superintendents of Insurance (similar to the NAIC) was formed. The association has been generally successful in achieving its goal, with a major stride toward uniformity made by the enactment in all provinces except Quebec of the Uniform Life Insurance Act, which deals with life insurance contract law.

The provinces maintain jurisdiction over matters which are mainly policyowner-related, including most marketing practices. The federal government is concerned chiefly with the solvency of federally registered companies. Thus, the provinces are responsible for the terms and conditions of insurance policies (which differ somewhat from policies sold in the United States) and for the licensing of agents. Further, a company that is federally registered must still obtain a license to conduct business in a particular province.

Every province requires a person to pass an examination before selling life insurance. Some provinces limit an agent's representation to a single insurer, although the trend seems to be going toward multi-company representation. Agents in Canada need not obtain separate licenses (as their United States counterparts must) to sell variable annuities and variable life insurance.

No Canadian law requires formal policy form approval, nor is approval of rates required. Provincial law prohibits unfair discrimination in rating practices and requires insurers selling participating life insurance to distribute fairly the surplus generated from such business. Limitations as to the maximum surplus that can be withheld from participating policyowners are contained in the Uniform Life Insurance Acts.

The system of regulation as evolved in the United States differs philosophically from that of Canada. The United States system can be characterized best as being relatively rigid, focusing on detail and restrictions. While the Canadian system also contains these elements, it relies more on telling insurers and agents what they must do rather than how they must do it. For example, Canadian insurers are subject to somewhat less stringent investment restrictions than are United States insurers. Because of this, Canadian insurers, on average, have earned more on their investments than United States companies.

Implicit in the Canadian system is more regulatory freedom coupled with a greater emphasis on self-regulation. The Association of Superintendents of Insurance develops guidelines on such matters as variable contracts, group accident and sickness insurance, and creditors group insurance. These guidelines do not carry the force of law, but are followed closely by the companies and thus affect their operations. In addition, the Canadian Life and Health Insurance Association (CLHIA) publishes recommended "initiatives" for their member companies to follow. These initiatives, also without the force of law, deal with such matters as providing a "10-day free-look" for life insurance and interim insurance agreements, which in effect extends the conditional receipt.

Of the 167 active life insurers in Canada in 1979, 145 were federally and twenty-four were provincially registered. The federally registered companies held 94% of the total life insurance in force in Canada.

Areas of Regulation Affecting Life and Health Insurance Marketing

Numerous insurance laws and regulations have an impact on life and health insurance marketing. Some relate specifically to marketing practices, while others relate indirectly. This section discusses several of the important traditional areas of government regulation: organization and licensing of insurance companies, expense limitations, rate regulation, policy forms, agent regulation, advertising regulation, and group insurance regulation. Since regulation of group life and health insurance is generally more flexible than regulation of individual life and health products, less attention is devoted to the group area.

Organization and Licensing of Insurers

At the most fundamental level of insurance, and therefore of life and health insurance marketing, is the insurance regulator's power over the formation and licensing of insurance companies. In the United States, insurance companies are incorporated by the states and standards for establishing a new insurer are set by the insurance code of each state. These standards vary considerably from state to state. For example, because of Arizona's low capital and surplus requirements, a large number of the almost 2,000 life insurers in the United States were formed in that state.

Newly formed domestic (in-state), foreign (out-of-state), and alien (non-U.S.) insurers must obtain a license before selling insurance within the state. The insurance commissioner uses not only clearly defined financial standards in deciding whether to grant an insurer a license but also has considerable latitude in imposing other, more subjective, criteria. For example, the quality and reputation of the incorporators and of management is of prime importance. Canadian regulatory officials have similar powers in determining whether to grant a certificate of registry (license).

Canadian life insurance companies can be incorporated under either federal or provincial law. The usual practice is to seek federal incorporation unless the insurer intends to transact business in only one province. Each province and the federal government have laws establishing minimum capital and surplus standards for the formation of new insurers.

Expense Limitations

One aspect of regulation which has an impact on the marketing of life insurance relates to the limits that New York and Wisconsin have placed on the amount of expenses that insurers may incur in connection with new individual life policy sales. New York insurance law is particularly important to insurance companies since it is extraterritorial. That is, an insurance company that does business in New York state must comply with many New York laws in all the other states in which it does business. For example, Section 213 of the New York Insurance Code has a direct bearing on the commission that can be paid to a life insurance agent who sells for a company that does business in the state of New York.

Generally, the New York commission limitation is 55% of the first year premium. Hence, an agent representing a non-New York-licensed insurer can receive higher commissions than an agent representing a New York-licensed insurer. These and other expense restrictions were the direct result of the Armstrong Investigation, which found excessive amounts spent for expenses by life insurers, especially as related to the acquisition of new business. While no study has investigated the extent to which these limitations influence the marketing of life insurance, little doubt exists that they have an impact. One effect is that some companies avoid doing business in New York. Others set up a subsidiary company in New York to conduct their business there, so that the parent company need not comply with the New York laws in the other states in which it operates.

Rate Regulation

The rates insurers charge have a direct bearing on marketing insurance products. Ideally, rates should be adequate, not excessive, and equitable (not unfairly discriminatory). Although a few states require that rates for the ordinary line of life insurance be filed along with an insurer's contract form, no laws in either the United States or Canada require "approval" of life insurance rates. A few states require approval of the rates of individually issued health insurance policies. Group insurance rates need not even be filed with insurance regulators.

Adequacy of Rates

Life insurance rates in the United States and Canada are, however, indirectly regulated through statutorily mandated minimum reserves and in the United

States by nonforfeiture requirements. These requirements are believed to minimize the chance of an insurer's charging inadequate rates, thus forcing it to draw upon its surplus.

Generally, group life and health rates are not subject to regulation as to adequacy, since it is believed that the sophistication of the group insurance purchaser and the seller are sufficient for each to protect its own interests. However, in the recent past, New York and Michigan provided that initial group life rates could not fall below a statutorily mandated minimum. Michigan repealed its law in 1969, and the New York law was significantly modified in 1973 to apply only to a group purchasing insurance for the first time and to groups requesting major changes in benefit design.

Reserve and nonforfeiture requirements for individual cash value life insurance have also been liberalized recently, resulting in lower premiums and values for many new policy series. Even more drastic reductions in premiums and values on new policies can be anticipated in the near future. These reductions will materialize as state legislatures enact versions of the 1980 NAIC Valuation and Standard Nonforfeiture Model Law and as Canadian laws are similarly liberalized.

This 1980 model law includes provision for a dynamic interest rate, unlike existing state laws which set a maximum interest rate to derive values. The new rate concept will allow insurers to make annual interest rate adjustments as economic circumstances indicate. Of course, any change would apply only to newly issued life insurance and annuity contracts. The model law also makes use of new mortality tables (1980 Commissioners' Standard Ordinary and others). The new tables reflect the improvement in mortality rates that has occurred since the preparation of the mortality table specified in the current law (1958 C.S.O.). Further, for the first time, separate mortality tables for males and females are included. Certain needed technical changes too complex and numerous to mention here also are incorporated into the new model law.

The NAIC Task Force responsible for the new law speculated that its timely passage by state legislatures could result in a further lowering of gross premiums and cash values by 1985. For example, calculations made by the Task Force suggest that gross premium rates for new ordinary life policies could possibly be decreased by 15% to 20% for males and up to 25% for females.

Even ignoring the 1980 model law, the current trend toward lower premiums means that agents, subject to a fixed commission schedule, must sell more life insurance to maintain the same absolute income level.

However, this also means that the assumptions used to derive policy values and premiums, although still conservative, may be more attuned to actual results. While life insurance policies may now be more competitive relative to other financial instruments, the changes may also mean that it is financially advantageous to some policyowners to replace older higher-cost policies, a development which would have the effect of promoting sales.

Non-Excessive Rates

Technically, an insurer may charge as high a premium for individual life insurance as it wishes, although it is said that price competition discourages marketplace excesses in this area, especially if competition is encouraged through effective cost disclosure. There are, however, some states that regulate individual health products closely to ascertain that the benefits bear a reasonable relationship to the premium charged. For example, they may specify that a specific type of policy have a loss ratio of at least 55½%.

Equity of Rates

Equitable pricing among classes of insureds is said to be promoted through competition and by requirements in a few states and by the Canadian federal government relating to maximum surplus accumulation, annual apportionment of surplus, and fairness in surplus allocation with respect to participating insurance. These latter requirements resulted from the Armstrong Investigation. Even so, the field of fairness in rates, especially as relates to surplus distribution, must be regarded as relatively unfettered by regulatory constraints. This is said to have created some inequities within the marketplace which are in need of special attention. For example, some insurers do not improve dividend scales for older policies even though experience would warrant such an improvement. Some insurers are said to design terminal dividend scales for the sole purpose of making their policies appear attractive from a cost standpoint.

Policy Forms

To the extent that life and health insurance policy forms are regulated, marketing is affected. In most states, individual life and health insurance policy forms must be filed with the insurance commissioner. In some states, the commissioner must specifically approve each form. In other states, if the commissioner takes no action, the form is approved, in effect, and may be used. In Canada, policy forms need not be approved except when a company is first licensed, although insurers usually file their forms with the regulators as a matter of courtesy.

Individual and group insurance policies in both the United States and Canada must contain certain provisions (e.g., incontestable, grace period, reinstatement clauses), although the exact wording is not mandated. In the

United States, forms may be disapproved if a commissioner believes any of the policy's provisions are unfair, deceptive, or otherwise not in the public interest. In recent years, regulators have also become concerned with the ease with which policies can be read by policyowners.

The policy loan clause is an increasingly important aspect of individual life insurance policy provisions. Life insurance policies with cash values are required by state law to provide that the policyowner has a right to receive a loan (technically, an "advance" on the policy proceeds) through his or her policy for an amount up to the policy cash value. Such loan provisions are optional in Canada, although usually included. This has been an attractive feature of cash value policies particularly in recent years, since the interest rates charged by insurers for these loans could not exceed 8% in most states. Some older policies have five or 6% interest rates. In Canada, policies are being issued with no ceiling on interest rates.

Many agents use the policy loan feature as a selling point by showing prospective purchasers how they may be able to take financial advantage of the combination of the low interest rate and a high marginal tax bracket to lower the effective cost of a cash value insurance policy. The approach involves a systematic plan of borrowing under the policy to pay the premiums. The interest on the loans can be made tax deductible, thus resulting in a lower-cost policy. This approach has been particularly effective for persons in moderate to high income tax brackets.

However, another new NAIC model law promises to diminish the attractiveness of the above marketing approach and the policy loan provision generally. This model law, already enacted into law in one state and pending in several others, provides for a flexible policy loan interest rate to be included in newly issued policies. The maximum rate an insurer could charge at any time would be based on Moody's Composite Bond Index. Of course, the interest rate established in policies already in force would be unaffected by the new law.

While for the long-term welfare of the life insurance business this approach must be viewed favorably, some agents may feel threatened and may find that a sales approach that centers on the loan interest rate is less appealing to customers.

Agent Regulation

The insurance codes of the states and the provinces provide that a person must obtain a license from the insurance regulator prior to selling life or health insurance. The person must also be authorized by an insurer to represent that insurer. Some states (e.g., Georgia) make a provision for a counselor's license for those who give insurance advice for a fee without selling insurance. The insurance laws in most states and Canadian provinces require the regulator to administer an examination to each person who desires to become a licensed agent, broker, or counselor. The examination tests the individual's mastery of the fundamental concepts of life and health insurance and of the applicable insurance laws and regulations. Upon passing the examination and upon meeting certain other requirements as to age, citizenship, and character, and, in some jurisdictions, education, the person is issued a license to sell, or provide advice regarding, life or health insurance.

Although most agent licenses are perpetual, they can be revoked or suspended by the regulator for sufficient cause. In the United States, the chief cause of license revocation and suspension, as well of agent fines imposed by the commissioner, is violation of a state's Unfair Trade Practices Act. These state laws, patterned after an NAIC model of the same name, were passed by all states shortly after the McCarran-Ferguson Act to ensure state compliance with the "proviso" clause of the McCarran-Ferguson Act (whereby the federal government does not involve itself in insurance matters so long as the states act in public interest), thus replacing the Federal Trade Commission's (FTC) authority in this area.

These state trade practices acts are designed to prevent numerous activities deemed to be unfair, including fraudulent, misleading, and unethical acts of agents and brokers: (1) rebating, (2) twisting, (3) misappropriation of funds, and (4) commingling of funds.

Rebating is the practice of an agent's (or insurer's) returning a portion of the premium (e.g., agent's commission) to an applicant for insurance. Rebating is illegal, since it is considered contrary to the maintenance of fair competition and equity among policyowners. Critics of the rebating prohibition argue that the prohibition is illogical in that it prevents buyers from negotiating fully with the sellers, as is the case with respect to non-insurance commodities and services.

Twisting refers to the practice of misrepresentation by an agent to induce a policyowner through misrepresentation to discontinue an existing life insurance policy and purchase a new one from the agent. In contrast to simple **replacement,** which is discontinuing one policy to purchase another, twisting is illegal. The purchase of a life insurance policy, while not a complicated transaction, may involve a complex array of financial data. The consumer can easily be misled, either intentionally or unintentionally, by an agent. In recognition of this fact, several states have promulgated a version of the two NAIC Model Replacement Regulations, which require the disclosure of certain information considered pertinent to the proposed replacement decision.

Agents often handle large amounts of their policyowners' money in the form of premium payments, dividend checks, and surrender and loan funds. **Misappropriation,** or misuse, of these funds even on a temporary basis is illegal. Related to misappropriation is the practice of **commingling** of funds. Agents are not to combine monies belonging to policyowners with their own funds.

Advertising Regulation

A state's Unfair Trade Practices Act prohibits misleading or false advertising related to a life or health insurance company or policy. Like many insurance laws, however, it is clarified by the insurance commissioner's promulgation of regulations setting forth specific prohibitions and guidelines.

In response to FTC pressure, the NAIC recommended in December 1955 a code for health insurance advertising. This code prohibited many misleading advertising practices and required disclosure of certain health policy provisions. The NAIC developed a Model Life Insurance Advertising Regulation in 1975. This regulation restricts the use of several misleading words and phrases. For example, the terms "investment," "profit," "founder's plan," "savings plan," and other similar terms may not be used in an advertisement if the effect of such usage would be to mislead a prospective purchaser as to the nature of the insurance product advertised. The regulation also mandates limited insurer and policy disclosure in advertising. Although only a few states have adopted a life insurance advertising regulation, some have considerably expanded the applicability and scope of their regulation (e.g., Georgia's regulation includes extemporaneous sales talks in its definition of advertising).

Group Insurance Regulation

The preceding pages have, where appropriate, included discussion about how group life and health insurance marketing is affected by regulation. However, additional aspects of group insurance regulation are also of importance to the marketing function.

For example, state law stipulates the groups that are eligible for group insurance (e.g., unions, employers, creditors, etc.). The minimum number of persons in a group to be considered for coverage under group insurance is usually established by law (common minimums are 3, 5, or 10 lives) as is the minimum proportion of the group to be covered (e.g., 100% of the group must be insured if the plan is noncontributory and at least 75% must be insured if the plan is contributory).

A few states place a maximum (e.g., $100,000) as to the amount of group life insurance that may be written on any one life, although the trend is moving away from the use of maximums. Some states establish a maximum rate (e.g., $.60 per $1,000 per month) an employee may contribute toward group life insurance.

Canadian group insurance was virtually unregulated until 1971 when the Association of Superintendents of Insurance began issuing rules which, in effect, establish requirements similar to those in many states. Further, since medical expense coverage is provided to each Canadian by the province, the market for medical expense benefits in Canada is limited to offering only benefits to cover the gaps in the basic government-provided coverage.

The trend in both the United States and Canada is toward liberalizing group requirements. Thus, while current standards undoubtedly inhibit an insurer's or agent's ability to penetrate some markets with group benefits as fully as possible, one can anticipate fewer strictures in the future.

U.S. Federal Initiatives Affecting Life Insurance Marketing

Just because the states are allowed by Congress to continue to be the primary regulators of the insurance business, it would be a mistake to conclude that no federal regulation of the insurance business exists. Recall that McCarran-Ferguson stated only that no federal laws would apply to the insurance business *unless* the law stated specifically that it did so apply. As discussed below, Congress has enacted several laws that state explicitly that they apply to insurance. Further, McCarran-Ferguson does not prevent investigations by federal agencies into the insurance business. Nor does it prohibit federal regulatory involvement where the states have failed to act. The insurance-related activities of several federal agencies are discussed below.

The Federal Trade Commission

The Federal Trade Commission (FTC) has been involved in enforcement of several laws and several investigations concerning the insurance industry.

The FTC was given the responsibility by Congress in 1970 of enforcing the Fair Credit Reporting Act (FCRA). From the consumer's perspective, this act provides three basic rights. First, it requires insurers to notify an applicant if an investigative consumer report may be prepared on him or her.[4] This notification usually is provided by the insurance agent via a detachable form appended to the life insurance application. Second, the act also gives a consumer the right to learn the "nature and substance" of the information

[4] An investigative consumer report is a report prepared by a consumer reporting agency (inspection bureau), which involves the collection of personal information (habits, character, general reputation, finances, etc.) from others (such as friends, employers, bankers, etc.).

maintained on him or her by the report preparer. Third, if a report is the basis in whole or part for an adverse underwriting decision, the applicant must be notified of that fact, advised of the report preparer's name and address, and advised of his or her right to find out the general content of the report.

The FTC has investigated alleged abusive marketing practices associated with Medicare supplement insurance and with the debit system of marketing life insurance. Another FTC initiative studied the use of life insurance policies by small businesses to fund pension plans and the claim that agents provide inadequate cost disclosure in connection with the sale of such policies. The recently released FTC staff report, *Life Insurance Cost Disclosure,* severely criticizes current cost disclosure practices and aroused a good deal of industry concern about FTC objectives. Some of the issues raised by this report are discussed in Chapter 4.

The Securities and Exchange Commission

The Securities and Exchange Commission (SEC) became involved in life insurance marketing when the Supreme Court ruled in 1959 that federal laws applied to insurers selling variable annuities.[5] The Court ruled that such annuities are securities under the Securities Act of 1933, that the separate accounts backing the annuities are "investment companies" subject to the Investment Company Act of 1940, and that sales personnel must be registered as security broker-dealers. In other words, the marketing of variable annuities is subject to joint federal and state regulation.

The SEC also asserts jurisdiction, along with the insurance commissioners, over the design and marketing of **variable life insurance** (VLI) in much the same way it does with respect to variable annuities. VLI policies provide for cash value and face amounts to vary with the investment performance of the underlying portfolio of securities. Although VLI marketing activity remains at a low level, many believe the product eventually will gain widespread marketplace acceptance. To date, the practical and regulatory problems associated with VLI—dual agent licensing and dual insurance company regulation—coupled with a sluggish stock market throughout the 1970s have stifled its growth, although at least two insurers are enjoying moderate acceptance of the product in the marketplace.

Internal Revenue Service

The Internal Revenue Service (IRS) is charged with enforcing several laws which have an impact on life and health insurance marketing practices. First,

---

[5] *SEC v. Variable Annuity Life Insurance Company of America et. al.,* 359 U.S. 560, (1958).

the IRS is responsible for enforcement of three major tax laws relating to life insurance policies and annuities: (1) income tax, (2) estate tax, and (3) gift tax. Life insurance and annuities enjoy special treatment under the tax laws. For example, life insurance death proceeds generally are received income tax-free and can be arranged to be estate tax-free. The gift of a life insurance policy to someone creates potential gift tax liability only on an amount approximately equal to the policy's cash value, rather than on the face amount. The interest credited to the cash value accumulation of life insurance policies and annuities enjoys income tax deferral. These and other tax aspects are often promoted as inducements to buy life insurance. A recent favorable private letter ruling, dated January 2, 1981, regarding E.F. Hutton Life Insurance Company's "Universal" life policy could mean that this tax deferral advantage could spark a significant growth in these types of "new money" products.

Second, the IRS, along with the U.S. Department of Labor, is charged with the administration and enforcement of the Employee Retirement Income Security Act of 1974 (ERISA). ERISA was passed because of a growing concern by Congress about the soundness of many employee benefit plans and about the fair treatment of employees under such plans. The act prescribes numerous requirements to be met by pension and group plans, many of which have an impact on life and health insurance and annuity marketing since many plans are partially or totally funded by insurance.

ERISA created marketing opportunities for insurance companies by creating the individual retirement account (IRA). Persons who are not covered under a qualified pension or government plan may establish their own personal retirement programs through an IRA. Individuals may make tax deductible contributions of up to $1,500 per year to an IRA. Earnings of the IRA are tax deferred. Many agents focus their sales in this market, with funding for the IRA provided through an annuity.

ERISA also liberalized a previous law, the Self-Employed Individual Tax Retirement Act of 1962 (more commonly known as the Keogh Act or H.R. 10), allowing greater contributions by a self-employed person to his or her retirement plan. Deductible contributions to a defined contribution Keogh Plan may not exceed the lesser of $7500 or 15% of the self-employed person's income. However, the lesser of $750 or 100% of earned income may be deducted on behalf of a self-employed person earning less than $15,000 per year. As with the IRAs, agents and insurers often view the Keogh plan as a marketing tool since insurance can be used to fund the plan.

ERISA reporting, disclosure, and other requirements have caused increased administrative work for employers. This may have discouraged small employers from offering some group benefits. On the other hand, the

ERISA requirements seem to have rendered the services of insurers and agents more valuable, thus, more desirable.

In addition to ERISA regulation, the IRS must promulgate regulations dealing with income tax consequences to employees of employer-provided group insurance. Section 79 of the Internal Revenue Code provides that up to $50,000 of group term life insurance may be provided tax-free to an employee by an employer. Amounts over $50,000 and group permanent life insurance are subject to certain income taxation. Revised group permanent life (Section 79) insurance regulations were recently promulgated, the effect of which is to require a redesign of many insurers' group permanent products and to force certain changes within existing plans.

Income tax law relating to group life and health insurance must be considered generally as favoring the marketing function. For example, premiums paid by an employer for group life and health insurance that benefits employees are income tax deductible to the employer. And, subject to the above-mentioned limit of $50,000 on group life only, employees need not report any of the employer contributions to group life and health insurance as income.

State Versus Federal Regulation: A Continuing Debate

As can be seen, while the states are the primary regulators of insurance marketing in the United States, the federal government's role is far from inconsequential. Marketing practices of life and health insurers and agents could be profoundly affected if the federal government in the United States chose to assume a more active role through the repeal or modification of the McCarran-Ferguson Act.

The debate as to whether the public interest is best served by federal or state regulation is an old one. Various investigations at the federal level have delved into the effectiveness and quality of state insurance regulation, the most recent being a 1979 study by the General Accounting Office. Recommendations have been made from time to time to repeal or modify the McCarran-Ferguson Act, as for example, those made in the 1978 report of the National Commission for the Review of Antitrust Laws and Procedures. Federal bills to accomplish repeal or modification have been introduced with little success over the years—the most recent such effort being the Insurance Competition Improvements Act, in 1980, introduced by Senator Howard Metzenbaum.

The federal versus state debate seems to have "cooled" following the 1980 election results and the changed congressional mood in 1981. However, if history is any indication, the debate is destined to become intense again in the future.

Although it is beyond the purpose of this chapter to discuss fully the pros and cons of state versus federal regulation, the following lists provide the reader with an idea of the complexity of the discussion. Some of the arguments made for continuing state regulation include:[6]

- Decentralization of government is a virtue in itself.
- State regulation already exists.
- States can be more responsive to local needs than can the federal government.
- Federal regulation would become cumbersome and perhaps create a rigid, arbitrary bureaucracy.
- Whatever uniformity is necessary has been and continues to be achieved through the NAIC.
- Effects of ill-advised insurance legislation are localized.
- States may serve as "laboratories" for insurance regulation.

On the other hand, arguments given in favor of federal regulation include:

- Lack of uniformity among state insurance codes and conflict in rulings create complications and added expense for insurers operating in several states.
- The expense of having to file financial reports in each state and maintain fifty-one separate insurance departments is high.
- Ill-advised legislation can be passed easily in states where legislators cannot devote resources to studying legislation as can the United States Congress.
- The political nature of the appointment or election of state insurance commissioners may produce poorly qualified regulators who are subject to undue local pressure.
- Conflicts arise between standard federal regulations and state rulings which affect insurer operations.
- Varying state requirements cause insurer inflexibility.
- Most insurers operate in many states, and states find it increasingly difficult to solve regulatory problems involving foreign and alien insurers.
- Insurance commissioners and state legislatures are sometimes overly responsive to domestic insurance companies' pressures to the point of placing extra burdens on non-domestic companies.

[6] *Issues and Needed Improvements in State Regulation of the Insurance Business* (Washington, D.C.: General Accounting Office, 1979) pp. 165–183 and Robert I. Mehr, *Life Insurance: Theory and Practice* (revised ed.; Dallas, Texas: Business Publications, Inc., 1977), p. 719.

The federal/state controversy will, no doubt, continue. The controversy could result in (1) the states' continuing to be the primary regulators of insurance, (2) the federal government's becoming the primary regulator of the insurance business, or (3) a system of dual regulation, akin to the Canadian approach, under which some types of regulations would be administered by the states and others by the federal government. Whatever happens, the impact on marketing of life insurance will continue to be felt. Even if the states retain primary jurisdiction, the continued threat of federal involvement has encouraged states to consider mandating more stringent marketing- and pricing-related regulations than those now imposed. Thus, it is critical that insurance marketers continue to watch developments in regulations on both the state and the federal levels.

Summary

Government regulation of the life and health insurance business remains extensive in the United States. Canadian regulatory requirements are less prevalent, although far from nonexistent. Much of this regulation in both countries has an impact on the marketing function by constricting some markets, restricting certain practices, and in some cases, creating marketing opportunities. This chapter has considered how some of the traditional aspects of government regulation have affected this function.

Chapter 4

The Impact of Consumerism on Insurance Marketing

Harold Skipper, Jr., Ph.D., CLU

One hears and reads constantly about the impact on business and government of the "new phenomenon" known as consumerism. To some, the "consumer movement" constitutes nothing but a few self-appointed consumer advocates seeking to make a name for themselves or attempting to promote their own viewpoints. To others, consumerism is bringing about a much-needed change in the way businesses view and respond to consumers' concerns and attitudes.

Actually, consumerism is not new but has existed for decades. Consumerism simply means that a business must deal with its customers and within its environment in an honest, fair, and open manner. Consumerism is not one person's or one organization's views; it is the collective opinions and attitudes of the public brought more forcefully to bear on business and government than has heretofore been the case. Consumers can bring more pressure to bear on business today than in the past because they are better educated and have easier access to information needed for decision-making. As a result, they will continue to demand better products at lower costs.

The impact of consumerism on the life and health insurance industry and its regulators has been significant. Consumerism is forcing insurance regulators to acknowledge that their role as consumer protectors goes beyond minimizing insurer insolvencies; it includes providing more useful day-to-day insurance assistance to consumers. The consumer movement is encouraging many insurers to change from a "product-directed" marketing strategy (fitting marketing practices—and the customer—to the products the insurer offers) to a "customer-directed" strategy (producing products—and adjusting marketing practices—to fit particular customer needs).

Public Attitudes

Because in a private free enterprise economy, the public's attitudes and concerns should ultimately determine what products and services will be offered, and how and by whom they will be offered, management must have an appreciation of these attitudes and related trends. Although the life insurance business has always spoken of its need to be aware of public attitudes and trends, as an industry, it was late to act on this need. Only within the last few years have steps been taken to determine the buying public's attitudes about the industry. The American Council of Life Insurance (ACLI) now sponsors two projects to monitor consumers' attitudes: (1) the Monitoring Attitudes of the Public (MAP) annual survey and (2) the Trend Analysis Program (TAP). The Canadian Life and Health Insurance Association (CLHIA) also tracks consumer attitudes, one recent effort being its *Data Base II* survey in 1977.

The MAP survey, conducted annually for the ACLI since 1968, involves having a national sample of adults respond to questions about the life insurance business, its products, and related matters such as views on economic security, business, and government (including Social Security). Related to the MAP survey is one conducted every other year by the ACLI on the attitudes of young persons aged 14 through 25. The Trend Analysis Program, produced at irregular intervals, studies emerging trends in American society that may have significance to the life insurance business.

These and other publications serve as the basis for the following discussion on the public's attitudes regarding (1) business, (2) government, and (3) the economy and economic security. Although the discussion focuses on attitudes of United States citizens, the general findings and trends reflect the attitudes of Canadians also.[1]

Attitudes About Business

The average consumer's attitude toward big business is perhaps best described as one of skepticism. For example, when asked if big business is overly concerned with profits at the expense of good service and good products, MAP reports a less than favorable public opinion of business, as shown in Table I.[2]

[1] G. M. Devlin, "Life Insurance in the 1980's", *Canadian Insurance/Agent and Broker* (November 1979), p. 80.

[2] *Monitoring Attitudes of the Public,* (Washington, D.C.: American Council of Life Insurance, 1979), p. 43.

TABLE I
Business Overly Concerned with Profits

	1968 %	1971 %	1972 %	1975 %	1976 %	1977 %	1979 %
Yes	44	49	47	57	58	52	50
No	20	19	19	14	16	15	18
No opinion	36	32	34	29	25	32	31

Young consumers (ages 14 to 25) expressed the same sentiments: 79% agreed that business is overly concerned with profits, the view being most widespread among college graduates (97%) and young people ages 22 to 25.[3] In addition, a majority of consumers believe that big business often takes advantage of poor persons in its pricing and selling of products, plays no constructive role in trying to control inflation, and is becoming a threat because of its greater political activity.[4]

Despite these negative views about big business, substantial proportions of consumers still believe that if it were not for big business, their standard of living would be much lower, although the percentage holding this belief shows a decline in recent years.[5]

Young consumers are positive in a related aspect of their attitudes toward business. Over three out of four (77%) believe business is responsive to the needs of consumers.[6] The percentage agreeing declines with increasing age.

Related to youths' attitudes toward business is their attitude regarding work, with 85% of young people sampled in 1978 expressing agreement with the notion that hard work almost always pays off.[7] This percentage is up from the 1974 (74%) and the 1976 (78%) results. These and other results from the same survey led its preparers to conclude: "Young Americans today are becoming noticeably more conservative in their basic attitudes toward life styles."[8]

Attitudes About Government

The public's attitudes about government are even more negative than its attitudes about big business. Increasingly, the public believes that private industry provides greater value in performing services than does government.[9]

[3] *Youth 78,* (Washington, D.C.: American Council of Life Insurance, 1978), p. 57.
[4] *MAP—1979,* pp. 44, 64.
[5] *Ibid.,* p. 44.
[6] *Youth 78,* pp. 57–58.
[7] *Ibid.,* p. 38.
[8] *Ibid.,* p. 7.
[9] *MAP—1979,* p. 58.

Much has been written recently about the "psychology of entitlement" that is alleged to exist among consumers, that is, the tendency of persons to consider certain privileges as rights even if not "earned." Consumers defy such stereotyping, however. It is true that large majorities of the public believe, for example, that they have a right to an adequate pension at retirement, to adequate support of dependents upon the death of the breadwinner, and to adequate health care.[10] Yet, regarding other, less essential benefits, the public believes generally that "it is all right that the *good* things in life should be distributed unequally, as long as everyone has an equal opportunity to compete for them."[11] Thus, the public seems to be saying that certain base-levels of security should be a right of every North American, but beyond that, they hold strong views in favor of equality of opportunity as opposed to equality of rewards.

Attitudes About the Economy and Economic Security

Americans believe inflation to be the country's most serious problem. A strong majority of consumers believe that the best way to fight inflation is by a general reduction in government spending. Yet, when asked in what major areas spending should be decreased, only a small proportion are in fact willing to support specific reductions. In four of the eight major areas (the elderly, health care, education, and the poor), a majority in 1979 supported an increase in government spending.[12]

Consumers are aware of the importance of personal financial planning and state a preference for saving money, rather than spending it, during inflationary times. Table II shows how the public claims to view buying patterns

TABLE II
Buying Patterns During Inflation

	Good time to: %	Bad time to: %
Save money	71	28
Buy life insurance	48	49
Buy stocks	33	62
Buy a house	33	66
Buy major appliances	32	66
Buy a new car	23	75

[10] *MAP—1974*, p. 6.
[11] *MAP—1979*, p. 60.
[12] *Ibid.*, pp. 59, 64–65.

during times of inflation.[13] If consumers' beliefs are reflected in their actions, one can understand why the housing industry often leads a recession.

The reader must use caution when considering the data presented above. These findings form a reasonable approximation of the public's attitudes rather than an exact representation. Even so, the ACLI believes the current mood of the public can be summarized as follows:

> Confidence in our leaders and major institutions is down. A growing majority seem to feel the nation's future will not live up to its past and there is increasing criticism of government. But, it is important to note that Americans are still quite satisfied with their own lives, and by and large confident in their own futures. . . .
>
> Despite the crisis in confidence, the public still expresses very strong support for our system of government and the free enterprise system.[14]

Consumer Concerns Relating to Insurance Marketing

With the preceding overview of the public's attitudes in mind, specific contemporary consumer concerns as they relate to life and health insurance marketing may be addressed. Consumers are "heard" in two places: within the private sector and within the public sector.

Within the private sector, consumers voice their attitudes and concerns through their buying habits. They buy what they like and can afford, and (usually) avoid that which they dislike or cannot afford.

The life and health insurance marketplace is not directed solely by consumers' buying habits, as the theoretically perfect market is described in economic textbooks. Therefore, consumers' elected and appointed representatives sometimes establish prohibitions or limitations on certain practices and products in the marketplace. This gives rise to a public sector voice of consumers expressed through their elected representatives. These representatives are expected to act in their constituents' interest by responding to their demands and by protecting them even if they are not fully aware of the need for protection. The preceding chapter addressed the traditional areas of this public sector voice. This chapter addresses contemporary aspects.

Space does not permit a discussion, or even a list, of all consumer concerns affecting life and health insurance marketing. The balance of the chapter discusses those concerns which, as viewed from the beginning of the 1980s, seem to be the most important to consumers and to government. The responses of insurers and the government are described also. The seven

---

[13] *Ibid.*, p. 67.

[14] *Ibid.*, p. 8.

areas of consumer concern that are discussed below are having or seem likely to have an impact on life and health insurance marketing. These are insurance products, policy readability, cost and benefit disclosure, privacy, equality, replacements, and agent qualifications.

Concerns About Insurance Products

The public believes strongly in the benefits of life insurance. A large majority believe owning life insurance is a necessity for the family wage-earner. Not surprisingly, a large majority of consumers believe life insurance is the best way of protecting a family financially against the primary wage-earner's premature death. Life insurance is the choice of a relatively low percentage of consumers as a vehicle for funding children's education (16%), retirement (16%), or emergencies (14%). Yet, only 22% of consumers disagreed that life insurance cash values are "one of the most important benefits of life insurance." Hence, although life insurance policies are viewed primarily as providing death protection, consumers are generally aware of the importance of policies' cash values.[15]

Consumers, primarily through their elected or appointed representatives, express concern about specific insurance products. These concerns center around cash value life insurance, products sold through the debit system, partial endowment insurance, cancer insurance, and Medicare supplements.

Cash Value Insurance

All forms of traditional cash value life insurance have been coming under increasingly heavy attack. Many of these criticisms are based on a mistaken understanding of the nature of cash value insurance (e.g., the belief that the practice of requiring a policyowner to pay interest on a policy loan is unfair), while others are based on valid arguments (e.g., high inflation erodes the value of many forms of cash value insurance).

Much of the controversy involves disagreement as to the "true nature" of the products and their appropriate uses. Some argue that traditional agents and insurers are biased in favor of cash value insurance sales, since commissions are usually higher for this form than for term life insurance, notwithstanding the fact that more term life insurance is sold than whole life. Anticipated changes in nonforfeiture and reserve requirements, as discussed in Chapter 3, will likely be the unintended cause of more consumer concern, since many types of existing cash value policies will appear less attractive relative to new products. Regardless of the merits of cash value insurance, as

[15] *Ibid.*, pp. 25 and 27.

a proportion of total new sales, its market share continues to decline in both the United States and Canada.[16]

Debit Insurance Products

Life and health insurance products specifically designed to be marketed through the debit system have recently been the focus of much public concern and debate. Problems alleged to exist within the debit system and many of its products are the high cost of benefits compared to other forms of insurance, high lapse rates, unfair contract provisions, overloading (the practice of selling a person more policies than he or she can afford), churning of policies (the practice of repeatedly selling a person new policies in place of old policies), misleading and high pressure sales tactics, and exorbitant profits. While acknowledging that some problems may exist, industry spokespersons forcefully defend the system and its products.

Consumers understandably are not generally aware of these alleged problems, although for one type of debit product—industrial life insurance—30% of consumers who said they were familiar with the product stated a preference for its sale being banned. At least one state (New York) no longer allows industrial life insurance to be sold in that state.

Several insurers have voluntarily withdrawn from the sale of industrial insurance, with some attempting to cease altogether the use of the debit system of marketing. Nevertheless, many insurers are still quite active in this market, stating a belief that the debit system is adaptable to a changing environment. They also point out that, too often, critics do not distinguish carefully between the debit system of marketing and its products. National figures indicate that what was a major segment of the debit insurance business, industrial life insurance, has decreased significantly in importance. Further, the expenses associated with marketing small policies through the debit system will likely continue to rise.

At some point, public policy makers could conceivably decide that the benefits provided under such small policies are deemed too small in relation to the premiums charged. The NAIC, for its part, recently appointed a Task Force and Advisory Committee to investigate alleged problems with debit products and the debit system. Its work was unfinished at this writing.

Partial Endowment Type Life Insurance

Since the late 1970s, some insurers and agents have been specializing in the marketing of partial endowment type life insurance. This insurance, sometimes inaccurately referred to as "deposit term" life insurance, is often

---

[16] *Life Insurance Fact Book,* (Washington, D.C.: American Council of Life Insurance, 1979), p. 14; and *Canadian Life Insurance Facts,* (Toronto, Ontario: The Canadian Life Insurance Association, 1979), p. 6.

marketed as a term-type product. The first year premium is higher than subsequent ones. The purpose of the high first year premium is to discourage early lapsation and to provide the selling agent with a commission higher than that which he or she would receive from the typical term policy. A modest endowment value is included in the policy, with the amount of the endowment usually set at a multiple of two or three times the excess of the initial premium over renewal premiums. This policy design lends itself to deceptive sales presentations, which implies the existence of a "deposit," or "additional" first-year premium (the excess of the initial over renewal premiums) that is "returned" to the persisting policyowner at double or triple the original amount. The product is often sold as an alternative to other cash value policies through a variation of the "buy term and invest the difference" approach.

Much partial endowment type life insurance is sold to replace existing cash value insurance. This fact, plus allegations of deceptive sales practices have resulted in ill-will within the life insurance business regarding the marketing practices associated with this product.[17] Thus, pressure is being exerted within certain states to promulgate special regulations aimed at this product alone.

Cancer Insurance

Another product causing concern to some is cancer insurance. A few health insurers market this specialized product which is designed to cover direct and certain indirect expenses associated with cancer. Some regulators and others have questioned the wisdom of allowing such specialized insurance policies to be sold, pointing out that the consumer's first need is for adequate major medical expense insurance, not insurance designed to cover only one peril. Marketing practices are also criticized because they are to said to focus on many consumers' extreme fear of cancer, especially if any history of cancer exists in the individual's family.

Insurers that market cancer insurance contend the product is demanded in the marketplace and that it serves to fill a valid consumer need. They contend that, while isolated marketing abuses may exist, generally the marketing practices are fair and honorable.

Medicare Supplement Insurance

The Medicare program of the United States federal government provides health care coverage for the elderly who are eligible for Social Security retirement benefits and for certain other classes of persons. Deductibles and

[17] Harold Skipper, Jr., "Perspectives on Partial Endowment-Type ("deposit term") Life Insurance: Implications for Regulators," *The Journal of the American Society of Chartered Life Underwriters,* Vol. 33, July 1979, pp. 10–25.

other internal limitations require the patient to bear some of the costs of medical treatment, a share which has increased in recent years. Medicare supplement insurance is sold by some life and health insurance companies to "fill the gaps" of Medicare (hence the term "medigap" insurance).

Criticism has recently been leveled at the quality of these products and at the marketing practices of some of the agents and insurers selling medigap insurance. The claim has been made that many agents play on elderly persons' fear of extraordinarily high hospitalization or physician bills and that overloading is common. Companies marketing medigap insurance respond that the insurance product is an important supplement to Medicare and that while some problems may exist with their marketing practices, they can be remedied.

The so-called Baucus Amendment to the Social Security Disability Amendment Act of 1980 provided that the states are expected to have established minimum standards for medigap policies by July 1, 1982. In response to the Baucus Amendment and other concerns, the NAIC developed a model bill and accompanying regulation which address the problems identified in the Baucus Amendment. For example, the bill limits the time period during which a pre-existing conditions clause can be applied and establishes minimum loss ratios. Because of the threat of imposition of federal minimum standards, at this writing at least thirty-three states had embraced the NAIC or a similar approach.

Concerns About Policy Readability

Related to public concerns about specific insurance products is a concern that the language used in life insurance policies is not clear to the lay person. In a recent MAP survey, of those who said they had tried to read a life insurance contract, about two in three reported having at least some difficulty.[18]

State and NAIC Action

By mid-1981, seventeen states had adopted legislation requiring that life and health insurance contracts marketed in those states must meet certain specified readability levels. Most of these laws are patterned after the NAIC Model Life and Health Insurance Policy Language Simplification Act, adopted by the NAIC in 1978. Type size and policy format are also included in some states' readability legislation.

The Model Act requires that life and health insurance policies be tested for and meet minimum standards of readability using the Flesch Reading

[18] *Ibid.*, p. 51.

Ease Scale. This test measures the number of sentences and syllables in a 100-word section of text, giving higher values to short sentences and simple words. A high score is supposed to indicate easy to read text. For example, a score of 30 to 50 is considered "difficult," while a score over 70 means "fairly easy." The NAIC Model Act mandates a minimum of 40, although several states have upgraded the standard to 50.

Unfortunately, the test is no guarantee of "reading ease." Dr. Rudolph Flesch himself said the test had shortcomings and expressed the desire that his formula not be taken too seriously since it was intended as a "rough estimate" only. Even so, the Flesch test is the one that has been embraced by the NAIC and the states, and it appears that other states will enact similar laws in the near future. The reader is cautioned that policy readability involves more than a formula. It involves appropriate policy organization and design as well as other considerations.

Insurer Action

In response to concern regarding readability, insurers have revised policies and other forms to make them more understandable. Many have done so to comply with new state laws while several are undertaking the action voluntarily. The Life Office Management Association (LOMA) and the Life Insurance Marketing and Research Association (LIMRA) have been active since 1977 in providing policy simplification guidelines to life insurers.[19] For example, LOMA/LIMRA publications provide guidance to policy drafters as to how to group and order policy provisions and how to avoid technical insurance terms. Emphasis is placed on effective graphics and policy design in addition to policy language "readability."

In Canada the CLHIA has prepared initiatives in this area, encouraging companies to make their policies more readable. There are no provincial regulations on this matter.

Concerns About Cost and Benefit Disclosure

The complex issue of life and health insurance cost disclosure has been the subject of much debate recently. Implicit in any meaningful cost and benefit disclosure system that an insurer may use are (1) the availability of certain data on policy benefits, and (2) a technique which permits comparisons of policy cost from the buyer's perspective. Any reference to "cost" or "price" below is meant to be from the buyer's perspective.

---

[19] See, for example, *A Guide to Writing Understandable Life Insurance Policies* (New York: LOMA, and Hartford: LIMRA, 1977), and later documents.

The Need for Cost Comparisons

Wide price variations for similar types of policies exist within the life insurance business. While some variation is to be expected in a private enterprise economy, significant variation is, according to accepted economic thought, indicative of a marketplace that is not functioning as efficiently as it might. This results in unnecessary costs to consumers and, in the long run, an inefficient allocation of society's resources. The producers of goods and services that are sold in such a marketplace are also injured by the reduction in the flow of money to that industry grouping.

The intelligent consumer will prefer to buy the lower cost of two similar products. Failure to do so suggests that the consumer (1) is ignorant of cost differentials, (2) has difficulty in measuring cost differences, or (3) is irrational.

No *prima facie* reason exists for concluding that life insurance consumers are irrational. Indeed, evidence suggests the contrary. In a 1975 survey, 85% of the respondents said they would compare policy costs if a standard comparison method existed.[20]

Evidence also suggests that consumers are generally unaware of differences in life insurance policy costs either because they do not understand what "cost" means or because they apparently believe differences are not great. Support exists for concluding that consumers have difficulty in measuring the cost of life insurance policies. In a 1975 joint ACLI/LIMRA study, 54% of the respondents mistakenly equated a policy's cost with its premium. The premium is a measure of the annual outlay for a policy rather than its cost. Cost includes all elements of a policy (dividends, premiums, cash values, and death benefits), not just premiums. Moreover, six out of ten said they had "some" or "a lot" of difficulty in determining whether they were receiving their money's worth.[21]

Less than half of consumers surveyed say that they believe they know enough about life insurance to evaluate an agent's recommendation.[22] Perhaps even more disturbing than consumer ignorance is a survey which showed that 48% of full-time life insurance agents and 56% of their supervisors believed there existed ". . . little difference in net cost for similar policies."[23]

---

[20] *MAP—1975,* p. 55.

[21] *Life Insurance Consumers: A National Survey of Cost Comparison Attitudes and Experience,* (Hartford and New York: LIMRA and Institute of Life Insurance [now ACLI], 1975), pp. 11–12.

[22] Roger A. Formisano, "The NAIC Model Life Insurance Solicitation Regulation: Measuring the Consumer Impact in New Jersey," *The Journal of Risk and Insurance,* March 1981, Vol. XLVIII, p. 59.

[23] National Association of Life Underwriters and Life Insurance Marketing and Research Association, *Survey of Agency Opinion,* (1976), p. 33.

This suggests that even if agents believed they should advise a client about cost differentials, about half of all life insurance agents would not know how to do so.

Consumers say they would use cost information if provided to them, but only a third believe agents give enough cost information. Of those who had bought life insurance from an agent, 43% said the agent had provided no cost information and 21% said they did not remember.[24]

In summary, life insurance consumers do not seem to be well-informed about life insurance cost differentials or about how to measure cost. As a result, the NAIC, many insurance industry persons, and others now support the concept of consumers' having access to adequate cost disclosure information. Disagreement exists, however, as to the form this disclosure should take.

Cost Comparison Methods

No known method of comparing life insurance costs takes into consideration all possible factors a consumer should consider in the purchase decision. Hence, it is important to supplement "cost" information with "benefit" information through a complete disclosure system. However, before discussing issues related to cost (and benefit) disclosure, the reader should obtain an appreciation for some of the more commonly discussed cost comparison methods. The focus here will be on those methods that have been supported by various influential groups or persons.

No cost comparison method purports to measure the cost of a life insurance policy for every consumer. Two basic classes of methods are used to measure a policy's cost. One class measures the cost using the assumption that a specific, but unlikely, set of circumstances occurs for the policyowner. These are referred to as **event specific** methods, and include the traditional net cost, the interest adjusted net cost, the Linton Yield, the cash accumulation, the yearly rate of return, and the yearly price methods.

The other class of methods, called **group average,** estimates an average cost of a life insurance policy to a group of policyowners. Unlike the event-specific methods, the group average methods utilize probabilities of death and lapsation and can never be the "true cost" for an individual policyowner. Of the group average methods, only the retention method, or variations of it, is discussed here.

Traditional Net Cost Method

The traditional net cost (TNC) method, an event specific method which has been in use for years, is the easiest cost comparison method to understand

[24] *MAP—1979,* pp. 53–54.

and calculate but also the most misleading. To arrive at a cost under the TNC method, one adds together the premiums over a stated time period (usually ten or twenty years) and subtracts from this figure the sum of the policy's illustrated dividends, if any. From this figure is subtracted the policy's cash value (and terminal dividends, if any) at the end of that period. Dividing by the face amount (in thousands) and the number of years in the stated time period yields the TNC per thousand per year.[25]

The TNC method was, and often still is, used to compare the costs of two or more life insurance policies. Although the traditional method can be helpful for illustrating cash flows and for determining income tax liabilities under a single life insurance policy, it is misleading because the method totally ignores the time value of money, thus resulting in a bias against certain policies. Moreover, the TNC can be easily manipulated by lowering dividends or cash values in the early years and increasing them in later years, thus appearing to lower the policy cost.

The Interest Adjusted Net Cost Method

The interest adjusted net cost (IANC) method was developed to correct the primary defect of the TNC method—ignoring the time value of money. An event specific method, the IANC method, like the TNC, assumes the policyowner survives a stated time period (e.g., ten or twenty years) and terminates the life insurance policy at that time (the event).

To calculate the IANC (also called the interest adjusted surrender cost index), the policy's premiums and dividends are accumulated at some assumed interest rate over the stated time period. The accumulated dividends are subtracted from the accumulated premiums. From this figure is subtracted the cash value (and terminal dividend, if any) at the end of the assumed time period. The result of this calculation is then divided by the accumulated value of one dollar for the time period and by the face amount in

---

[25] The formula for the TNC for a period of n years is:

$$TNC_n = \frac{\sum_{t=1}^{n} P_t - \sum_{t=1}^{n} D_t - CV_n}{(\text{Face})\ (.001)\ (n)}$$

where

n = number of years.
P_t = premium in policy year t.
D_t = illustrated dividend or other nonguaranteed premium credit in policy year t.
CV_n = guaranteed cash value plus terminal dividend at the end of policy year n.
Σ = the "sum of"

thousands.[26]

The IANC method can be used to compare only policies of similar type, since premium levels and cash values vary greatly among dissimilar policies. (Note that the TNC method is a special case of the IANC method with an interest assumption of zero.) The IANC method has other drawbacks, too. For example, the method is subject to manipulation in much the same way, although to less an extent, as the TNC method. It, like other event specific methods, provides a valid measure of cost only if the unlikely event occurs.

The Linton Yield Method

The Linton Yield (LY) method is an event specific method that solves for an implicit rate of return only within a cash value policy. All life insurance cost comparison methods must make some arbitrary assumptions to derive a measure of policy cost. The IANC method assumes an interest rate and solves for the "cost of insurance." The LY method, on the other hand, assumes a "cost of insurance" and solves for a policy interest rate implied by that assumption.

The assumption as to the cost of insurance may be in the form of a standardized set of yearly insurance costs (e.g., yearly renewable term rates) or in the form of the rates and values applicable to any other policy. The LY method was developed to allow comparisons of any two dissimilar policies and is frequently used to compare a "term plus side fund" plan to a whole life policy. A "term plus side fund" plan—sometimes referred to as a "buy term and invest the difference" strategy—involves having the buyer purchase a lower premium term policy rather than a higher premium cash value policy and then investing the difference between the premiums for the two policies in a "side fund" to accumulate at interest. In this context, the *difference* between the premiums of two policies (e.g., the term premium and the higher whole life premium) is accumulated at interest each year. Thus, total outlays for the two plans are held equal each year. The face amount of the lower premium policy is hypothetically reduced each year so that the sum of the "side fund" and the reduced face amount exactly equals the face amount of

---

[26] The formula for the IANC for a period of n years is:

$$IANC_n = \frac{\sum_{t=1}^{n} P_{t(1+i)}^{\,n-t+1} - \sum_{t=1}^{n} D_{t(1+i)}^{\,n-t} - CV_n}{(\text{Face})\,(.001)\left(\sum_{t=1}^{n} (1+i)^t\right)}$$

where

i = assumed interest rate

and other variables are the same as in footnote 25.

the higher premium (e.g., whole life) policy. Thus, total death benefits for the two plans are held equal each year.

The interest rate necessary to cause the accumulated value of the annual differences in policy premiums (the side fund) to be equal to the higher premium policy's cash value (plus regular and terminal dividends, if any) at the end of the period of analysis is known as the Linton Yield. Stated differently, the LY is the rate of return that must be earned on a hypothetical side fund in a "term plus side fund" plan so that the value of the side fund will be exactly equal to the value in a higher premium cash value policy at a point in time. The higher the LY, the less expensive is the higher premium (e.g., whole life) policy relative to the alternative plan (e.g., term plus side fund).

The LY method can be used to compare any two dissimilar policies and, if a standard set of term rates is used, LYs of similar policies can be compared easily. Any ranking of similar policies based on IANC closely parallels a ranking based on the LY method.

The LY method has been criticized because its calculation is so complex as to require a computer and because the results are sensitive to the term rates chosen. Hence, if relatively high term rates are used, one can generate a relatively high LY figure and vice versa. Furthermore, little agreement exists as to what constitutes "appropriate" term rates.

Cash Accumulation Method

Also an event specific method, the cash accumulation method (CAM) is actually a variation of the LY method. The only difference is that the CAM accumulates the "differences" in premiums at some stated interest rate that is not necessarily the rate that causes the side fund to be equal to the other policy's value. Thus, the accumulated premium differences will likely differ from the value in the higher premium policy at the end of the stated time period.

The CAM suffers from the same criticism as the LY method in that calculation requires a computer and results are sensitive to the term rates chosen. If illustrated on a yearly basis, however, the CAM permits convenient annual comparisons between the side fund ("cash") accumulations and a cash value policy's surrender value. The CAM can be structured to reflect more accurately the buyer's after-tax rate of return and its impact on the decision as to whether to buy a whole life policy or a "term plus side fund" arrangement.

Yearly Rate of Return Method

The yearly rate of return (YROR) method solves for the internal rate of return that would be necessary to make benefits available for a particular policy year equal to the investment in the policy for that year. The "benefits" under a life insurance cash value policy are the cash value and dividend at the end of the policy year being analyzed plus the expected value of the net death benefit for the year. The "investment" for a particular policy year is the premium paid that year plus the cash value at the beginning of the year. Hence, the YROR is derived by dividing the annual policy "benefits" by the corresponding year's "investment" and subtracting one from this quotient.[27]

The YROR is analogous to a marginal rate of return for a cash value policy while the LY is analogous to an average rate of return. The calculations can be done without a computer. However, yearly "costs of insurance" are needed for both methods. The YROR can be helpful to the person who is deciding whether to retain a policy for another year or who is interested in seeing how a policy performs on a year to year basis. Policy design manipulation is also easily revealed by this method. This method should be used only for policies with cash values and should be interpreted cautiously when a policy has very low cash values, such as when a cash value policy is first purchased.

Yearly Price of Protection Method

While the YROR assumes a mortality cost (or price of protection) and derives a marginal return figure, the yearly price of protection (YPP) method assumes a rate of return and derives a marginal price figure. The yearly price represents an estimate of the cost, in a given year, of the net protection (face amount less cash value) provided under a policy. It is found by (1) subtracting the change in cash value for that year from the net premium (premium less dividend) for that year, (2) then adding to the resulting figure a factor to adjust for the time value of money, and (3) dividing the result by the net death protection in thousands.[28]

The YPP is analogous to a marginal cost for a life insurance policy while

---

[27] The formula for the YROR for policy year t is:

$$YROR_t = \frac{CV_t + D_t + (YP_t)(F_t - CV_t)(.001)}{P_t + CV_{t-1}} - 1$$

where

YP_t = assumed yearly price of insurance

F_t = face amount in policy year

and other variables are the same as in footnote 26.

[28] The formula for the YPP for policy year t is:

$$YPP_t = \frac{(P_t - D_t) - (CV_t - CV_{t-1}) + (P_t + CV_{t-1})}{(F_t - CV_t)(.001)}$$

where variables are the same as in footnotes 25, 26, and 27.

the IANC method is analogous to the average cost. Use of a computer is not necessary to derive YPP figures. Advantages of the YPP method are the same as those of the YROR method. While the YROR method is to be used only with policies which have cash values, the YPP method may be used fairly with both term and cash value policies. However, the YPP method should not be used on a policy whose cash value equals or exceeds its face amount (such as may be the case with a retirement income policy). Further, it should be interpreted with care for a policy whose cash value is near its face amount.

Retention Method

The retention method of cost comparison is a group average method that provides the consumer with an estimate of the proportion of premiums paid for a policy that will be retained by the insurer to cover expenses, profits, and contingencies. This is accomplished by (1) calculating the present expected value of future premiums (i.e., the sum of future premiums over a specific time period discounted for interest, mortality, and lapsation); and (2) subtracting from this amount the present expected value of the policy's future benefits. "Benefits" under a policy are net death protection, cash values, and dividends. The present expected value of future benefits is found by discounting the component parts for interest, mortality, and lapsation.

The lower an insurer's retention the better the policy for the consumer. Criticism of the retention method centers on its complexity and its sensitivity to the needed assumptions. Further, many question the applicability and usefulness of group average figures to any particular individual.

Cost Comparison Limitations

Other event specific and group average methods exist.[29] The above have been singled out for discussion since they enjoy more support in 1981 than other methods. Even so, all cost comparison methods have limitations, many of which were discussed above. One particularly important limitation is that all methods rely on policy dividend illustrations or other nonguaranteed values of policies. Since such values are not guaranteed, cost comparisons among participating or other policies containing nonguaranteed elements or between such policies and nonparticipating policies should be interpreted cautiously. This is not to say that such comparisons are invalid, but rather that relatively small cost differences are not significant.

[29] For discussions of these and other methods, see *Analysis of Life Insurance Cost Comparison Methods,* (Society of Actuaries, 1974) and *Report of the Joint Special Committee on Life Insurance Costs,* (New York: Institute of Life Insurance, 1970) [*Joint Committee Report*].

Other potential limitations include the fact that some cost comparison methods (e.g., the IANC method) can be used to compare similar policies only. Further, some event specific methods focus on one or two policy years only, possibly ignoring other equally important years. All methods must make some arbitrary assumptions to derive costs. These assumptions may not be appropriate for the buyer. All methods ignore the potential tax implications of policy termination to the purchaser. Finally, and of great importance, no method is capable of factoring into the cost formula the quality and integrity of the insurer or agent.

History of the Cost Disclosure Issue

Although recommendations for improving cost disclosure were made as early as 1908 by the Wisconsin insurance commissioner, significant activity on the issue did not occur until the 1960s, beginning with the actions of Senator Philip A. Hart.

The Hart Subcommittee

Arguments that consumers needed more complete policy cost and benefit information were at first met unenthusiastically by the insurance industry. Later, in 1968, when the late Senator Philip A. Hart proposed to introduce Truth-in-Life Insurance Legislation unless the life insurance industry responded to the problem of providing insurance customers with adequate cost and benefit information, an eleven-member industry committee was appointed to study the issue and make recommendations.[30] In 1970, the committee, after examining numerous cost comparison methods, concluded that the most suitable was the interest adjusted net cost (IANC) method. The traditional net cost (TNC) method was explicitly found to be inappropriate. Although industry associations did little to publicize or support the committee's report, momentum for the use of the IANC method built, and a few life insurers voluntarily included IANC figures in their ratebooks and sales material. Senator Hart's subcommittee held hearings again in early 1973 on the adequacy of policy information available to consumers and on marketing problems within the insurance business. The subcommittee undertook a detailed study of individual insurer lapse ratios, agent turnover, sales practices, and policy costs, publishing its findings in four volumes.[31]

---

[30] *Joint Committee Report.*

[31] Senate Subcommittee on Antitrust and Monopoly, *The Life Insurance Industry—Parts 1, 2, and 3,* (Washington, D.C.: G.P.O., 1973) and Senate Subcommittee on Antitrust and Monopoly, *The Life Insurance Industry—Part 4,* (Washington, D.C.: G.P.O., 1974).

NAIC Action

With the exception of a couple of states, state insurance department interest in the disclosure issue was also minimal at first. However, in 1972 an NAIC Task Force on Life Insurance Cost Comparisons and an Industry Advisory Committee (AC) were established to study the form cost disclosure should take. As a result, the NAIC adopted a model disclosure regulation on an interim basis in mid-1973, and a final version in 1976. This final version, the Model Life Insurance Solicitation Regulation, incorporates an expanded version of the IANC method for cost comparisons. Over thirty-five states now require cost and benefit disclosure similar to that required in this model regulation. Its details will be discussed later in the chapter.

Since the adoption of the NAIC Model Life Insurance Solicitation Regulation, other groups have studied the cost disclosure issue and marketing problems within the life insurance business. The United States House Subcommittee on Oversight and Investigations held hearings in 1978 and released a report critical of the NAIC disclosure approach.[32] In addition, the report discussed other marketing problems including the existence of wide cost variations of policies and high lapse rates. This report recommended the use of the CAM for cost comparison purposes, rather than the IANC favored by the NAIC.

The FTC Report

The Federal Trade Commission (FTC) staff also investigated marketing problems in the life insurance business, releasing its report in 1979.[33] This report identified several "consumer problems" in life insurance marketing:

1. The rate of return consumers received on the "savings" component of cash value insurance policies is often very low.
2. Consumers lose substantial amounts of money through termination of whole life policies within the early years of coverage.
3. The cost of similar life insurance policies varies widely.
4. Consumers often receive a small amount of protection against premature death relative to premiums paid for ordinary insurance.

Several reasons were cited as causes of these consumer problems.

1. The methods used to evaluate the cost of insurance are complicated and difficult to use.
2. Consumers are unable to determine the real cost of insurance.

---

[32] *Life Insurance Marketing and Cost Disclosure,* (Washington, D.C.: G.P.O., 1978).

[33] *Life Insurance Cost Disclosure,* (Washington, D.C.: FTC, 1979).

3. The absence of cost information reduces competition.
4. The agency system exacerbates the competitive problem because of agent ignorance and a commission structure that favors whole life insurance.

The FTC report presented detailed recommendations by the FTC staff as to how these problems could be remedied, one of these remedies being the adoption of the LY method of cost disclosure.

The FTC staff report has caused more turmoil within the life insurance industry than any other recent issue. Criticisms of FTC staff tactics abound, and the industry has testified vigorously against the report on the grounds that:

- Adequate price competition exists within the life insurance business as witnessed by an industry with over 2,000 insurers and by decreasing life insurance prices.
- The cash value of a life insurance policy cannot be compared fairly to a savings account, as the FTC has attempted to do.
- Adequate cost disclosure *is* provided through the NAIC Solicitation Regulation.
- Cost variations are not so great as they appear to be because insurers compete in different markets and have different mortality, investment, and expense patterns.[34]

To counter the FTC's involvement in insurance activities, the industry supported a successful amendment to the 1980 FTC authorization bill that exempted the insurance business from the FTC's investigative powers unless the investigation was specifically requested by a majority vote of either the House or Senate Commerce Committees. The amendment effectively ended FTC insurance projects including those on cost disclosure, replacement, debit insurance, underwriting practices, and the McCarran-Ferguson Act.

The NAIC Model Life Insurance Solicitation Regulation

Over thirty-five states require cost and benefit disclosure to prospective life insurance purchasers as recommended in the NAIC Model Solicitation Regulation. The regulation requires an insurer to provide a *Buyer's Guide* and a *Policy Summary* to all prospective life insurance purchasers before accepting

[34] See, for example, Blake T. Newton, Jr., "The Misleading Report on Life Insurance Cost Disclosure of the Federal Trade Commission Staff," *The Journal of the American Society of Chartered Life Underwriters,* Vol. 33 (October 1979), pp. 12–22 and "Life Insurance Business Sets the Record Straight at Senate Hearing on FTC Study," *Council Review,* Vol. 4 (October/November 1979), p. 11.

the applicant's initial premium, unless the insurance company provides a ten day or longer unconditional refund offer, known as a 10-day free look. If the company provides the refund offer, the Buyer's Guide and Policy Summary may be delivered with the policy.

The Buyers Guide

The Buyer's Guide is a document which purports to help prospective purchasers (1) decide how much life insurance to buy, (2) decide what kind of policy to buy and, (3) compare the costs of similar life insurance policies. The language of the Guide is mandated by the regulation.

The suggestion in the Buyer's Guide for choosing the right amount of life insurance is general, advising the consumer ". . . to figure how much cash and income your dependents would need if you die." The Guide explains the three types of life insurance—term, whole life, and endowment—pointing out positive and negative aspects of each. Next, the consumer is advised that "your chances of finding a good buy are better if you use two types of index numbers. . . ." The consumer is admonished: "*Look for Policies With Low Index Numbers.*" These index numbers are contained in the Policy Summary.

The Buyer's Guide explains the distinction between participating and nonparticipating life insurance, includes a general description of the Life Insurance Surrender Cost Index (the name used by the NAIC for the IANC) and the Life Insurance Net Payment Cost Index (described below), and advice on how to use them.

The Policy Summary

The Policy Summary is a document containing the disclosure information on the specific policy being considered by the consumer. The name and address of the insurance agent (if any) and the insurance company must appear on the Summary, along with the generic name of the insurance policy (e.g., "whole life insurance").

The Policy Summary must contain certain policy data for the first five policy years, and for representative policy years thereafter, sufficient to illustrate clearly the pattern of premiums and benefits. These years must include the tenth and twentieth years, plus data for "at least one age from 60 through 65 or, if earlier, policy maturity." The data required to be shown separately for the basic policy and for each rider for each of the above specified years are:

- the annual premium.
- the guaranteed death benefit.

- the total guaranteed year-end cash surrender values.
- illustrated cash dividends (need not be shown beyond the 20th policy year).
- guaranteed endowment amounts.

In addition to the above policy data, the effective policy loan interest rate must be stated. Of prime importance is the requirement that the ten- and twenty-year surrender cost and net payment cost indexes must be provided. The surrender cost index is the name given by the NAIC to the IANC method. The procedure to calculate the indexes is mandated by the regulation. A 5% interest assumption is to be used. The net payment cost index is calculated in the same manner as the surrender index except that cash values (and terminal dividends, if any) are omitted. Thus, the payment index attempts to measure the average annual outlay associated with a particular insurance policy over a ten- or twenty-year period.

If the policy is a participating policy, another index, the Equivalent Level Annual Dividend (ELAD), must be disclosed. The ELAD represents the average annual illustrated dividend for the policy, recognizing the time value of money at 5%. It is intended to show the consumer the proportion of the cost indexes of a participating policy represented by dividends. It is calculated by accumulating the annual illustrated dividends at interest and dividing the result by the appropriate annuity factor to obtain a level annual equivalent to the (non-level) illustrated dividends.

The Solicitation Regulation requires an agent to inform any prospective purchaser of the full name of the company for which he or she is acting as a life insurance agent. The sales person is prohibited from using terms such as financial planner, investment advisor, financial consultant, or financial counseling in such a way as to imply the agent is generally engaged in fee-for-service advisory business unless that is actually the case. The use of the TNC method of cost comparison is prohibited except to show a policy's cash flow pattern.

NAIC Task Force Criticism of the Model Regulation

The NAIC Solicitation Regulation has been the object of considerable external criticism. The NAIC, mindful of these criticisms, formed a Task Force in mid-1979 to solicit comments on the issues and evaluate the regulation. The Task Force report, released in December 1980, provided another criticism of the existing disclosure system.

The Task Force stated that a life insurance disclosure system should promote three policy objectives. First, it should aid consumers in purchasing reasonably priced insurance policies that suit their needs. Second, enough accurate, reliable information should be provided to consumers to assure a vigorously competitive market. Third, undesirable market behavior should be discouraged and market performance should be enhanced.

In general, the Task Force found that the existing solicitation regulation did not sufficiently meet these objectives and that it was "seriously deficient" in the following ways:

- It does not permit comparisons of dissimilar policies.
- Providing six indexes (surrender cost, net payment, and ELAD for ten- and twenty-year durations) confuses many consumers.
- By focusing at ten- and twenty-year durations only, it ignores other cash values and, hence, creates an environment that encourages manipulation in policy design.
- The index numbers themselves have no intrinsic meaning to consumers, except in relation to other policies.
- It fails to provide consumers sufficient guidance regarding determining suitable policy choices.
- The disclosure that is required at the time the purchase decision made is insufficient.
- It fails to give existing policyowners the right to receive certain policy data on their policies.

As a result of these and other deficiencies, the Task Force concluded that the interest adjusted method has become outmoded. The Task Force said it believed that the current system must be abandoned altogether and a completely new disclosure system—on three levels: (1) "upfront", (2) at policy delivery, and (3) periodic—instituted in its place.

"Upfront" Disclosure

To supply disclosure at the first level, the task force recommended that before a prospective purchaser signs an application for insurance, the agent should provide a Buyer's Guide, a suitability form, and a preliminary policy summary in a specified format. The suitability form is to be completed by the consumer, or the agent for the consumer, to assist in determining the consumer's life insurance needs. The information in the preliminary policy summary falls into two categories. First, certain non-cost information must be provided, including a description of the policy and an abbreviated table of premiums, dividends, death benefits, and cash value information for certain years. Second, the summary would contain a probable cost index (a variation of the retention method) for the policy, which the prospective insured could use for comparative price shopping. The Task Force also recommended a change in the interest rate to be used in developing cost indexes from the current NAIC requirement of 5% to 8%.

Disclosure at Policy Delivery

The second level of disclosure is that which is provided upon policy delivery or, if requested by the prospective purchaser, at any time before. This full policy summary includes the probable cost index for the policy, a table showing the premium amount for each payment mode, and a detailed listing, referred to as a **ledger,** of policy information for each of the policy years one to thirty.

This full summary would also include probable annual cost figures for each year. The probable annual cost represents a variation of the company retention method, except that it attempts to measure the cost, from the policyowner's perspective, of the annual (as opposed to aggregate) dollar amounts retained by the insurer for expenses and profits. Yearly rate of return figures are also to be included in the policy summary, as is a separate table showing summary information based on the retention method.

Disclosure at Policy Anniversary

Finally, the Task Force recommended that each insurer should be required to provide to each policyowner on or about each policy anniversary a notice containing:

1. Ledger statement information, including the probable annual cost and the yearly rate of return for the preceding year;
2. information showing such ledger statement information for the next year;
3. a statement that the insurer, for a stated reasonable fee, will provide the policyowner an up-to-date policy summary on request; and
4. the total amount of policy indebtedness, if any.

The Task Force's report was "received" (neither accepted nor rejected) by the NAIC at its December 1980 meeting. The future of the proposal is in question at the time of this writing, with some further changes almost a certainty.

With few exceptions, the life insurance industry now strongly supports the NAIC Solicitation Regulation, arguing that it offers consumers sufficient cost and benefit disclosure, and that the detailed information proposed by the Task Force would increase company expenses without a concomitant increase in consumer usage of the information provided.

Proponents of fuller cost disclosure hope that as agents and consumers become better informed about differences in life insurance policy costs, consumers would look to buy lower cost policies. Agents would then put pressure on companies to improve performance in their policies.

Cost Disclosure in Canada

The Canadian Life and Health Insurance Association (CLHIA) in June 1975, recommended to its members that they make cost information available to prospective purchasers on request. The Canadian system is similar to the NAIC Solicitation Regulation except that the interest rate used in Canada is 6% instead of 5% as used in the United States. To date, the Canadian approach to cost and benefit disclosure can be described as voluntary insurer action, with companies cooperating with the CLHIA-recommended procedures.

Concerns About Privacy

Privacy ranks high as an issue of concern to the life and health insurance business in general and to life and health insurance marketing in particular. The public believes firmly in its "right to privacy." This right to privacy includes not just the right to be free from overly intrusive prying into one's personal life but also the right of the consumer to be free from the abuse or misuse of personal information by business and government. Heightened concern about threats to personal privacy may have stemmed from the increasingly common practice of substituting written records for direct contact between the individual and the government or a business. New information technology further contributes to the potential for privacy abuses.

Public Attitudes

Consumers' concern about their right to privacy has increased steadily throughout the 1970s. Three out of four Americans now believe that the right to privacy is as important as "the rights of life, liberty, and the pursuit of happiness."[35] One-half of the consumer population is worried about how government and business use personal information. Large majorities of consumers believe that:

- Some people are prevented from getting fair treatment because past mistakes are kept too long on their record (81%), and
- Americans begin surrendering their privacy the day they open their first charge account, take out a loan, buy something on credit, or apply for a credit card (76%).

[35] These and other survey results, unless otherwise stated, are from Louis Harris and Associates, Inc. and Alan F. Westin, *The Dimensions of Privacy,* a National Opinion Research Survey of Attitudes Toward Privacy, (1979).

One out of five Americans (19%) believes that he or she personally has been a victim of an improper invasion of privacy with 14% of the American people claiming to have avoided applying for a job, credit, or insurance because they did not want to provide certain information about themselves. Of that 14%, over nine in ten said their action stemmed from a belief that the request for information was unfair.

Most consumers (72%) believe that information-intensive organizations collect more sensitive information than is necessary. Drawing from a list of eighteen private and public sector organizations, organizations ranked as follows for asking for "too much personal information":

Organization	Percent saying "too much"	Rank (out of 18)
Finance companies	45	1
Credit bureaus	44	2
Insurance companies	38	3
IRS	38	4
CIA	34	6
FBI	33	7
Banks	29	10
Census Bureau	24	13
Local police	23	14
Physician	11	18

Although two-thirds of the public believes that new laws and organizational policies "could go a long way to help preserve our privacy," one-half of the public believes the main responsibility should rest with the people themselves.

Consumers want to be told how information about themselves will be used (97%) and told in writing why each item of information is needed (74%). A large majority (91%) believes that an organization should obtain an individual's agreement before information from a file is given out to other organizations for purposes other than that for which it was collected. Further, they believe they should have the ability to see and verify information on them held by others.

When asked what information life insurers should *not* have the right to obtain, the majority of consumers responded as follows:

- lifestyle (77%)
- moral character (71%)
- income (70%)

- existing insurance (63%)
- criminal history (60%)
- previous insurance claims (55%)

Interestingly, the majority of insurance executives agreed that information on lifestyle (58%) and moral character (53%) should not be collected, as did the majority of insurance commissioners (lifestyle [73%], moral character [76%]). Consumers do believe life insurers should be able to collect information on such items as drinking habits, type of employment, sex, age, health, and medical history. Moreover, 65% of consumers and 55% of insurance commissioners believe that the types of information insurers can collect should be determined by law.

Background of the Privacy Legislation

Concerns over the impact on personal privacy of the "new information technology" were expressed through the decade of the sixties. This concern led to several studies and to passage of two major federal privacy laws: the Fair Credit Reporting Act (FCRA) in 1970, which was discussed in the preceding chapter, and the Federal Privacy Act of 1974, which created the Privacy Protection Study Commission.

The Privacy Protection Study Commission

In addition to granting major privacy protection to citizens in their dealings with federal agencies, the Privacy Act of 1974 created the Privacy Protection Study Commission (PPSC) to study the information practices of several industries and, where appropriate, to make recommendations as to needed change. The PPSC released its landmark study in July 1977,[36] covering a number of industries as well as certain aspects of governmental informational practices. Regarding the insurance industry, the Privacy Commission concluded that insurance consumers were not provided with adequate privacy protection. As a result, the commission made seventeen specific recommendations for change, some of which are that:

1. Applicants for insurance should be given an elaborate notice which explains the agent's, insurer's, and any insurance-support organization's information collection, use, and disclosure practices.
2. Insurers and agents should identify clearly those items of information which were desired for uses unrelated to the insurance transaction at hand.
3. Consumers should have a right to have access to the information

[36] *Personal Privacy in an Information Society* (Washington, D.C.: G.P.O., 1977).

about the consumer which was maintained by agents, insurers, and insurance-support organizations and a corresponding right to request correction of that information.

4. Agents, insurers, and insurance-support organizations should be prohibited from making disclosures of information about a consumer without the consumer's consent, with certain exceptions.
5. Standards be established for authorization forms used by life and health insurers to obtain information from physicians, hospitals, etc.
6. Applicants for insurance should have the right to be interviewed in connection with the preparation of an investigative consumer report.
7. Consumers should be told why insurance was denied them or offered to them at a higher than standard rate.

Implicit within the Privacy Commission's recommendations were criticisms of state insurance commissioners for insufficient action on privacy concerns. As a result, the NAIC appointed a Task Force in mid-1977 to review the Privacy Commission's recommendations and, if appropriate, to develop a response to the report findings. After two years, the Task Force developed the NAIC Insurance Information and Privacy Protection Model Act, adopted by the NAIC in 1979. Amendments to the act were adopted in December 1980.

The NAIC Insurance Information and Privacy Protection Model Act

The NAIC Model Privacy Act enjoys broad insurance industry support, with both the American Council of Life Insurance (ACLI) and the National Association of Life Underwriters (NALU) supporting it. State activity on the bill has begun, with Arizona, California, Illinois, Montana, and Virginia having enacted the bill as of early 1981. It appears that other states will adopt some version of the Model Act within the next couple of years. If this occurs, some modifications must be made with respect to insurers' marketing practices.

The act is a lengthy and complex document, perhaps the most complex ever adopted by the NAIC. Within the operative sections of the Act are found variations of most of the Privacy Protection Study Commission's insurance recommendations listed above. Despite this, the NAIC Model Privacy Act has been criticized for representing mainly the interests of the insurance industry and for providing less privacy protection than that recommended by the PPSC. It is further argued that adequate privacy protection should be the right of every United States citizen, and, as such, the state by state approach alone will not provide sufficient guarantees.[37]

The NAIC and insurance industry spokespersons have disagreed, arguing that the state approach should be given a chance to prove itself and that as a first step by the NAIC in the privacy protection arena, the NAIC Model Act, while not as strong as it could be, represents a good compromise and a worthwhile initial effort.

The Fair Insurance Information Practices Act

President Jimmy Carter's administration was sensitive to the PPSC recommendations and developed a federal minimum standards privacy bill to be applied to the insurance industry. President Carter's Fair Financial Information Practices Bill, Title V of which was the Fair Insurance Information Practices Act (FIIPA), was introduced into Congress in November 1979. With the 1980 elections, near-term prospects for a federal privacy insurance law appear slight. The FIIPA, however, did enjoy some life insurance industry support, although the support was not as broad-based as that for the NAIC Model Act.

The FIIPA covered many of the same general areas as the NAIC bill, except that it omitted provisions contained in the NAIC bill dealing with certain underwriting practices. The federal bill differed from the state (NAIC) model bill in that it did not cover as many of the Privacy Commission's recommendations as did the state bill; yet in certain key areas, it would have provided stronger privacy protection for consumers than the NAIC Model Act.

A unique feature of the federal bill was that it would not have created a federal regulatory agency to enforce the law. If a consumer's privacy rights had been violated, based on the standards of the act, the consumer would have had to have recourse to the courts to seek an appropriate remedy. Further, if an insurance commissioner of a particular state desired, he or she could (although need not) have enforced the provisions of the act.

The FIIPA was criticized for not striking an appropriate balance between the rights of consumers and insurers. Some provisions were criticized for being too strong and likely to cause unintended disruptions within the industry. Segments of the insurance industry oppose any federal bill in the belief that it could constitute the beginning of federal insurance regulation.

Proponents of the bill argued that, as a national issue, privacy rights should rest at the federal level, even if enforcement were at the local level.

[37] Harold Skipper, Jr., "An Analysis of the NAIC Model Privacy Act," *Best's Review,* Life/Health ed., Vol. 80 (March 1980).

They further argued that a federal bill would have provided more protection to insurance consumers than the NAIC Model Act.

Effect of Privacy Legislation on Insurance Marketing

Support exists for some form of privacy legislation. As a result, it seems reasonably certain that further privacy legislation will be forthcoming in the not too distant future. This will necessitate agents' and insurers' making alterations to applications and other forms (e.g., authorization forms), plus developing a lengthy notice to be given to each applicant. Additionally, because a right of access would be created, agents and insurers may have to make some changes in the way that information is maintained in order to accommodate any consumer requests. Since a consumer would have the right in most cases to learn the reasons for any adverse underwriting decision, special care will have to be exercised by both agents and insurers in notifying applicants when sensitive information is the basis for an adverse decision.

With respect to information already in their own files, many insurers have taken steps to deal with the privacy issue by developing guidelines for their own operations. These guidelines for internal use often start with a statement acknowledging that final responsibility for ensuring the privacy of policyowner records rests with the company itself and that development of procedures to accomplish this is a matter of high priority.

The guidelines themselves deal with the following general areas:

1. What information should be released at the request of various inquirers (policyowners who are also insureds, policyowners who are not insureds, insureds who are not policyowners, spouses, beneficiaries, assignees, attorneys, the IRS and other governmental agencies, etc.).
2. What kind of authorization should be required before releasing information (signed requests, phone requests, etc.).
3. What type of identification should be required (verifiable signature, identification code, etc.).
4. What employees should have access to the various kinds of information (underwriting, policy issue, policyowner service, actuarial, marketing personnel, etc.).

At least some companies have established procedures to inculcate employees with an appreciation of the importance of treating information gained in the course of work with a high degree of confidentiality.

Privacy in field offices is also a matter of concern for two reasons. First, privacy legislation will apply to agents and field offices as well as to the home office. Second, privacy standards will be more difficult to enforce with respect to field offices and agents. This is partly because of the decentralized operations and partly because of the difficulty in knowing what information is available in a field office; some of the information may even be stored in agents' personal files.[38]

Aside from the threatened state and federal bills, many life insurers, sensitive to the changing expectations of consumers, have instituted voluntary programs to assure informational privacy. For example, Aetna Life and Casualty, in March 1976, adopted a "Code of Privacy Principles and Standards," which established information handling guidelines to be followed by all Aetna personnel. The Equitable Life Assurance Society was also an early leader in the privacy area, having adopted a set of "Privacy Principles" in March 1976. Other life insurers have demonstrated concern for action by taking leadership positions by establishing voluntary guidelines.

Concerns About Equality

"Equality" is a changing concept. What is fair today may be deemed unfair by society tomorrow. Moreover, what constitutes equality in life and health insurance in contemporary North American society is ill-defined.

Public Attitudes

The public generally believes that the principle of classification for life and health insurance rating purposes based on individual risk characteristics is fair although a significant proportion believes it unfair. When asked to react to specifics of their concept of fairness, majorities of consumers said it was fair to deny a person a loan because of a poor credit record (83%), to charge a person with two or more accidents a higher automobile insurance premium (74%), and to charge higher life insurance premiums to persons who work in hazardous occupations (67%) or who have had a heart attack (57%). They believe women (65%) and persons who do not smoke (60%) should pay less for life insurance. Yet, consumers generally believe it is unfair to charge women more for pension plans (57%) and to charge handicapped persons more for life insurance (70%).[39]

Demand has been growing for laws addressing discrimination based on disabilities (including blindness, mental retardation, and epilepsy), sex, lifestyle, marital status, location, and/or age. The 1978 United States Supreme Court's *Manhart* decision, which prohibited different pension benefits for

---

[38] *Privacy and Consumerism: Facing the Issues*, Operations and Systems Report #59 (Atlanta: Life Office Management Association, 1981).

[39] *MAP—1979*, p. 38.

men and women, has spawned additional questions on sex-based classifications. While much of this activity is not directly aimed at the life insurance business, it takes little imagination to realize the likelihood of the life insurance business' practices coming under scrutiny and criticism.

Potentially the most important recent legislative initiatives in this area are nondiscrimination acts of the types recently introduced into the United States Congress. These bills would prohibit discrimination in insurance issuance, underwriting, or rating based on sex, race, color, religion, or national origin. Such legislation enjoys broad support and its passage would cause major changes in the way insurers price life and health insurance and annuities.

NAIC Responses

The NAIC recently adopted a modified version of an older regulation that prohibited unfair discrimination based on blindness. The new regulation, adopted at its June 1979 meeting, is titled, "A Model Regulation on Unfair Discrimination in Life and Health Insurance on the Basis of Physical or Mental Impairment."[40] The regulation prohibits an insurer from refusing to insure or charging a higher rate to an impaired person, except where an actuarial or other reasonable basis exists for doing so.

The NAIC is now reviewing questions involving rate distinctions in life and health insurance based on sex. The NAIC Model Unfair Trade Practice Act already prohibits the denial of insurance coverage solely because of sex or marital status. That the NAIC is also considering proposals to prohibit rate distinctions based on sex and marital status in automobile insurance suggests that implications of any such change to the life insurance business should be considered carefully.

Insurer Responses

Some life insurers have been reviewing their underwriting criteria in light of society's pressures to abolish rate distinctions. For example, Teachers Insurance and Annuity Association recently announced that an applicant's sex would no longer be a factor in annuity ratings, although some problems are being experienced in implementation.

The reader may feel "uneasy" with the move to alter time-honored insurance selection and classification practices. Because life insurance underwriting is far from an exact science, the impact on future mortality and morbidity of some underwriting criteria in use today is not well understood; some criteria may actually be irrelevant. The pressure being exerted on the

---

[40] Wonder what the readability index of this title is?

life insurance business may cause companies to try to prove the relevance of some of their underwriting and pricing criteria. But relevance is not the only issue. Some groups in society seem to believe that certain classes of information—regardless of relevance—should not be used for decision-making purposes. Yet, in defending the industry's position, insurance industry spokespersons sometimes overlook this distinction between relevance and propriety.

Concerns About Insurance Agents' Qualifications

Most individual life and health insurance in the United States and Canada is sold by insurance agents. The cliché that "life insurance is sold, not bought" is still probably valid, although recent evidence suggests that this may not apply as broadly as many believe. For example, the sales of direct response life insurers have grown rapidly within the past decade. In one (non-random) study of consumer buying habits with respect to life insurance, fully 35% of those who had purchased insurance recently stated that they had initiated the purchase.[41]

Agents remain the backbone of the life insurance industry. They are the spokespersons for the life insurance business from the perspective of most consumers. Indeed, to many consumers, agents are the life insurance industry. Clearly, therefore, the public's perception of agents is of great importance. In turn, the ability of agents to advise and service their customers influences public attitudes.

The Public's Attitude Toward Agents

The public continues to believe agents are an integral and valuable part of the life insurance purchase decision. Six out of ten consumers believe it would be a mistake to eliminate the agent, although a substantial proportion of the public (42%) would prefer to buy life insurance from a bank rather than from an agent and one in four young people believe it is best to avoid a life insurance agent if possible.[42]

Although most consumers (54%) apparently believe agents to be knowledgeable, some ambivalence exists. For example, only 13% of consumers disagreed with the statement that "poor people are often the victims of unethical agents . . ." and only 19% disagreed that "most life insurance agents take advantage of your concern about your family. . . ." In each instance, however, one in three consumers had no strong opinion one way or another.[43] The contrasting views that agents are needed by consumers, yet

[41] *Buyer-Initiated Sales and the Agency System,* LIMRA Research Report 1979–4 (1979), p. 2.

[42] *MAP—1979,* pp. 16 and 46; *MAP—1974,* p. 49; and *Youth 1978,* p. 26.

[43] *MAP—1979,* pp. 47–48.

that they take advantage of consumer needs, are reflected in the two most frequently chosen adjectives used to describe agents: "knowledgeable" and "manipulative."[44] In summary, the agent is viewed as a valuable asset to the life insurance purchaser, although much room exists for improvement.

Insurer, Agent, and NAIC Responses

One key to improvement in the public's uncertain attitude toward life and health insurance agents seems to rest to some degree on upgrading agents' knowledge and professionalism. Many believe that upgrading can be achieved in two ways: first, by imposing stricter agent licensing requirements and second, by imposing continuing education requirements. As mentioned earlier, to obtain a license to sell life insurance in most states, a person must pass an examination. The rigor of these examinations varies considerably from state to state, with some examinations requiring minimal preparation and others demanding demonstration of a deeper understanding of insurance fundamentals. A trend towards strengthening these examinations appears to be emerging, although to date results have been inconsistent. Most agents express support for more rigorous licensing requirements, although it is not clear whether most insurers share this same commitment.[45]

A few states allow an applicant for an agent's license to sell life insurance on a temporary basis without passing an examination. Allowing an untested and unproven person to advise consumers on such an important matter as their life insurance is now generally recognized as not being in the public interest. Most states now have either eliminated the temporary license altogether or restricted its use.

A second trend in agent licensing requirements appears to be emerging in the form of pre-licensing and post-licensing formal education or training requirements. Several states are now investigating the desirability of mandating such requirements. The NAIC adopted an Agents Continuing Education Model Regulation at its June 1978 meeting. Pressure seems to be on the side of requiring applicants for life insurance licenses and, to a lesser extent, already licensed life insurance agents to demonstrate a higher level of competence.

The importance of formal education requirements suggests that insurers may have a somewhat more difficult time in the future in recruiting life insurance agents and that more emphasis will be placed on agent quality.

---

[44] *Ibid.*, p. 17.

[45] Lawrence T. Bauman, "Selling the Salesman: Creating a Stronger Field Force," *Best's Review*, (October 1976).

Insurers, the various insurance trade associations, educational institutions, and others may find greater demands placed on them to provide such training. Agents of the future cannot, as their predecessors may have, survive on personality alone. The public is increasingly demanding greater competence from its advisors, and insurance agents will not escape this increased expectation level.

Concerns About Replacements

The very mention of the word "replacement" evokes strong opinions and emotions within the life insurance business. Replacement activity is believed to be at an all-time high and still increasing. Some insurance regulators, executives, and agents have expressed alarm over this trend, arguing that life insurance consumers are losing millions of dollars by switching policies. Others argue that replacement is often in the consumer's interest and that an existing life insurance policy is no more sacred or immune to replacement than any other consumer purchase. Some agents and insurers are said to have a marketing strategy based on replacement of existing whole life insurance.

Background

The so-called replacement debate is not new. In the past, the industry generally viewed replacement as being synonymous with twisting. By 1911, pressure was so great to do something about the problem that a special conference was held on conservation. In 1914, the NAIC voted to require every insurance application to include a statement by the applicant as to whether replacement was involved in the sale.

In 1930, an industry committee on replacement was formed to recommend solutions to the high lapse and replacement rates experienced during the Depression years. This committee developed an intercompany agreement among ninety-four insurers as to methods of dealing with replacement, but the agreement ended in 1941 because it was found to be anti-competitive.

The 1970 Model Replacement Regulation

In 1970, the NAIC adopted the first Model Replacement Regulation. This regulation requires an insurer (or agent) to provide the consumer contemplating a replacement with (1) a notice, and (2) a Comparison Statement.

The notice points out that "as a general rule, it is not advantageous to drop or change existing life insurance in favor of a new policy." It then lists some of the potential disadvantages to replacement, such as the fact that the incontestable and suicide clauses will begin again under a new policy.

The Comparison Statement provides the consumer with comparative data on the existing and proposed policies to assist the consumer in his or her decision as to whether to replace. These data include death benefits, premiums, illustrated dividends, if any, and cash values at specified future time periods as well as certain other policy information.

The 1979 NAIC Model Replacement Regulation

The NAIC adopted a revised replacement regulation at its December 1978 meeting. This new regulation represents an improvement over the previous regulation in that it presents a more balanced approach to a policy replacement. For example, the 1979 regulation—unlike the 1970 model—presumes nothing as to the propriety of replacements, neither condemning nor condoning the practice. It, however, is otherwise patterned closely after the older regulation in that it, too, requires a notice and a comparison form.

Both the older and newer versions of the regulations have shortcomings. Critics claim that the regulations constitute a road map as to how to replace. On the other hand, claims are made that the regulations discourage many justifiable replacements because of the time-consuming task of completing the comparison form; in other words, the regulation itself stifles competition. Others point out that the disclosure form provides much policy data, the usefulness of which is, at best, questionable and, at worst, counterproductive. The fact that the replacement regulation provides for no cost comparison method is also regarded as a major flaw.[46]

In one recent study, it was found that numerous justifiable replacements probably could be made.[47] As price competition within the life insurance business increases and as more lower-priced policies are offered, replacement activity will likely increase. High inflation and high interest rates will tend to be the indirect cause of more replacements.

Summary

The life and health insurance industry and its marketing practices are undergoing close scrutiny by the public and the government. The industry is in a period of transition, the culmination of which still is unclear. The adage that "there are no problems; only opportunities," indicates that many insurers will make use of the opportunities presented by the transition period.

This transition for the life and health industry is merely a part of a larger

---

[46] See, generally, Harold Skipper, Jr., "Cost Disclosure in Life Insurance Replacement," *Journal of the American Society of Chartered Life Underwriters,* Vol. 80 (October 1980).

[47] Harold Skipper, Jr., "Replacement Vulnerability of Older Nonparticipating Life Insurance," *Journal of Risk and Insurance,* (December 1980).

transition in American society. Professor George Cabot Lodge of the Harvard Business School wrote recently:

> The United States is in the midst of one of the great transformations of Western civilization. What is happening is that the old ideas and assumptions which once made our great institutions legitimate, authoritative and confident are fast eroding. They are slipping away in the face of a changing reality and are being replaced by different ideas and different assumptions which are as yet ill-formed, contradictory and shocking. This transition is neither good nor bad. There is the possibility of plenty of both. The point is simply that it is taking place.[48]

Some of the data discussed earlier in this chapter suggest that the business community may be out of step with the views of the consumer. Perhaps, in some instances, consumers are simply poorly informed and, therefore, hold unreasonable or erroneous attitudes. If so, the industry must seize the opportunity to communicate clearly and accurately enough correct and relevant information so as to diminish such misunderstandings. On the other hand, perhaps changes in the attitudes and perceptions of many insurance executives and agents are needed to assure the industry's profitable survival by satisfying the needs and addressing the values and attitudes of a changing, more knowledgeable and demanding consumer marketplace.

---

[48] George Cabot Lodge, "A Culture in Transformation: Toward a Different Societal Ethic," TAP-12, (New York: Institute of Life Insurance, Fall, 1975), p. 3.

PART II

PRODUCT, MARKET ANALYSIS, AND SUPPORT

Chapter 5

Product Development

R. C. Dowsett, FSA, FCIA, MAAA
R. G. Boeckner, FSA, FCIA, MAAA

Once a life and health insurance company has agreed on a marketing plan, it must then begin to consider the products it will develop to meet the needs of the markets it has chosen to address. These products will play a critical role in the company's efforts to achieve market penetration. Thus, proper product design and development are essential elements in the marketing process.

Product Development in Life and Health Insurance

The products of a life and health insurance company may not be as apparent to the consumer as those of a manufacturing company. Life insurance companies provide financial security in various forms to their customers. Tangible benefits are provided in terms of dollars paid upon the occurrence of the event insured against, such as premature death, disability or retirement. The actual piece of paper containing the contract, the policy, describes the amounts of the benefits to be paid by the company, the conditions under which they will be paid, and the price to be charged to the customer (the premiums). However, the piece of paper is not the life insurance company's product. Rather, the product—be it life insurance, retirement insurance, or health insurance—is really the coverage stated in the contract wording. A life insurance company's **portfolio** of products is the total array of life, health and retirement coverages provided by all of its contracts.

Product development is an ongoing process involving the organized research of consumers' wants and needs, the design of the various concepts to be combined into a final contract, and the determination of the price to be charged for the benefits provided. Procedures performed by such diverse areas as the legal department and the various administrative departments contribute to the final policy form that is issued to a customer. Thus, the product development process combines theoretical concepts and procedural activities.

Product development does not just happen—a concerted effort must be made; nor does it occur only in the initial stages of a company's existence. At any point in its history, a company may introduce a new product in reaction to the everchanging environment in which it operates. This environment includes such factors as competition, government action, and changes in consumers' life styles. In addition, all companies regularly update the rate structure for their existing products to reflect changes in the same environmental factors. While product development is a key element in the marketing process, at this point it should be emphasized that attractive products cannot by themselves make a company successful. All the aspects of a company's total marketing operation such as home office marketing support, home office sales management, and field sales operations, must be strong.

In this chapter, the subject of product development for individual life and health insurance will be examined with theoretical as well as practical considerations in mind. While the company's technicians can design what they believe is the best product available, if the public will not buy it or if its sales representatives will not sell it, all efforts are in vain. The required consistency of the product design activity with the company's marketing philosophy will be stressed and product design objectives will be outlined. Then, objectives to be considered when setting the price for a life or health insurance product will be discussed.

A theoretical model of the product design process will be developed, and important practical considerations that may require deviation from the model will be pointed out. The model is described in detail since effective product design requires the involvement of many talents from various areas of the company at the appropriate time. The chapter concludes with an examination of the trends which may affect product development in the future.

Goals of Product Development

As discussed in Chapter 2, all companies establish corporate objectives, although many companies may not have formal written objectives. Traditionally, a life and health insurance company seeks to help its clients achieve financial security by providing risk-sharing mechanisms for the risks of premature death, sickness, disability, and old age.

A company's marketing plan will be established within the framework of the overall corporate objectives. For example, the relative emphasis in a company's corporate objectives on sales versus service may affect the level of expense that must be incorporated in the price of its products. If a company stresses low rates to its clients, then it probably prefers to provide a minimum level of service in order to keep the expense component of its rate structure small. On the other hand, if a company decides to emphasize the service it provides to its clients, it may have to accept a less competitive rate structure in order to cover its expenses. If a company stresses low premium rates, then its sales people must understand that it may not have the expense loadings available in its products to provide the best fringe benefits, the best located field offices, the best estate planning support personnel, and the best sales promotion material.

Corporate objectives relating to such factors as the acceptable degree of risk-taking, the emphasis on satisfying sales force needs versus buyers' needs, and the concern for a high-quality image may also affect marketing objectives.

Before the product development process can begin, a company must establish goals for its development activity. The company will likely establish objectives for the types of products it will offer—*product design objectives*—and objectives for the general rate characteristics of its products—*product pricing objectives*. For example, a company could choose between offering a complete spectrum of level and decreasing term life insurance products or offering only one or two yearly renewable term plans (a product design objective). In addition it could decide to compete vigorously in the term market with very low premiums or alternatively, it could decide to build greater profit margins into its term rates (a product pricing objective). In this section both product design and pricing objectives will be discussed.

Product Design Objectives

Once a marketing strategy has been established that is consistent with the company's corporate objectives, then the broad guidelines are in place for the process of product design, and decisions about the products to offer can be made.

Three simple examples may serve to illustrate how product design can be affected by corporate objectives. Company A has a career agent sales force and plans to market to middle income families. Its products' rates would likely be high enough to support service by A's agents to its policyowners. Its product portfolio might contain only a few basic plans. If its policies have a small average size, it might combine various benefits in one package in an effort to keep administrative costs down in relation to the total premium for the policy. Company B brokers life insurance through casualty agents to the owners of small businesses. It needs somewhat more sophisticated products than Company A, but these products should not be too complex because the casualty agents may not normally sell much life insurance business. Company B provides support services such as computerized sales illustrations and basic tax planning tips to its brokers but probably will have little direct contact with its policyowners. Company C plans to broker large amount policies in complex estate planning situations through very sophisticated life insurance brokers. Usually such companies have very competitive (i.e., low) rates. The broker may be an expert in business, tax and estate law, but the home office must have some expertise in these subjects, and an extremely sophisticated product line is necessary. In order to keep rates low, the home office will probably not offer direct service to the policyowner and very little sales support to the broker. Any required policyowner service would be done through the broker.

Responsibility for Setting Product Design Objectives

A company's marketing strategy will usually be developed by the senior marketing officers and then approved by senior management. Establishment of product design objectives that are consistent with the marketing strategy is a joint effort of the marketing department and the product design actuaries.

In many cases the product design objectives may only represent practices that have been accepted over a period of time. For example, a company may have always based its sales effort on participating products with high premiums, high dividends and high cash values, without ever formally stating this. In other cases product design objectives may be formally established by a policy committee. For example, if a company sells its products through career agents, a policy committee may emphasize the development of products that would appeal primarily to the family market. A company may have a formal expense ratio objective. A policy committee may translate this expense ratio objective into a product design objective to develop products that can be handled by simple administrative systems in order to keep unit expenses low.

A company's investment department may have an objective for investment in securities that stresses high yields and downplays liquidity. This objective might allow the product designers to develop products with a heavy savings element where the higher yields from private placements are used to achieve competitive interest yields.

In any event, some understanding must be reached so that the actuaries do not waste time designing and pricing products that the sales people find their clients do not want, while the sales people desperately need particular new products for the company's traditional markets.

Product Design and Company Objectives: An Example

Let us consider two possible new products a company may wish to introduce and note how they may relate to various company objectives. One product is a single premium immediate annuity with rates based on the interest yield on new investments as opposed to the interest yield on the company's total portfolio of assets. The other new product to be considered is a yearly renewable term life insurance plan to be sold at low premium rates with a very high minimum policy amount.

The annuity would support the corporate objective to provide consumers with vehicles for financial security against the risk of old age, while the yearly renewable term plan would provide consumers with vehicles for financial security against the risk of premature death. If the company has sold only life insurance in the past and no retirement products, then the introduction of the annuity plan represents more of a deviation from its traditional marketing philosophy than the yearly renewable term plan does.

The annuity plan may give a company with career agents an additional product to offer their clients who are nearing retirement. The new term plan may have little appeal in the family market because its high minimum amount would lead to premiums higher than the average family could afford. Thus, the term plan may be inconsistent with a company's philosophy if the company stresses the family market and sells through career agents. However, the term plan might well appeal to sophisticated buyers served by brokers.

The yearly renewable term plan may fit into existing administrative systems with only limited modifications being required. On the other hand, introduction of the single premium annuity may require the company to develop new procedures to make fixed income payments on a regular monthly basis, possibly causing problems in meeting unit expense objectives.

The new money annuity may require a significant investment of surplus by the company to establish actuarial reserves based on statutory interest rates much lower than the interest rates assumed in the premium. The surplus invested may be released very slowly in the future. The term plan would not likely require a significant surplus investment and might begin contributing new profits to surplus sooner than the annuity. Therefore, surplus growth objectives can also be a consideration in determining which product to develop.

The company's investment objectives may also be a consideration in product development. The new money annuity may require expertise in aggressive investing in long-term private placements to obtain higher interest rates. The term plan would generate relatively few assets and these could probably be invested in the same manner as the company's traditional life insurance assets. Table I summarizes these two product examples.

Organization for Product Design

The product design function is usually handled as a staff function (''off-line'') for two reasons. First, staff may find it easier to develop a completely new product than line personnel. Line personnel may be too committed to the

TABLE I
How Two Different Products Satisfy Various Company Objectives

Type of Company Objective	Single Premium Annuity	High Minimum Amount Yearly Renewable Term Life Insurance
Corporate Objective	Provides vehicle for financial security in old age	Provides vehicle for financial security against risk of premature death
Market to Serve	Aimed at those nearing retirement	Aimed at wealthier sophisticated buyers
Administrative Costs	Extensive new monthly payment procedures may be required	Few systems modifications needed
Surplus Growth Objective	Significant investment of surplus for actuarial reserves required	Significant surplus investment not needed
Investment Objectives	Aggressive investing necessary to obtain high yields	No change from whole life investment

company's traditional products to consider new, untried products. Changes in the product mix may be necessary for the company's future survival. Particular lines of business may have to be eliminated because they are no longer growing and profitable. Such decisions are best initiated by the staff who have no vested interest, as line personnel might, in continuing to offer unprofitable existing products.

Second, the design of innovative new products requires extensive research, which is best performed as a staff function. Often it may be necessary to develop several approaches to a new product before getting the right combination of features. The success rate for new products is far from 100%, causing companies frequently to "go back to the drawing board." Companies continually make modifications in existing products, making ongoing research a necessity. Since a company's whole marketing thrust is not likely to be built on one particular new product, there needs to be a line organization in place to continue to sell the company's "tried and true" products while the new products are worked into the portfolio by the staff.

Effects of the External Environment

The environment of the early 1980s has several characteristics which affect product design. The majority of these characteristics are part of the social, economic, legal, and competitive environments. Ideally, an individual in the marketing research unit continually scans the external environment and forecasts trends, so that the company can develop products to take advantage of new opportunities.

Influence of Social Factors

A very high percentage of married women are now in the labor force. While this situation reduces the need for traditional forms of insurance on the "male breadwinner," many companies have designed joint life plans for families who are dependent on two incomes for their standard of living, where the death benefit is payable on the first death, whether husband or wife.

Changes in the structure of the family unit are affecting product design. Financial security needs change as children are born, grow up, and then leave home. The new **adjustable life** products (policies whose face amount, premiums, cash values, or duration of coverage can be changed at the insured's discretion to adjust to the temporary or permanent changes in the insured's economic status or lifestyle) may be the answer for a buyer whose family situation changes several times during his or her lifetime. Such flexible coverages might also fill the needs arising from recent changes in family structure as exemplified by the serial marriage life-style.

Influence of Inflation

Inflation was a significant consideration in the economic environment through the latter part of the 1970s and shows no sign of decreasing to historically normal levels in the decade of the 1980s. This trend has created problems for companies stressing level premium whole life insurance plans. Clients are reluctant to pay premiums in today's dollars for benefits payable in deflated dollars tomorrow. There is a severe increase in companies' expense ratios, since premiums calculated several years ago do not contain sufficient expense loadings to cover today's inflated administrative costs.

Several solutions have been proposed to overcome the problems caused by inflation. Traditional means of increasing coverage by applying dividends to purchase paid-up additions or one year term insurance additions have not been able to keep up with inflation very well. **Variable life insurance** (VLI), which relates benefits to equity values in a portfolio separate from the general investment portfolio, was introduced several years ago. VLI has a greater potential for cash value and death benefit coverage growth than does whole life insurance. Premiums remain level, but death benefits and cash values of the increase or decrease with investment performance. Sales have been relatively disappointing since the introduction of VLI, perhaps because there have been many instances in recent years where equity values have decreased while the rate of inflation has increased. In the early 1970s, a few companies developed level premium life insurance with coverage that increased automatically as the Consumer Price Index increased, but sales of these plans have not been as high as hoped, perhaps because the initial premium charged is high for the initial coverage provided. These examples indicate that product designers who are able to anticipate changes in the environment still may not develop successful responses to such changes. It is never easy to predict how buyers will react to a new product.

Influence of Government

One of the major environmental influences on product design is government at the state, provincial and federal levels. The bulk of governmental influence arises from regulation of the life insurance business. However, in some cases government is a competitor and in other cases a creator of new opportunities for the industry.

Product designers need to recognize the legal restrictions on product design due to government regulations. These include the various state nonforfeiture laws which lead to minimum values for life and annuity contracts; the required minimum ratios of claims paid under health insurance contracts to the premiums paid for such contracts imposed in some states; and deficiency reserve regulations, some of which are out-of-date and lead to surplus strain for companies who attempt to price their products competitively.

As a competitor, the government has tended to be the provider of an ever-increasing basic floor of protection, especially for lower-income individuals. The United States Social Security System provides significant pension and disability benefits to workers, and valuable death benefits to their survivors. This has created problems for private disability insurance carriers in particular because portions of their potential market are being eroded. In order to guard against overinsurance when government benefits are added to those paid by private plans, some companies now review their issue limits annually to reflect regular increases in government benefits.[1] In Canada, the

---

[1] Daphne Bartlett, "Effective Product Management," *Best's Review,* November 1979; E. Paul Barnhart, "The Effect of Social Security Legislation on Voluntary Individual Health Insurance," *1976 Society of Actuaries Part 6 Study Notes.*

government provides basic retirement coverage through the Old Age Security System. Additional pension benefits are provided to workers through the Canada and Quebec Pension Plans. These latter plans also contain death and disability benefits of a significant amount, although the determination of disability is quite strict. In Canada, the provincial governments provide basic hospital and medical care benefits. The United States government has been considering national health insurance. Passage of such legislation drastically reduces markets for private insurance carriers.

Product designers for companies whose marketing philosophy involves products with low average policy amounts for clients with lower than average incomes must bear in mind government's past tendency to increase the coverage it provides, thereby eliminating the need for these groups to purchase coverage from private companies.

On the other hand, government can also create opportunities for new products, primarily through tax regulations. H.R. 10 and ERISA have encouraged the marketing of retirement plans in the United States. In Canada, Registered Retirement Savings Plan legislation has led to large increases in sales of retirement plans.

Income tax relief for employer-sponsored group life insurance has not only encouraged sales of group life insurance to large employers but also has spurred the "Section 79" market for smaller employee groups in the United States,[2] although the twists and turns in government policy have made it difficult for companies to stay in the Section 79 market.

The major problem with designing products that capitalize on government action is that the government can always change the regulations or the laws, perhaps significantly altering market opportunities. Development costs for new products may not be recoverable. Advertising material may have to be thrown away. Existing policies may have to be modified, and extensive administrative changes made so that previously issued cases do not lapse.

Influence of Competition

Competition for life and health insurance companies comes from other insurance companies and other industries. Competition from other companies can be in the form of price, product features, underwriting, and policyowner service, and can have a significant impact on product design. A company must respond to the actions of its major competitors when they develop a

[2] Section 79 is that section of the United States Internal Revenue Code which states the requirements to qualify for the special tax treatment applicable to group insurance situations. Individual insurance products have also been developed to qualify under Section 79.

product that threatens its market share. Pressure on product designers is also created when a competitor develops an exciting new product, thus creating an innovative image for itself. The sales force may request a similar product, and the product designers may have to respond to the challenge just so the company does not appear to be falling behind.

One critical decision in product design is a determination of when a company should quickly respond to competition and when it should wait to see how the market will respond to its competitor's new product. If the product is too radical a departure from tradition, the public may not understand it and thus not buy it. If high start-up costs or development expenses for administrative systems are involved, the company may decide to wait to see if a competitor's product is a success before committing itself to similar expenditures.

Some major companies have the philosophy of being just behind the leading edge on any new product. They wait for another company to introduce a new product, convince the regulatory authorities to approve the new policy forms, and educate agents and the public about the virtues of the new product. If that product turns out to be successful, the companies watching strive to bring out an improved version of it as quickly as possible. While some may feel that this approach is somewhat parasitical, it is also quite pragmatic. Companies cannot patent or copyright their new ideas since, except for the cash benefits ultimately provided, life insurance is an intangible product.

Since there are approximately 1800 life insurance companies in North America, the company must determine who its significant competition is in its chosen markets. Otherwise, it may dissipate its resources by vainly trying to be the best company in all product lines in all geographical areas.

The company's sales representatives can provide regular information about whom they perceive to be the competition. Both articles and advertising in trade publications may make the marketing research area aware of companies with similar marketing philosophies.

A small regional company may introduce a new product, but its competitors may choose not to follow because the innovator does not compete nationwide. Stock companies selling only nonparticipating insurance may stress products with low gross premiums and not try to compete directly with mutual companies selling only participating insurance.

In addition to competition from within the insurance industry, competition from outside the insurance industry can have an effect on product design. Competition due to government provision of benefits has been mentioned. Many savings institutions compete successfully for dollars that previously went to traditional life insurance products, thus diminishing the market for life insurance. This forces life insurance companies to respond with creative product designs to maintain their market share. For example, life insurance companies have introduced low-load annuities with interest credits based on new money yields to compete in the retirement market with other savings institutions.

Product Pricing Objectives

When a company actually comes to the point where it must set rates for the products it has designed, it will have to consider its pricing objectives. An example of an overall pricing objective might be to have premium rates at key issue ages, such as 25, 35, and 45, that are among the three best (lowest) of the twenty-five largest life insurance companies offering the same product. More specific pricing objectives will relate to the assumptions to be used for the various factors that are incorporated in the premium formula. A manufacturing company might consider factors such as the cost of raw materials, labor costs and desired profit margins in calculating the price for one of its products. For a life insurance company, risk and profit factors are the chief items incorporated into its rate structure.

Risk Factors

The risk factors include not only the specific contingency being insured against but also the elements of interest, expense and persistency. The product designer must consider the relative impact of these factors on premium assumptions.

Contingency Being Insured

The particular contingency being covered will be specified by the product under consideration. For life insurance, mortality is the chief contingency; for health insurance, morbidity. In determining the mortality factors to use for life insurance, the product designer must be aware of the company's underwriting philosophy—is it liberal or conservative? Does the company accept large face amounts without requiring a medical examination? If the company sells insurance by direct response with little or no attempt to eliminate poor risks, its mortality will be higher than that on business that has strict underwriting standards.

Morbidity experience on disability insurance varies depending on the waiting period and benefit period of the coverage. It is also affected by economic conditions such as higher rates of business failures or higher rates of unemployment.

Interest

Interest that the insurer can earn on the assets accumulated under a policy may be a significant risk factor for a product such as level premium whole life insurance that has a sizable investment component, but will have very little significance for a product such as yearly renewable term insurance. The interest factor is extremely significant for products with relatively high investment elements, for example, annuities. Companies have to decide whether they will assume the interest rates earned on "new money" investments or on the entire portfolio of assets in the calculation of premium rates for particular products. Will an adjustment be made in the form of higher premiums or lower dividends to reflect lower interest rates earned on policy loans compared to other available investments? The product pricer may also want to consider trends in future interest rates in the product rate structure.

Expenses

Several types of expenses contribute to risk factors and thus have to be incorporated into the pricing structure. These include compensation, administration, overhead, lapse assumption, and taxes. If a field force is involved, direct compensation of the sales force, including commissions, and indirect acquisition expenses, such as the cost of recruiting, training and financing agents, must be included. There may be volume incentives for agents. Fringe benefits and expense allowances for field personnel have to be covered. Sales remuneration may differ depending on whether the company uses a general agency system or a branch managerial system. A general agent may be paid for sales alone, while a branch manager may have remuneration factors based on the recruiting and training of new agents as well as sales. Section 213 of the New York Insurance Law places a limit on the sales remuneration which can be paid. If a company sells in New York, this must be considered. If a company markets by direct response, it will have little or no sales remuneration expense, but its advertising expense will be high and it may use the savings from sales remuneration to offset expected higher mortality.

Administrative expenses need to be covered by premiums also. These include policy issue and underwriting expenses, as well as renewal administration, policyowner service, claim and change processing costs. Expenses in the home office and in the field offices must be included. Renewal expense loadings take into account collection costs for renewal premiums, and also reflect the company's philosophy about the quality of policyowner service it wishes to provide (the more money allocated to policyowner service, the better the service that can be provided).

An expense item beyond the control of a company that must be covered in the rate structure is taxes. The premium tax, generally charged at the state or provincial level, can vary by product as well as by state. Federal income tax charged to the company has to be provided for within the rate structure. There are also miscellaneous licenses and fees charged by various government authorities that have to be recovered from the rate structure.

The most difficult expense factor to deal with is that related to overhead. This includes the cost of various functional areas in the home office such as personnel or corporate accounting where the basis of incurring costs is not obviously related to a policy or block of policies. Items such as home office rent must be provided for. A company may adopt the philosophy that a new product line will not be charged its full share of overhead until a sufficient volume is built up to provide a reasonable amount of available expense loadings generated by the premiums.

A **lapse assumption,** an assumption of the annual probability of voluntary termination of the contract by the policyowner, must be made for most lines of business in order to determine if initial expenses will be recovered. A high lapse rate indicates poor persistency, whereas a low lapse rate indicates good persistency. Such an assumption should be based on the company's own experience if possible, since lapses can vary significantly by product (term insurance versus permanent insurance), the premium mode (annual versus monthly), and perhaps distribution system (brokerage versus career agent). Pension products may exhibit high terminations at attained ages between 60 and 65 due to early retirement. Economic conditions can also affect lapse rates. Poor business conditions lead to lapses of business coverage. High rates of unemployment lead to lapses of family coverage.

In establishing any risk factor assumption, a company can choose to project improvement or deterioration in that factor. Some companies are more conservative (or more averse to risk) than other companies and reflect this in their projection philosophy by assuming deterioration from current experience, and vice versa.

Profit Factors

The profit objectives to be incorporated into a product's pricing structure must be consistent with the corporate goals established for profits from the particular line of business being priced. A stock company whose corporate objective is to provide a specific return to its shareholders may express its profit objective as $X per thousand of face amount, as Y% of premiums or as a specific deduction from the interest rates or contingency rates assumed in calculating premiums, for example, the interest assumption to be used is the rate earned on the total portfolio of assets less 1/4% for profit margin.

A stock company may use more sophisticated profit objectives than those above. Profit objectives could be related to the amounts of surplus invested in a line of business, bringing in return-on-equity concepts. For example, the company may wish to earn 15% per annum over the life of a policy on the first year investment of surplus in the new policy. A company can also relate its profit objective to agent's commissions so that the agents are motivated to adopt goals consistent with those of the company. For example, it may incorporate in its pricing structure an objective that the present value of profits to be earned over the expected duration of the policy will be equal to 50% of the first year commission on the policy.

For a mutual company, or the participating business of a stock company, corporate philosophy may be related to policyowner dividends. For example, a company may choose to charge high gross premiums leading to high policyowner dividends. A company may decide it should pay out all profits on participating business as they are earned, in the form of dividends. Or, it may feel that a certain portion of participating profits should be retained by the company as a permanent contribution to the surplus of the enterprise, thereby providing greater financial protection to all generations of policyowners.

A company may adopt profit objectives which vary by line of business reflecting the different degrees of risk in the various lines. For example, interest gains on the assets underlying a block of permanent whole life business may be used to offset inflation in administrative expenses. For a block of term insurance the asset build-up is much smaller and interest gains cannot be used to offset expense inflation. Thus, term business could be considered riskier than permanent business and as a result have a higher profit objective than whole life. Similarly, nonparticipating business could be considered riskier than participating, and again justify a higher profit objective.

Competitive Factors in Pricing

Just as a company must consider its competitors in designing a product, it must also consider its competitors in establishing pricing objectives. Unlike most consumer goods, which are used immediately upon purchase, the benefits of life and health insurance are paid sometime in the future. Thus, as discussed in the previous chapter, price comparisons of different policies are difficult to make.

There is a great deal of price competition in the life insurance industry, but, as mentioned previously, companies also compete by providing unique products or by providing varying degrees of service. While life insurance brokers may compete by shopping to obtain the best possible price for each client, career agents with long-established mutual companies may compete by developing a lasting relationship between their clients and their companies. Direct mail companies compete with companies using sales representatives by providing convenience to their purchasers as well as trying to be price-competitive.

Consumers do not purchase life insurance with high frequency, as for products such as toothpaste, a new automobile or even automobile insurance. Many consumers are probably not aware of the price competition that there is in the life insurance industry, and they may not know how to tell which policy is more expensive. Also, consumers usually have little experience with the varying degrees of service provided by different companies and thus have difficulty comparing that aspect.

For consumers who do shop around before purchasing insurance, a company may stress its low **interest adjusted cost.** This involves the use of the interest adjusted net cost method (IANC) for cost comparison, as discussed in Chapter 4. Here, a client considers the difference between premiums paid and dividends credited plus the cash values available at particular times, giving due regard for the time value of money. Other companies may stress low continuing cost, sometimes known as the **interest-adjusted payment.** Such companies will place emphasis on the difference between premiums paid and dividends credited, again with due regard for the effects of interest. In addition, those companies may provide low cash values on the grounds that the consumer should really be interested in the continuing cost of the protection purchased, not the cost on surrender. Only an individual purchaser can determine which factors are most important in his or her own case.

A company may decide that because little shopping is done by buyers of small face amount policies, its prices can be less competitive in that category. However, plans with high minimum face amounts (over $100,000) may be sold in a very competitive market, and a company will try to keep its prices for these policies as low as possible.

Other Factors in Product Pricing

A company's rates for each product should be consistent with those for other products in its portfolio. For example, if a company introduces a joint term policy that provides benefits on the second death of two lives, then one would expect the premium on the joint plan to be lower than the sum of the premiums for two single life term policies on the same two lives. Products with differing average sizes may incorporate expenses in their rate structure in a fashion leading to inconsistent premium rates. In other words, a $10,000 life policy from a block with a small average size may cost more than a $10,000 policy from a block with a large average size.

At some point the actuary has to be concerned about the adequacy of the total rate structure. If the risk and profit assumptions are chosen properly, all premiums should be adequate. However, the individual setting prices may decide to smooth some of the risk factors or some of the resulting premium rates. This may require the development of a **model office**[3] with various combinations of forecast sales experience that can be tested to ensure that the whole block of business will have an adequate rate structure. It is dangerous to contemplate artificially pricing one product higher to compensate for inadequate premiums for another product. Changes in the distribution of either product's sales could cause serious problems.

The price-setter should be concerned about potential changes in the pricing factors, especially if it is anticipated that the premium rates will be in effect for a significant period of time. An actuary who is pricing guaranteed cost nonparticipating insurance must project factors far into the future, as well as consider current experience. In pricing annuities it is quite common to project inflation in expenses and improvements in mortality throughout the income-paying period.

Last but not least, the actuary considers whether there are any legal constraints that affect the rate structure. In discussing the influence of government earlier in this chapter, the concept of minimum claim ratios for health insurance business was mentioned. Many states have specific cash value requirements for deferred annuities that can put a constraint on the net premiums assumed in the pricing structure. Since the minimum required cash values may be a function of the annuity's gross premiums, it is not possible to determine precisely if the cash values are adequate until the premiums have been calculated. A few iterations may be necessary until a final scale of gross premiums is determined that will in every case ensure that the policy's cash values are greater than required. Despite these constraints, the combined effects of all the other pricing factors almost invariably ensure that no two companies have exactly the same premium rates.

The Process of Product Development

In the first part of this section, a theoretical model of the product development process will be described. Practical procedural aspects, which flow from the theory, will be covered in the second part of the section.

---

[3] A **model office** is a model made up of a small number of hypothetical situations such as combinations of issue ages and face amounts, that in total will reproduce reasonably closely the entire range of cases that will occur in real life.

A Product Development Model

The model described here focuses on the roles of the various people involved in the product development process and may not apply to every company. Particular features of the model will vary depending on the operating philosophy and resources of the actual company under consideration.

The Role of Field Personnel

Companies with sales representatives find that their field people are the members of their organization closest to the needs of the consumer. The field sales representatives are the chief, and in many cases the only, contact between the company and the buying public. Therefore, almost all product design ideas for these companies originate in the field. In addition, field people are generally the first to become aware of better rates and better products provided by competitors. They can also give guidance about the relative emphasis to be placed on rates versus level of service. Thus products must appeal to the field force and reflect their perception of the buyer's needs. As one company's actuary has stated, "our market is not individual clients but the agents and general agents who represent us."[4]

Companies actively encourage their field people to point out developing problems with their current portfolio of products and to submit new product ideas. If a company's entire sales force is demanding a new product, the chances of its success are substantially better than those of a product developed entirely by home office product designers.

The local agency heads, either branch managers or general agents, are often the vehicles for transmitting the views of agents to home office. They may summarize or edit field comments in order to foster a better home office reception. They may have more time to formulate product design concepts than does the agent or broker who is actually occupied in writing new business. The agency head can communicate to the home office through regional field management the agents' perceptions of a new idea: Will it have a broad or limited market? Will agents have difficulty selling it?

The agency head can also be extremely useful in helping to "sell" new products to the sales force. Ideally, a company should let the local agency head run training courses on new products for agents or brokers. If the agency head is convinced that a product is good for the buyer, his or her enthusiasm can be transmitted to the sales representatives. Local introductions at the same time result in a coordinated launching at minimum cost. Some home offices produce audiovisual presentations and make these

[4] R. E. Hunstad, private communication, February 15, 1980.

available to the field; others bring members of the field force into home office schools to learn about new products.

Some companies have officially designated field advisory councils which meet at scheduled times in the home office. Successful advisory councils provide positive input distilled from their field associates into the product design and rate setting process. They also provide feedback on other aspects of company activity that can affect the field, such as underwriting philosophy and policyowner service. Unsuccessful advisory council sessions can be highly negative if they consist of complaints from the field about rates that are too high, remuneration that is too low and the absence of any good product development. While such sessions may occasionally help to clear the air, on a frequent basis they can poison field–home office relationships unless improvements are made.

The Role of Home Office Personnel

In the home office, senior management with the overall responsibility for particular lines of business (for example, vice president, individual insurance operations) will set the policies for their divisions on such matters as growth and profit objectives for specific product lines. Subsequently the line heads may review major new products and rate revisions for consistency with line objectives. They can be most valuable in helping to resolve conflicts that may arise in product development.

The head of agency operations (agency vice president) will set overall sales objectives and may be involved in establishing sales objectives for a particular new product. He or she will definitely have to approve any changes in marketing philosophy required by a new product as well as review any changes in remuneration philosophy that it may entail. The agency vice president is often the conduit of concepts from the field to the product design actuaries regarding new products and rates, especially if there is no field advisory council in the company.

The head of the marketing department develops the overall marketing plan for a new product, especially activities related to its introduction to the field, field training and sales promotion. The marketing head may be the originator of new product ideas and may direct the development process. He or she should review the product during the various stages of a new product's development to ensure that it still follows the intended marketing concept. Note that in some companies, the same person may be head of agencies and marketing.

Marketing Research

A company's marketing research unit may identify a market need requiring a specific new product before the field force does. Staff members should continually monitor the *Monthly Survey of Life Insurance Sales in the United States and Canada,* produced by the Life Insurance Marketing and Research Association (LIMRA). The marketing research unit analyzes the market's buying power by county with information provided by outside sales research organizations and compares it to the company's corresponding market share. This could identify areas where a particular new product might have some appeal or areas where the company's market penetration could be improved. The marketing research unit can also monitor the sales success of existing products and suggest that remedial action be taken for products whose sales seem to be decreasing.

Material from the Trend Analysis Program (TAP) and the Monitoring the Attitudes of the Public (MAP), produced by the American Council of Life Insurance (ACLI), will provide clues to the changing external environment and its possible effects on a company's products. The marketing research unit may keep rate comparison studies indicating the company's competitive cost position, and it may maintain summaries of significant features of competitive products.

In practice, there are many who believe that the "grass-roots" market research done every day by a company's field force is generally more pertinent to the product design team and more current than the most elaborate study done by highly educated but theoretical home office market researchers.

On occasion, if revolutionary concepts are involved, a brand new direction in marketing philosophy, such as the introduction of adjustable life, may be initiated in the home office. However, this probably happens only in the company that originated the product. Any other companies introducing the new product are likely to have it brought to their attention by their field personnel. Even the originating company may have developed the revolutionary product based on general concerns expressed by its field personnel.

The marketing research unit can also play a role in field testing a new product before it is introduced on a widespread basis. However, field testing of new insurance products is difficult, and actual cases are rare. Life and health insurance is not like many consumer products that customers can try and determine quickly whether the product is better than the product of a competitor. A consumer product can be test marketed in selected areas and modified or eliminated if the consumer perceives problems or sales are inadequate. Field testing is not so simple for insurance products. For various reasons, the company may conclude that a full scale introduction of a new product is just as good as going through a period of test marketing. Exposure to the field force for comments and possible subsequent redesigning may be an acceptable substitute for test marketing. Consumer interviews can take the place of "live" testing.

Once the general characteristics of the new product have been determined, the company will consider its distribution. If the company's existing distribution system can readily serve the new market, then it is quite a bit easier to add a new product to the current portfolio. If a completely new distribution system is necessary for the success of a new product, consideration should be given as to whether or not the market is large enough to justify the expense of developing the new distribution system. For example, a company that has always used a career agency system may have developed a new product that would best be sold by a direct mail approach. It must consider the expense of developing the new system, and the potential losses if it fails. Analysis of the potential sales of the new market can be done by examining the experience of other companies in similar markets. Consumer interviews might also be useful for this purpose. Marketing research plays a role in all of these activities.

Actuarial Department

The actuaries, the company's product engineers, must be involved early in the product development process, so that they can properly understand the basic concepts of the product in order to price it appropriately. They must allow for the risk factors that best apply to the product and incorporate the agreed-upon profit objectives in their pricing. The actuaries may develop alternative rate structures reflecting variations in minimum sizes, different remuneration patterns and various underwriting philosophies. Some companies may use premium rates that are **banded,** that is, one set of premiums per thousand for policies up to a certain face amount and a lower set for policies over that amount. The minimum size of the policy to be issued on the new plan will determine the average size for expense loading purposes. For example, if the minimum size policy is $2,000, then the average size policy might be predicted to be $10,000. On the other hand, if the minimum size policy is $25,000 then the average size policy might be predicted to be $50,000. In the first case the per policy expenses will be a greater component of the premium per thousand than in the second case. Expenses that are constant for each policy no matter what its size may be covered by some companies through a policy fee.

If a field force is involved in a new product's distribution, decisions made regarding the balance between remuneration paid in the early years and remuneration paid in renewal years should reflect the company's philosophy regarding the relative importance of sales and service. Many companies pay most of the remuneration in the early years to emphasize to the field force that sales are important. Such companies may not stress service or may provide service through salaried employees. While reducing remuneration helps to lower a product's price, if the level of remuneration is unreasonably low or inconsistent with other products offered by the company or its competitors, the field force may not sell the new product.

The actuaries must consider the number of females in the potential market. Since females have a longer life expectancy than males, companies often have separate schedules of life insurance premiums for males and females, with the female rates being lower. The actuaries also consider the pricing effects of various cash value and dividend scales.

By providing the variations in price that correspond to each of these items, the actuaries make it easier for those in the marketing area to make decisions regarding the product's characteristics. As mentioned previously, the actuaries are concerned with the effects of technical regulations relating to new products, such as nonforfeiture laws. They may also draft policies if the legal area does not have this responsibility.

Legal Department

The legal department's involvement in product development centers around policy drafting, policy filing, and making sure that all applicable product laws are complied with.

Policy drafting is a part of the initial product design work. The legal area reviews the policy wording, especially the non-actuarial provisions. In addition, the lawyers may be responsible for ensuring that the contract conforms with any applicable readability rules. Many companies are voluntarily moving to more readable policy forms in all territories in which they do business.

In addition to the legal department, administrators in both the data processing unit and the policy service units should review the policy draft provisions at an early stage. The discipline of reducing the new product idea to actual policy wording often helps to clarify design problems and may reveal potential claim handling difficulties. If the new product cannot be made to fit into the company's data processing systems, it might have to be administered by costly manual systems. Minor variations in the product design may minimize future administrative costs. Change in the policy draft can be made more easily later when the draft is close to its final version.

The legal department may have the entire responsibility for the policy drafting activity, including filing with state insurance departments. In Canada policy forms do not usually require approval by the provincial insurance departments unless they are variable contracts. Depending on the particular state, the requirements may include sample cash values and calculation formulas to demonstrate compliance with standard nonforfeiture laws, sample or complete schedules of premium rates and perhaps even proposed dividend scales. Some states require certificates signed by top management that the new form has been carefully checked against the requirements of the particular state. A readability evaluation may have to be included with the filing.

If a new product is extremely radical, such as a variable whole life policy, it may not be approved until new regulations or even new laws are passed in a particular state. As a result of such a situation, for a period of time, some companies offered policies with three different policy loan rates, 5%, 6%, or 8%, depending on the state in which the policy was to be issued.

In addition to state insurance department approval, some products may require other approvals for various reasons from bodies such as the Securities and Exchange Commission (SEC) or the Internal Revenue Service (IRS). For example, companies selling variable life insurance policies or variable annuity policies may be required to obtain approval of the contract, and the sales material to be used with it, from securities regulators. In Canada, variable contracts and associated information folders must be approved by the provincial insurance departments before they can be introduced. Certain contracts in Canada also require approval from the provincial securities commissions. Policies sold in the H.R. 10 market or as Individual Retirement Annuities under ERISA may require IRS approval. Policies designed to be used in particular tax situations may require private letter rulings from the IRS, including Section 79 plans.

Sales Promotion Department

The sales promotion unit is often not involved in the process until the final design is almost established. One of its functions is to design sales material that may be oriented either to the agent and broker or to the ultimate consumer. The unit may create advertisements for the trade press, develop special sales support illustration material, design information kits for agents, or even run sales campaigns featuring the new product.

For direct response companies, the sales promotion function is extremely important: material must be designed that explains the product to the potential buyer and influences him or her to respond positively and immediately. Some companies use outside advertising agencies, especially if direct consumer advertising or direct mail solicitation is involved. An outside agency may assist internal sales promotion personnel in developing sales material.

Education and Training

For a company with an agency force, the agent training and education unit can often be a key factor in the introduction and promotion of a new product. Many agents develop the habit of always selling a favorite plan, and they must be convinced of the new product's strengths. If agents do not understand the product, they may not even try to sell it. The training and education department may design audio visual presentations. It may develop a presentation to be used by the local agency head at meetings, showing where the new product fits into the overall portfolio. A company may develop a prepared sales presentation for agents to use with their clients. If a company is in the brokerage market, it will strive to educate its general agents who in turn will have the responsibility of educating brokers about the new product.

Education of the field service staff may also be necessary if there are particular application procedures to be followed. For example, many states have regulations regarding sales illustrations, and the field administrative staff may be required to monitor compliance. Some of these rules vary from product to product (e.g., whole life versus annuities), or from state to state. If a company has decided to conform (voluntarily) to the model sales disclosure regulations in all states in which it operates, some decisions may be required about this procedure, which must be communicated to the field staff. Policyowners may direct questions to the field administration personnel some time after they have obtained their policies.

If the new product involves significant development and introduction costs, the comptroller may wish to establish a separate budget for it. Special reporting of the financial results of the new product may be required. If so, new accounting procedures must be developed. If a broad new line is being developed, an entire set of accounts may have to be established.

Procedural Considerations for Product Development

The preceding discussion centered on theoretical considerations of product development. Certain procedural steps must be included in the process, such as the development of a critical path for activity, test marketing, and monitoring sales.

The Critical Path

One of the initial steps is the development of a critical path specifying all the stages in the product development process along with the required time for each event. A critical path allows various events to take place at the same time. Before the first event on the critical path, the field sales representatives have identified a market need and relayed it to their home office supervisory contacts, then to the marketing research department. Home office personnel in turn will have decided that satisfying this need meets the overall corporate objectives and fits the company's marketing philosophy. Table II outlines the stages of a critical path and who might have responsibility for completing them. A "new money" single premium annuity is used as an example. Decisions that might be made at certain points are shown in brackets. The time

TABLE II
Critical Path For Development and Introduction of New Money Single Premium Annuity

Event	Responsibility Assigned to	Elapsed Time To Complete
1. Develop general marketing plan including introduction activities	Marketing	1 week
2. Consider if existing distribution system appropriate for new product [decide whether greater emphasis on brokerage sales is needed]	Agency Vice President	1 week
3. Select risk factors assumptions and calculate test premiums using various assumptions [decide to test using commissions of 3% and also 2.5%]	Actuarial and Investment	2 weeks
4. Initial policy draft	Actuarial	1 week
5. Review initial draft		
— for conformity to regulations	Legal	1 week
— for potential servicing problems	Policyowner Service	1 week
— for computer systems modifications	Data Processing	1 week
6. Check product against general overall marketing and corporate objectives	Marketing Vice President	2 days
7. Approve remuneration structure [decide on commission of 2.5% of premium plus volume bonus]	Agency Vice President	1 week
8. Set specific sales objectives considering acceptable surplus strain [decide on $40 million new single premium]	Marketing Vice President Corporate Planning Actuarial	2 weeks
9. Design sales material	Sales Promotion	3 weeks
10. Design field training material	Agent Training	3 weeks

TABLE II (cont'd)

Event	Responsibility Assigned to	Elapsed Time To Complete
11. Revise policy draft to final version for filing	Actuarial	1 week
12. Revise computer system	Data Processing	4 weeks
13. Carry out policy filing and approval process	Legal	2 months
14. Revise policy form to reflect state insurance department concerns and refile if necessary	Legal and Actuarial	3 weeks
15. Set up new account codes for annuity product	Accounting	1 week
16. Expose test version of product to field [Feedback may lead to repetition of some previous events]	Marketing Research Certain Agencies	3 weeks
17. Develop final design reflecting field comments [decide to expand number of available income options—refiling of policy form may be necessary]	Actuarial	2 weeks
18. Print introduction material including rate manual pages, training material and sales promotion material	Sales Promotion	3 weeks
19. Announce final version of product to field and home office departments	Marketing, Promotion	2 days
20. Hold introduction training sessions for agents and brokers	Local Agency Heads	1 week
21. Review actual sales compared to original objectives; modify product if necessary [decide to improve rates because interest yields have increased and original rates no longer competitive]	Marketing Actuarial	6 months to 1 year 6 weeks

shown for each stage is only for illustration purposes and will vary depending on the characteristics of each particular company. A product development team should be able to come closer to its time estimates for each stage with each successive product introduced. The total elapsed time to develop and introduce the new product is not the sum of the time required for each of the events since many of the events can happen concurrently. The company may even choose to set up a temporary task force where normal reporting responsibilities are suspended for a period of time to coordinate the various product development activities. Despite the most careful organization, unforeseen problems and delays will cause deadlines to be missed; thus, extra time for these delays should be built into the path.

Data processing systems modifications provide an example of an event where work can start before the final details of the new product are known. Even regular rate changes may require systems updates. The earlier this work can be started the better, so that the ultimate introduction date can occur as soon as possible.

Printing activities are a second example of events that can begin before all the final product details are determined. Even before rate manual pages are produced, sample policy forms have to be printed for filing with the state insurance departments. A sufficient number of policy forms, and even application forms if they are new, must be printed in time for the planned sales activity. There may also be special sales promotion, introduction, education, and illustration material to be printed. The design and drafting of all the printed material should be started during the policy design process, so that optimum use can be made of available printing facilities.

One important activity that is largely outside the control of a company operating in the United States is the process of obtaining policy form approval from the various state insurance departments. Since filing requirements vary among the various states, most companies employ an expert on filing procedures who is familiar with all the variations. Several states require that approval of the new policy form be granted by the company's home state before they will grant approval. For this reason, companies often find it best to file with their home state first.

During the filing process it often becomes apparent that the responses, concerns, and level of expertise vary widely from state to state. Many state regulators are quite helpful to companies filing new products where the benefits are obvious for the insurance-buying public. Insurance regulatory authorities in some states will quite frequently help companies through the legal complexities. Other state insurance departments may take a literal interpretation of the existing regulations and turn down a new product initially until they can be convinced that it fits within the existing legal framework or until the regulations can be modified to accommodate the new product. Negotiations in these latter states can be very time-consuming and frustrating for those with the responsibility for the approval stage.

Often in the filing process a company may be required to make changes in policy wording. While for administrative ease it is best to try to keep variations in wording to a minimum, it is not uncommon for companies to end up with five or six, or even more, versions of the same policy to be used in different states. If the variations in the product from state to state are significant, for example, different policy loan rates, then different rate manual pages may be necessary for each version of the product.

Test Marketing

The introduction of the new product should be well planned. Field testing may or may not be part of this process and therefore may or may not be on the critical path.

If a company decides that it will test market a new product, it must first establish definite criteria for success before beginning the test marketing period. It would determine if the new product is one that should have a widespread appeal in all agencies or if it is one that will serve selected markets only. For example, contingent life policies, separate policies to which all the lives insured are a party and which insure several members of a partnership or corporation, are assumed to appeal to the sophisticated business market. Test marketing in a cross section of agencies may support or disprove this belief.

When Minnesota Mutual Life Insurance Company introduced Adjustable Life in the United States in the early 1970s, it did some pilot marketing in a few agencies in its home state. That company's main concern was its ability to cope administratively with the widespread introduction of such a revolutionary new product. After a few months of sales in one state, Minnesota Mutual distributed questionnaires to its field force and its clients to get reactions to the new concept. On the basis of the results of the questionnaires it decided to continue to offer Adjustable Life, but still introduced it only gradually until the administrative concerns were resolved.[5]

Monitoring Sales Success

After a product has been on the market for a period of time, management must determine if its actual sales success has met the original objectives. Companies may use as criteria for success the new face amounts sold, amount of new premium income, amount of profits from the new product or

---

[5] R. E. Hunstad, private communication, February 15, 1980.

new line of business, or even combinations of these and other criteria. No product can be considered successful unless the buying public, the sales representatives, the actuaries and the marketing department are reasonably happy with the design, the remuneration schedule and the pricing.

In determining whether a product is successful or not, it should be borne in mind that a company will spend a certain amount of money on the development of new products every year. Product research and design are going on continuously. For a major new product, the company may wish to keep track of its specific development costs to determine if ultimate sales recover the original investment. Any additional administrative costs due to a particular new product are monitored and minimized wherever possible. Since not all products are successful, it should be remembered that each product must contribute an amount greater than its own development costs, that is, the successful products must pay for the failures.

After a product has been on the market for a short period of time, the company may wish to modify it in light of actual sales experience. It is necessary to continually check the sales record of the product and study the assumptions underlying its rate schedules. If the sales of a particular product begin to decline, it may be that its rates are not competitive and improvements in some of the risk factors may allow rate decreases, thereby boosting sales. Perhaps agent compensation is not sufficiently attractive. A competitor may have introduced a similar plan with additional features that the company should emulate.

Profits on the block of new sales may be less than planned due to higher mortality or morbidity experienced, poor investment results, or other poor experience. The company can try to correct the cause of such poor risk experience, perhaps by tightening underwriting. It may seek higher-yielding investments. These alternatives should be considered before deciding to increase rates. However, it may find that it has no choice but to increase rates.

A product which has been in the portfolio for a lengthy period of time may be given a needed face-lift by adding new features. For example, the maximum attained age to which a yearly renewable term plan may be renewed might be extended from age 65 to age 75 or even to age 100. Such "repackaging" might give the product additional sales appeal.

At some point a product may actually have outlived its usefulness and will have to be removed from the portfolio. "Jumping juvenile" plans were introduced in the mid-1940s.[6] These took a few years to become successful,

[6] A child is insured for an initial amount of coverage until an age such as 21 at which point the coverage increases significantly, perhaps to five times the initial amount.

but eventually almost every company came out with its own version. More recently sales of such plans have decreased as people have begun to question the need for insuring young children. Dropping a plan at the end of its life cycle may create problems if there are some agents who have been making most of their sales on the product to be eliminated. However, if on the whole a product cannot support itself no matter what changes are made, it must be withdrawn from the market.

Trends in Product Development

As indicated earlier in this chapter, product development is a continual activity. Changes in the environment lead to changes in products and even to changes in the way a company organizes itself for product development. This section discusses some trends that are visible currently and that are likely to occur in the near future.

The External Environment

Some environmental changes that are taking place may lead to significant changes in product concepts. Factors such as a mobile population and inflation are especially important to product developers.

Families are changing their place of residence more frequently than in the past, providing a challenge to insurers to keep track of their policyowners in order to keep existing coverage in force. Thus, companies may find it appropriate to increase premiums to incorporate assumptions of higher lapse rates than they have experienced previously. Home service companies will be especially affected by this trend.

The average family income continues to increase—in many cases, much faster than the rate of inflation. Thus, insurers may be dealing with buyers in need of more sophisticated products than in the past. However, a major factor in the increase in family income is the increase in the number of workers in the family. Insurers are changing their thinking regarding the protection needs of the family where there may be two equally significant wage earners. More and more companies are developing and promoting joint life coverages. Families with a standard of living based on two incomes need disability insurance on each wage-earner.

During periods of high inflation, many of the traditional products of life insurance companies do not appeal to the public because there is a reluctance to pay premiums in today's dollars, in return for fixed future benefits payable in depreciated dollars. The endowment plan which combined death coverage and guaranteed maturity values has almost gone the way of the dinosaur. Instead of buying permanent whole life insurance, some people buy term insurance to cover their death protection needs and invest in alternative savings vehicles. In an effort to retain saving dollars, more life insurance companies will introduce flexible premium deferred annuities with relatively high credited interest rates to compete against the products of other savings institutions.

The traditional guaranteed nonparticipating whole life product with its fixed premiums and benefits is becoming more difficult to sell, since there is no opportunity for the purchaser to obtain the benefits of higher interest earnings. Participating insurance, in which there is some opportunity for the buyer to enjoy the effects of higher interest earnings while at the same time be exposed to the risk of higher expense loadings, has more appeal than nonparticipating insurance.

In the future the public might be willing to do without interim guaranteed values in exchange for higher ultimate guaranteed values in their coverages.

Since it takes time for trends in the environment to become established and evaluated, companies have to be cautious in their product design. The insurance-buying public (and the sellers of insurance) have been fairly conservative in the past with respect to completely new products. Since development costs are so high, most companies wait to see if a trend is merely a short-term fad or whether it indicates a permanent change in the environment before initiating specific new product development.

Trends in Products

The trends discussed above indicate that products will change in response to changes in the environment. Recent experience in Canada exemplifies product trends that are common in all areas of North America. Group insurance in Canada has grown from 37% of total life insurance ownership in 1970 to 44% in 1979. For individual insurance, term (as opposed to permanent) has expanded its market share from just over half (55%) in 1970 to almost two-thirds (70%) in 1979. Because of tax incentives for policyowners, premium income from annuities has grown significantly. The annuity products themselves have changed in design to have lower expense loads and returns that more closely reflect the interest returns on new investments.[7]

Mortality improvements are making underwriting at advanced ages more likely. Whole life policies are being issued to people in their eighties, and even term insurance is being underwritten at higher and higher issue ages, into the seventies in some cases. Term insurance is also being renewed to higher and higher ages. Most companies now active in the term market have a yearly

---

[7] Gerald M. Devlin, *Canadian Insurance/Agent & Broker*, Canadian Life Insurance Association, November 1979.

renewable term plan that is renewable to attained age 100 although the renewal premiums become quite substantial. At younger ages, accidental death is becoming a relatively more significant cause of death. Specific accidental death coverage may become increasingly popular. These are two examples of changes in mortality affecting product offering.

As increased Social Security benefits act to eliminate the private disability insurance market for low-income wage-earners, companies are increasing their issue limits for higher income groups.

While inflation continues to be a key concern to North Americans, new products may reflect the belief that the public may be more willing to take risks. VLI, which directly reflects equity performance, may finally gain acceptance. Products with built-in cost of living adjustments are becoming more widespread. As data processing systems become capable of coping with all its variations, adjustable life and other flexible product concepts, should take hold. With the diminishing emphasis on whole life insurance as a savings vehicle, the public will readily accept lower minimum nonforfeiture values in return for lower continuing costs of protection.

Special packages of coverages may be developed more widely for use in salary savings or payroll deduction schemes as companies seek ways to serve the lower-income market in the most economical manner.

In the United States H.R. 10 and IRA regulations (RRSP in Canada) may be liberalized and these changes may lead to significant increases in annuity sales if life insurance companies can develop products that compete with other savings institutions. They may have to put more stress on the ultimate income benefits of their products if they cannot compete with other vehicles during the accumulation period. Annuity sales in the United States have already increased due to H.R. 10 and ERISA legislation. More and more companies will be introducing products which qualify in some way for tax relief to take advantage of specific provisions in the tax legislation.

Some mutual companies have introduced investment generation concepts into their policyowner dividend structure. This leads to interest rate assumptions in dividend scales that vary depending on the actual calendar years in which premiums are paid. Such "new money" concepts have been common in the annuity area for some time. These concepts may also be expanded to level premium whole life policies.

Several stock companies have introduced policies with a low current premium but which contain provisions allowing the company to change rates in the future, either up or down, but never greater than a specified maximum. This ability to increase rates if future experience calls for it allows nonparticipating insurance to be sold without the actuaries' having to build excessive contingency margins into the rate structure.

With the increased emphasis on a healthy life-style many companies have introduced discounts for non-smokers and for people who exercise regularly. On the other hand, the simplified underwriting concept, under which only a few health questions are asked on the application form and very little underwriting is done, is an innovation designed to reduce the cost of acquiring business as expenses rise. The rate structure assumes that mortality on such business will be worse than that for normally underwritten business, but expense savings as a result of not having to underwrite each case are used to offset the excess mortality.

Organizational Changes for Product Development

Earlier in this chapter a number of field and home office personnel involved in the product design process were identified. Many different divisions in a typical company's organization structure are involved in the process. Several companies have attempted to reduce the number of areas involved by assigning product-pricing actuaries to their marketing areas. Typically, the product actuaries report to marketing vice presidents who are not necessarily actuaries. The product actuaries will recommend new products and do the pricing work using actuarial assumptions that have been approved by the corporate actuarial area. The final rate schedules may require corporate actuarial approval as well. By situating the product actuaries in the marketing area, it is expected that products will be designed that more closely meet the requirements of the company's marketing plan.

Other companies establish product task forces to which representatives from key areas are assigned, and normal reporting lines are suspended. These task forces are often headed by a marketing person. They may include representatives from areas such as agency, systems, administration and actuarial. Such a task force might be responsible for researching the needs for the new product, developing the first rough draft of the product design and determining the key elements involved in the product introduction. A representative from each area will be responsible for those items which are related to his or her particular area's expertise. Once a new product has been formally introduced, then the task force may be disbanded, and members reassigned to their normal duties.

Summary

Product development is a key part of a life insurance company's marketing effort. Both the qualitative design features and the quantitative pricing features of a product must fit with the company's overall objectives. While it is important to be aware of the theoretical considerations of product design, one must never lose sight of the practical concerns. Many areas in a company's home office and field offices should be involved in product development. The true success of a product does not lie in how well it is designed, but rather in its acceptance by the marketplace and its contribution to the profits of the insurer. Active marketing research is one essential element to successfully developing a new product or adapting an existing one. Thus, product development should be an ongoing activity.

Chapter 6

Special Markets

Harry G. Bubb, CLU

The concept of market segmentation is an important one in marketing. A market segment (or target market or specialty market) is a narrowly defined group of potential buyers, capable of being reached or communicated with. Market segmentation is the process of dividing a large market into these smaller market segments. Life and health insurers engage in **target marketing** by choosing a market segment, identifying the market segment's perceived needs and developing a marketing mix that will meet those needs. The members of a target market have certain needs in common, which may be met by a product, or group of products, or with a common delivery system, such as an individual or group sales approach.

Special (target) markets for life and health insurance can be grouped into two general classifications: markets for business insurance and markets for personal insurance. Markets for business insurance include professional corporations, partnerships, sole proprietorships (including conventional corporations), and owners of small businesses.

Markets for personal insurance include estate planning, high-income non-professionals, families, college students (both graduate and undergraduate), members of non profit associations (for tax-sheltered annuities), singles, women, retired persons and the "45 to 64" age group, and substandard prospects.

Each of the first two markets to be discussed—professional corporations and owners of small businesses—has needs that can be met by the general category of business insurance as well as unique characteristics that differentiate one from the other.

Professional People

The professional market consists of those who practice or are employed in a recognized profession, such as medicine, law, and accounting. Professional people have needs that make them excellent prospects for life and health insurance products. They usually earn high incomes, which create needs for financial planning to prepare for retirement, to minimize the burden of income taxation, and to minimize the burden of estate taxation. Adequate health insurance, such as disability income, is also needed by this group.

In recent years, income and estate tax considerations have spurred many professionals to incorporate their practices, although sole proprietorships and partnerships still remain important markets. In many circumstances, incorporation permits financial planning techniques that shelter substantial amounts of income from taxation.

Preparation for Retirement

Whether their practices are corporations, partnerships, or sole proprietorships, professionals have special needs in relation to their retirement planning. In contrast to owners, or employees of large businesses who have access to deferred or supplemental retirement benefits through their employers, professionals are expected to provide for much or all of their own retirement. Their needs center around ways of setting aside tax-exempt or tax-deferred income now for later use in retirement years. Owners of small firms have similar needs.

The obstacle faced by professionals and owners of small firms in their retirement planning is a simple lack of money. Whereas large corporations can fund retirement income from expected future profits due to stability of income and credit ratings, professionals and small business owners generally lack this option. In addition, the problem of business continuation intensifies the difficulties involved in retirement planning.

The insurance industry has responded to the need for tax-deferred retirement income by developing a variety of plans to help professionals prepare for retirement. Many of these plans are related to tax legislation, and indeed were created to take advantage of it. The products used in these plans may be retirement income policies (which include insurance), retirement annuities (which do not include insurance), or combinations of the two. More frequently, the product used will be an ordinary life-type contract sold in conjunction with a "side fund" which may be invested in any reasonable and legitimate investment vehicle.

Income Tax Considerations

As much as possible, retirement plans for professionals are designed to qualify as tax-favored, so they can be funded with pre-tax income. Some of the plans in use in the United States are presented in the following list.

1. The standard qualified pension and/or profit-sharing plan, provided for in Sections 401–404 of the Internal Revenue Code, in which contributions are tax-deductible by the employer.
2. H.R. 10, or Keogh, plans for self-employed persons.
3. Individual Retirement Accounts (IRAs), for employees whose employers do not provide a tax-qualified retirement plan.
4. Non-qualified deferred compensation plans. Because they are "non-qualified," they can therefore be discriminatory—that is, employers can make the plan available to whomever they choose, without concern for the IRS requirements that may apply to qualified plans.
5. Thrift plans. These are "qualified" plans—and are often supplementary to other retirement plans. Like other qualified plans, they are tax-sheltered to the extent that interest earned, and any employer contributions, may be tax-deferred. Again, as with other qualified plans, employee contributions would be made from "after-tax" dollars, although earnings on such employee contributions would be tax-sheltered until withdrawn.

In Canada, private pensions are given more favorable tax treatment than in the United States. Employees receive a tax advantage on their contributions to employer-sponsored plans. Registered Retirement Savings Plans (RRSPs) are available to all workers, and offer higher tax-deferred dollar limits for qualified plans than Individual Retirement Accounts in the United States.

While all *self-employed* professionals may avail themselves of the benefits of the Keogh Act, *incorporated* professionals may install "employee" pension and/or profit sharing plans for themselves and their employees (secretaries, technicians, nurses, and so on). Employees of non-incorporated professionals are a market for IRA plans. The sale of these various plans offers professional life insurance agents one of the most practical approaches to this market.

Estate Planning Needs

Professionals are also in need of estate planning services. Estate planning is generally regarded as a personal insurance decision and will be discussed in the section of this chapter that deals with personal insurance.

In addition to retirement and estate planning, professionals need health insurance, including overhead indemnity or business interruption coverage, and group life and health coverages.

In recent years, insurance agents have made special efforts and have developed special approaches to serve the professional market. Some agents represent such organizations as the Physicians Planning Service, which provides various types of administrative assistance to medical personnel. Other agents form their own corporations and work on a team basis with other professionals (such as attorneys or accountants) who provide services related to financial planning.[1]

Owners of Small Businesses

While the number of professionals in the country is substantial, the number of small businesses is also very large and comprises a market that is more visible and more easily approached than the professional market. In addition, this market has many of the needs of the professional market, although the business and financial agreements that must be considered are, if anything, even more complex.

There are 3.4 million small businesses in the United States, "small" being those establishments with fifty or less employees. Of those 3.4 million, 56% have no group insurance at all, and 70% have no business-related life insurance. Business insurance sales possibilities exist in disability income coverage, funding for buy-sell agreements, retirement plans, and so on. While many areas may overlap, there is a tremendous market for multisales to a single prospect.[2]

Business Continuation

Just as professionals, business owners need to make provisions for estate liquidity and tax reduction. There are other needs that are unique to small businesses. One of the main problems faced by business owners is the continuation or favorable disposition of their businesses after their death or disability. If this problem is not anticipated and planned for, the owners may find that the work of a lifetime may evaporate, leaving heirs and survivors with nothing to live on.

For sole proprietors, the problem may be relatively simple. If there are family members or skilled assistants who could take over the business, it may continue without interruption. Even so, those who take over the business, whether family members or employees, need the money to purchase it—unless they inherit it from the deceased. Otherwise, they may simply remain

---

[1] Jack Trudeau, "The Initial Step into the Medical Market," and William R. de Lashmutt and William P. Squire, Jr., CLU, "Selling to Professional Corporations—A Team Effort," *Life Association News,* (May 1973).

[2] William E. Robertson, "Small Business Is Big Business for Insurance," *Best's Review,* Life/Health ed., (June 1979), pp. 26–30.

employees of the owner's heirs, and those heirs may be forced to assume managerial duties for which they are unprepared.

When there are no children or employees ready to take over, a buyer for the deceased owner's portion of the business must be found. Failing this, the sole proprietor's survivors may find themselves inheriting only the proceeds from a forced sale which may result in a loss of the firm's physical assets.

For business owners who are partners, the problems are similar but more complex. Essentially, when a partner dies, unless other arrangements have been made in advance, the business must be terminated and its assets sold (at a possibly ruinous loss) or the business must be continued under a new agreement by the owner's heirs, by the owner's surviving partners, or by a combination of the two. The death of a stockholder in a closely held corporation presents similar problems.

Long experience has shown that, unless the deceased owner's heirs have some special qualifications, the most desirable solution to this problem is usually for the surviving partners or stockholders to purchase the interest of the heirs. But this is often impractical unless plans have been made to provide the surviving partners or stockholders with the necessary funds for such a transaction.

Fortunately, life insurance can be utilized to solve the problem of business continuation. For the sole proprietor, if there are no children to inherit the business, it is often a matter of reaching an agreement with an employee to buy the business when the proprietor dies. The funds to make this purchase can be provided by life insurance on the proprietor's life. Even if the employee lacks the funds to pay the premiums on this life insurance, arrangements can be made whereby the proprietor advances all or part of the premiums. Bringing about the funding for such an arrangement so as to realize the maximum financial advantage for the insured is frequently a challenging problem, and it is one of the reasons why the professional life insurance agent is so valuable to clients. Agents are aware of the possible problems and can objectively and knowledgeably advise clients.

In the case of the partner or stockholder, the application of life insurance to the problem of business continuation is more complex than for sole proprietors because of the law and because of the number of people involved. The methods used to handle a business continuation problem will often depend on the size of the business. Where only a few stockholders or partners are involved, it may be convenient for each owner to purchase insurance on each of the other owners' lives. For example, in a firm with only two owners, each owner could easily purchase a policy insuring the life of the other owner. But where a number of owners are involved, it may be advisable for the partnership or corporation to own one policy on each owner, with the partnership or corporation named as the beneficiary. Whatever the technicalities, the principle is the same: life insurance provides the funds with which surviving owners can buy out the interest of the deceased owner from the heirs. In this way, the business can continue uninterrupted, avoiding the possibility of unwanted participation by well-meaning, but inexperienced, outsiders.

It should be added that properly drawn **buy-sell** agreements (whether between the owners of the business as individuals, or between the business as an entity and its owners) are also a necessary part of a business continuation insurance plan. These agreements, drawn by an attorney, specify the conditions (e.g., death, or disability for a certain length of time) under which an owner's interest in a business would be sold, to whom it would be sold, and the price to be paid for it.

Business continuation problems can also arise when a business owner is disabled. In this connection, a properly drawn business continuation insurance agreement should also contain disability, and possibly medical expense coverage, plus some provision for buying out the owner's interest if disability should become permanent and prevent a return to work.

Key Person Insurance

Many companies employ individuals who make vital contributions to their businesses, and whose absence could lead to substantial financial loss, or even failure. Such key persons, whether owners or not, occupy important executive positions and perform duties requiring a high level of skill and judgement. Insuring against the loss of these people's services through either death or disability is an important aspect of business insurance, known as **key person insurance.**

While all corporations have key people, the largest ones (those in the Fortune 500, for example) are usually well-situated financially to stand the financial shock caused by the loss of a key person. This is not true of many smaller businesses, professional corporations, and close corporations. For such firms, therefore, key person insurance may be a necessity to indemnify the firm for the loss it will suffer if a key person dies or is disabled.

In addition, life insurance can be used to fund retirement benefits for key persons, so that it will be more difficult for competitors to lure them away. This is an important consideration, since key persons who are not owners can be lost just as effectively if they leave to take another job as if they die or become disabled.

Among the losses which key person insurance helps guard against is loss of the company's credit. For example, the line of credit which a bank extends to a small firm often reflects its judgement of the firm's earning power, which in turn often depends on the presence of one or more key people who keep the firm going. The loss of one of these key people could lead a bank to revise, perhaps drastically, its assessment of the business, and this could shorten the line of credit the bank is willing to extend.

Further, it is expensive to replace a key person. A new person must be trained to assume new duties, and income may be lost while this new person acquires the expertise needed to do the job. Or, a key person may be hired from another firm—but it may be necessary to pay a higher salary and higher fringe benefits to hire this new key person away from his or her previous position.

Finally, one must consider the financial loss that may result if customers and suppliers lose confidence in the firm following a key person's death or disability. Customers may feel the firm's product or service will no longer be delivered on time, or that it will be of lower quality. Suppliers, who are often a source of credit in that they may be patient about payment of bills by good firms, may also cause a problem by stopping or cutting deliveries. Key person insurance can help in this case by providing funds to the firm as it rebuilds confidence or demonstrates that the loss has not undermined the company's operation.

Key person insurance can help offset any or all of these risks by providing funds to the employer in the event of the death or disability of the key person. Through a careful analysis, a value for the key person's services can be arrived at in all these categories, and the potential losses can be estimated.

Some mention should also be made of a sophisticated business insurance planning device which enables a company to offer a key employee low-cost, permanent life insurance with growing cash values—and still recover all of its cash outlay. This device is known as split dollar insurance. There are two major split-dollar systems—the collateral assignment system and the endorsement system. Using the collateral assignment system, the key employee, as the insured, owns the policy, selects the beneficiary, and pays the premiums with the proceeds of a loan from the employer. The loan is secured by the policy itself. The death benefit is paid to the designee, subject to repayment of the loan to the employer. In the endorsement system, while there are many variations, the basic plan specifies that the company pay the entire life insurance premium and keep the right to that part of the proceeds equal to its total premium payments. On the insured's death, the corporation gets all of its money back. The insured's family gets the rest of the proceeds.[3]

---

[3] William B. Lynch, *How to Get the Most Out of Your Private Corporation*, (Pacific Consulting Corporation, 1980), p. 33.

Estate Planning

In addition to the desire to reduce current income tax payments and to prepare for retirement, professional people and owners of businesses frequently need counsel on estate planning. Many of them can anticipate accumulating a substantial amount of wealth, which they will naturally want to preserve for their loved ones. Yet, estate taxes at death can be high and, since a great many estates tend to be short on liquid assets, the necessity of paying these taxes can lead to severe estate shrinkage if proper plans have not been made. Estate planning is designed to alleviate such problems.

The foremost consideration in estate planning is the objectives of the person who is accumulating the estate. These objectives may be as simple as making as much money as possible, and that is indeed a typical objective. Beyond this, the person may have other objectives, such as leaving properties to heirs in relation to their needs and abilities, a bequest to a favorite charity, and so on. Some people will put primary emphasis on minimizing income taxes during life, while others will put primary emphasis on building an estate for heirs. In any good estate plan, the objectives of the person building the estate must be known, understood, agreed upon, and accounted for.

The first step in proper estate planning is the elementary task of executing a will. Failure to do so means that at death the estate owner's assets will be disposed of according to law, with little consideration given to the individual needs of heirs, or to conservation of as much of the estate as possible for them. While executing a will is a necessary first step, it is in itself inadequate for the purpose of estate conservation. While a will may be effective in minimizing estate taxes, it cannot assure that money is available to pay the taxes when they become due. For this purpose, more extensive estate planning is desirable.

Ideally, the one who initiates the estate planning process (frequently an agent of a life insurance company) brings together experts in law, accounting, and financial planning to analyze an individual's assets and recommend steps to maximize the creation, accumulation, conservation, and proper distribution of wealth.

The tools of estate planning include such important documents as wills, trusts, instructions to the estate's executor, and—in most cases—permanent life insurance. Permanent life insurance is a particularly valuable tool in estate planning because it can provide the liquidity necessary to pay estate taxes, otherwise valuable assets may have to be sold, perhaps at inappropriate times, at prices that may be drastically below their fair market value.

High-Income Non-Professionals

The mere possession of substantial wealth or property may in itself create a need for insurance services, quite apart from the business or profession one engages in. Private investors (such as in real estate or equities), and others who have inherited wealth, are examples of this kind of prospect. These affluent individuals will generally have a minimum annual income of $100,000, including earned and unearned income.

Affluent individuals generally have the same needs for insurance that professional and business people have. Some 87% of affluent individuals have life insurance. They have special needs for estate planning to conserve their assets for their survivors, and they may also need to shelter current income against taxation. Once contacted, such prospects can be approached and counseled on life insurance needs in much the same way as professionals and business owners, except that frequently there is no need to consider forms of business or corporate organization.

While such individuals may have little need for disability income coverages because of unearned incomes, they have the same need for major medical coverage that other people have. A major illness can have an impact on even a substantial estate, and wealthy people will want to protect themselves against this hazard just as others do.

People in this market category are not as conveniently contacted as professional people or owners of small businesses. An agent cannot simply look in the phone book or drive through commercial areas to secure leads for prospects. However, this market is well worth reaching. One of the most popular ways is to offer special seminars on financial or estate planning. Seminars may be expensive, but can prove rewarding. Of course, the most common method is by referral from other clients.

Families

The family has been one of the major markets for life and health insurance for years, yet there still remains great potential for insurance sales. It has always been clear that the death of the breadwinner—traditionally the father—would create financial problems for the survivors. Traditional roles have been changing, with women becoming more involved in contributing to the income of families. To help solve the problems of loss of income, insurance companies have learned to analyze a family's income needs and to project the amount of insurance that would be necessary to meet those needs for a specified time if the breadwinner were to die or become disabled. The approach has been to sell both disability insurance and a mix of term and permanent life insurance that would be adequate to meet future needs.

Dual-Income Families

In recent years, the growing prevalence of the two income family has complicated the traditional sales approach to the family market. The resulting higher incomes have created a need for more insurance protection, creating opportunities for sales that have not yet been realized. Specifically, there is a greater need than ever before to insure the lives of employed women, many of whom are married and have children. The death of these breadwinners would have substantial economic impact on their families and should be insured against in the usual manner.

As of 1977, 47% of the married women in the United States were employed, and their contributions raised the median family income from $16,267 (with only the husband working) to $19,327 (when husband and wife were employed). Yet one study shows that the average size of new policies issued to married employed women was only $15,480, compared to an average size of $33,472 for new policies issued to married employed men. The difference between the amounts issued to husbands and wives remains even after accounting for age, income, and occupation. For example, a woman earning between $15,000 and $25,000 is sold an average size policy of $22,400, while the average size policy for a male earning the same is $34,000.[4]

A factor that must be taken into account is the growing popularity of group insurance, which leads many families to underestimate the need for personally owned insurance. Heads of families, men and women alike, need to be aware that group insurance will terminate at retirement, and may be terminated even earlier in the event of loss of employment. The later in life this happens, the more difficult it will be to replace this insurance with personal insurance. Of course, the need for insurance decreases to some degree when children grow up and leave home, but even in retirement years a need for insurance for the surviving spouse remains.

Reaching the family market is accomplished by using any of the available distribution systems that will be discussed later in the text, including personal contact by agents, direct response, and even distribution by savings banks in certain states.

College Students

As of 1980, college students numbered approximately eleven million (over 9½ million undergraduate students and nearly 1½ million graduate students) and thus comprise one of the largest markets in the country. It is a

[4] Cheryl D. Retzloff, "Protecting a Family's Lifestyle . . . The Total Income," *Managers Magazine*, (LIMRA, August 1979), pp. 12–13.

market whose members either need or will shortly need life insurance for a variety of reasons, such as mortgages, children's education, or family income. Furthermore, college students are generally concentrated on or near campuses, in dormitories, fraternities and sororities, and thus are relatively easy to locate and contact. In addition, while they usually lack economic means to purchase substantial amounts of insurance at the moment, many of them will be among the higher income groups in the future, either as members of professions, like medicine and law, or as successful executives and entrepreneurs.

Success in life insurance marketing always requires a degree of far-sightedness and adaptation, but this is especially true of the college market. Because the present insurance needs and economic means of students are limited, most companies that specialize in this market make some kind of initial premium financing available to students. This financing typically consists of loans or notes to be repaid by specific dates, and at specified interest rates.

A good deal of thought has also been given to the design of products that will be uniquely suited to the college market. For example, some companies offer guaranteed issue policies, which are issued with minimal underwriting information in order to assure competitive costs and efficient placement of coverage. Another popular product for this market is the guaranteed purchase option, attached to a standard policy, which enables insureds to purchase a stated amount of insurance at specified dates in the future without offering evidence of insurability. This option has been well-received because, for a low cost, policyowners can be assured of the ability to increase insurance protection to meet their growing needs.

Many companies that are active in the college market use policies that have been specially designed for students. Some whole life policies include short-term endowments that mature to pay off the loan that financed the initial premium. Other policies have large dividends in the early years that serve the same purpose.[5]

In addition, there has been some discussion of marketing guaranteed insurability coverage for college students, in which the option would be separated from the life insurance product. In effect, the students would not be purchasing life insurance but rather the right to purchase life insurance in the future, regardless of their health at those later dates.[6] This would guaran-

---

[5] LIMRA *News and Trends,* Bulletin #122, (March 18, 1977).

[6] Leonard L. Berekson and Patricia A. Strong, " The Case for Group Marketed Insurability Coverage for College Students," *Best's Review,* Life and Health edition, (November 1978), p. 10ff.

tee a 20-year-old who purchases the option later insurance coverage even if he or she becomes uninsurable or a substandard risk.

A LIMRA study indicates that relatively few companies are currently active in the college market. Of those that are, their marketing strategies vary. Only a few companies have a special sales force, or a separate home office department with exclusive responsibility for penetrating this market. In most of the few active companies, serving the college market is essentially a sideline.[7] The college market can be reached by agents who approach each prospect individually, or by using direct response methods.

In addition to individual sales to college students, group sales are used for this market. In this approach, all students of a college, or of a particular organization within a college such as a fraternity or alumni group, are given an opportunity to purchase group coverage within a certain period of time after the offer is made. The offers are made through direct mail and group presentations in order to reach as many students as possible, but no attempt is made to reach each student individually, as would be the case with the individual marketing approach.

Members of Non-Profit Associations

People who work for non-profit organizations that are tax-exempt, such as charities, hospitals, schools, colleges, and universities (including publicly operated school systems at any level from primary to university), represent a special market that has great potential for the insurance marketer. All bona-fide employees of such associations or organizations are eligible to have their employers purchase "tax-deferred" annuities for them. The rationale behind this benefit is to encourage employers to help their employees in these organizations plan for retirement.

Technically, the employee does not make the purchase of the tax-sheltered plan, which is also known as a "403(b) Plan" after the IRS code section authorizing it. It is the employer who makes the purchase, and for this reason the agent must approach the employer. If the premiums for the annuity are to come from an increase in the employee's salary, then the employer will have to be convinced of the value of this approach. More frequently, the premiums are obtained by "reducing" the employee's salary. That is, the employee's salary is reduced by the amount needed for the premiums. In this case, the employer is effectively providing only an administrative service and will usually agree to let an agent approach the employees.

The key concept of these plans is that employees are being given an

[7] LIMRA, *op. cit.*

opportunity to buy annuities with before-tax dollars. Purchasing annuities with before-tax dollars can mean a substantial savings to employees, and allows them to prepare for retirement at a lower cost than would be the case if they purchased a similar annuity under any other circumstances. Generally, 20% of the year's current pay (16.7% if by way of salary reduction) can be set aside tax-free each year, although adjustments must be made for past service and for previous tax-free contributions.[8] The tax advantage also applies to all but a nominal amount of the premiums paid for certain life insurance policies, and to amounts invested in mutual funds.[9]

Since this market consists of a relatively small number of employers and a large number of employees, it is in some ways ideal. The eligible organizations are easily located, and the first approach can be made during normal business hours. The employees themselves are also relatively easy to approach, and usually this can also be done in the daytime.

The people for whom the annuities are purchased are usually middle-income people. While they will probably not have much need for high-level estate planning, they may become prospects for family insurance planning. Once they have been approached through the tax-sheltered annuity sale, they should be more easily approached for other insurance and financial planning sales.

Singles

Single people without dependents constitute a major and growing market for insurers to consider. As of 1978, one-fifth of all households consisted of persons living alone. The number of men living alone, 6.4 million, had risen 79% since 1970, and the number of women living alone, 10.4 million, was up 42%.[10]

The young singles market consists primarily of people in their twenties who are not presently married. Excluding college students, most of the people in this market are in the early stages of their careers, and while their incomes are generally not high at the moment, they are likely to eventually earn higher-than-average incomes. Further, many of them look forward to marrying and raising families.

As a group, young singles do not have a high awareness of the need for life or health insurance. And indeed, their present need is not as great as exists in the other markets. Although the young singles market might include some divorced or widowed people with children, the market consists gener-

---

[8] *Tax Deferred Annuities for Employees of a School, Hospital, Charity, etc.*, (R&R Newkirk, 1979–80), p. 2.

[9] *Ibid.*, p. 3, 4.

[10] *Current Practices* (LIMRA, August 1979), p. 2.

ally of people with no dependents. Still, young single people are not without a sense of responsibility, and they are generally receptive to the thought that they will eventually need life insurance. Once this future need is understood, they realize that there are great advantages to buying at least some insurance while they are still young. First, premiums will never be lower, since they increase with the age of the insured. Second, since the issuance of insurance depends on the buyer's health, a change in the applicant's health could affect the ability to qualify for insurance in the future.

Since young singles often have both limited financial resources and limited immediate needs for insurance, base policies with some kind of guaranteed insurability rider are frequently best suited for them. This allows them to begin their insurance program modestly, but guarantees them the right to purchase additional coverage in the future as their needs increase.

Women

At first glance, the designation of women as a separate market for insurance may seem inappropriate. One may ask: If there is a women's market, why is there not a men's market? There are, after all, roughly as many women as men in the population. Further, it can be reasoned that, despite the rapid social changes of the last few decades, many women remain full-time housewives, with no separate and independent incomes. Insurance bought on their lives is properly part of the standard family insurance market. Why then should women be designated a special market for life insurance?

While the reasons stated above make a case for continuing to regard women as components of the family market, there are equally convincing reasons for looking at women in a completely different light. First, a substantial and growing number of women are gainfully employed. In the United States, approximately half of all eligible women, about 40 million women, are so employed. Of these, about 13% are single heads of households, and about a third are married.[11] A similar trend is occurring in Canada.

Second, while women generally earn lower incomes than men, women exhibit a wide range of earning power, and many professional women and executives are highly paid. Many are successful entrepreneurs with substantial estates. However, as we have seen, women are generally insured for much less than men with comparable incomes. It is this fact that makes women such an important target market, for if women have the same insurance needs as men, clearly their needs are not being met.

Basically, the same insurance products that are needed by men are also

---

[11] Rena Bartos, "What Every Marketer Should Know About Women," *Harvard Business Review*, (May–June, 1978), p. 73.

needed by women. Interestingly, one company's research indicates that women prefer whole life to term insurance.[12] The same company has found that women are receptive to the tax-sheltered annuity. Whatever the product, women buy for much the same reasons as men: to create an estate, to pay final expenses, to prepare for retirement, and to indemnify family members for the loss of their income or services.

Women need the same financial planning services that men do. Since there is no single best insurance product for women, sales people who want to succeed must undertake the same fact finding interviews and financial analyses for women as for men.

It is important to be flexible in sales approaches to women because their life situations are as variable as men's. Some are single, some are married; some are working only temporarily before starting a family; some are career women, and will remain so, even if they later have children. They may be professionals or business owners; they may have large estates. Until a specific prospect's situation has been determined, it is necessary to refrain from drawing conclusions about the kind of insurance needed.

Retired Persons and the 45 to 64 Age Group

Insurance marketers have tended to market to people in their early and middle years, but lately more attention has turned to those in later life. Data provided by the advertising agency of Kenyon and Eckhardt show that people over 65 years old constitute 20.3% of all households in the United States. This group accounts for 11.9% of all spending power, and for 7.1% of all discretionary income. And, in recent years, more people have been able to take "early retirement," frequently beginning as early as age 55. Furthermore, a major organization, the American Association of Retired Persons, has been created to serve the needs of this segment of society. The Association's bi-monthly publication, *Modern Maturity,* now has some seven million subscribers. Clearly, people of retirement age constitute an economic force to be reckoned with, and both they and life and health insurance marketers have a common interest in meeting their needs.

The same information indicates that people in the 45 to 64 age group constitute 33.6% of all United States households, with 52.8% of the nation's discretionary income. Their mortgages are likely to be paid, children are grown, and wives are likely to be working. They are generally concerned about planning for their retirement. In addition, prospects in this age group

---

[12] "Everything You Thought You Knew About Selling to Women, But Didn't," (Travelers Insurance Company brochure, 1978).

are considered "experienced, less fad-oriented, less likely to feel peer group pressure, and more likely to want facts and demonstrations before buying."[13]

Clearly, retired persons and individuals who are 45 to 64 constitute target markets with economic resources not to be ignored. There is a potential for life insurance sales to this market that is being successfully realized by some companies.[14]

It is true, of course, that social security programs in the United States and the Canada and Quebec pension plans in Canada meet at least part of the needs of a substantial portion of the over-65 market. Yet, despite the high premiums for life insurance for this age group, there are many who feel they need to purchase additional protection. Many realize belatedly the need for whole life insurance, and among the affluent there is often a substantial need for life insurance for estate planning purposes, as well as the ability and inclination to buy insurance for children or grandchildren.

In addition to life insurance, health insurance is a major need of people in this age group. Again, for people who are eligible for Social Security in the United States, a substantial part of this need is provided by Medicare, which provides stated benefits for hospitalization and medical procedures. There are, however, gaps in this coverage in such areas as deductibles, co-insurance, and any amounts over stated limits. Many private companies do offer special "medigap" policies to provide coverage to supplement Medicare.

Both direct response techniques and the individual agent system have proved workable in selling to this market. Agents who properly qualify their prospects by determining need, insurability, and financial ability can offer individually tailored programs for certain selected people, and many companies reach a larger section of the market with media advertising of products designed specifically for this market.

Substandard Risks

Approximately 10% of the population of the United States consists of people who, for one reason or another, are not eligible for life or health insurance at standard rates. These people comprise a group we will call the substandard market. In most cases, the reason is some impairment of health, such as a heart problem, but other factors are also involved. Some substandard risks are so classified because of a hazardous occupation and still others are placed in this category because of social factors or habits that might reduce life expectancy. While companies set age limits for issuing policies, age is not in

13 "Discovering the Over-50 Set," *Business Week,* (November 19, 1979), p. 194–195.

14 Richard J. Sayre, "Who Needs Life Insurance After 65?" *Life Association News,* (September, 1979), p. 89.

itself a basis for substandard ratings. Age may, however, complicate other factors, such as poor health.

Surprisingly, the largest life insurance companies have not played a leading role in serving the substandard market. Most of the leading specialists in this field are middle-sized companies that have developed special techniques for dealing with the substandard segment of the general market.[15]

One of these techniques is reinsurance. While this insurance specialty was developed to help companies avoid excessive (but not necessarily substandard) liability, it has proven a convenient resource in the substandard market. Rather than ask one of its agents to approach several other companies in order to provide a valued client with the desired insurance coverage, a company will accept the coverage with one policy, then make its own arrangements to reinsure with one or more companies. This arrangement gives the insured the convenience of one policy and one premium, allows the company to spread its risks, and enables the agent and company to enjoy greater client loyalty.

Of course, insurance companies also have a different premium structure for substandard risks. There are, in fact, various ways of arriving at rates for these risks. A flat extra premium (permanent or temporary) may be assigned; in this case, for example, a person may simply be charged $10 per thousand more than a standard risk. Another method, less popular today, is simply to add one or more years to the substandard risk's age, thus requiring the insured to pay the premium of a person one or more years older. But the multiple table pricing system is the one most generally used for impaired risks. In this approach, the premium is based on the plan, the age of the insured, and the average mortality of people in the insured's risk classification, compared to standard risks for the same plan and age.[16]

In addition, some companies have issued special policies or have revised standard policy premium structures for a special class of risk, such as smokers.

One of the problems of selling to the substandard market is obtaining enough data to determine how high a substandard rating is needed. Once preliminary data shows the existence of higher than normal risk factors, additional reports or investigations may be needed to determine how high an extra premium must be charged. Some of these reports can be ordered without the applicant's permission; others, such as medical reports, may

[15] Warren B. Eller, "Trends in the Underwriting of Substandard Life Insurance Risks," (paper presented to the Western Risk and Insurance Association, January 7–9, 1979).

[16] Gaylord L. Paine, "Risk Selection and Substandard Risks," *Life and Health Insurance Handbook,* 3rd ed., (Richard D. Irwin, 1973), p. 208.

require prior authorization. In addition, current laws require release of underwriting information to the applicant, except that an insurance company may decide to release medical information only to a physician of the applicant's choice.

Summary

The foregoing analysis is by no means a complete discussion of all the markets available to life and health insurers. However, the subjects that are covered in this chapter represent the major markets that are generally recognized as important to the insurance industry. An understanding of how these special markets are determined will enable readers to identify characteristics of other special markets that may become important to insurance marketers. Types of employment, health, income, and future income potential are among the factors that determine these different markets. And each segment holds its own challenge for life and health marketers.

Chapter 7

Marketing Support

Harvey W. Rubin, Ph.D., CLU
Guy E. Webb, Jr., CLU

The definition of marketing support varies among life and health insurance companies. Many activities can be included in this category, but all have a common element: central operation at the home office.

In order to understand the subject of marketing support, the reader must first be acquainted with the structure of marketing departments in life and health insurance companies, the factors that affect this structure, and the home office agency and marketing department. These are presented before going on to a discussion of marketing support as provided by agency services, marketing research, and other departments such as policy issue and the legal department. Agency services, a major component of marketing support, includes the functions of advanced underwriting, field electronic data processing services, and agent licensing, among others.

The primary mission of any financial institution, whether a life and health insurance company, property and casualty insurance company, commercial bank or savings and loan association, is first to determine its clients' needs; second, to develop, distribute and stimulate demand for its products; and third, to serve customers who have bought its products.

All of the great product designs and research are useless if the public is not aware of the company's product. Actuarial research and development, underwriting processing efficiency, and claim promptness are of little value if no one is willing to purchase the product. Creating this awareness and willingness is one responsibility of the marketing organization.

The duties assigned to the marketing department influence how the department structure is deliberately organized or how it develops over a period of time.

Factors Affecting the Marketing Structure

Both internal and external conditions have an influence on a life and health insurance company's marketing organization. Some examples of external factors are competition, consumerism, regulation, and economic and social factors. These factors, and some of the ways in which the marketing organization is affected, are discussed below.

External Factors

The financial marketplace is composed of the various financial institutions and the financial instruments they sell. The nature of the financial marketplace is quite important to a life insurance company since the products it sells are financial instruments.

The financial marketplace of yesterday is gone. Yesterday's financial world was marked by a slow-paced, steady, and uncomplicated way of life. Today, our economy is marked by constant upheavals, cyclical upturns and downturns, and double-digit inflationary spirals that seem unending.

Today's insurance marketplace cannot help but reflect this new environment. This environment is marked by Social Security's meeting the needs of the middle and lower economic classes; the enactment of the Employee Retirement Income Security Act (ERISA) in 1974 and several modifications since; one-stop financial planning to include every financial service from the purchasing of insurance to the buying of stocks; the introduction of "split dollar," "Section 79," and close corporation stock redemption plans; and retired lives reserve.

The consensus of the leading authorities in the life insurance industry is that the marketing structure must have the flexibility to be able to respond quickly and effectively to the financial world affected by the external factors of competition, consumerism, regulation, the economy and social factors.

These external factors make it more important than ever before that the marketing organization have an awareness of its environment through a public affairs department. The function of public affairs is discussed in detail in the following chapter. Often the issues addressed by public affairs have been brought up by state or federal governmental agencies or representatives. Thus, the organizational structure of the modern marketing department would reflect the above considerations.

Competition

The functions of financial institutions have become less than clear. Previously, an individual's stockbroker bought and sold equities exclusively. One's bank and savings and loan association administered checking accounts and processed automobile loans and home mortgages. Individuals are now being actively pursued by these same institutions to become life insurance clients. If one-stop financial planning is truly the wave of the future, then life and health insurance companies must make the proper organizational changes. This might include organizing the agency/marketing department to support the distribution of equity products on the same level as is currently being done with non-equity products.

In the past, competition from other marketers of financial instruments for savings dollars simply did not exist. Today, national stock brokerage houses aggressively market life insurance and annuities. Now, almost every monthly statement from stockbrokers includes literature on the virtues of life insurance and annuities, indicating an effort to become the primary distributors of all types of financial instruments to a select market. Brokerage houses are apt to target their marketing efforts to business persons (small business owners as well as medium and large business owners), professionals and high-income non-professionals. Most studies show that the life insurance industry has not effectively tapped market.

Another source of increased competition for savings dollars is commercial banks and savings and loan associations. Competition is coming from the high-interest saving vehicles such as the thirty-month certificate and money market mutual funds, as well as from efforts by some banks and savings and loan associations to market insurance through wholly owned insurance agencies.

The organization may add a risk management service to the marketing department which will analyze all the financial risks of a client, whether this analysis indicates a need for life insurance, property and casualty insurance, self-insurance, or specific types of investments. The risk management service may then design an overall financial portfolio to provide a solution for the risks to which the client is exposed.

Consumerism

The true cost has not always been as apparent with the purchase of financial services, as with the purchase of other services such as medical treatment. The true net cost of financial instruments can not be determined until the instrument is sold in the case of a stock or until the policy actually matures in the case of life insurance.

Consumer pressure for privacy, cost disclosure and other issues has prompted many life and health insurance companies to organize their marketing departments to be conscious of consumer needs. As mentioned earlier, many companies have created a public affairs department. This department may make education in the community one of its responsibilities.

Regulation

Before the age of consumerism, the regulatory efforts of state insurance commissioners and the federal government could be described as passive.

In most states, regulatory actions almost always addressed property and casualty insurance matters. Few regulatory actions touched on life insurance. This is not the case today. For example, as a reaction to various consumer group pressures, states have become quite active in determining what sales literature may or may not say or imply, as well as proper policy language, wording, and interpretation. A staff attorney will usually be assigned to review all sales literature generated by the marketing department to make sure it contains no misleading or confusing statements.

Economic and Social Factors

In the late 1970s, inflation became the number one economic topic. Since by their very nature life insurance and annuity contracts provide future enjoyment of one's income at the sacrifice of present enjoyment of that income, the buying power of that future benefit is quite important to the policyowner. Developing new insurance products whose benefits will retain their buying power in a time of double-digit inflation is an additional challenge for today's marketing and product development departments.

In the insurance trade press, one constantly reads of the changing lifestyles of potential and current clients. The rise of "me-ism" seems to be an integral part of the thinking of the age group between 20 and 40. The concern is with acquiring and preserving wealth for oneself as opposed to the transfer of that wealth to others. To a large extent, life insurance has been marketed in the past as a unique financial instrument to protect the transfer of this wealth. However, many companies now are actively marketing retirement annuities in order to appeal to this more self-centered philosophy.

Single professional women have achieved new stature in the business, professional, and civic communities. In recognition of this, some companies are establishing separate departments for sales to the women's market. The director of the women's market also sometimes assumes the role for the active recruitment of women agents.

Single-parent heads of households are also a relatively new social phenomenon. Many are women who have had little prior experience in managing personal finances. Life and health insurance companies must find ways to serve this market, perhaps by offering more financial counseling.

The traditional marketing organization within life and health insurance companies that was virtually free from external factors and pressures is a relic of the past. Because of increasing competition, changing value systems, consumerism and regulation, and economic conditions, the marketing department of today must be a constantly changing one if the company is to keep abreast of the marketplace and anticipate external factors that will influence the destiny of the company in the future. Marketing departments need to monitor and respond to external factors in order to be effective.

Internal Factors

Life and health insurance companies' marketing departments are affected by internal factors such as management philosophy and objectives, and individual talent available to the company. The manner in which the company chooses to react to internal factors is dependent upon senior management philosophy. This philosophy is in turn determined by senior management's assessment of the current and future marketplace and the internal talent available to implement the most suitable marketing strategy for these markets.

Another internal determinant of a company's organizational structure is the type of company that it is or desires to become: an ordinary insurance company, a combination company, an industrial company, a brokerage company, a captive association company such as the Farm Bureau, a direct response marketer, or some combination of all. For example, combination companies usually have a separate ordinary agency department and combination agency department but a common marketing support function because, in many respects, both departments have the same requirements for sales literature and promotion material. Because of the different markets served by the two departments, specialized sales material will be required for each as well.

Captive association companies such as the Farm Bureau, sell insurance to their members. The association members are already pre-disposed to purchase insurance from the association's life company since they are already purchasing other services from the association's other companies such as farm equipment and seed. Thus, the marketing department essentially provides internal support and direction for the field force. Some companies have extensive in-house agent training programs and aggressively solicit life insurance sales through heavy distribution of sales literature to their members.

An ordinary company sells insurance solely through agents. Therefore, the marketing department must be organized to handle such activities as soliciting new policyowners, servicing present policyowners, training, educating, and updating a relatively sophisticated agency force, and monitoring the changing demographics of the marketplace. Product innovation is also an important activity of this department. The primary concern is that of selling insurance products. Thus, a department titled "agency sales" is frequently the division that has responsibility for the sales function. Other elements on the organizational chart for an ordinary company's marketing department would include departments in such functional areas as advanced underwriting, sales promotion, advertising, product development, marketing research, meetings and conventions, training and education, and field communication. These departments are sometimes grouped under the heading "agency sales," or "marketing," depending on the company. Many companies combine agency sales and marketing into one department, and, for purposes of discussion, this chapter will also present agency and marketing as one department.

In many companies such departments as product development would be located in departments other than marketing. However, the trend in modern marketing companies is to place it within the marketing department. The important point to remember is that these functions exist within the corporate structure and not necessarily the department in which the particular function is located. Functions are transferred quite frequently from one department to another, and therefore cannot safely be assumed to belong to one specific department indefinitely.

The Home Office Agency and Marketing Department

The agency and marketing department is the focal point of all sales activity within a life and health insurance company that distributes its product by direct sales. Sales generate premium income for investment in securities, real estate and mortgages; generate the cases for review by the underwriting department and their issuance by policyowner services; generate the requirement for data storage and retrieval by the data processing center; generate the required legal analysis and decisions; and generate the necessity for corporate financial planning and control. Thus the saying, "Nothing happens until the sale is made" is certainly true since it affects all operations of the company. In a sense, marketing supports the entire corporate structure.

Agency sales may be sub-divided into four basic distribution systems: ordinary, home service, combination, and all-lines. A **director of agencies** at the home office level usually directs the activities of the agencies, whatever the method of distribution. The managers of individual agencies are called **agency heads.**

Management in Ordinary Agency Companies

Ordinary companies rely solely on career agents to distribute their products. Ordinary agents and agencies sell only regular premium notice business. Agency heads play an integral role in the overall marketing structure. The agency head is the link between field office and the director of agencies at the home office. Agencies are generally grouped into regional divisions. In ordinary companies, the agency head is either a general agent or a branch manager. The difference between the general agent and the manager, not nearly so marked today as in the past, is found in the contractual arrangements and risk/reward factor. A more detailed discussion of these types of agency heads will follow in Chapter 10.

Career Agent

While both branch managers and general agents sell or personally produce sales themselves, most depend upon the hiring of full-time agents to represent their companies and to be members of their agencies in order to obtain a large volume of production. The career agency system and its variations is the subject of Chapter 10.

Brokers

In addition to agents in an agency, general agents and managers will appoint brokers. A broker is a licensed life insurance salesperson who does not have a regular producing contract with the particular company and agency. Brokers will sometimes send two or three sales a year to an agency or they may allocate many sales to an agency. Chapter 11 will discuss the activities of brokers and describe their relationships to home office operations.

The agency head will normally appoint a brokerage manager if the company actively solicits brokerage business. The brokerage manager reports to the agency head. All brokerage business is submitted through the agency head in the same manner as any other business.

Personal Producing General Agents

Personal producing general agents, or PPGAs, are a cross between a broker and a general agent. PPGAs are usually given "long" contracts with little or no home office financial backing and are allowed the privilege of appointing brokers to produce business through their agency. PPGAs may represent any number of companies and may have PPGA contracts with all of them. Chapter 10 discusses their function more completely. Usually, a PPGA will appear in the organization structure in the following manner.

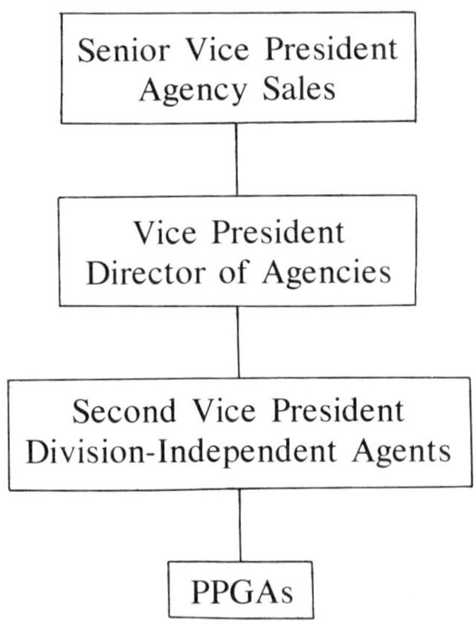

Management in Home Service Companies

Life and health insurance companies organized on the debit or home service system have agents who sell only weekly premium or monthly debit ordinary (MDO) business. Agents are expected to collect premiums in person from policyowners on a weekly or monthly basis.

In essence, the marketing organization in the home service system is a premium collection system. Debit companies offer relatively few types of policies. Advanced underwriting is a type of support that is typically not required for debit insurance companies. Agents and managers are the basis of distribution in this system and much of the home office function involves support of their activities.

Management in Combination Companies

Life and health insurance companies may be organized by combining both ordinary and debit sales. These companies are known as combination companies. The agent may sell to either one or both types of customers. In reality, most combination companies are organized in almost the same fashion as ordinary companies since debit premium collections have been automated. A typical combination company organization chart would not be significantly different from that of an ordinary company organization chart.

Some agency/marketing people perceive a great difference between the ordinary agency and the combination agency; however, in other people's minds the difference is minimal. The perceived likenesses or differences will affect the marketing organizational structure somewhat. In some companies, the combination agencies and the ordinary agencies are kept separate with distinct marketing support systems for each. In other companies, the same marketing support system is used by both types of agencies.

Because of the accounting procedure historically associated with weekly or monthly premium collection, the combination home office clerical task was enormous. Organizational conformity was mandatory with very little room for innovation and creativity. In essence, the home office was structured to be that of a large collection agency and not a sales organization. There was no requirement for the marketing support functions, and certainly the motivation to adopt an aggressive corporate marketing strategy was non-existent.

As a result of this original strictness and discipline, combination agencies, regions and divisions are more formal than their ordinary counterparts. However, combination companies having both ordinary and combination agencies are blending the methods that were successful for each system. Combination and ordinary agency operations are becoming increasingly similar because economics and inflation have increased the average size policy sold. The sophistication of the consumer and the wide use of checking accounts have spurred the practice of agents to blend the ordinary and combination approaches to selling into one.

Management in All-Lines Companies

Companies which sell property and casualty insurance, such as homeowners and automobile and commercial insurance, may also sell life and/or health insurance. Such companies are known as multiple-line or all-lines companies. Two major approaches to all-lines marketing are the exclusive agency system and the independent agency system. Both established life and health insurance companies and property and liability insurance companies have diversified into all-lines marketing so that they may serve a broader market.

Organization for Group Insurance and Pensions

Group insurance and pensions may be marketed within the agencies just like any other life insurance or health insurance product. However, because these are specialty products, companies are often organized with division or regional managers for group insurance and group pensions who have particular expertise. These company representatives generally work closely with the agencies by providing proposals and back-up information, often making sales calls and sales presentations with the agents. This is an example of organization by product line. Brokers and PPGAs may also be involved in the distribution of group and pension products.

Because the individual pension business, IRAs, H.R. 10, tax-sheltered annuities, and corporate pensions are somewhat different from group pension sales, administration is handled by a separate staff in the home office and is not often located within divisions or regional areas. This is a centralized staff function. It is felt that efficiency of operation can best be achieved by allocating the resource personnel on an "as needed" basis.

Agency Services

A life and health insurance company with an agency system for distribution of its products cannot exist without adequate logistical support. Whether this support for the agencies is the responsibility of one department, frequently called agency services, or by various departments in a company, the support is essential. This support includes field financing, field properties and leasing, agent licensing, agency statistics, advanced underwriting, and field electronic data processing. Education and training of the agency force is frequently grouped in agency services.

In charge of agency services will usually be a senior officer at the home office who has overall responsibilities for the above functions as well as the administration of the agency budget and personnel. Decisions to be made include setting policy for the areas of field financing, field properties and leasing, and agent licensing; gathering agency statistics; providing total guidance for all non-sales-related activities in the agencies; and setting compensation for each agency's clerical staff that is competitive within the community in which the particular agency operates. The officer's primary task then becomes one of establishing the budget and administration of agency personnel.

The functions listed above as agency services could be considered corporate responsibilities, rather than marketing responsibilities, depending on the company. For example, in some companies field properties and leasing is a corporate function rather than a marketing department function.

Field Financing

The field financing staff handles non-contractual bonuses and expenses which are reimbursable to the field, prepares and reviews the budget for home office agency and marketing, and reviews financing plans for the agency field force. In addition, the staff must ensure that its compensation plans are competitive within the industry, including the following: new PPGA contracts, community service agents' programs, special incentive recruiting programs, experienced agents' financing plans, sales managers' compensation contracts, contract updating, and schedules of commissions for new product lines. The function of field financing is headed by a director with staff assistants. The size of the staff is dependent on the size of the agency field force.

Field Properties and Leasing

The leasing and refurbishing of field offices are handled by a director at the home office. Staff responsibilities include monitoring all legal ramifications of leasing, updating leasing, aiding local management in locating office space, handling all office equipment and furniture on an initial buying basis and a refurbishment basis, standardizing all field offices, preparing all real estate mortgage aspects for the field when the offices are being relocated, and supervising telephone and janitorial services for all offices. Thus, the director is usually a Certified Property Manager.

Agent Licensing

All agents in the United States must pass the required state license examination for both life and health insurance, and this is strictly enforced by the agent licensing staff. The agent licensing staff helps new and experienced agents obtain and renew licenses to sell insurance from the state insurance departments. The director of agent licensing and the staff have responsibilities that include: administering the licensing fees and applications at the point of employment of the agent; differentiating the filing forms to meet the various requirements of many states; and monitoring the continuing (annually renewable) licensing requirements of each agent. The company does not pay either the initial or the renewal license fee. Agents can be licensed to sell life only or health only. Once the agent is licensed, the company contracts with the agent. Some states require that an agent surrender his or her license to the company upon termination and thus the staff must facilitate this action. Some Canadian provinces combine life and health examinations.

Temporary licenses, issued once only to new agents, are valid for thirty, sixty or ninety days depending on each state's requirements. In some states, temporary licenses are not permitted. In Canada, temporary licenses are not issued.

Precontract orientation (PCO) is an arrangement whereby a prospective new agent spends time in the field with an established agent before contracting with the company. It is designed to help prospective agents make an informed choice about a career selling insurance. The use of PCO cuts agent turnover and expenses, thereby making it possible to reduce premiums. An increasing number of companies would like their agents to go through PCO. However, states are setting tighter licensing requirements and in some cases will not allow an agent without a license to go in the field even if that agent is accompanied by an established agent.

Agency Statistics

Life and health insurance companies keep records of agent performance in terms of sales, agent and management turnover, and agent recruiting (the number of prospective agents contacted, tested, approved by the home office, entered into pre-contract testing, and finally employed). Keeping these records is a function of agency statistics personnel. The type of statistics collected determines the size of the staff as well as the organizational makeup. This group of people also generates statistics on agents who qualify for various company conventions, achievement awards, and honor councils. The agency statistics section also compiles monthly reports on each agent, sales manager and agency to show sales volume, premium volume, persistency, percentage gain, and ranking in the company. Thus, the type of reports and their sophistication determines the classification of the individuals employed in the agency statistics section.

Advanced Underwriting

The marketplace for the life insurance product is becoming more and more complex. The solving of business insurance problems often involves the use of Section-79 plans, split dollar plans, retired lives reserve, key person insurance, buy-sell arrangements, and pension plans. Such business solutions invariably involve the services of the advanced underwriting department.

In addition, the constantly changing tax laws have made estate planning critical for almost every individual of moderate wealth. The advanced underwriting department, sometimes also called estate planning, provides the analysis for such important individual cases.

The advanced underwriting department is charged with the support of the agency field force in the areas of estate planning and business insurance. To that end, agents are encouraged to seek assistance from estate planning and business insurance specialists in the home office.

Home office assistance from the business and estate planning staff and attorneys may include:

1. Case preparation based on the data collected by the agent from the personal insurance prospect—an analysis of this data is conducted and recommendations are made on the best way to conserve the prospect's estate, minimize the tax consequences, and provide income in the event of premature death, disability or retirement. A sales illustration, or proposal, contains the analysis and recommendations.
2. Case preparation based on the data collected by the agent from the business insurance prospect—an analysis of this data is conducted and recommendations are made as to the best way to provide continuation of the business if a key person dies or becomes disabled, to fund buy and sell agreements, and to provide employees benefits under a pension plan, split dollar plan, or retired lives reserve.
3. Joint case work with the agent—personal assistance is provided to the agent by estate planning and/or business insurance personnel in presentations to the prospect.
4. Field computer service support for proposals—an agent has access to a terminal whereby data is collected from the prospect, fed to the computer proposal service, and recommendations are returned in moments on a computer printout.
5. Regional and agency advanced underwriting seminars—seminars provide the agent with the latest in tax laws and life insurance products designed to fund estate and business insurance plans. Technical instruction is provided on the applications of the various life products.

Thus, the function of the advanced underwriting department is to provide technical sales support to agents in the advanced markets.

Field Electronic Data Processing

The age of automation affected every industry in the decade of the 1970s. In the life and health insurance industry, electronic data processing is used in the field to prepare sales illustrations and to assist in policyowner service and general agency activities.

Complicated tax laws, requirements for integrating social security benefits with private insurance plans, numerous business situations in which life insurance may be used, and the advent of exhaustive estate planning make hand calculation of individual sales illustrations much too difficult and often inaccurate. Thus, many companies are making available to the field the accuracy and speed of data processing equipment.

Sales Proposals

Computer-produced sales illustrations are accurate, consistent, personalized, and conform to legal requirements. The fact that computers are fast is of great value also. An agent with a strong prospect does not want to wait a week or ten days to receive a complicated quotation from the home office advanced underwriting department. This is especially true when the agent can receive the desired information within an hour by using a computer terminal or a minicomputer. Agents need to concentrate on sales rather than on clerical tasks. A terminal in the agency allows agents to devote more of their time to sales.

A terminal can be installed in an agency to allow agents access to the computer in the home office. Once an agent has fed into the terminal the business or personal data, a computer printout is available almost instantaneously, showing the amount of life insurance required to fund a particular situation.

The alternative to having a terminal in the agency office is a portable terminal. This portable terminal is actually carried by the agent to the client's home or business, is plugged into the telephone line at the client's residence or place of business; and an illustration is provided in the same manner as that generated by a terminal in the agency.

Minicomputers and agency terminals can calculate needs analysis, business evaluations, and estate tax planning programs. Ledger sheets on company plans as well as ledger sheets on other companies' plans may also be obtained through the use of appropriate software. Some of these minicomputers print out illustrations and others use a voice response which the agent records and then uses to personally prepare an illustration.

Agents using electronic data processing report favorable responses from prospects. There seems to be more validity to a computer recommendation that the prospect purchase an additional $200,000 of insurance as opposed to an agent's hand calculations which make the same recommendation.

Several brands of minicomputers are now available to agencies, although the cost is still fairly substantial. Some companies make arrangements to share the cost of time usage. Other companies arrange for agency managers to pay for time usage themselves or to split the cost among their agents.

Policyowner Service

In addition to preparation of sales proposals, computers and terminals in agencies can aid policyowner service. Terminals or computers in agencies can instantly recall clients' files, indicate desired coverage, generate form letters, and make automatic yearly reviews of clients' coverages and recommendations. Also, the computer can keep lists of prospects on file.

Agency Activities

Aiding the sales and service function are the primary purposes of a computer terminal in an agency. However, terminals also improve accounting functions in the field such as payrolls and commissions. Generally speaking, the accounting functions are incidental to the sales and service activities mentioned above.

The high cost of terminals and minicomputers is still a deterrent to universal adoption, and agents with their own portable terminals are not typical. But, by having a terminal available in the agency on a sharing basis, easy access to computers for sales proposals is more possible than ever before. Costs for the computers and their usage have become more economical over the years. Computers which cost tens of thousands of dollars in the past are sold today for a few thousand dollars. There will be much greater usage in the future of the minicomputer.

Training and Education

The training and education of a company's agents is a function vital to its operation. The financial world of today requires the sales person to become more and more knowledgeable about various sophisticated financial instruments. Agents must be prepared to answer questions about all financial instruments and their uses for particular situations, and must have the ability to combine the instruments into an overall financial strategy. The initial preparation of a new agent and the continuing education of established agents is fully described in Chapter 16.

In addition to conducting schools and seminars, another major responsibility of the training department is the provision of guidance for the selection of agents, sales managers, and managers. Agent and management tests are developed by this department for use in the selection of future agents and managers. Tests developed may be as simple as measuring job interest or as intricate as measuring the job stress an applicant is capable of enduring.

To support the various schools, seminars, and development programs, an extensive amount of publications is required. Normally, the education and training staff will develop and write the educational material, with the graphics department providing the illustrations.

The field training process is a mixture of basic training and advanced training with the object being to continue to increase the level of expertise of the agent. The education is not restricted to the classroom; the approach emphasizes practical experience. Field training will be discussed in detail in Chapter 16, Recruiting, Training, and Contracting.

Marketing Research

The responsibilities of the marketing research department in a life and health insurance company cover a wide range of issues. Marketing research should provide guidance for senior management decision-making. In this sense, the function of marketing research on the corporate level is strategic planning—to determine the direction the company should take.

In addition to strategic planning, marketing research is used to answer questions on internal operations. Some of the internal questions marketing research seeks to answer are: What are the income and demographic trends in the country and in the regions in which the company operates? What are the potential markets for the life and health company's products? In what geographic areas should the company expand its present agencies, start scratch agencies, and combine existing agencies? What is the agent retention rate? What are the job attitudes of the field force? These questions are a few examples of those which marketing research is designed to answer.

Marketing research is also concerned with competition. Are other companies' products competitive? Are other products being marketed in a unique manner? What types of distribution system do competitors use? What new products are being developed by competitors, and when are they scheduled to be introduced into the marketplace? These are just some of the questions that marketing research seeks to answer about competitive factors.

The Marketing Research Procedure

Marketing research begins with a definition of the problem. It is essential that a clear definition is developed. For example, agent retention may be low, but the problem that needs to be studied is the reason for agent turnover and possible solutions.

After defining the problem, a review of the research on related problems already in progress or completed is undertaken. The success and roadblocks encountered in past research are considered. The researcher must then initiate a research study design. The research study design involves the examination of all facets of the marketing problem beginning with the formulating of an hypothesis, the designing of questionnaires to test the hypothesis, and the interpreting of the statistical results.

A variety of statistical techniques may be used to process the data gathered, ranging from the most simple quantitative technique to the most complex. Regardless of the methodology applied, the primary objective of marketing research is to document alternate courses of market strategy and implementation to senior management.

Upon interpretation of the statistical results, researchers may draw conclusions on the course of action the company should take with regard to the marketing question under consideration. Presentation of these conclusions to management should be made in a form that can be understood by its intended audience. Management can then use the findings to choose the course of action that the company should take.

Using the Findings of Marketing Research

All the research in the world is useless if no one is aware of the findings. Thus, it is quite important that the marketing research department make the results available at agency and company meetings and seminars in order to motivate agents and managers to action. Research can and will have meaning to the field force if the research studies and the implications of the conclusions are discussed. For example, if the researcher can discuss untapped markets and offer documentation, the field force will listen to the ideas presented and can initiate action. This increases marketing research's credibility with other areas in the company. Thus, an effective marketing research department will be organized not only to conduct research, but more importantly will have a staff which can make creditable presentations to the field force both in oral and written form.

The marketing research department should have a staff which can present the research methodology and findings orally for critical evaluation at industry and academic meetings. Life underwriters associations, general agent and managers associations, and CLU society meetings are also groups which marketing research personnel can address. Publication of the research should appear in academic and professional journals, monographs, and books. Only in this manner can the department's research be subject to peer group scrutiny.

Applications of Marketing Research

The marketing research department can be very effective if it adopts an active research approach. This active research approach automatically includes several responsibilities: identifying markets, examining consumer behavior, evaluating the effectiveness of promotion, examining the quality of business, measuring expenses, and analyzing agency statistics.

Identifying Markets

The first responsibility is the identification of markets using demographic data and other segmentation methods. Knowledge of market segments and characteristics is essential. Of importance to agents are the neighborhoods in a given community whose population has the need for insurance and the disposable income to purchase the life insurance and annuity products.

Many companies do not have a formal marketing research department to gather and analyze demographic data. Marketing research can still be conducted by employing outside consulting firms, by attending industry meetings sponsored by the National Association of Life Underwriters (NALU), the Life Insurance Marketing Research Association (LIMRA), and the American Council of Life Insurance (ACLI), and by subscribing to studies conducted by these organizations.

Examining Consumer Behavior

Another responsibility involves the examination of consumer behavior in purchasing life and health insurance. Through the sampling of the marketplace, agents, and policyowners, the researcher can be well aware of the desires for new products by the public. Specific questions about consumers may be asked: What benefits are the most important to the prospective purchaser? How important a consideration is the price of the policy to the potential purchaser? At what market segment should specific products be aimed? What trends in consumer behavior are likely in the short-, intermediate-, and long-run? The answers to these questions influence the product development stance of the company.

Evaluating the Effectiveness of Promotion

A third responsibility of market research is the formal investigation of the general effectiveness of company advertising and sales promotions. One aspect to be studied is the frequency of consumer exposure to advertising in all media on a national and a local level. Advertising and sales promotion are directed just as much towards agents as they are towards potential customers. Marketing research applies quantitative measures to evaluate how successful these media are in achieving motivation of agents and consumers.

Studying the Quality of Business

The marketing research department contributes knowledge on **lapse rates** (policies not staying in force) and conservation (the tendency of policies to stay in force). It does little good to have elaborate advertising and sales promotion programs that produce a high volume of sales if the business does not stay in force. Marketing research needs to find out how its company's lapse rates compare with industry-wide figures. Reasons for policyowners' lapsing their policies should also be studied. The heart of the market researcher's job is to study the actual conditions to see where improvement is needed.

Measuring Expenses

Another responsibility of marketing research is expense analysis. How much does it cost to generate sales? What is the break–even point for each agency? Is each product line expected to show a profit? If a product line has very high expenses, can it be eliminated, thereby cutting losses? Are there product lines that are necessary to the generation of other sales and therefore cannot be eliminated regardless of expenses associated with them? Which expenses are not contributing to the sale of the products and therefore should be eliminated? What are the profit centers of the company and what should be their minimum level of contribution to profits?

Analyzing Agency Statistics

Marketing research departments in agency companies must also measure the activities of its agencies. Since the life blood of an agency company is the constant inflow of premium dollars, the activities of the agency are quite important. Such activities include recruiting and selection, training, prospecting and closing, and the retention of agents by field management.

The number one priority of the agency manager is the recruitment, selection, and retention of agents. Most companies publish reports which contain the recruiting standings of all agencies for each month. These are distributed to all agencies. Recruiting as a management activity is discussed in Chapter 17.

Most companies also have a monthly agent turnover and net gain statement for each agency and division. This is the true measurement of the success, or lack thereof, of the agency in the retention of its agents. Marketing research plays an important role in generating these figures.

The Direction of Marketing Research in Life and Health Insurance

Every division within the company establishes its own objectives based on the direction in which the company is likely to move in the future. Through marketing research the company is able to measure its actual success in the marketplace in comparison with its potential for success. Thus, the idea of using marketing research for today and tomorrow involves not only the classic role of conducting research on internal productivity, but also, and perhaps more importantly, research on the potential for the company's interaction with the business and civic community. The internal role of marketing research needs to be expanded so that the researcher may earn credibility and respect in the field by instructing in home office schools, seminars, meetings, and conventions, as well as by visiting all the agencies at least once a year to present research findings which will provide the motivation for the implementation of the marketing strategies by the field. In other words, communicating the results of the research and helping to implement the findings is an integral function of marketing research.

Marketing Support From Departments Outside Marketing

Marketing support comes from areas that are not traditionally considered marketing in themselves, such as legal, actuarial, policyowner service, policy issue and the field force. In many companies, the legal department must approve the policy language, advertising, and public statements about company positions on certain issues. Such a formal policy may apply to materials and speeches made outside of the company as well.

When new products are initiated, the cost projections are made by the actuarial department. Although distribution and product design are marketing decisions, pricing products involves actuarial input. The actuarial department must also approve the calculations contained in policies and advertising.

Policyowner service maintains a direct contact with the policyowner. Providing good service—prompt, accurate, courteous—to policyowners is critical to the retention of a company's existing and future business.

Thus, the marketing effort is a joint undertaking which crosses over department lines. In agency companies, the whole reason for being of the home office is to support the entire field force in generating sales and premium volume.

Directions of the Marketing Department

The insurance industry is expected to change in the future to reflect changes in the needs of the markets it serves. The directions to which life and health insurance companies' marketing departments are looking include direct response sales, the provision of financial planning, the sale of equity products, and the sale of property and casualty products.

Direct Response Sales

Many companies that are involved in the sale of the life and health insurance do not use an agency system. Direct response companies that use print media to sell their products are examples of such companies. While the direct response system of distributing life and health insurance is the subject of Chapter 15, it should be noted here that the marketing organization of such companies is different from agency companies. There are generally no estate planning or pension planning departments, and of course, no agency department. Advertising and promotion are emphasized.

Financial Planning and Counseling

Many insurance industry experts state that the trend is to providing consumers with total money management services, rather than a particular product. The service would be one of financial planning and counseling. This concept entails designing a financial strategy for the client by combining all financial instruments, including life insurance, stocks, mutual funds, real estate, and similar instruments to meet the financial objectives of the client.

Most insurance companies have the internal expertise from which to draw to establish such a financial planning and counseling service. Already in the corporate structure are people with the expertise in investments, taxes, estate planning, and insurance. The risk management director would enlist the various in-house experts, thereby utilizing a significant segment of the corporate financial planning talent.

Those individuals offering the financial planning service would be reimbursed for their efforts on a fee basis; in essence, they would be salaried employees rather than commissioned agents. The alternative to using straight salaried employees is preparing the existing agency field force for such a responsibility. To a certain extent, this process would involve making agents aware of the necessity of having a working knowledge of all financial instruments in addition to life and health insurance.

Mutual Funds and Other Equity Products

As a step toward total financial planning, some life companies in the early 1960s began selling mutual funds and encouraged their agents to become licensed to market these equity products as well as others. In 1974 when the stock market reached its lowest point since the Depression, the value of these funds decreased substantially. The result was that mutual funds fell from favor with both agents and clients alike, and the field force reverted to selling only life insurance.

But, today financial institutions such as banks and stock brokerage houses are competing for the insurance premium dollar by emphasizing their ability to provide total financial services for the client; these institutions are having a significant impact on the marketing philosophy of the life insurance company. Many life companies have begun offering insurance products which are indexed according to the bond market, cost of living index, or other variable standards. Thus, the marketing organization will require people with expertise in the various financial instruments and not just in insurance.

Property and Casualty Insurance

Some industry leaders believe that if a life and health insurance company and its field force are going to prosper in the 1980s, they must offer property and casualty lines. Many life companies have already begun to market property and casualty insurance in an effort to provide their agents with an additional source of prospects and of income. More will be said on this subject in Chapter 12.

Summary

A life and health insurance company's marketing department is organized so that work can be grouped into separate manageable tasks. Organizing simply involves arranging the functions to be performed and the personnel to perform them. Organizing the marketing support function is far more comprehensive than simply drawing lines and boxes: the organization must encourage the maximum effectiveness of the functions.

The organizational structure of the marketing department has developed over the years to motivate the sales force to sell its products and to motivate the public to purchase its products. Life insurance sales are a function of the number of quality people contacted, either by agents or promotional pieces, and the marketing department's role is to facilitate this effort. Agents must be motivated to call on prospective buyers. This motivation is achieved through the establishment of several support areas within the marketing department—market research shows which markets to contact and where they are; advanced underwriting provides complicated sales proposals; education and training imparts the knowledge necessary for the agent to serve his or her client; and the agency sales department provides the distribution system for the product.

The financial marketplace is constantly changing. Thus, the evolution of the modern marketing department is a reflection of our socioeconomic processes. Financial planning and counseling under the umbrella of risk management, are functions which must be considered as part of the marketing organization chart of the future.

The following chapter is a continuation of this chapter's description of marketing support. Its focus is the communication aspect of this topic.

Chapter 8

Marketing Support – Communications

Harvey W. Rubin, Ph.D., CLU
Guy E. Webb, Jr., CLU

One important function of marketing support in a life and health insurance company is marketing communications. Since the perceptions of a company by the marketplace are significant factors in that company's success, communications is a major responsibility of management.

Marketing communications must be a well-planned effort. The specific group to which the communications are directed and the message contained in the communication are the two basic decisions to be made in marketing communications.

This chapter addresses three major tools of life and health marketing communications: advertising, sales promotion, and public relations. Internal company communications is included here for discussion, and although it is generally not regarded as a duty of marketing *per se,* it is viewed as a responsibility of corporate communications, which overlaps with marketing communications. Internal company communications also includes communication to home field personnel and office employees. Personal selling, also a communication tool, is discussed in Part III, Distribution Systems.

Corporate Communications

Increasingly, insurance companies are expected to become opinion-makers and leaders in the business community. This requires that a company stay informed about current issues and problems. Government regulations, consumerism, and increasing competition from other financial institutions make it imperative that a company communicate its position on respective issues in an effective manner.

As a result of external factors and the need for insurance companies to address the issues, many companies are changing their structures by consolidating all the departments which must deal with their "publics" into one department. This new department, controlled at the corporate level, is sometimes termed corporate communications. In corporate communications, it is recognized that a company must keep all of its publics informed of relevant topics, such as company philosophy, involvement in community activities, and the value of life and health insurance products.

The publics that those in corporate communications must be concerned with consist of a wider range of groups than the audience of marketing communications. Marketing communications are generally directed to potential or present policyowners, the field force, or the general public, that is, the consuming public. The publics of corporate communications include the consuming public, as well as employees, regulatory bodies, and, in stock life insurance companies (as opposed to mutual), its investors. In more detail, these publics include:

- company employees
- field agents and managers
- company management
- board of directors
- the community
- potential policyowners
- present policyowners
- governmental bodies, including the city government
- state and federal legislators
- shareholders
- investment intermediaries
- brokers and independent agents
- educators on both the primary and secondary levels
- special interest groups, including minorities and the handicapped
- public interest groups and consumerists

Each of these publics has different interests in a company, and, thus, each needs varying types (and messages) of communication. Management must be aware of these needs and make a commitment to provide the information that is needed through corporate communications.

The forms of marketing communications that will be discussed here include: advertising, sales promotion, and public relations. Internal company communications will also be described.

Advertising

Life and health insurance advertising is perhaps the most visible form of mass communication to the public. It can be seen in virtually every medium: print, broadcast, and outdoor advertising, to name only a few. Just as with advertising of consumer goods, advertising life and health insurance can take many forms, purposes, and messages. The variations in these will be discussed here.

Objectives of Advertising

A specific life and health insurance advertising campaign may have one or more objectives. Possible objectives are (1) to build the company's public image, (2) to introduce a new product, service, or marketing strategy, (3) to shape the public's opinion on certain insurance issues, (4) to encourage agents and brokers to sell the company's products, and (5) to make consumers receptive to the company's agents when they make sales calls, among others. **Product advertising** and **institutional advertising** are two types of advertising widely used by insurance companies to achieve these and other objectives.

Product Advertising

Product advertising is heavily weighted toward informing consumers of specific products' attributes. Because descriptions of specific plans can be technical and therefore complicated to consumers, most product advertising only highlights the features of insurance plans. Advertising for a specific product usually tries to stimulate curiosity in the product or to make the consumer aware of the product. A related objective is to make consumers receptive to a sales interview.

Product advertising in life and health insurance does not generally concentrate on trying to stimulate **selective demand** (the demand for a specific plan of a company—for example, Company X's ''Premiere'' Whole Life Plan). Rather, **primary demand** (the demand for a general category of plans—for example, whole life insurance) is more easily stimulated through life and health insurance advertising.

Institutional Advertising

Advertising that is designed to enable consumers to identify with the company is known as institutional advertising. A company may want to promote the life and health insurance industry itself by pointing out that the industry has protected millions of families through financial planning and has provided capital for businesses through its investments. It may want its name associated with the growth and development of a community. Perhaps a company wishes to state its position on a particular consumer concern or point out the advantages of owning life and health insurance. Institutional advertising is the term used for each of these examples. Television networks generally do not accept strongly worded messages if a company takes an advocacy position in institutional advertising; however, they will accept broad promotional institutional advertising.

Life insurance companies are heavy users of institutional advertising. One reason for this may be the emphasis the prospective buyer places on the stability and favorable reputation of an insurance company. Institutional advertising can be used to convince the buyer that a company indeed has these qualities, even after the purchase has been made.

Advertising Strategies

Advertising in a life and health insurance company, depending on the company's size and markets, may be one or a combination of several types: national, local, and cooperative.

National Advertising

National advertising programs are generally conducted by large companies. Objectives of national campaigns may be (1) to promote the name of the company to the public, thereby easing the way for agents, (2) to introduce a new product or program, and (3) to enhance the image of their life and health insurance products with consumers so that they are receptive to future selling efforts. Sometimes the advertising simply promotes an intangible but desirable quality of the insurance company which it wants the public to recognize. This is perhaps of most value to the company's own field force because it opens the door for agents.

Media used in national advertising programs may be weekly magazines, newspapers, radio, and television, each targeted to specific types of consumers, using knowledge of the medium's audience. Advertising in trade journals is generally used to inform the producers (agents and brokers) that certain products are available, with the idea of securing sales from these agents and possibly recruiting them.

National programs are expensive. The only limit to the expense is what the company itself may feel it is willing to spend. Many companies run a several-million-dollar-per-year national advertising program.

Local Advertising

Local advertising generally promotes more specific features than does national advertising. The message may be one of promotion for the local agency. It may be an ad of congratulations to members of the agency who qualified for company honors, i.e., leading producers club, or Million Dollar

Round Table (MDRT) qualification. The advertisement may promote a particular product, a particular agent, the agency and the company.

Local advertising generally uses such media as radio, local magazines, newspapers, billboards, as well as high school and college yearbooks, civic club programs, and sponsorship athletic teams. This kind of advertising may be done by the company on behalf of its local representation or it may be done by the local sales agency on its own.

Local ads which promote agents or agencies tend to generate more tangible results in the less densely populated areas—in fact, the smaller the community, the better the local advertising is received by its targets. In large metropolitan areas, the more effective ads seem to be the ones that promote the solidity of the company and the availability of insurance coverage, rather than promotion of an individual agency.

Cooperative Advertising

Cooperative (co-op), or personalized advertising, is a joint venture using company dollars as well as those of the agent or agency. Because advertising is a very expensive item and every agent and agency wants all the advertising a company will allow for its area, available funds must be effectively and equitably distributed. Typical programs allow the agency to share the cost with the company on a 50/50 basis with maximum cost limits.

Co-op advertising may be used with promotional items (or advertising specialties) that are used by many companies, such as umbrellas, road atlases, flower seeds, and golf balls, all prominently displaying the company's logo and name. Agents generally purchase these items below cost from the company, which maintains an inventory and makes them available to the sales force.

There are several advantages of co-op advertising: (1) it encourages genuine initiative on the part of local representatives, (2) it stretches the advertising budget for the company, and (3) the company does not have to choose the locations it will direct its advertising to in addition to any national program, because its own agents will make that decision.

Media Selection

Life and health insurance advertising appears in a wide variety of media. The choice depends on the company's advertising objectives, its resources, and target markets, and the nature of the media.

Radio is frequently used for local advertising, especially in small towns. It is effective in reaching specific target markets and is economical due to the size of market that it can reach.

Television is a very expensive medium and most life and health insurance companies make limited use of it. It is generally used only for national advertising campaigns. It is generally not considered for local advertising because of its high cost and the desire to allow individual agencies to design advertising programs that meet their own needs and objectives.

Advertising aids or novelties, such as caps, baby bottles, and calendars are frequently used by life insurance companies to remind consumers of the company. These novelties are an important medium by which companies reach a wide, although selected audience. Agents may distribute the articles according to their personal marketing plans.

Among other advertising aids are direct mail programs in which agents furnish lists of prospects to their home office. The home office then mails policy information and an offer for a gift (for example, a road atlas or wallet. Prospects must return a reply card to the home office to receive their gift). The gifts are sent to the agent for delivery to the prospect. This approach provides an opportunity for an agent to present a gift to a prospect with the ultimate objective of making a sale. Typically, the company shares the cost of the direct mail program with the agents, perhaps paying for the preparation of the letter and the cost of the gift, while the agent pays for the postage. The cost-sharing method is used so that the agent will feel that the company is helping him or her with the costs of an expensive program. It should be noted that this direct mail program employs the services of an agent and is thus differentiated from direct response marketing which does not use the services of an agent.

Advertising may be accomplished by sponsoring a coffee break at a large civic meeting and prominently displaying signs of the local agency or company; paying the cost of printing the local Junior Chamber of Commerce program for a special event; or acting as one of several sponsors for a local college athletic contest to be televised within the home area. Advertising may be accomplished by any actions which give the company or the agency a good public image.

Limitations and Restrictions on Advertising

Virtually all companies require their advertising—company-paid or cooperative with agencies—to be produced or approved by the company's marketing, public relations, and legal representatives to avoid inaccuracy, poor taste, or legal entanglements. Many state insurance departments have advertising codes pertaining to life insurance companies which limit or restrict the kinds of advertising they may undertake. There are restrictions on words that may be used. For example, "deposit" may not be used to mean a premium paid. The word "profit" may not be used when describing the excess of cash value over premiums paid at certain durations in the life of the policy. In some states the policies must use generic names when referring to its policies. For example, a company may want to call its whole life policy with a minimum face amount of $100,000 its "Vanguard" policy, although the company may not do so in certain states. The policy would have to be called "Whole Life." In some states, sales brochures that will be presented to the public or illustrations that will be shown to the public must be filed with the insurance commissioner's department before such material may be used in a sales interview or be distributed to the public.

Advertising Budgets

Advertising can encompass a several-million-dollar-per-year budget on a national basis including television, popular national magazines, and radio. Many companies conduct very large national advertising campaigns, employing professional ad agencies to design, implement, and, in large measure, administer such programs.

Advertising budgets are determined in a different manner by different companies. Some companies use measures of quantitative factors, for example, a percentage of first-year premium. Others look at past expenditures and raise or lower the current year's budget depending on other expenses for other programs or availability of funds. Or, the company may not be committed to a fixed-dollar amount and may evaluate the current advertising program for a given year on the desired objectives for the year: sales of a new product, recognition of the company among the public, or perhaps, a new image.

The Advertising Department

The advertising department may be positioned somewhere in the marketing organization. It may handle both home office and field advertising and also a national program. In some companies, the advertising department is a part of the corporate communications group, which has responsibilities in sales promotion, field magazine publications, and even home office publications and communications. Its positioning is generally a result of the company's overall viewpoint on the importance of advertising and how large the advertising budget is.

The organization of advertising and sales promotion departments is sometimes controversial. One opinion holds that advertising is a corporate function that is a distinct unit and therefore should report directly to the president. Another is that since the ultimate objective of advertising is to create demand for the company's products and thus, sales, it is therefore a marketing function and should be placed within the marketing department.

Ad agencies are used by both large life and health insurance companies as well as small companies. Typically, if the company is advertising a planned program in many different geographic areas, an ad agency is used to handle details such as billings, buys, and media placements. If a company does not have a widespread advertising program, the company usually produces its own advertising.

Sales Promotion

Sales promotion, the second tool of marketing communications, is an activity whose objective is to encourage sales. In life and health insurance, the sales promotion efforts are directed mainly to field agents, although consumers are also targets for sales promotion. Sales promotion activities include planning conventions and meetings, running incentive programs for agents to increase production or conservation (including contests, awards, and other recognition), direct mail programs to gather prospects, and supplementary sales materials. Sales promotion directed to agents generally has one of three objectives: (1) to make it easier for agents to sell (through sales aids such as visual sales tracks), (2) to help them to sell more (through sales campaigns), and (3) to recognize their accomplishments through special programs (conventions and leaders' clubs).

In some companies, sales promotion may be part of the corporate communications division. But, as with advertising, the organizational location of sales promotion depends upon the size of the company and the importance placed on that activity. Generally, sales promotion departments report through the marketing department because of the coordination that is needed with so many other functions of marketing. These functions would include meetings, sales kits, and coordination with new products.

Sales Aids

Sales aids are a major tool of sales promotion. They are designed for agents to use with potential policyowners and include brochures explaining policies, visual sales kits which help an agent "walk a prospect through the sale," audio-visual cassettes to be used in promoting sales, mailers, and sales proposals which employ preprinted ledger statements. A specifically designed sales piece based on a request from a field agent may originate in the advanced underwriting department, in conjunction with sales promotion. Frequently, sales tracks are prepared by the department in the company that trains agents.

Sales literature is prepared at the home office and is mostly used at point of sale and left with the prospect. Sales literature may include pamphlets describing a particular policy, illustration forms giving the policy's cash value and particular features, and ledger sheets giving a year-by-year description of the policy's cash value, net surrender cost and premiums from issue age all the way to retirement age or beyond. Also visual sales tracks are used to explain the need as well as the solution to a particular problem.

Sales Campaigns

Sales campaigns are directed at the field force and are typically handled by the sales promotion department; most companies have sales campaigns from time to time. Many companies have a **fast start** sales campaign in the first sixty days of the year, a **policyowner service month** to contact all policyowners for service in mid-summer, and a **fast finish** contest in November and December. These campaigns typically give agents gifts of merchandise or, in some cases, cash, trips or even extra credit toward qualifying for the company conventions as incentive awards.

Sales contests and campaigns are also conducted in individual agencies at various times during the year to act as incentives to increase production. Campaigns are extremely popular with many agents since they are receiving additional rewards and compensation. Sales campaigns generate excitement and competition for achievement among peers, not only to boost sales but often to raise agents' morale.

Agent Recognition

Sales promotion is also very much involved in agent recognition. The purpose of agent recognition is generally to give the agent a positive self-perception. Each month (or more often) most companies produce some type of publication or listing of agents' sales for the month, year-to-date, honors within the company (prorated for the month) and honors within the industry (National Quality Award and NSAA). Sales promotion may use a data system to keep up with an agent's volume (MDRT, premium, commission credits), persistency (which is becoming more important than ever before), and rankings among agents and agencies.

Conferences and meetings also have the objective of increasing the agent's own self-perception—to try to motivate the agent to become the best in his or her profession. Through recognition, the company is rewarding the agent in front of his or her peer group.

Life insurance companies probably spend considerable time, effort, and money on conferences and meetings. There are good reasons for this. Sales people are motivated and influenced by incentives and information at group meetings. Because agents are so spread out in their locations, they are very much interested in and look forward to gatherings of their own company people for sales or educational meetings. Agents also learn from their peers; sometimes this is more effective than home office presentations as a way of motivating agents to increase production. These meetings serve to rebuild the enthusiasm of those involved in the sales function. Communication, education, recognition, and loyalty are the themes that run through all meetings of marketing personnel.

There are many different kinds of meetings. Starting at the local level, agencies typically have a weekly meeting at which they discuss sales results, exchange routine information, and perhaps have a training period on a particular company policy, procedure or sales technique. On a regional basis, some companies have meetings periodically to discuss sales results, plans for the future, and perhaps any new programs the company is introducing.

National meetings are generally sales conventions for which the participants have been qualified to attend. Qualification is frequently based on one of three factors in an ordinary company: an agent's volume, paid-for premium, and submitted business. Weekly premium business is generally measured by the increase in the account from week to week. Most companies establish qualifications according to a minimum amount of Million Dollar Round Table (MDRT) volume and/or minimum premium income and/or minimum first-year commissions paid to the agent. National sales conventions are different from those on a local and regional level in that they are constructed both to entertain and educate as well as to communicate and to build loyalty among the agents. Any local, regional, or national meetings could be used for purposes of sales training, product planning and introduction, and market planning.

Generally the responsibility for these meetings falls in a conference planning unit under the marketing services or agency administration department. The company-wide meetings may range from very simple meetings to elaborate ones in foreign countries utilizing well-known speakers and entertainers. Section 602 of the IRS code and New York State's proposed Regulation 93 have imposed restrictions on a company's ability to take deductions for such trips, and management must be aware of the implications to the company.

Public Relations

The third major tool of marketing communications is public relations. Public relations is a broad term for the function that encompasses the management response to the needs of a number of groups within the general public. Generally its activities are (1) media relations, (2) community relations, and (3) industry relations programs. Media relations activities include the production of information for use by newspapers, magazines, radio, and television about the officers and activities of the life or health company. Community relations involves representing the company in its dealings with its corporate and community neighbors. Industry relations activities include educational and information exchange with other companies through insurance industry associations such as LIMRA, LOMA and agent organizations such as the National Association of Life Underwriters.

Public Affairs

The regulatory climate in which a life company must operate is influenced to a large degree by regulators' attitudes towards the insurance industry. Public affairs activities are usually a refinement of general public relations functions with emphasis upon legislative and regulatory concerns. A public affairs department is responsible for developing communications programs which present the company's viewpoint in the resolution of issues and concerns raised by consumers or other industries in public debate. Often the issues addressed by public affairs have been brought up by state or federal governmental agencies or elected representatives. Sometimes public affairs departments also have responsibility for media relations, community relations, and industry relations.

Many companies have representatives on joint industry-insurance commissioner committees. The National Association of Insurance Commissioners (NAIC) provides a format for discussions of common insurance regulatory problems and develops model insurance bills and regulations. These are efforts toward creating mutual understanding and solutions to industry-wide problems that give regulators and legislators the benefit of company/industry expertise.

Not only is an insurance company employee a part of the insurance community, he or she is also a part of the entire business and civic community. A function of public affairs in the community is to involve the company in an active role in the community. In order to have maximum visibility, many companies require their officers to serve on civic, business, and insurance industry boards and committees. Other members of a company are encouraged to participate in these organizations both as a source of self-fulfillment and company pride.

If a company is to accomplish all that a public affairs department dictates, its employees must be well-educated on current issues. A company must be committed to taking the necessary steps to keep its employees well-informed.

The Relationship of Public Relations and Public Affairs

Public relations and public affairs activities in many companies are an outgrowth of the marketing operation. They help to assure a favorable public opinion of the company and its products which makes the job of the field force easier in representing the organization and selling its products. A few marketing managers retain direct control over public relations and public affairs. However, the trend is toward control by senior management over these departments. This trend has been accelerated by an increasing need for management to monitor and respond to pressures from the insurance, business and community environments.

In addition to responsibility for control over or liaison with public affairs and public relations, the marketing manager of a life or health company frequently has charge of advertising and sometimes of internal communications to employees. In many companies, the internal communication function is still retained by the personnel manager. However, the trend is toward establishment of a corporate communications area which has responsibility for public relations, public affairs and company publications directed at managers and employees. This corporate communications function is controlled at the top of the organization. Usually the manager of corporate communications has direct access to the chief executive officer. Whether or not he or she has direct accountability for the activities of public relations, public affairs, and corporate communications, the marketing manager must maintain close ties with those areas of company operations.

Internal Company Communications

While not tools of marketing communications as are advertising, sales promotion, and public relations, internal company communications are essential for effective operations. A company must promote its products and philosophy to its field force and employees, just as with consumers. Publications are widely used by life and health insurance companies to communicate to agents, field managers, and home office personnel.

Publications to Agents

Company publications to field agents may take many forms: monthly production bulletins, weekly bulletins during sales contests, semi-monthly management newsletters, quarterly management magazines, and monthly field magazines. Field magazines generally contain articles written by agents in the field or home office department heads, about such subjects as tax changes and industry news. Company anniversaries, production clubs, and agents' sales standings are also major subjects of these magazines. They may take on a very professional look and are edited and published by individuals with expertise in journalism. The aim of all field publications is to give the field force information or incentives which will help it be more productive and give better service to the policyowner. It is essential that agents themselves are convinced of the value of specific plans before they can begin to sell the plans to any potential policyowner.

Company agents or home office personnel who are recognized and accepted as creditable make good contributors for the magazine. Production figures, sales leaders, honor club promotion, and educational articles are typical subjects. Good field magazines can contribute much to the productivity of a company. Poorly done field magazines project a poor company image to the field force. Both field and home office magazines can do much to communicate a feeling of pride in the company and in being "on the team."

Publications to Field Managers

Most companies also have some form of informational publication for managers, whether it is a monthly manager's magazine or a bi-weekly management newsletter. Generally, company field magazines give little publicity to managers' accomplishments; instead as much promotion as possible is given to agents to give them a heightened sense of importance. The manager's magazine or newsletter generally carries information about recruiting of agents, training, supervision, motivation, and changes in company rules as well as announcements of new products and procedures.

Publications to Home Office Personnel

Home office publications may be newsletters that give information on company events, social events (employees' social events such as picnics), civic involvement (employees' participation in local blood drive), or company business (announcement of new work hours). Newsletters are frequently distributed weekly.

A monthly home office magazine may present company news from a home office viewpoint. However, the field viewpoint is not overlooked: a home office magazine gives the home office staff a perception of the field's position and attitude. Service anniversaries, industry/educational opportunities and recognition are some subjects of home office magazines.

Summary

Marketing communications are important to the overall operation of a life and health insurance company. Advertising, sales promotion, and public relations each makes unique contributions to marketing support. Personal selling, a fourth marketing communication tool, an important element in life and health marketing, is frequently viewed as the foundation of life and health insurance distribution.

Chapter 9

Group Insurance Marketing

William G. Williams

Up to now, much of the discussion has focused on the marketing of individual insurance. This chapter will discuss the marketing of group insurance, which encompasses the sale and service of an extensive product line of group life, health and pension coverages.

All insurance might be called "group insurance" in that it is based on the statistical law of large numbers. True group insurance, however, adds a new dimension to insurance underwriting. In return for an adequate participation level or "spread of risk" within a group of persons, underwriting for each individual in that group can be virtually eliminated. Thus, coverage is provided for everyone in the group regardless of past health history. In addition, it can be looked upon as a method of mass marketing and servicing of insurance whereby many persons are covered by a single contract with an insurer, thereby reducing acquisition and administrative costs. Stated an other way it may be described as follows:

> Group insurance is an economical way of providing protection against the financial losses caused by death, disability, medical care expense, or retirement to a changing group of individuals (employees), who are associated with the policyholder (employer) by some common relationship other than insurance. Typically, the benefits, rights and obligations of the parties are stated in a master policy which is issued by the insurer to the policyholder for the benefit of the individuals, who receive a certificate of insurance which summarizes the benefits and principal provisions of the group plan.

The marketing of group insurance is complex and highly technical. It involves interaction of various insurance company experts and specialists in such functions as actuarial, administrative, claims, communications, contracts, electronic data processing, reinsurance, underwriting, and sales. In addition, the influences of employers, unions, associations, trustees, agents, brokers, and consultants, as well as state and federal laws and regulations on group insurance marketing, are strong, frequently divergent, and sometimes complicated. Group personnel must be trained continuously to keep pace with both technical advances and the changing sales and service environment.

In a chapter of this scope it is impossible to cover all of these areas in depth. The purpose of this chapter is thus to promote a general understanding of group insurance marketing, rather than to describe every variation and alternative that exists in the business.

The importance of group life, health and pension coverages can be illustrated by showing their growth as contrasted with individual life, health and pension coverages. While most group life insurance is term insurance and does not build insurance company assets as rapidly as cash value forms, it constitutes an ever larger proportion of the total life insurance in force. Table I shows the changing relationship between group and ordinary life insurance in force.

TABLE I
Life Insurance in Force in the United States
(000,000 omitted)

	Group		Ordinary	
Year	Certificates	Amount	Policies	Amount
1910	—	—	6	$ 11,783
1915	*	$ 100	9	16,650
1920	2	1,570	16	32,018
1930	6	9,801	32	78,576
1940	9	14,938	37	79,346
1950	19	47,793	64	149,116
1960	44	175,903	95	341,881
1970	80	551,357	120	734,730
1980	118	1,579,355	148	1,760,474

* Fewer than 500,000.

In 1950, group life insurance accounted for 20% of all insurance in force. By 1980, the ratio had reached 44%.[1]

Group health insurance, like group life insurance, was first underwritten in 1911. Table II illustrates the remarkable growth of group health insurance in the United States since 1940 when valid statistics became available.[2]

[1] *1981 Life Insurance Fact Book,* The American Council of Life Insurance, (Washington, D.C.).

[2] *Source Book of Health Insurance Data,* The Health Insurance Institute, (Washington, D.C.), 1980–81. This is also the source for Table II.

Table III shows a comparison of group pensions with individual insured pension plans. It is readily apparent that the majority of people covered by pension plans administered by life insurance companies are covered by group pension contracts.[3]

TABLE II
Number of Persons with Hospital, Surgical and Major Medical Coverage by Type of Policy in the United States (000 Omitted)

	Insurance Companies					
End of Year	Hospital		Surgical		Major Medical	
	Group	Individual and Family	Group	Individual and Family	Group	Individual and Family
1940	2,500	1,200	1,430	850	N.A.*	N.A.*
1950	22,305	17,296	21,219	13,718	N.A.*	N.A.*
1960	54,416	22,181	55,464	16,025	26,454	1,607
1970	80,505	26,658	81,549	17,961	81,962	5,414
1980	94,263	34,384	96,692	17,707	110,809	7,313

* Major medical expense insurance was introduced nationally by private health insurance companies in 1951.

TABLE III
Pension Plans in the United States with Life Insurance Companies in Force at Year-End

Year	GROUP*		INDIVIDUAL**	
	Number of Plans	Number of Persons	Number of Plans	Number of Persons
1950	2,620	2,225,000	8,650	530,000
1960	8,710	4,360,000	23,630	1,115,000
1970	25,300	8,080,000	264,210	2,500,000
1980	106,170	19,460,000	204,300	6,520,000

* Includes Group Annuities, Deposit Administration Plans, Immediate Participation Guarantee Plans, Terminal Funded Group Plans.

** Includes Pension Trusts, H.R. 10 Plans, Certain Profit Sharing Plans and Miscellaneous Plans.

† H.R. 10 Plans, Tax-Sheltered Annuities, IRAs, etc, not available.

[3] *1981 Fact Book,* The American Council of Life Insurance, (Washington, D.C.), 1981. This is also the source for Table III.

Characteristics of Group Insurance

One way to describe the nature of group insurance marketing is to make comparisons with the marketing of individual insurance in a number of specific areas. Two characteristics of group insurance which are distinctly different from individual insurance are the contract and cost of insurance.

The most obvious characteristic that distinguishes group insurance from individual insurance is the insuring of a number of persons under a single master contract. The insurer and the policyholder are the parties to the contract; insured individuals have a defined relationship to the policyholder, for example, an employer-employee, union-member, or creditor-debtor relationship. The individuals do not receive a policy but instead receive individual certificates of insurance, or certificate-booklets, that serve as evidence of their coverage under the master policy.

The cost of group insurance is normally lower than the cost of individual insurance because the costs of underwriting, selling, administering, and servicing group insurance require a smaller percentage of the insurance premium than is required in individual insurance. For example, group underwriting is considerably less expensive than individual underwriting because the group selection process seldom requires health questionnaires, medical examinations or inspection reports to establish insurability. Administration is also more economical than in individual insurance because the insurer deals with a single entity (the policyholder), generally all covered employees are actively at work, and payroll deductions provide a simple way to collect any required contributions of the insured individuals.

Marketing Aspects

The marketing of group insurance differs from individual insurance in several aspects: the nature of the group market, selection of risks, market research and product design, pricing, advertising, distribution, and servicing.

The Nature of the Market

The marketing area for group insurance tends to be limited to urban areas where a sufficient number of eligible groups (e.g., individual employers, unions, multiple employers, trade associations) exist and can be solicited at a reasonable cost. The marketing area for individual insurance has almost no geographic limitations. There simply needs to be a sufficient number of prospects and insured individuals to support an agent or broker.

The group insurance buyer (the person who chooses an insurer) is generally more sophisticated in insurance knowledge, buys less on emotion and more on price and service than the buyer of individual coverages. Often there is pressure on the buyer to provide group insurance, stemming from competition within the industry and/or labor-management negotiations encouraging the buyer to purchase insurance. The individual buyer, on the other hand, frequently buys only because of a motivating sales presentation by an agent.

Selection of Risks

When marketing a product, the seller must identify potential markets, decide in which markets to sell the product, and develop ways to select the best prospects in the preferred markets. In individual insurance, the insurer follows a selection of risks process (underwriting) that uses health and occupational questionnaires, medical examinations, and inspection reports to determine insurability. Group selection, on the other hand, is normally not concerned with the health, morals, or habits of any one particular individual; instead, group selection is aimed at determining whether a defined group of lives, or what is even more important, an aggregation of such groups of lives, will yield a certain predictable rate of mortality or morbidity. Thus, the home office group insurance underwriter is responsible for selecting group risks which will be acceptable to the insurance company, taking into consideration legal requirements and the insurance company's underwriting rules and general philosophy. The group insurance selection of risks process consists of:

1. Analyzing each group with regard to its underwriting characteristics, that is, the group as a whole with respect to type of prospect (e.g., single employer, union, trade association), nature (industry), size (total number of eligible employees), employee turnover, geographic location, and financial stability.
2. Evaluating the characteristics of the individuals making up the group with respect to age, sex, occupation, and income.
3. Determining that the contract applied for can be legally issued in the jurisdiction in which it is to be written.
4. Ascertaining that the plan to be provided can be satisfactorily administered by both the policyholder and the insurer.
5. Establishing premium rates that can be expected to produce a reasonable contribution to the insurance company's surplus account, and that employers will find feasible to contribute to on behalf of their employees.

However, even before starting the group underwriting process, the group insurance underwriter has determined that certain conditions exist.

Insurance Incidental to the Group

There must exist a cohesive group established by a strong, mutual continuing interest other than that of obtaining insurance. In general, groups formed primarily for the purpose of obtaining insurance are not eligible groups within existing statutes.

Flow of Persons through the Group

There must be a steady flow of new persons through the group as older employees leave, in order to keep within predicted mortality and morbidity rates and attain desired profitability and persistency. Otherwise, the group will contain a disproportionate number of unhealthy and aging lives, and adverse selection will result.

Automatic Determination of Benefits

Group insurance underwriting rules require that a plan have an automatic basis for determining the amount of benefits applicable to an individual, beyond the control of the employer or employees. Thus, the eligibility requirements and benefits must be formulated on the basis of conditions pertaining to employment, under some uniform plan, which precludes any selection by individuals of amounts or benefits and prevents any undue concentration of risk in a few classes or a few individuals. For example, the amount of group life insurance is usually related to the individual's earnings or job classification.

Broad Participation in the Group Plan

In order for the insurance company to obtain a proper spread of risk, a substantial percentage of the eligible persons in a given group must enroll in the group plan. Standard legal and/or underwriting requirements usually call for an enrollment of at least 75% of those eligible for the plan if it is contributory, and 100% if noncontributory (employer-pay-all). Unless a high degree of participation as well as a steady flow of new persons through the group is maintained, a disproportionate number of unhealthy lives will be present in the plan, the average age of the group will increase and the average unit cost of the insurance will also increase.

Significant Sharing of the Cost by the Employer

A cost to the insured employees that is low in relation to other comparable forms of insurance, and not subject to wide fluctuations, encourages participation by making the plan more attractive to eligible employees. For these reasons, there should be significant third-party sharing of the cost, that is, cost-sharing by the employer. In many cases, cost fluctuations can be absorbed or at least minimized by adjusting the employer's contribution, rather than by increasing the employee's contribution rate. Today, because of inflation and the escalating cost of medical care, some employers are establishing the employee cost for health insurance as a percentage of the cost so that as inflation drives the cost up, the employee's share also goes up.

Efficient Administration of the Group Plan

In the group business, unlike individual insurance, the policyholder is involved in the day-to-day details of administering the group plan. Thus, a single, centrally located administrator, who is able and willing to assume responsibility for administration, enrollment of new lives, collection of contributions, remittance of premiums, keeping of records and assistance with claims, will generally assure efficient administration of the group plan. Further, in a contributory plan, there must exist a simple, routine method, such as payroll deduction, for collecting the contributions of the insured employees and remitting them, together with the employer's share of the cost, to the insurer.

Market Research and Product Design

Unlike individual insurance marketing, specific market and product research and development projects in group insurance marketing have been, and often are, initiated by large buyers. For example, Montgomery Ward & Co., Inc., has been credited with the idea of both group life and group health insurance upon which group insurance was founded in 1911. The basis for many new products and funding concepts in group insurance has been the development of tailor-made benefits at the request of a specific policyholder (e.g., International Harvester Co.—group paid-up life insurance; General Electric Co.—group major medical expense insurance; Caterpillar Tractor Co.—minimum premium plans; General Motors—survivor income benefits). Often the employee benefits resulting from labor-management negotiations in major blue-collar industries affect present products or represent future product trends for the group insurance industry. For example, survivor income benefits, dental coverage, psychiatric benefits, prescription drug benefits, vision care expense benefits, and group pension plans were developed as a result of such negotiations.

More flexibility exists in product offering for a particular group insurance prospect or policyholder than for an individual prospect. Insurance companies are able and willing, on cases of sufficient size or premium volume, to hand-tailor contracts to meet the specifications of informed buyers and the influence of competition. In contrast, the buyer of individual insurance coverage must select one or a combination of plans from an existing portfolio.

Product Pricing

Because life and health insurance are generally based on the concept of one-year term insurance, rates are usually guaranteed for only one year. Since group pensions, and most individual policies, cover a period of more than one year, rates are set for a much longer period, often for life. Premiums for both group life and health and individual insurance are determined by such characteristics of the group or individual as age, sex, and occupation, but group life and health insurance also use such characteristics as income level, type of industry, and geographic location. The principle of experience rating, the process of determining the premium rates for a group case wholly or partially on the basis of that group's own experience is also an important factor in determining premiums for group insurance. Previous life and health claims experience (the premiums paid and the claims paid out over the three most recent complete policy years) of the group may be considered by an underwriter in order to establish initial and subsequent group life and health rates, if the group is large enough to give credible experience.

Group life, health, and pension rate calculations often are quite complicated and when done at the point of sale may be tentative until the final enrollment results are known, whereas individual insurance rate calculations in the field are relatively simple and usually final.

Advertising

Because of the difference in the degree of sophistication and the influences that motivate the group buyer compared with the individual buyer, advertising and sales promotion play a less significant role in group insurance marketing. Thus, there is relatively little advertising in the general media: newspapers, radio and television, or popular national publications. Instead, advertising is directed to employee benefit buyers and consultants through ads in trade publications and other specialized periodicals. Since emotion plays a small role in the purchase of group insurance, the group buyer usually secures competitive proposals and is less influenced by advertising and sales promotion approaches than is the individual buyer.

Distribution

Channels of distribution for group insurance consist of group representatives (salaried home office employees), consultants, and third-party administrators (professional insurance administrators), as well as commissioned agents and brokers. Although the majority of group cases (plans) are sold through agents, more premium income by far is produced by brokers and consultants who either specialize in or have specialized employee benefit departments for group insurance and tend to handle larger cases.

Sales of individual insurance are most often conducted in the buyer's home and frequently in the evening, with the exception to this being in sales to business and professional people. In most instances, group sales take place during business hours at the buyer's place of business, where greater opportunities exist for selling all forms of insurance.

Servicing

Group service consists of the initial enrollment of all eligible lives, installation of the group plan (explaining administrative procedures, the claims filing procedure, contract benefits, terms, and limitations) and making scheduled service calls to check the administration of the plan. It also includes unscheduled service calls to solve plan problems relative to administration, claims, or benefits. To the insurer the most important service call is the annual renewal sale, because the group policy must remain in force for approximately three to five years with good experience for the insurer to recover the acquisition cost (initial contracts, booklets, expenses).

The greater administrative duties required of the group policyholder necessitate more service than for the individual policyholder. Also, frequent benefit plan changes are likely to occur on a group case, whereas the plan of insurance sold under an individual policy seldom changes. Furthermore, the usual term nature of group coverage and the intense competition result in much more frequent transferring of coverage from one insurer to another than in individual insurance. In the final analysis, the group policyholder measures the costs of insurance against the services provided by the insurer and its representatives. With costs on the rise, the quality of service has become of greater importance to policyholders and thus to the persistency (renewal) of group business.

Group Life and Health Insurance Coverages

Through the years, the group insurance industry has responded to continually changing social and economic conditions by making available to consumers numerous forms of group life and health insurance coverages. In addition to group life and health insurance, this section will discuss group pension plans, the three coverages commonly offered by the life insurance industry.

Group Life Insurance Coverages

The purpose of group life insurance is to provide financial assistance to the beneficiary or beneficiaries of a deceased employee. At the current time, the following are the most popular group life insurance coverages being marketed to eligible groups: group term life insurance, group creditor life insurance, and group survivor income benefit insurance.

Group term life insurance is one-year renewable term insurance and is by far the most common form of group life insurance. This coverage may also be provided for an insured spouse and eligible children under a separate dependent group life insurance contract.

Group creditor life insurance is a form of decreasing term insurance provided on a one-year renewable basis. It is generally sold as a protection for installment loan borrowers and mortgagors with the insurance covering the amount of the outstanding loan made by creditor firms.

Group survivor income benefit insurance (SIBI) is one-year renewable term insurance which provides payment to a beneficiary in the form of a periodic income to supplement a basic plan of group term life insurance, Social Security survivor benefits, death benefits under pension plans, and personal savings.

Group Health Insurance Coverages

Most group health insurance coverages are designed to reimburse the insured individual for losses incurred because of nonoccupational accidents and sicknesses. Only nonoccupational accidents and sicknesses are covered because Workers' Compensation and occupational disease laws generally provide benefits for occupational accidents and diseases. As with individual insurance, group health insurance benefits may be broadly classified: (1) accidental death and dismemberment insurance, (2) disability income insurance (short or long-term), and (3) medical care expense insurance coverages, (basic medical care, major medical, dental, and others).

Group Pension Plans

Nearly one-half of all workers in commerce and industry in the United States and three-fourths of all government civilian personnel are now enrolled in retirement plans other than Social Security. The number of participants is estimated to be over 51 million. Of that number, 25.9 million at year-end 1980 were covered by private pension plans administered by United States legal reserve life insurance companies. The majority of the people covered by these life insurance company pension plans are under group pension plans, such as group deferred annuity plans, group deposit administration contracts, group immediate participation guarantee contracts, and guaranteed investment contracts.

The Group Insurance Marketing Operation

Just as in individual insurance, the group insurance marketing operation is a total system of interacting business activities, including sales and service, actuarial activities, underwriting, claims and administration, which are designed to plan, price, promote, and distribute need-satisfying products and services to policyholders and prospective policyholders. This operation includes group life and health insurance, often group pensions, and may be organized as a fully integrated group division with the responsibility for overall group marketing activities headed by a senior officer of the company.

Marketing objectives in group insurance are usually set by the executive in charge of the group division, in accord with the overall objectives of the company. The marketing plan of the group division, which normally covers one year at a time, is the direct responsibility of the officer in charge of the group sales department.

The annual marketing plan guides the company's group marketing activities toward attaining specific sales and service objectives (e.g., amount of new group life, health and pension premium; volume of new group life insurance; number of new group cases). This plan tells what is to be done, when it is to be done, and who is to be responsible for carrying out the various activities. The elements of a marketing plan can be combined in many ways, and the successful marketing executive is the one who can find the most profitable mix for the company through a careful study of markets, pricing, products, promotion, channels of distribution, market research, and the available resources of manpower and money.

The group insurance marketing operation implies a corporate state of mind that insists on the integration and coordination of all corporate activities for the basic company objective of producing maximum long-range corporate profits and contributions to surplus.

Group Insurance Markets

Generally, each group-writing company assesses its strengths and weaknesses and directs its marketing activities toward the markets in which it is strong. Further, it develops the products, services, and marketing techniques that are and will be most effective in those specific markets.

The markets for group insurance may be characterized by type and size of groups. In broad terms, all organizations that meet the various legal and underwriting criteria necessary to constitute a group for group insurance purposes represent this market. Practical considerations make it more meaningful to divide the vast category of "groups" into more manageable segments, that is, in terms of specific markets (types of groups), such as (1) individual employers; (2) multiple employer-trusteed health and welfare plans (Taft-Hartley groups), trade associations, multiple-employer trusts

(METs); (3) labor unions; (4) creditor groups; (5) professional associations; and (6) miscellaneous groups. By dividing this vast market into smaller categories, individual group insurers can decide which markets to sell in and then tailor their products and services to compete for those groups.

Individual Employers

Individual employer groups, as prospects for group life, health and pension products, comprise by far the largest share of the group market, representing about 90% of all group policies in force. This market, which includes proprietorships, partnerships, and corporations, consists of all sizes of individual employer groups. For example, approximately 80% of all group insurance policies in force are on groups of less than 100 employees, 10% on groups of 100 to 500 employees and 10% on groups of 500 or more employees.

Most insurers consider groups with less than 50 employees to be small groups. In the small group market, where experience rating is not used extensively, price is always an important consideration in choosing an insurer. However, a good price alone does not always assure that a particular insurer will be chosen; benefits offered are important as well. To attract and hold highly qualified employees, small companies must be able to offer "large company" employee benefits, such as $1,000,000 or unlimited major medical coverage. Thus, for companies to be successful in the small group market, the insurer needs to offer attractive benefit features and services at the lowest competitive cost.

In the large group market, where partial or full credibility is given to each group's actual claims experience by the insurer, buyers are very interested in net costs and want to know how much of their premium dollars will be retained by the insurer to cover expenses, contingencies, and profits (retention), and how much will be returned in the form of benefits, dividends, or retrospective premium adjustments. When projecting these costs, an insurer will attempt to prove that the dollars retained for commissions, premium taxes, administrative expenses, contingencies, and a margin of profit are appropriate in the context of a properly administered program. Another factor of importance in the large group market is an insurer's flexibility with regard to coverages and administrative procedures, since many employers expect various features (benefits and services) that the insurer may not consider standard. Thus, this market considers it important that an insurer have a technical staff with the talent and experience to develop new and unusual coverages as well as facilities to provide administrative flexibility.

Multiple Employers

Another small but important market for group life, health, and pension products is multiple employer groups. Trusteed health and welfare plans, plans for trade associations, and multiple-employer trusts are used for this segment of groups.

Trusteed Health and Welfare Plans

As a result of a collective bargaining agreement between one or more unions and one or more employers, group insurance benefits may be provided to members of a union under the terms of a trusteed health and welfare plan (i.e., a Taft-Hartley trust). These plans represent about 2% of all group insurance contracts in force but a much higher percentage of total group premium volume, as these tend to be very large cases. Brokers and employee benefit consultants play a dominant role in selling and servicing coverages to groups of this type, and some work exclusively in this market. Trusteed health and welfare plans are usually purchased on the same basis as plans for large individual employer groups, that is, at a low net cost and with administrative flexibility on the part of the selected insurer.

Plans for Trade Associations

In most states a market exists for insurance where the employers have a common business interest by being members of a trade association. In this market, the group life or health policy is issued directly to a trade association (or to the trustees of a fund established by two or more employers in the same industry) to enable small member firms to offer their employees "large company" group insurance benefits. These cases are usually controlled (handled) by brokers or consultants and administered by the association or a third-party administrator. Generally, member firms pay only for employee coverage (not dependent coverage), therefore, low premiums, liberal coverages and administrative concessions are important features for insurers who wish to compete in this market, which accounts for less than one percent of all group policies in force.

Multiple-Employer Trusts

Multiple-employer trusts (METs) are legal entities in the form of trusts (e.g., finance, insurance and real estate trust; retail trade trust; wholesale trade trust) sponsored by an insurer, an agent, or an administrator for the purpose of marketing group life and health insurance to employers with a small number of employees, for example, two to nine employees. The entity is established with a trust company, or with trustees domiciled in a state chosen for its legal environment (e.g., the state permits the insuring of groups with less than ten employees under a single master group policy). This enables the insurer to issue a policy to one legal entity, the trust, in the state of the trust's domicile. Multiple-employer trusts are an attractive vehicle for providing group life and health benefits at low cost to small firms, which normally would either not qualify for group insurance, or not qualify for insurance on a favorable underwriting and cost basis. Full-time career agents and small general lines brokers are the usual marketers of METs.

Unions

Coverage under a group life and health insurance policy issued directly to a union to cover members in good standing is not widely marketed because most unions have the majority of their benefits provided through collective bargaining agreements under the provisions of the Taft-Hartley Act. One reason for most unions' receiving their group benefits as a result of collective bargaining is that federal law prohibits an employer in interstate commerce from making payments directly to a union for the purpose of providing group insurance. Thus, when a policy is issued directly to a union, insurers utilize a low-premium, low-benefit approach, since the most important consideration for the union in a "member-pay-all" plan (i.e., the only source of funds to pay premiums is union dues) is the lowest "going–in" or gross cost.

Professional Associations

Professional associations are composed of individuals in the dental, medical, legal, and teaching professions. Typically, these associations are covered by large group plans, which are established on a state-wide, regional or national basis, and marketed through highly specialized broker-consultants. Insurers who are successful in this market often establish a separate department for this type of business, because it usually requires direct mail solicitations as well as participation by a large, willing agency force in enrolling (for a fee) eligible members. Low premiums are typical for these plans, which comprise a relatively small part of all group life and health contracts in force, and are written on a "member-pay-all" basis.

Creditor Groups

Group life insurance and disability income coverage can be provided for debtors of a creditor (e.g., bank, finance company, savings and loan association, credit union). Specifically, credit life insurance provides that in the event the debtor dies the outstanding balance of the loan will be paid to the creditor. Credit health insurance provides that if the debtor becomes totally disabled the insurer will pay to the creditor the amount of the debtor's monthly installments. Effective sales strategy with large creditors is frequently based on existing business or personal contact with someone in that particular organization. Today, because of statutory rulings and regulations, some insurers have withdrawn from this specialized market.

Miscellaneous Groups

The category of miscellaneous groups includes associations of employees, fraternal society members, college alumni groups, savings account depositors, and veterans organizations. Not all state statutes permit such groups to be covered by group life and health insurance, and the business generated is usually not significant to the insurance industry from the standpoint of premium volume. Because of the underwriting problems inherent in these types of groups (e.g., poor participation, high acquisition costs, selection against the insurer, high administrative costs), few insurers are active in these markets. However, as in all "member-pay-all" situations, the insurer with the lowest premium tends to have the most appeal.

The Marketing of Group Insurance Plans

The actual selling of group insurance plans in a life insurance company is usually planned, coordinated and supervised by the group sales department, which is generally completely independent of the individual, or ordinary, department. The group sales department is composed of both home office and field personnel. This section discusses two aspects of selling group insurance: the group marketing representative system and the actual sales process.

Group Marketing Representatives

The marketing activities for group insurance are conducted through group representatives, agents, brokers, employee benefit consultants, and third-party administrators. A description of these representatives, their functions and methods of compensation are outlined below.

Group Representatives

Group representatives are usually salaried home office employees of the insurer, specifically trained in the techniques of selling and servicing group insurance plans. The group representative's more important sales functions are (1) working with agents and brokers in developing group prospects, (2) preparing field group proposals, (3) securing data from a prospect and submitting it to the insurer's home office with recommendations for a proposal, (4) presenting group proposals, (5) assisting in the closing of group cases, (6) assisting in the enrollment of employees under new group cases, and (7) keeping the home office informed of competitive developments in the group business.

In addition, the group representative performs many functions relating to the servicing of existing group insurance plans. These include (1) setting up administrative procedures for new policyholders, (2) making regular service calls on in-force cases to assist in their administration and plan modernization, (3) placing necessary rate increases on in-force group cases, and (4) taking action to retain present policyholders.

Group representatives generally are compensated on a salaried basis, or salary plus an incentive bonus for group production in excess of goals or allotments. The importance of bonus compensation varies from insurer to insurer. A few insurance companies provide no bonus whatsoever, while others use a bonus as the main method of compensation. Under a typical plan, overall bonus payments may range between 10 and 50% of pay, with the maximum payout to any individual limited to one times salary.

Bonuses paid to group representatives will vary by case, but are usually based on a percentage of the commissions paid to agents or brokers, which may include only first-year commissions or both first-year and renewals. The formula used in determining this percentage may be weighted to give special emphasis to the sale of specific products or markets. Today, the trend is to provide extra compensation for good persistency and profitability, and sometimes to reduce compensation for lack of persistency and profitability.

Agents

Insurance agents under contract with an insurer to sell its full line of products play an important role in group insurance marketing, particularly with employer-employee cases of fewer than 100 lives. The agent usually locates the prospect and calls on the insurance company's group representative for technical sales assistance in selling, installing and servicing the group program. Some agents concentrate their sales in group insurance and become specialists in one or more segments of the market and, as a result, require little assistance from the group representative.

Agents and brokers are usually compensated for group production on the basis of commissions, a percentage of the premiums arising from their sales. However, group commissions are a much lower percentage of the premiums paid than the commissions for individual insurance. Generally, they grade down as the size of the annual group premium increases. On large group cases there may even be "negotiated" commission arrangements. These arrangements involve the policyholder, agent or broker, and the life insurance company, which has to file such arrangements with the pertinent insurance departments for review and approval. Decreases in group commissions are the result of intense competition, the participation of salaried employees (group representatives and home office personnel) in sales and service activities, and the larger premium per sale usually generated by a group case.

Brokers

A broker is an insurance specialist who usually handles all the insurance needs of his or her clients. Although the function of brokers is similar to that of an agent of an insurer, brokers are independent solicitors who are actually agents of the insureds and who place business with a number of insurance companies. Brokers may confer with group representatives in drawing up specifications and reviewing proposals for group plans; however, in most instances, the broker actually sells the program to the client.

Some group sales come from general lines brokers, who are usually small, local operators with a background of property and liability insurance. Often the group representative finds that these general lines brokers can be valuable contacts, as they usually possess a good degree of control over their clients but need technical assistance with group insurance.

Although the small-volume broker sells and services part of the market, the largest percentage of group insurance, from a premium standpoint, is controlled by specialized group brokers or consultants and by the larger brokerage firms with specialized group departments. Contacts with individuals at a high level in the group give them a decided edge in handling the larger group accounts. Their specialized technical knowledge and knowledge of the client's operations make them well-qualified in this area. A number of the largest brokerage and consulting firms are nationwide organizations with offices in principal cities throughout the country. Such firms are particularly adapted to serving the needs of large clients whose organizations are widespread geographically. The group broker (1) assists the client in designing the benefit plan, (2) secures and analyzes proposals from insurance companies, and (3) assists the client in the selection of the insurance company.

Brokers, like agents, are compensated on a commission basis by insurance companies for the sale and service of group insurance. However, in recent years there has been a trend toward special negotiated commission sales on large group cases in order to reflect the degree and type of service rendered to the group buyer.

Employee Benefit Consultants

This terminology is often applied to individuals or firms who specialize in the design, sale and service of employee benefit plans. These individuals or firms may perform the same services as the large brokers with specialized group departments and may be compensated by commissions. However, the compensation of employee benefit consultants may also be on a fee arrangement with the client, that is, according to the services provided. Regardless of compensation, the distinction between consultants and brokers in the employee benefit field is more a matter of semantics than of substance.

Third-Party Administrators

A third-party administrator is a professional group administrator who handles the administration, which may or may not involve claim payments, of one or more group plans (usually association or labor-management negotiated groups) on a contract fee basis. Normally, third-party administrators do not perform the usual functions of brokers relative to the securing of group coverage; rather, they are concerned with the administration of the group plan purchased. Some third-party administrators are also licensed as brokers and perform both functions.

With the growth of multiple-employer trusts (METs), fully self-funded and partially self-funded plans, third-party administrators are becoming increasingly involved in their administration, including claims processing, for employer groups. They are reimbursed on a contract fee basis for their services.

The Marketing Process

Group insurance marketing demands imaginative techniques within a very competitive market. Coordinated efforts among the group sales and other insurance company departments, such as actuarial, administration, claims, contracts, systems, and underwriting are needed. The group marketing process, which involves both initial and continuing sales and service efforts by all involved, can be divided into at least eight distinct steps: prospecting, interviews, proposal preparation, sales presentation, enrollment, installation, administration and service, and the renewal sale.

Prospecting

Effective group prospecting includes a planned approach to reach those who are in a position to say "yes" or "no" to the purchase of group insurance, usually key executives. Prospects must be developed logically and qualified (must meet the insurer's underwriting rules) carefully. **Cold canvassing** (prospecting without known contacts) of individual employers can be successful, especially with small groups, but it involves time and usually many disappointments before success. Large group prospects are difficult to sell to unless a good contact with a key person exists or can be established.

Although group representatives may prospect for group buyers themselves, most group representatives get their prospects for new group insurance clients through agents and brokers. Groups representatives typically find that relatively few agents and brokers have the necessary group knowledge and contacts, and the majority of the group training effort is usually spent with these individuals. In working with agents and brokers, group representatives attempt to establish close working relationships with them and to train and motivate them in prospecting for group insurance.

When group representatives obtain their prospects from large volume brokers, brokerage and employee benefit consultants, the approach must be different from that described above. Here, training of the broker, account executive or consultant is usually not needed, and the group representative seeks to establish as close a personal working relationship as possible. The group representative demonstrates his or her own ability to the broker or consultant and attempts to encourage the placement of group insurance with his or her particular life insurance company because of its capabilities, facilities, and services.

The Interview

An essential element of a successful effort is securing the information needed for plan design and proposal preparation during the first and subsequent interviews. Group sales interviews are similar to interviews for other sales. The salesperson must have a sales plan and be prepared during fact-finding interviews to talk the buyer's language and (1) ascertain the prospect's needs, attitudes and desires, (2) determine the amount of money available to purchase a group plan, (3) motivate the prospect to consider a group insurance proposal, (4) obtain the factual data needed to develop a proposal that will provide sound benefits at a competitive price, (5) anticipate and answer the prospect's objections, and (6) instill in the prospect confidence in the salesperson's ability, and the insurer's competence, to provide group insurance benefits, costs and services that are most advantageous to the group.

Very few group sales are closed during the first interview. In fact, a successful first call will usually lead to another, scheduled, interview during which further details are discussed and data obtained from the prospect in order to prepare a written proposal. During these interviews, such matters as the prospect's degree of satisfaction with present insurers, coverages, services or rates may be discussed as well as collective bargaining requirements, time deadlines, and management's objectives. The data used in preparing proposals normally include an employee census relative to the age, sex, salary, occupation, family status, and geographic location of each eligible individual; the amount of the employer's contribution; and, if there is any group insurance in force, a description of that plan, its experience (benefits, rates and claims) for each line of coverage (e.g., life, disability income and hospital-surgical major medical benefits), if possible, covering the three most recent complete policy years.

Preparing the Proposal

The preparation of a proposal involves evaluating the prospect's needs, designing the plan of benefits, calculating the applicable rates, and assembling the plan and benefit description and rates, in an attractive sales document. For cases from agents and small brokers, final plan design is a blend of the client's desires and the recommendations of the agent, broker, and group representative. The group representative's influence is strong in these situations, although for cases of fewer than ten lives a limited number of plans may be available, which lessens the opportunities for flexibility in plan design.

Proposals for both small and large cases generally contain the following information:

1. General information about the insurer, for example, position in the life insurance industry (ranking by volume and premiums in force), financial strength, and available insurance products and services.
2. A brief description of each coverage included in the group plan.
3. A schedule of the rates and premiums quoted for each coverage.
4. A complete description of the eligible employees and dependents to be insured under the proposed group plan.
5. Any underwriting assumptions and requirements pertaining to the plan of benefits.

In addition, large case proposals may include a net cost or retention illustration of the proposed group program (usually covering a five- or ten-year period). Most salespeople agree that a carefully prepared, well-designed and attractive proposal is a valuable sales tool in the group marketing process.

On cases of all sizes from large brokers and employee benefit consultants, it is customary for them to request quotations on the basis of fairly rigid plan specifications which they have worked out in consultation with the client. Group representatives have little influence on plan design unless they are able to work with the broker or consultant at a very early stage and so affect the drawing of specifications.

While most proposals are prepared in group field sales offices, the underwriting function, except for small standard cases, is normally done in the insurer's home office. The home office group underwriter evaluates the data and recommendations of the group representative, approves or modifies the proposed benefit plan, sets the rate level and specifies any special conditions pertaining to the case. One of the most important considerations in setting the rate level for an experience-rated case is the evaluation of the previous claim history, if any, of the prospective group. If the case is currently insured, the claims experience of the present insurer must be analyzed in detail (e.g., the most recent three years, if available), and cost projections made to establish the proper rate levels to be charged for the type of benefits proposed.

The Sales Presentation and the Close

With small groups, the group representative may personally help the soliciting agent or broker in presenting the proposal and closing the sale because of the need for technical expertise. When quoting on large groups for which several insurers are competing, group representatives generally do not have the opportunity to present their company's proposal directly to the client since this function usually is handled by the prospect's broker or consultant. In most cases, however, group representatives review their company's proposal with the broker or consultant prior to having it analyzed by the broker and submitted to the client with the broker's or consultant's recommendations regarding a proposed insurer.

In the final evaluation of the proposal, general considerations of the clients and their agents, brokers, or consultants, are the insurer's facilities, experience, and reputation. Specific considerations are the insurer's constructive plan design, degree of compliance with plan specifications, and suggestions of alternatives. Special weight usually is given to the competitive position of the insurer's rate quotation and net cost illustration, if pertinent to the sale.

A net cost illustration is based on premium and claim assumptions (often specified by the prospects or their advisors) and other factors applicable to the group under consideration. The illustration is developed by applying the insurer's current experience refund methods and charges to the experience assumptions chosen, on a year-by-year basis, for a specified period, such as five or ten years. It is important to remember that net cost illustrations are not customarily made for smaller cases because the individual claims experience of such groups is not actuarially credible and, therefore, does not entitle them to receive an experience refund. When net cost illustrations are used, the prospect must be cautioned that experience refund exhibits are merely illustrative of financial results that may be achieved under the insurer's refund formula, provided that assumptions are realized. They do not illustrate the variations in the range and quality of service from one insurer to another, which can be considerable.

Whether the group is large or small, the sale is closed when a signed application and the first month's premium are secured from the new group policyholder.

The Enrollment

After the sale is closed, the new insurer selected to underwrite the group insurance program makes arrangements with the policyholder to place the benefits in force by obtaining the required enrollment of the employees. If the program is noncontributory (where the premium is paid entirely by the policyholder), all present eligible employees are automatically insured, provided they are actively-at-work on the effective date of the plan. If the program is contributory (where the cost of the benefits is shared by the policyholder and his employees), generally both statutory and underwriting considerations require that a minimum of 75% of those employees eligible to participate in the plan must enroll in the program. The most essential element in the enrollment is the active support of the new group program by the employer and the use of key personnel in securing the signed employee enrollment cards. A normal enrollment might occur as follows: the insurance company prepares an announcement letter or booklet for use in explaining the plan to the employees, meetings are held to present the plan to employees, employee enrollment cards are distributed, and key employees follow up to obtain the signed enrollment cards.

Once the enrollment procedure is concluded, an application for benefits is completed by the employer, and signed employee enrollment cards and any special instructions are forwarded by the group representative to the home office so that the case may be processed.

The Installation

When the signed master application, first month's premium and enrollment cards arrive in the home office, final rate calculations are made based on the actual enrollment and the master policy; individual certificates and administrative materials are then prepared for delivery to the group representative and installation of the case. It is at this point that the group representative, often accompanied by the agent or broker, performs a vital service for the insurer by spending sufficient time with the policyholder or the policyholder's administrative representative to explain all aspects of the installation process. Inadequate explanation of these important functions can lead to misunderstandings and errors that could later result in policyholder dissatisfaction with the insurer. During the installation process, the group representative delivers the master policy, individual certificates and administrative materials and thoroughly reviews all details of the plan's administration (e.g., premium billing and accounting; enrollment of new employees; claim forms and filing procedures; termination benefits). Proper installation is essential to the future success of the group program and to the relationship among the insurer, policyholder, and agent or broker.

Administration and Service

If a group insurance program has been properly sold and installed, the policyholder's need for intensive service from the insurer is lessened. Periodic calls by the group representative and agent or broker to the policyholder are required to assure continued control of the business and to help eliminate minor problems before they become serious dissatisfactions. On large, more complex cases, frequent visits are sometimes necessary.

Good service contributes greatly to increased policyholder satisfaction and lessens future conservation problems. Poorly serviced policyholders are prime targets for sales efforts by other insurance companies, agents and brokers. Most service calls involving routine administrative matters, claim procedures and the collection of data required by the underwriters, may be made by the group representative on the policyholder's administrative personnel. Calls involving new or revised benefits, experience refunds and rate increases are usually made by the group representative on the policyholder with the agent, broker, or consultant. Frequent and considerate service also helps maintain good agent, broker, and consultant relationships.

The Renewal Sale

Since group life and health insurance is usually written on a one-year renewable term basis, each renewal is a separate and distinct sale. It is the renewal of good business that generates profits on sales, because in the early years of the case little or no profits are generated. Unquestionably, the most important service call made by the group representative and the agent or broker together is the annual renewal sale.

Some of the conservation techniques which have been found to bc effective in renewal selling are as follows:

1. Explanation of the general methods of pricing group insurance benefits.
2. Routine review (at least once a year) with the policyholder of the benefit structure relative to adequacy, local conditions, competition, and the current economic situation.
3. Analysis of census data, service call reports, and claims incurred for the renewal presentation, and development of recommendations for corrective action (schedule changes, elimination of "first-dollar" benefits, increased deductibles or coinsurance, or inclusion of needed contractual limitations) where problems are evident.
4. Presentation of the potential disadvantages of transferring the group to another insurer (the high costs of acquisition must be incurred again; rarely, if ever is the same coverage made available

to the policyholder; the possibility that some employees will lose benefits in the transfer due to changes in benefit limits; and the possible application of preexisting conditions provisions by the new insurer.

A successful sale is the result of good teamwork by the home office, the agency manager or general agent, the agent or broker, and the personnel in group sales and claim offices. Conservation begins when the initial sale is made and continues throughout the entire life of a group case.

Competition

The actions, attitudes and decisions of a life insurance company's competitors must be constantly researched and monitored. Group insurance is subject to intense competition from many sources in addition to other private insurance companies, including Blue Cross and Blue Shield plans, health maintenance organizations (HMOs), proponents of self-funded plans, banks and trust companies.

While among the competitive factors are the technical aspects of plan design, cost considerations and administrative services, the most significant competitive factor is the cost of the group program. Generally, at the point of sale group marketing is more competitive than individual marketing, particularly in the area of cost. With the exception of the buyer of business insurance or a large policy, who is apt to make cost comparisons among several insurance companies, the individual buyer with a limited knowledge of insurance often buys from the insurance company of the agent who appeals and motivates on a personal level. In contrast, the group buyer, who may have considerable knowledge of employee group benefits, usually reviews proposals from a number of insurers and places heavy emphasis on comparative costs and available services before selecting an insurer.

Unlike the practice of cost disclosure that exists in individual insurance, there are no published premium rates and costs for group insurance companies. Although information is available at state insurance departments and occasionally from agents, brokers, consultants and group representatives, meaningful comparisons are very difficult to develop. This is due to the competitive underwriting evaluation processes of the different individual group insurers (e.g., establishing of final premium rates for the benefits and services being provided, and the application of experience rating techniques). Nevertheless, group buyers continue to demand bids from various types of insurers, which greatly intensifies competition.

Competition from within the industry is created by innovations in products, service, and cost differences. Since basic group insurance coverages are fairly standard among private insurance companies, one competitive factor is the development of a new type of coverage or the expansion of an existing benefit. If the remaining insurers feel the new or expanded benefit is saleable and can be offered profitably, they will usually include it as part of their portfolios and the benefit then will become a standard part of the benefit package offered by most insurance companies.

Services are important competitive factors. An insurer's reputation, based on past performance, in areas such as claim processing, communications, general innovation, and computer systems, can be the deciding factor in choosing the underwriting company. In addition, the technical competence and personality of the group representative is an intangible but important factor in competition.

Perhaps the most significant factor in competition among private insurance companies is the cost of the group plan. The group insurance prospect usually reviews proposals from a number of insurers, placing a great deal of emphasis on comparative costs. The annual rerating of most group life and health insurance policies and the experience refund concept on large group plans are additional characteristics of group insurance which foster an ongoing consideration of price by the group buyer.

Today, various ways to improve a policyholder's cash flow (e.g., retrospective and deferred premium arrangements, minimum premium plans, and administrative-services-only arrangements) have become factors in competition among insurers for large group cases, along with products, services and costs. These cash flow arrangements influence the cost of a group plan by making available to the group buyer money that would otherwise be paid, or retained, under the group contract.

Blue Cross and Blue Shield Plans

Generally, competition between Blue Cross/Blue Shield plans and private insurance companies often resolves into one of price, as there is little difference, if any, between the benefits provided by the Blues and other insurers. Because of their general tax-exempt status, and the advantage of discounted hospital charges in many areas, Blue Cross/Blue Shield plans may be more cost competitive than insurance companies. Private insurers have a competitive advantage over the Blues in their ability to (1) offer group buyers a total package of group benefits, including life, disability income, medical care as well as pensions, which results in administrative simplicity and cost savings of having one insurer; (2) tailor benefits to meet specific needs of the buyer; and (3) offer more uniform benefit programs and services to local, regional, statewide, national or international accounts.

Health Maintenance Organizations (HMOs)

Another source of competition for private group health insurance plans, especially in the medical care market, is the health maintenance organization (HMO). An HMO is an organized system of health care that provides a full range of health maintenance and treatment services to a voluntarily enrolled population within a defined geographical area, generally through employer sponsored plans. The HMO concept, which is not new, has been stimulated by the Federal HMO Act of 1973 in the United States.

Self-Funded Plans

Further competition for private group insurance plans is found when companies themselves provide for all or part of their own insurance needs through self-funding. Self-funding is a modification of conventional methods of funding group insurance plans while guaranteeing comparable benefits and is primarily intended for large employers whose savings can justify the additional work required. As employers went to self-funding their insurance needs, insurance companies endeavored to participate in this self-funding by devising various arrangements with the companies. Arrangements for self-funding can be divided into cash flow alternatives that are part of a fully insured arrangement (e.g., retrospective premium adjustments, extended grace periods) and those programs that make the benefit plan either fully or partially self-funded (e.g., minimum premium plans, administrative-services-only and high deductible major medical plans). Because of possible unfavorable tax consequences for group life insurance, only group health insurance is amenable to partial or full self-funding.

Whether a group policyholder decides to self-fund depends upon a variety of factors, including comparative costs and the ability of the policyholder to find substitutes for an insurance company's services (carrying the risk, administering claims, providing accounting services, and providing actuarial advice). An example of a self-funded plan is a minimum premium plan where an employer self-funds (non-insures) the bulk of expected health claims, while the insurer provides protection against health claims in excess of a specific level. By self-funding the bulk of its claims, the company may avoid the premium tax on a substantial portion of its medical care costs. An extension of this concept is for an employer to assume the full burden of the insurance risk, with the insurer providing an administrative-services-only arrangement under which the insurer provides claims paying and other administrative services on a fee basis. Through such innovations, insurers demonstrate the capabilities of the private insurance industry to respond to the varying needs of the marketplace.

Banks

Banks and trust companies present additional competition for group insurers. While banks have become involved as third-party administrators for group health insurance, their competitive presence in group insurance is most evident in the funding and administration of private pension plans. Under trust fund plans, contributions made by employers or their employees are deposited in trust funds which are normally held by banks or trust companies, either as corporate trustees or as custodians acting on behalf of individual trustees. In either case the banks invest the funds and pay the pension benefits to those entitled under the plan.

Group Insurance Marketing Trends

Many challenges involving group insurance are now on the marketing horizon and the future undoubtedly will bring others. To meet these challenges, insurers will have to increase their marketing research, develop innovative products to fit employer needs, improve agent training, explore new markets, and possibly develop new or modify existing distribution systems. A look at present and emerging trends in group life, health and pensions gives one an insight into the future of group insurance marketing.

Mounting inflation in the past decade has had a tremendous impact on every facet of the insurance industry, group insurance included, affecting policyholders, agents, brokers, consultants and insurers alike. For policyholders, the escalating inflation of doctors' fees and hospital and other medical and dental care charges has eroded the value of their group life, health and pension coverage by increasing their expenses. Inflation has caused premiums and loss ratios to rise to the point where agents, brokers and consultants, are meeting increased client resistance to present plan approaches while their clients demand new techniques to combat rising benefit costs.

For insurers, inflation has forced acquisition and claim costs up at nearly double the general rate of inflation without a corresponding increase in agent, broker or consultant productivity. This problem has resulted in narrower operating margins, minimal profits, cash flow problems, and in some cases, withdrawal from a market.

Unless inflation is brought under control, some form of indexing (e.g., allowing for benefit increases tied to increases in the Consumer Price Index) of group life and pension benefits might become common. This approach may increase the cost of doing business, resulting in an increase in the cost to the consumer, which would compound an already disturbing trend.

Trends in Group Life Insurance

Several changes in the way group life insurance is offered may make the product more flexible. Under a flexible group term life insurance plan, a basic benefit level (e.g., one times salary) may be established on a noncontributory basis for all employees with a series of optional modifications. For example, additional employee group term life insurance equal to one, two or three times salary, dependent group term, high amounts of 24-hour travel accident insurance, or survivor income benefit insurance may be available on a contributory basis. In the future, high amounts of group term life insurance may be available to employees at any age; that is, no reduction formulas would be applicable at any time. On the other hand, high amounts of group term may be replaced by relatively modest amounts of group term for transitional purposes at the death of an employee, augmented by survivor income benefit insurance for an employee's spouse and eligible children.

Trends in Group Health Insurance

As congressional debate over the merits of a national health insurance program continues in the United States, a number of trends are emerging that directly affect the marketing of group health insurance. First, there is an increasing demand by the public for benefits designed to provide greater protection against all forms of hospital and medical care costs, including catastrophic costs.

Second, cost containment has become a major concern of all involved in the marketing and buying of health insurance. Among the ways in which insurers have tried to control costs and the increasing use of medical care services has been the expansion of major medical expense insurance, but with an emphasis on providing less costly out-of-hospital care; higher deductibles and co-payments; coordination of benefits; outpatient X-ray and laboratory examination benefits; skilled nursing facility benefits; home health care benefits; preventive care benefits; ambulatory care benefits; second surgical opinions; and pre-admission testing. In addition, insurers have encouraged the establishment of medical society review committees and hospital utilization committees to examine the type and quality of care patients receive. In particular, insurers support the concept of peer review inherent in the Professional Standards Review Organization (PSRO) legislation and have urged its extension to all patients—not just Medicare and Medicaid patients.

Third, the private insurance industry is participating in the development and operation of HMOs, offering consulting advice, financing, marketing expertise, administration, reinsurance, or a combination of these services to the new organizations.

Fourth, new types of benefits such as dental, prescription drug and vision care are now being written in an attempt to help fill the demand for more comprehensive medical care expense coverage. In addition, Medicare, with its broad range of coverage for persons age 65 and over, plus the Age Discrimination in Employment Act (ADEA), which generally prohibits age discrimination in private employment for people between the ages of 40 and 70 with respect to, among other things, group insurance and retirement plans, have influenced employers and unions to provide comparable comprehensive health care protection for their active employees.

Fifth, there is the continued growth of health insurance marketing by mail and other mass media. Most common is the mass marketing of term life, accident coverage, and hospital indemnity plans to customer groups and associations of individuals. After the master sale is made to the sponsoring organization, enrollment of individuals is effected through direct mail and such mass media as newspapers, magazines, radio, and television.

Finally, both federal and state governments in the United States are assuming an increasing role in health insurance. Among the more recent laws affecting the health insurance industry are: the HMO Act of 1973, which legislated an alternative delivery system for health care benefits; the pregnancy benefit law, which mandated that pregnancy and its complications be treated the same as any other sickness insofar as medical benefits to be provided; and mandated benefits for alcoholism and drug abuse.

Trends in Group Pensions

The major development in the group pension field is the substantial increase in flexibility made available under group pension contracts. Insurers are now in a position to tailor their contracts to the specific needs of the employer. Employer demands for greater flexibility in investment policy and in the timing of contribution payments have led to a strong preference for the unallocated type of contract in the group pension market. Today, insurers have designed contracts that provide an investment facility for pension contributions, and it is not mandatory that annuities be purchased under these contracts. Alternative funding arrangements can be used.

Since pension plans have already been established by most large employers, the future extension of private pension coverage depends largely on the extent to which programs are started by smaller employers. The enactment of the Employee Retirement Income Security Act of 1974 (ERISA)—which requires, among other things, more liberal vesting provisions, more stringent funding requirements, and guarantees arrangements for insuring accrued pension credits—may deter further expansion of private defined benefit plans among small employers. In addition, the existence of individual retirement accounts (IRAs), which allow individuals to set up their own retirement plans when they are not covered by a qualified plan, may have the effect of lowering the growth of private plans among small corporations.

Although it is difficult to determine to what extent such developments as ERISA and ADEA will encourage or discourage the growth of pension plans among small employers, it seems reasonable to conclude that the number of new plans established each year will continue to grow, but at a slower rate than experienced in the past.

Because of increased administrative complexity and cost, some insurance companies have simply abandoned selling pension plans to small companies and are concentrating their energies on providing investment-only-services and products for the large company market. Investment business has the advantage of higher cost margins and it is an area in which insurance companies have particular skills and expertise. Investment services and products can be particularly attractive when they are coupled with certain types of guarantees that only insurance companies can offer. In all probability these services and products will continue to expand and will enjoy increased usage in the coming years.

Summary

Group life, health, and pension products generally require different marketing considerations from individual life and health insurance. This is a result of the nature of group insurance and the specific markets for the products. The selection of risks, product design, pricing, advertising, distribution, and servicing all have unique applications to group life and health insurance and pensions. These are important areas of insurance and are increasing in importance. Successful marketing of group insurance requires an understanding of their inherent complexities as described in this chapter.

PART III

DISTRIBUTION SYSTEMS

Chapter 10

The Career Agency System

Jack E. Bobo, CLU, FLMI

The career agency system is the backbone of the distribution mechanism for life and health insurance products. While there are many distribution systems within the insurance industry, none has contributed as much or continues to account for as much total volume of business as the agency system.

The career agency system is a network of management personnel and sales and service support personnel structured to distribute life and health insurance products. This system involves the sale and service of insurance products on a personal basis, usually one-on-one (agent to buyer). Both individual and group insurance products are distributed through the career agency system, although with group insurance and related products, the agent deals directly with the group policyowner rather than with each insured.

The basic functions of the career agency system are (1) the recruitment and training of sales persons (career agents) and (2) the directing of their activities to sell and service various insurance products in a professional way. At any given time, the system will employ a large number of agents at each stage of development.

Some of the marketing techniques that today are separate from the agency system were originally pioneered by agents. Examples would be credit life insurance and large group insurance cases now handled directly by insurance companies. The agency system has been innovative over its lengthy lifespan, finding new applications for existing products, and creating pressure to develop new products to meet the changing needs of the public.

During the 1970s, a steady evolution of the career agency system into a more diffused marketing concept occurred. It was as if the Age of Specialization had somehow been reversed. In the past decade, many career ordinary agents broadened their range of services—both as a function of their individual choices and to conform to the new products and marketing strategies embraced by their companies. These changes will become evident as the career ordinary agents' activities are described in detail. The overlap between the activities of the agents and those of other insurance practitioners is explained in succeeding chapters.

Functions of Career Ordinary Agents

As its name indicates, the heart of the career agency system is the agent. The agent is the point at which the public and the insurance company most often meet. Agents vary in many ways, but all are involved with the sale of insurance products and are involved with rendering continuing service to those who make such purchases.

Sales

The sales process of career agents involves many steps. Agents must be thoroughly familiar with the products they sell before they begin to look for prospective clients. Only after this search, called prospecting, is complete will agents visit prospective clients, determine their specific needs (fact-finding), and make the sales presentation.

Products Sold and Method of Operation

Today, career agents sell and service a wide variety of products. Almost all career ordinary agents sell both life and health insurance, in both individual and group policy forms. In addition, many sell individual and group annuities. A career agent's marketing strategy is influenced by the client's needs, as well as by the products that are sold. For example, a whole life policy can be used in a pension plan, an estate plan, for family protection, or as a simple education plan.

Certain life insurance and annuity products provide variable benefits and have characteristics that resemble securities. For this reason, agents who sell these products are required to obtain a license which reflects product knowledge and imposes market conduct similar to that required of securities sales people.

In recent years, a significant number of agents who sell property and liability coverages have added life and health insurance products to their portfolios. Simultaneously, many career life/health agents have become

Ireland isn't the smallest country in the world, but it is not the largest, either. From looking at maps, I found that during World War II Ireland was neutral. Ireland has an interesting culture and it is very alien in comparison to ours. We do have things in common with Ireland, though. We speak the same language as the people of Ireland. There are many books on Ireland and it is an easy country to research. There are many maps of Ireland which will be helpful in my paper. I want to learn about my ancestors, why they may have left Ireland, what they did when they lived in Ireland, and many more things. I don't want to do any other country. Actually, Ireland is an island off the coast of Europe. These are all reasons I want to do Ireland.

By
Susan
Hughes

3rd Period

Why I am Delecting this Country

Europe
Asia
Africa
Austraila

I want to write on Ireland because my ancestors came from Ireland and I would like to learn more about the country. It isn't large and it isn't small but it is very interesting. There are so many things to learn about it, like how many people live in the country, what the Irish do in their spare time, how they live, the average age of the Irish, what they learn in their schools we don't learn in ours, what encouraged the tale of the leprechaun, their ghost and goblins compared to ours, and many more things.

It is not a very large country, but they have a different way of life and different beliefs. Our major religion is christianity, their's is Roman Catholicism. There is so much to learn.

licensed to sell property and liability insurance, either for affiliates of their life insurance carriers or for other property and liability carriers.

Product Orientation

Agents' methods of operation are often governed by whether or not they concentrate on a particular use of one or more types of products. As agents from different product backgrounds move into a common market, they tend to retain their original orientation. Therefore, some agents who are expanding their product line will approach the market differently from other agents doing the same thing. For example, the life-oriented agent typically views basic life insurance coverage as a long-term, or permanent, need that can often be taken care of with a single policy covering multiple needs over a life cycle. Thus, where economically practical, permanent products such as whole life are favored. The property/liability agents, on the other hand, are likely to be term insurance-oriented, because all the products they had sold prior to branching into the life field were essentially single need forms of term insurance. Very often, these single needs could be covered by policies that were renewable either annually or at most every three years.

An examination of the mix of term and permanent coverages in force among the various types of companies offers strong evidence of this phenomenon. At times this difference in product orientation produces a deep philosophical conflict between agents and companies tilted towards these opposing points of view. Intense competition is the inevitable result, and one of the consequences in recent years has been a substantial rise in the number of policies being replaced because of this differing view of the role of insurance products.

Prospecting

Like other businesses, life insurance companies must continually search for new customers. In insurance, potential customers are prospects, and the activity of finding them is prospecting. In the agency system, forms of prospecting vary considerably with the skill and experience of the agent and the market being served. No matter what form prospecting may take, there is no disputing its importance, for a flow of new customers is essential to an agent's quest for success and security.

The principles of life insurance are such that it is not as difficult to sell as is generally supposed. The primary problem that agents face is finding enough people with whom they can seriously discuss the logic of these principles as it may pertain to them (the prospects). An agent's primary need is to have prospects. Seldom, if ever, does a person enter the insurance business with a ready-made clientele. Thus, prospecting ability is an early and continuing determinant of an agent's success.

A new and inexperienced agent resembles an octopus, reaching out in all directions to identify prospects or a market in which to work. Experienced agents are selective in this activity, having developed either a particular market or a method of easily identifying good prospects.

Qualifications of Good Prospects

Although life and health insurance enjoy wide acceptance and use, not everyone is always a prospect. An individual must meet four preliminary qualifications in order to become a good prospect for the insurance sale: the prospect must (1) have a need for insurance, (2) be able to pay, (3) be insurable, and (4) be approachable.

First and foremost, the individual must have a *need* for insurance. Some of the time the prospective insured will be aware of a need for insurance, but more often, he or she will not realize the need. Thus, a major part of the agent's sales task is to develop in the prospect an awareness of the need for insurance. This is perhaps the most difficult and demanding of all the functions an agent performs and requires particular skill, especially considering the natural reluctance of people to contemplate the more unpleasant uncertainties of life such as death and disability.

Next in importance is the individual's *ability to pay* for the insurance required. Helping the prospect find the premium for needed insurance also represents a creative role for the agent to perform. For example, a prospect may have limited cash but may have an employer who is willing to pay the premium as a loan to the employee. The agent may suggest such a cooperative effort to meet the ability-to-pay requirement of a prospect.

Once the need for insurance and ability to pay are established, the individual must also be *insurable,* that is, he or she must satisfy certain underwriting requirements—most often by providing evidence of comparatively good health and morals—before the insurance company will offer a policy.

Finally, the prospective insured must be *approachable.* Many people, otherwise qualified to purchase insurance, never become prospects because their jobs (celebrities of one sort or another, for example) or their dispositions isolate them from unsought contacts. Thus, many prominent people have died with little or no insurance or estate planning because of their inaccessibility.

Prospecting Methods

There are almost as many ways to prospect as there are personalities and characteristics of agents. Particular methods of prospecting suit agents according to their individual characteristics. For example, calling unannounced on prospects may stimulate one agent while it terrifies another. Or, the telephone may be one agent's best friend and the mortal enemy of a second agent. A new agent must reach in all directions to seek methods of contacting prospects in ways that are economical and best suited to his or her own particular style and talents.

Until agents acquire a certain amount of knowledge about insurance products and their use, they are handicapped. At times, agents may be in the presence of a prospect with a fairly complex problem (or need) which insurance may solve, but new agents may lack the knowledge to recognize that the problem exists. Therefore, prospecting by new agents centers around identifying relatively obvious and simple needs, such as mortgage insurance, spouse insurance, or educational plans. This leads to what is often referred to as **package selling,** for it entails putting a simple plan into a standardized presentation, then looking for people who can use it.

For simple needs prospecting, an agent may use direct mail, sometimes called mass marketing, which has the single objective of obtaining an interview with a prospect—selling the product comes later. There are two general direct mail prospecting techniques used by agents. The first of these is a mass mailing of a semi-personalized letter or brochure to a large number of people, lightly screened, with a message of general appeal. The second entails the use of a **pre-approach letter,** more personalized and more narrowly targeted to potential prospects who are likely to be able to use the specific idea featured in the letter.

In the first technique, a general mass mailing, the prospect shows interest to the agent by replying to the mailing—a 2% to 5% positive response is expected. This expressed interest enables the agent to follow up in a relatively strong position, either by a visit or by phone. To obtain the desired number of interviews with prospects, the agent must mail many letters and be somewhat creative in producing lists of potential prospects that will increase the percentage of repliers.

The pre-approach letter, like the mass mailing, also has as its purpose the securing of an interview on a favorable basis, but differs in that it requires the agent to follow up in every instance, rather than allow the prospect to respond. The follow-up is usually done by telephone, though some agents call in person.

The pre-approach letter, signed either by the agent or a home office official, can concern simple or complex ideas. Most successful agents continue to use pre-approach letters, adapting them to increasingly sophisticated prospects with ever larger problems to solve using greater amounts of insurance.

Among the many other forms of prospecting tried by agents is the **cold call.** A cold call is any call where the agent has not made prior contact in some form and is an effective method of prospecting for some agents. The ratio of such calls to sales varies widely, depending to a large extent on the skill of the agent. The potential effectiveness of the cold call, also called cold canvassing, will vary depending on the likelihood of finding qualified prospects. For example, some companies encourage their field forces to canvass new housing subdivisions, basing the strategy on a probable need for mortgage insurance. Or, experienced agents may make unannounced calls on businesses as they look for group or business insurance prospects.

To achieve the same sales results, the less-skilled agent must make many more cold calls than the one who has mastered the technique. Cold calling is a very time-consuming prospecting method, and in most instances, gives way to more productive methods as the agent becomes better established. However, like the pre-approach letter, the cold call remains at least a part of most successful agents' prospecting patterns throughout their careers.

As an agent builds a clientele over time, several factors begin to ease prospecting problems. First of all, the ability to recognize prospective needs increases with experience in serving the needs of current policyowners. Because of this increased sensitivity to a person's needs, the agent's heightened personal observation skill becomes an effective tool in generating alertness to situations where a sale may be made. For example, as the agent is exposed to different life-changing situations among his or her clients, such as the formation of a new partnership, marriage, the birth of a baby, a promotion, or inheritance, interest will be triggered because each event creates new financial pressures which can be eased by insurance.

Another factor working in favor of the established agent is the willingness of present policyowners to refer their agent to their friends, relatives, and associates. When an agent impresses on a client the value of insurance and that agent's services, the client will deem it desirable for others to have an opportunity for similar help. This attitude makes it possible for the agent to obtain referrals to well-qualified prospects who can then be contacted on a favorable basis.

Obtaining **referred leads** is one of the methods of prospecting most preferred by agents, for referrals are a source of prime prospects. Occasionally, clients will offer such leads voluntarily, but more often agents must ask for them. In requesting referred leads, an agent will usually ask a client about other people who may have experienced a life-changing situation such as those listed above. In time, some clients become quite adept at recognizing those times when their friends should be talking to an agent about their personal or business insurance. When these clients are alert to advise their agent of these instances, they become very important centers of influence and multiply the agent's own efforts. The agent with numerous centers of influence has solved the prospecting problem and can be regarded as truly established. It is generally accepted that most effective prospecting results from referred leads.

The sale requiring the least amount of prospecting effort is usually the repeat, or additional, sale to existing policyowners or to members of their immediate families. Because the agent/client relationship is already established, access to the client on a favorable basis is usually very easy. To the extent that agents can concentrate on referred leads and repeat sales, they can spend more time rendering client service. Good service, in turn, leads to more referrals and repeat sales. Thus, the amount of prospecting required diminishes as the cycle of sales is set into motion.

As agents gain experience, they sometimes concentrate their marketing efforts in a particular market, such as farmers, doctors, professional athletes or workers in a large industrial complex. Working exclusively in a particular market aids in prospecting. By understanding the unique problems of a particular market, an agent can earn a reputation as an expert, resulting in even greater access to members of that market. In a similar fashion, other agents may specialize in marketing a particular product, such as pensions. Their prospecting, made simpler by their expertise, would center on the markets for pensions.

As one can tell from the foregoing discussion, prospecting is one of the most important aspects of the sales process. An agent must have someone to whom to present sales ideas. Agents survive and prosper, in large measure, because of their ability to develop a prospecting method and to use it effectively. There is no one right way to prospect, rather each agent must develop a unique system that works effectively. Because of rising costs of such things as fuel and postage, new methods of prospecting may be expected in the future. New technology is presently being applied to identify prospects more quickly for agents to call on. Automatically dialed telephones are an example of such technology, though their use today is still too limited to make a firm judgement about their viability. There is no doubt, however, that some new technology will be needed to help agents of the future manage the prospecting problem.

Fact-Finding

Fact finding refers to the set of activities initiated by agents designed to lead to an eventual sale. The fact-finding activities include sales calls, estate planning and sales presentations. Each of these steps are essential for successful selling.

The Sales Call

The sale of many products is fairly simple and the process is often neatly structured. This is not the case with life and health insurance. Insurance products may be simple packages with only one sales call needed, or very complex cases involving many calls that extend over a long period of time. Complex sales may involve many other persons besides the buyer and the agent. Accountants, lawyers and trust officers are often consulted for sales of complex products, whereas in the sale of simple products, the prospect may wish to consult only with the spouse.

However, in most instances common elements exist in all sales calls, whether the presentation is made entirely in one call or in a series of calls. Typically, in a sales call, the agent gathers facts about a prospect to ascertain what, if any, need for insurance exists. Needs are determined by the problems or objectives the prospect has. In all cases, these needs have to be identified, clarified and agreed upon by the prospect. Alternate solutions to solving the problems or fulfilling the objectives must be explored. Insurance must be presented as a solution, or, in some instances, as the only solution.

In a sales call, the agent must impress upon the prospect the importance of acting on the solution(s) presented. The agent seeks to motivate the prospect to act quickly so that the exposure to risk that has been revealed is minimized. If the prospect agrees to purchase insurance, the agent then sets into motion the underwriting process and reassures the prospect that a wise purchase has been made.

If the prospect fails to act, the agent must continue to probe to find areas of sensitivity that will prompt the prospect to buy. This is a very delicate process and often is responsible for the negative images associated with life insurance people. It is very difficult to help most prospects face the realities of living and dying.

The sales call itself may take place in the shade of a farmer's tractor or in the boardroom of a large corporation. Most calls, however, take place in the home or office of a prospect. Many career agents, as they become established, are able to bring prospects into their own offices for the sales call. This offers distinct advantages and many agents strive for this approach. When the sales call takes place in the agent's office, competition from television, ringing telephones, playing children and other distractions, is eliminated. Coming to an agent's office also implies that the prospect attaches a more serious purpose to the sales call than if it occurred in another place. An agent is also better able to structure a presentation using resources available in the office such as audiovisual equipment or computer terminals.

Estate Planning

Agents also offer a wide variety of estate planning services. Estate planning sometimes consists of simple programming, whereby a client's financial objectives are coordinated into a comprehensive plan that considers all the client's assets. These "simple" estate plans usually cover contingencies that would arise from disability, retirement and death.

Estate planning can be significantly more complex, especially where it involves the development of plans to conserve substantial estate assets. An agent working with complex estate plans must know about laws governing the taxation and distribution of large estates, and must also be able to work well with the estate owner's other advisors—lawyers, accountants and trust officers.

In the process of developing such an estate plan, extensive service work on existing insurance may be required to assure the best tax treatment, or to meet other objectives. Thus, estate planning could be very time-consuming and, needless to say, highly unprofitable if it were not for the large dollar amount of sales that often result from this type of service work.

The Sales Presentation

The key action in any sales effort is the presentation of the product (plan) being offered for sale. Variations of insurance sales presentations (particularly life insurance) are infinite, limited only by the creativity of the agent. These presentations range from a few numbers scratched on a piece of paper to voluminous proposals costing thousands of dollars to produce.

It should be noted that frequently sales calls and sales presentations are combined. It may not be necessary for an agent to make more than one visit to a prospect, especially when a simple product is being presented or when an agent is calling on a present policyowner who desires his or her portfolio to be updated.

The package sale is perhaps easiest to describe to prospects. Since this sale involves a single idea, the presentation is usually a carefully rehearsed explanation of the plan or idea. Usually referred to as a **sales track** or "canned" presentation, it is best suited to new or inexperienced agents and imparts a degree of expertise in a very narrow area. Limiting new agents to this type of presentation helps them to be productive in their early months and reduces their chances of getting into complex sales situations beyond their expertise. The package sale is usually made with company-prepared sales illustrations that typically comprise an agent's sales kit.

The sales kit, or technique book as it is sometimes called, can be individualized by agents as they become more experienced. Sales tracks and illustrations are more often developed by the agent rather than the company and tend to be tailored to the market or markets being served. Many of the presentations are a blend of ideas the agent receives from the company and from other agents who have achieved a high measure of success.

Veteran agents continue to use presentations that resemble package selling, but are more sophisticated than those used by neophytes. An example would be large policies on juveniles sold to their well-to-do parents or grandparents. It is often said that any sale to a specialty group eventually takes on the characteristics of a package sale because the agent tends to create it, then follow an identical sales track on almost every sales call. Agents working the military market, where the needs and ability to pay are similar among a broad group of prospects, would be another example.

Every sales presentation, however, does have common characteristics. In all cases there is an *illustration*—in some graphic form—of the product being proposed, and an *explanation*—written, verbal, or both—of what the product will do and how it works. Finally the sales presentation involves *motivation* of the prospect to make the insurance purchase.

Sales illustrations present, in graphic form, the problem to be solved or dream to be fulfilled, a display of the cost elements (usually some type of ledger statement), and the mechanics of the insurance plan being proposed and range from the very simple to the highly complex. Illustrations may be developed by the agent as the sales presentation unfolds. The agent may list the elements on a chalk board, with an overhead projector, or more often, simply on a pad of paper. More formal proposals are carefully assembled in advance by the agent. Other sales presentations are made with the use of standard material in an agent's sales kit. The illustration gives the agent an opportunity to be a merchandiser and to tailor the plan being proposed to the prospect.

A primitive illustration with an excellent verbal explanation is more likely to be successful than a complicated illustration that only the agent understands. Fancy illustrations may be impressive, but standing alone they do not sell insurance. The prospect must understand what is being proposed. A good explanation would ordinarily include both verbal and written comments of a non-technical nature. The most successful agents tend to use very simple illustrations, even for complex subjects, which require very little explanation.

Agents must also use motivation in combination with illustrations and explanations. If the prospect fails to purchase, all other aspects of the sales presentation have been useless. Some prospects are moved to action by logic, others by emotion, and some by a combination of both. During the presentation, the agent must decide the proper approach to each prospect.

Many good agents who execute flawless illustrations and explanations fall short of the mark because they simply do not know how to ask the prospect to buy. Often the reason for this failure lies in the agent's fear of being rejected if the prospect does not act affirmatively.

In selling, analogies and motivating stories often bring the world of reality to the prospect. Agents who are good motivators master this technique and are able to relate, in a non-threatening way, situations that are similar to the prospect's own circumstances, where inadequate insurance caused undesirable results for others. Examples frequently used are partnerships that were liquidated when a partner died, widows who were forced from their homes, or disabled persons without sufficient income. Obviously, emotional appeals carried to the extreme would likely be regarded as scare tactics. Scare tactics tend to be ineffective in the long run and also contribute to a negative image of insurance agents. Therefore, agents must be very careful and professional in using this approach.

The sale is the ultimate objective of the career agency system. All other activities are secondary to this objective. The sales call, therefore, becomes the central event and the sales presentation becomes the process whereby the objective is reached. Both sales calls and presentations vary according to individual differences in agents and the markets they serve. The purpose of the call is to gather facts so that a sales presentation can be made. The sales presentation itself should illustrate and explain the proposal and motivate the prospect to make a purchase.

The features of prospecting and fact-finding are also present in other agency distribution systems such as brokerage systems and all-lines systems. These systems are described in subsequent chapters; however, the activities of the sales call and presentation are basically the same as for career agents.

Service

One of the career ordinary agent's most important functions is policyowner service. The line between service and sales is sometimes unclear because service is closely tied to maintaining a policyowner's interest in the plan or policy. Policyowner service by agents can be divided into two broad categories: contractual and non-contractual.

Contractual Service

All policies contain certain legal rights or privileges that may be exercised by the policyowner. Just a few examples of these are the right to change a beneficiary, select a settlement option, take out a policy loan, change the mode of premium payment, repay a policy loan, withdraw dividends, or change the dividend option. Such rights are contractual in that the rights and the conditions and procedures for obtaining them, are spelled out in the policy contract itself.

Thus, in purchasing a policy an individual has, in effect, also purchased a bundle of rights that require future performance (service) if elected by the policyowner. The insuring company is ultimately responsible for delivery (performance) of these contractual services. In the career ordinary system, much of that service function is normally delegated to the agent.

Very often, it will be the agent who initiates a request for service, usually as a result of periodic reviews of a client's (or prospect's) present insurance. Specifically, the agent's primary service function is to be alert to a policyowner's needs, respond to requests for service, obtain and have executed the proper forms to make the desired policy changes, and transmit the forms to the insurance company (or companies). Then, after the insurance company has made and recorded the requested change, any required documents are returned to the agent, who delivers them to the insured.

In some instances, the agent's service role is performed by another party, such as an attorney, trust officer or funeral director (in death claims). In such instances, a fee for the service, charged to the beneficiary, is not uncommon. The agent, however, does not charge the client for these contractual services; they are generally covered by his compensation package.

All studies regarding the contractual service aspect of the life insurance business show general public satisfaction with the service performance of both companies and agents. In addition, the studies indicate a strong public preference for agent service.

Non-Contractual Service

In addition to contractual services, policyowners need and expect other services for which there is no real legal entitlement. For example, an agent may make periodic reviews of existing policies to ascertain their continued adequacy and suitability, summarize cash value holdings and dividends from numerous policies, explain new products, advise on tax law changes that affect life insurance or estate holdings, analyze cash flow of future premiums, and/or change ownership.

These non-contractual services, while they are service, are frequently considered to be more of an adjunct to the sales process than pure policyowner service. The reason for this is that, in the process of a regular review of a client's insurance program, an agent is likely to uncover a need for additional insurance, in addition to necessary policy changes, thus creating a sale.

In this type of situation, the agent, employing the same kind of sensitivity used in prospecting, looks for life-changing situations that may require a revision in the policyowner's total insurance program. Examples of such situations include the formation or dissolution of a partnership, marriage and divorce. All such occurrences require an agent to provide serious counseling to ascertain if changes in existing insurance are required.

A need to revise a policyowner's insurance program may arise when a company introduces new products, or even entirely new product lines. Typically, when this occurs, agents will try to inform present policyowners of the new developments, along with advice as to the extent to which the new products may be of benefit to them or their families. This process often triggers the sale of new insurance, as well as changes in current policy options.

Problems of Policyowner Service

Despite the fact that the public has expressed general satisfaction with the insurance industry's performance in delivering contractual services, complaints do arise. For the most part, such complaints center around the failure to deliver non-contractual services, such as annual reviews, or a lack of financial advice to beneficiaries after a death claim is paid. The root cause of almost all the instances where service rendered has fallen short of the public's expectation has been a weakening of the contact between the insured and the agent. The weakening of contact can be categorized as either a systemic problem or as a weakness in individual motivation.

Systemic Problems

Agents and clients lose touch with one another for a variety of reasons. One is the mobility of today's population that tends to separate policyowner and agent, for one or both may relocate to another part of the country. Though such a separation does not necessarily mean a break in contact, in most instances it does. Perhaps the greatest single cause for the break in contact is the turnover in the field force. Each year a large number of agents quit, die or retire; and when these agents terminate, their policyowners become *orphans*. Unless the orphaned policyowners are "adopted" by another agent, they are not likely to receive the benefits of continued service.

Most companies try to assign orphan policyowners to active agents so that this vital contact can be maintained. However, though such efforts are often helpful, the second agent is not always able to establish the same trustful relationship achieved by the first agent. Thus, though the contact has been established, it may be weak.

The problem of orphan policyowners, though of great concern, may not be as acute as some perceive it to be. Most agents, as they establish a client relationship, assume responsibility for servicing all of an insured's policies, not just those they sell. Therefore, the orphan of one company may be well-served by an agent from another.

Unfortunately, though, this process can be impeded by a lack of cooperation from some companies. For example, an uncooperative company may receive requests for service information from agents of other companies, and may send the information or forms not to the servicing agent, but directly to the policyowner or to one of their own agents, who may or may not have a relationship with the policyowner. This can be very irritating to the servicing agent because the appearance of another agent can add a competitive element when new business is also being written. For this reason, the policies of companies who engage in such practices are often neglected, because agents do not like to stir up competition deliberately.

Companies defend this practice on the basis that they can best protect their business from replacement by limiting service to their own people. This seems to be a high price to pay, for, while it may protect a company, it does so at the expense of service to its policyowners.

Individual Motivations

Another problem associated with inadequate policyowner service is a tendency for the agent's motivation to provide long-term service to fade while the cumulative service needs of policyowners increase. This, of course, also creates an additional problem with persistency. A fall-off in service can lead to lapsed or replaced policies, for neglected clients are more likely than serviced clients to give up their current policies when faced with a shortage of funds or advised to cancel an old policy in order to purchase a new policy.

This problem of weakening motivation can be traced in part to the structure of the agent's compensation package. The compensation emphasizes sales, through much larger first-year commissions than those for later years. Service fees during the later policy years are either small or nonexistent, and the agent has less financial incentive to continue to service policies that have long been in force, sometimes for decades. This is particularly true where there is no possibility of selling additional insurance to the long-time client.

The neglect of policyowners' service needs is not merely a function of the financial motivation of the agent, though. A conflict may arise when an agent, who over many years has built a clientele of hundreds or even thousands of policyowners, becomes so burdened with service duties that selling time—the primary source of income—is seriously diminished. Thus, the agent has three solutions: (1) hire an assistant to perform the service duties—a decision which is itself an economic consideration; (2) face a drop in income and continue service responsibilities; or (3) allow service to policyowners to suffer in return for more selling time.

The problem is brought into sharp focus in a replacement situation. An agent attempting to replace an old policy with a new one is eager to earn the new sales commission plus renewals. The agent whose policyowner is considering replacement, however, has only renewal commissions, a small service fee, or perhaps no financial incentive at stake. Thus, agents will sometimes vigorously defend existing insurance purely on principle—to protect their policyowners from an unwise decision while risking their own incomes. Unfortunately, economic considerations may eventually overcome altruism, and many agents may finally push new, perhaps unneeded policies because they can make more money from sale.

Service Incentives

Perhaps the best assurance of continued adequate service comes from an agent's early training that emphasizes a commitment to a career based on selling through service. The truly professional agent views policyowners as individuals, each with a strong claim to continued quality service. However, the same agent views service responsibilities in the aggregate, and realizes that though one client may require more service than another, an average service commitment allows agents to concentrate on sales as well as on service.

This commitment to service is an intrinsic part of the professional career agent. The professional agent will learn to work efficiently by taking advantage of the time-saving techniques that were developed as a response to the problem of selling versus service time. Thus, the agent will be able to assure performance of service while retaining enough selling time to make a good living.

One example of a time-saving technique is the standard change of beneficiary form. Developed in 1978 as a joint venture by the Life Office Management Association (LOMA), the National Association of Life Underwriters (NALU), and the American Council of Life Insurance (ACLI), this standardized form, which is acceptable to most companies, has greatly simplified the procedure whereby an agent reports changes in beneficiary designations to numerous companies.

Standardized forms for other policyowner service needs are currently being worked on. In the meantime, companies have taken other positive steps to increase the incentive for agents to maintain policyowner service, and additional proposals are also being considered.

Among the steps designed to minimize a decrease in long-term service are (1) persistency bonuses paid to agents by companies in order to provide motivation for continuing service, (2) payment of a service fee to agents assigned to orphan policyowners, and (3) increased agent training in "humanizing" the settlement of death claims. Training is available from some companies, and also from industry associations such as the Million Dollar Round Table (MDRT). Most companies have persistency requirements in addition to production requirements to attain the company's production club (honor council) requirements.

Some agents have begun charging a fee for non-contractual services such as estate planning or executive counseling. Agents who have adopted this technique report considerable success, observing that their clients tend to have more regard for advice they have purchased than they do for free advice.

A small number of companies also have been experimenting with direct service, which puts the service burden on the company rather than on the agent. Another proposed solution is a restructuring of agent commissions. This proposal would provide less "up-front" compensation, and more deferred commissions, thus creating a greater financial incentive for long-term service to the policyowner. However, this solution, if introduced suddenly, is likely to encounter considerable resistance, for compensation patterns are difficult to change without causing serious dislocations among the field force.

Better communication techniques and computer technology offer much hope for future streamlining of the service function. However, while salaried company personnel may ultimately be able to relieve the agent of much of the "paper burden," it is unlikely that the agent will or should be entirely removed from the service process. This is especially true in the non-contractual service area, which is almost entirely an agent function.

Ultimately though, service is a vital part of an agent's responsibility. Good service leads to sales because new needs may be uncovered in the process of rendering service, and sales, of course, lead to future service. Problems in rendering service are numerous, but the break in contact between agent and policyowner dominates the problem area. Primary causes for lack of contact are agent turnover, population mobility, compensation patterns and general neglect.

Structure of Career Agencies

Just as the agent is the link between the insurance company and the public, the field office is the link between the agent and the company. The field or general office is "home base" for most ordinary agents, and it is in this office that much of the training takes place. Many of the support services that an agent relies on are also located there. There are two basic types of field offices: the branch office and the general agency.

Some agents have office space in the field office, but because it is not practical to establish such an operation in every community, other agents have office space closer to their homes. These agents are referred to as detached agents. In most instances, detached agents receive some type of rental subsidy to equalize their treatment with those housed in the field office. Whether based in the general office or working on a detached basis, the agent looks to the field office for market support, to process new business and to assist in the servicing of existing business.

The individual in charge of a field agency is either a branch manager or a general agent (GA), depending on whether the company is structured on a branch office or general agency basis. A general agent is an independent entrepreneur who has contracted with the company, while a branch manager is an employee of the company. Whatever the title, though, this person has supervisory responsibility over all persons working in or out of that office. The manager or GA sets the tone for the entire office, and often it is this supervisor's success that is the major determinant of the level of success achieved by the company in the field office's locality.

Among the more important responsibilities of the GA or manager are the motivation of those working in the agency and the recruitment and training of new people (both sales and clerical). Much of this work will be delegated to others, so the selection and training of supervisory personnel becomes crucial to the success of the agency.

One way to accomplish delegation of duties is through the unit management concept. Under this structure, the field office is subdivided into smaller sales units, each headed by its own supervisor. The consolidated office structure is retained for back-up services. Unit managers recruit and train their own agents, with varying degrees of support from other members of the agency staff. Typically, unit managers are also personal producers, so very often there is some kind of joint financial arrangement among the agents within each unit.

Regardless of the field office's structure, agents will become less dependent on the office and its staff for sales assistance as they gain knowledge and experience. With increased experience, agents will either move toward some phase of management or increasingly regard themselves as independent entrepreneurs. In general, agents' levels of independence tend to increase in direct proportion to the levels of success they achieve.

Branch Office

If the local field office is headed by a branch manager (or general manager), the managerial system of distribution is being employed. Under this system, branch offices are established in key locations throughout the company's marketing area. These branch offices function as extensions of the home office.

The general or branch manager, supervisors and all clerical personnel in branch offices are employees of the insurance company; agents attached to the office, though, are more often considered "independent contractors" once they have progressed beyond the initial company financing period. While agents can be company employees, more commonly they work as independent contractors because they are paid on a straight commission basis. Thus, they are in complete control of their own time and effort. In all instances, however, the agent is under contract to the company rather than to the branch office.

The insurance company pays the branch office expenses, such as rent and equipment costs. However, all expenses are carefully budgeted, and prior approval from the home office is required before an unusual expenditure can be made. Thus, the branch manager and all employees are subject to the type of control normally exercised by an employer. In consequence, any employee is subject to transfer, and territories can be changed at the discretion of the home office.

The branch manager is paid a base salary, but usually can derive additional income from an incentive compensation program. For example, the manager may earn bonuses if the office achieves predetermined benchmarks of performance, such as exceeding volume quotas, recruiting successfully, vertical growth of existing sales personnel, or persistency of business that is better than the company's average.

Companies that use the managerial system do so because of the control and flexibility it allows them to have in their total operations. Standards are more easily set and maintained, overall marketing strategy is more readily controlled, yet flexibility required for different locations and personalities is retained.

General Agency

If the local field office is headed by a general agent, then the general agency system is in use. General agency systems vary to a considerable extent, and in recent years have taken on many of the characteristics of the managerial system.

In the traditional sense, though, general agents are similar to franchisees. They are vested with certain general powers to represent the insurance company and to develop new business within a defined territory. That territory may be exclusive, overlapping, or non-exclusive.

Since general agents are independent entrepreneurs, the insurance company's control over their activities is limited by the terms of their contracts. Usually, the company cannot unilaterally transfer a general agent, nor can it redefine territories except as permitted in the original contract.

General agents also employ all personnel in the field office, and the agents are under contract to them. In this situation, the agents are still considered independent contractors, but their relationship to the insurance company will depend on the terms of the contract between the general agent and the company.

All salaries, commissions and office expenses are paid by general agents, whose incomes are derived primarily from commission overrides—the differential between payments made by the company to the GAs, and the amount the GAs pay their agents. GAs may also receive income for some of the service functions performed by their offices, such as a collection fee for renewal premiums paid by policyowners to the local office. The collection of renewal premiums is one of the basic powers vested in general agents.

Recent Modifications

This traditional GA system was advantageous to companies because it allowed them to open new territories at significantly lower cost. Since the general agents bore all local expenses, and since they were paid on a direct commission basis, the company's investment could be kept to a minimum. The general agents, on the other hand, were offered great opportunities, but with considerable personal financial risk.

Under today's competitive pressures, however, the general agency system in its purest sense no longer works effectively. Competition for agents, back-up personnel and business have required that substantial sums of money be expended at the outset. Few general agents are able to meet this kind of financial commitment, and so, increasingly, the company must make the initial investment.

As companies increase their investment in general agencies, they also exercise a greater degree of control over a general agent's activities. Thus, some of the general agent's former independence has eroded, and today it is not uncommon to see employees of company-subsidized general agencies considered employees of the company rather than of the general agent.

In most instances, the company's investment or subsidy to a new agency is temporary and may be in the nature of an advance to be repaid over a period of time. And, as the initial subsidy is repaid, the general agent's independence is usually asserted. Thus, as general agents become more established, they operate less like branch managers and more like traditional general agents.

Companies may be structured with field offices as true branch offices, as traditional general agencies, or as one of the various hydrids in between. An agent's activity is not particularly affected by a company's choice of organizational structure. Adequate or inadequate support can arise under any of the systems.

Contracts and Compensation

The agent/company relationship is a function of a company's contract with the agent—which specifies certain terms of the relationship. Compensation arrangements are also stated in the contract. A description of these two important subjects follows.

Contracts

Most ordinary life agents are introduced to the insurance business by a sponsoring company. Thus, though they may become legally independent contractors, loyalty to the sponsoring company continues to be strong.

However, a certain amount of loyalty may be mandated by the terms of an agent's contract. For example, some companies require an **exclusive right** to its agents' business, while others demand the option of **first refusal.** In the latter case where a company refuses an application or will accept it only on a substandard basis, the agent is then free to shop among other companies for the best policy for the prospective insured. Enforcement of this type of provision varies widely among companies, and even within companies.

Exclusive company contracts and first-refusal practices have declined in recent years, largely because of two independent movements. First, consumerists have pressed for agents to emphasize client loyalty ahead of company loyalty. The consumerists advocate that agents should always shop around on behalf of their clients in search of the best protection plan at the lowest cost.

In addition, sophisticated agents, particularly those who belong to professional organizations and have pledged to place their clients' needs before their own, see themselves as professionals dedicated to client service rather than as salespeople representing a single product line. In general, companies have responded to these changing attitudes by relaxing their rules regarding the placement of business with other companies.

Whether this trend will ultimately benefit either the consumer or the agent remains to be seen. Though comparative shopping has its advantages, skeptics are quick to point out that companies with career field forces are not likely to continue to incur the significant expense of recruiting and training agents if these agents tend to place a large portion of business with competing companies. This is particularly true of the competing companies using brokers, who hold down their product costs by eliminating their own training programs. Brokerage systems are discussed in Chapter 11. Thus, critics say, the long-term result could be a dramatic shrinkage in the size of the field force. In addition, because of the many variables, shopping around for life insurance policies often creates confusion, and a confused prospect is not likely to buy. Only the future holds the answer as to whether the "shopping-around" movement will gain momentum or the pendulum will swing back towards single-company representation. No studies to date have indicated significant public dissatisfaction with current marketing practices by career agents.

Compensation

The most important support that an agent receives from a company is compensation. Agents' compensation is comprised of both cash and non-cash benefits. All agent compensation bears a direct relationship to the premium income being generated by new sales and renewal premiums from business previously written.

Cash Compensation

The major emphasis in all agent compensation packages is on sales, rather than on other matters such as service, although the degree of emphasis does vary among companies. This heavy emphasis on sales has provoked some criticism to the point that it may affect the agent's productivity by coloring his or her judgements when making recommendations to prospects. This problem is exacerbated by the fact that among most companies the commission rate varies among types of insurance plans.

The argument regarding objectivity can also be made with respect to other fields. For example, lawyers' or doctors' recommendations for legal or medical services affect the income of those practitioners in precisely the same way. In the final analysis, the degree of professionalism of the agent is the best determinant of objectivity.

In addition, it has been observed that emphasizing sales in a compensation package is not inappropriate, for selling is the agent's primary function. There is nothing to be serviced until a sale is made, so the weight placed on sales in an agent's compensation package is, for the most part, justified.

Variations in compensation among types of products and companies do exist. For example, a typical career agent's contract with a company doing business in New York State provides a first-year commission of about 55% of the first-year premium. Additional commissions are paid on renewal premiums, as they are paid to the company by the policyowner, up to ten years. The true nature of renewal commissions is often misunderstood. Some contend they are deferred sales commissions while others look upon them as fees for continuing service. The fact is that they are a blend of both, with emphasis varying by company. Renewal commissions may be on a flat schedule of 5% to 7% a year, or graded down from the second-year high of 15% to 20% to lower levels in succeeding years.

High first-year commissions provide an immediate incentive for producing sales. On the other hand, renewal commissions have a cumulative effect over time and provide an incentive to the agent to keep business in force year after year. Thus, the renewal commission structure encourages a better aggregate quality of business by motivating the agent to provide consistent service to policyowners.

While the foregoing represents typical cash commission schedules of companies doing business in New York, it does not reflect the practices of companies not doing business there. Some non-New York companies who do not recruit and train agents use the savings thus realized to increase commission schedules as a means of attracting business from agents of other companies or from agents with no particular company affiliation. Such companies are usually referred to as brokerage companies. The types of commission schedules offered by these companies vary considerably, but have in common a higher level of cash payments than career agent companies, with a heavier concentration on the "front end" (early policy years). Despite the presence of literally hundreds of such companies offering enticing commission arrangements, most career ordinary agents place the bulk of their business with their primary company.

Frequently, that portion of the renewal commission which is attributed to sales is **vested** in the original selling agent. This means that the amount is payable whether or not the agent remains active with the company. In other cases, all or a portion of the renewal commission may be forfeited if the agent terminates association with the company.

That portion of the renewal commission regarded as a **service fee** is typically 2%, and payments often extend beyond the period for which deferred sales commissions are paid. However, payment of service fees stops when an agent terminates. In an effort to improve policyowner service, a few companies have begun reassigning forfeited service fees to other agents who are actually performing the service. However, the results of such efforts have been mixed and there is no clear trend in this direction at the beginning of the 1980s.

Persistency bonuses are becoming an increasingly popular form of cash compensation. Business that persists is very important to a company, because, depending upon the type of policy, it usually takes two to seven years for a company to recapture its acquisition costs. Early lapses are particularly costly. To the extent that agents can be motivated to protect policies against unjustified lapsation, persistency bonuses are good business for all concerned—policyowner, agent and company.

Some persistency bonuses are affected by the amount of policy loans outstanding against the policies sold by an agent. Company experience reveals a higher incidence of lapsation among policies that have had all or most of their cash values borrowed against. Furthermore, it can be argued that such policies are one step removed from lapse and should not qualify the agent for bonuses tied to the quality of business.

Non-Cash Compensation

In addition to compensation from the company in form of cash, agents also receive non-cash benefits which relate to the amount of business being generated. Any comparison of compensation among companies which deals only with cash payments is therefore incomplete. Ordinarily, these types of benefits are provided only by the agent's primary or sponsoring company.

Perhaps the greatest variance in agent compensation occurs outside the normal commission stream. Examples are fringe benefits, such as group life and health insurance and retirement plans, and support services. The fringe benefits offered by major companies can be quite substantial and are a significant cost factor to companies. Support services vary by company and are also somewhat dependent on the size of the field office to which an agent is attached. Large offices with substantial volumes of business are more likely to be equipped with technical tools and labor-saving devices.

Examples of the kinds of support services available for use by agents are secretarial assistance, word processing equipment, mail service, computer terminals and dictating equipment. Office space allocations or rental allowances for detached agents are usually determined by some formula that relates to the agent's production.

Support services have become a major factor in overall income considerations. This is because the purposes that insurance products serve today are more complicated and the continuing service more demanding than in prior years. The pension market is a good case in point. An enormous amount of service work is required just to satisfy federal regulations governing pension plans. The agent without computer assistance is at a serious competitive disadvantage when selling and servicing this type of business.

Sales conventions, which are both in the nature of reward and education, are also offered to agents based on their production. Typically, companies have several levels of production requirements to qualify for attendance at these meetings (i.e., the higher the production, the better the location of the meeting). Modest levels of production might qualify an agent for a regional meeting fairly close to home, whereas high levels of productivity would qualify for attendance at a national or international conference.

Compensation Regulation

From a regulatory point of view, the most dominant influence on agent compensation is Section 213 of the New York State Insurance Code. This section regulates an insurance company's overhead expenses and particularly specifies the maximum allowable commission payment. Section 213 not only imposes limits on total commissions payable as a percentage of premium, it also contains certain inside limits, most notably those on first-year commissions. Those companies not wishing to conform to the terms of this regulation elect to use subsidiary companies for their New York operations, or choose not to do business in that state.

Because this regulation extends to all business done by all companies operating in New York—whether or not the company is domiciled there—its impact on commission schedules is enormous. The number of companies doing business in New York, and thereby directly affected by Section 213, is relatively small, comprising less than 20% of all life insurance companies. However, the total volume of business generated by these few companies is substantial compared to the total volume produced by the entire industry; these companies therefore assume a dominant position. Thus, anything that affects New York companies influences the entire industry.

Companies not operating in New York are relatively free of regulatory pressures with respect to sales commissions. Therefore, the principal constraint on the amounts they pay is competitive pressure. Enhanced commission scales are used as a feature to recruit new agents and attract brokerage business from established agents of other companies and those with no company affiliation.

Career Path Support

As agents climb to success, their careers are influenced by many persons. The critical early years expose the agent to a fairly structured support system, developed for the recruiting and selection process and for early days of field training. Later education and training are somewhat less structured as different agents choose different paths in their growth and development. Chapter 16 details this aspect of an agent's support system. Aside from compensation, all of this activity is also geared to achieve the kind of recognition described in Chapter 9. Recognition is a powerful motivator and the career agent is afforded ample opportunity to achieve it.

Trends in the Career Agency System

A few years ago, the trend in the ordinary distribution system was to decentralize by opening many smaller field offices, both branch offices and general agencies. Presently, that trend seems to have reversed, and the movement is toward fewer, larger agencies. For example, there exist at present some "super agencies" that produce volumes of business in excess of $100 million annually. Several factors seem to be influencing this trend among ordinary agencies.

First, the availability of qualified management personnel is limited, and quality managers are becoming increasingly difficult to find. The obvious reservoir of such personnel is the existing field force (agents). However, the talents required of a good manager are not the same as those needed by a successful salesperson, and not every good agent will make a good manager.

Second, the financial rewards of successful selling often exceed those available to management. Still another factor is that the capital investment required of an agent is ordinarily less than that demanded of a general agent. Also, the GA faces a greater potential for loss. So, many qualified candidates are simply not attracted to the management challenge.

Perhaps the most significant factor in this trend toward fewer, bigger agencies, is the interaction between competition and technology. As previously noted, today's experienced agent requires extensive back-up services—particularly computer capability—when working such complex markets as pensions. Also, competitive pressures in the marketplace to keep administrative, and ultimately policy, costs down have forced companies into high technology operations involving very expensive equipment. It is simply not economically feasible to equip many small agencies with the kind of hardware necessary to use such services.

Thus, the type of agency structure likely to evolve will be the large regional field office with all the technology, specialized personnel, and service capability necessary to support a number of nearby satellite sales offices.

It should be obvious from this discussion that the career ordinary agency system is far from being monolithic. The variations are numerous, largely because of the wide range of marketing strategies and products used by the many companies that employ ordinary agents. While this conglomeration of strategies intensifies competition in the marketplace, it also brings with it the potential for abuse. Replacement activity is viewed by many to be an abuse of the variety of marketing strategies available.

Intense competition is based not on price alone, but also on conflicting ideologies and product orientations. These conflicts manifest themselves in issues such as the appropriateness of existing insurance and whether or not it should be replaced with new policies or with a combination of products.

Judgement in replacement matters is often influenced by more than a single set of values, which makes peer review of existing insurance programs particularly difficult. For example, if one believed that double-digit inflation is a permanent condition, one would make a different financial decision from the decision one would make if he or she thought such inflation to be temporary.

To date, most of the emphasis in judging competitive products in comparison to already existing insurance has centered on cost. However, those who have served on agents' ethics committees can attest that, in almost all peer review instances, the decision process is not that simple. As new products are designed to accommodate changing economic conditions, value judgements concerning product suitability and agents' recommendations are likely to become even more complicated.

Personal Producing General Agents

A subdivision of the career ordinary agency system is the structure headed by a personal producing general agent (PPGA). The PPGA system was developed as a result of certain conditions that minimized the effectiveness of a general agency. For example, small populations in some localities did not justify the expense of maintaining a field office, and detached agents in these places did not derive the full benefit of a general office that was located sometimes hundreds of miles away. Agency development was therefore difficult. PPGAs, who were first personal producers, were thus authorized to recruit and develop a sales force as large as their finances and the size of the area could accommodate. This concept seemed to fill the void in isolated areas and was adopted by a number of companies as a means of expanding without a major investment. Because PPGAs received commission overrides on personal business as well as on the business produced by any agents under contract, operations could be maintained economically without the support services of a regular field office.

Current PPGA Concept

Today PPGAs are independent contractors, and their ties to their home offices are not nearly as strong as branch managers' or general agents'. Since they are already experienced when they sign their PPGA contracts, they do not get, nor do they usually need, much training. This is particularly true when a PPGA is affiliated with a number of companies. What training the agents do get is usually limited to familiarization with the company's products and procedures, and is conducted by a field officer or regional manager.

In recent years, the use of PPGAs has expanded. Because of the enormous costs associated with recruiting and training new agents and maintaining field offices, some companies—especially smaller and newer ones—have abandoned the traditional approaches to marketing. Instead, they offer PPGA contracts to established agents who have already demonstrated a pattern of success. The savings of the cost of developing a field force from scratch have enabled such companies to offer agents the extra financial incentives of commission overrides and overhead allowances.

At first, most PPGA contracts gave the company a fairly exclusive right to a producer's business. However, such arrangements are disappearing. It is now not uncommon for an agent to have a PPGA arrangement with a dozen or more companies, making this system similar to the brokerage system which will be described in Chapter 11.

Despite the fact that the PPGA system is growing in popularity, only about 7% or 8% of the industry's sales volume is produced through it, according to estimates made in 1977 by the Life Insurance Marketing and Research Association (LIMRA).[1] However, several large companies have shown increased interest in the PPGA system since the cited report. These companies see the PPGA technique as a means of lowering policy costs as well as a way to attract a field force without a major investment in training. Thus, unless some new trend develops, continued growth in the number of PPGAs is very likely.

The PPGA system's primary advantage to any company, large or small, is its tendency to hold down costs. Inasmuch as nothing is paid to the sales force until a sale is made, the company risks very little capital in development costs. These savings can be used to design more competitive products, attract a field force via higher compensation arrangements, or a combination of both.

An agent may have a PPGA arrangement with one or more companies in addition to the agent's contract with a primary company, making it even more attractive. There are cases, though, where the PPGA arrangement replaces the relationship held with the agent's former primary company. Severing such a relationship is usually motivated by a desire for greater freedom of operation, higher compensation, and/or the opportunity to work in a highly specialized market.

Structure of a PPGA Organization

Insofar as personal production is concerned, the PPGA operates in exactly the same fashion as the career ordinary agent. The only real difference is in the procedure whereby business is processed. Instead of dealing with a field

[1] *Census of Life Insurance Sales Personnel,* 1980–3, (Hartford: LIMRA).

office, the PPGA will work through a regional office, or perhaps directly with the home office.

However, responsibility for controlling the office and staff rests squarely with the PPGA, although some overhead expense allowance is usually received as part of the PPGA contract. Commissions, both current and deferred, are generally fully vested, and are not normally linked to future performance. The PPGA does have the option of recruiting and training agents, but in most instances is under no compulsion to do so.

Development of a PPGA Sales Force

A closer tie to the home office exists when the PPGA system is employed in its original format, and not just as a means of attracting brokers. In such a case, the company may offer the PPGA financial assistance in starting up an operation, and/or with the financing of recruits.

Under this original system, the PPGAs are generally required to meet certain predetermined qualifications before they are offered a PPGA contract. These qualifications may be membership in the Million Dollar Round Table, proven ability to produce quality business, and other criteria indicative of a pattern of success. This type of PPGA is closely akin to a general agent.

Proponents of the PPGA concept cite statistics that show the concept to be satisfactory for reasons in addition to the elimination of training expenses. For example, LIMRA studies show that thus far companies have experienced less turnover among PPGAs than among career agents, and that the persistency of PPGA business is better. There are obvious reasons for these statistics. Since only experienced agents become PPGAs, the negative factors of high turnover from early failure and poor quality business produced by inexperienced agents are eliminated.

The foregoing description highlights the obvious attractions of the PPGA system to both company and agent, but there are disadvantages, too. From the company's viewpoint, the problems are in the areas of agent loyalty, continuity and motivation.

Because in recent years the principal growth in PPGAs has come through attracting experienced agents away from companies that are investing heavily in the development of sales forces, the PPGA concept has become increasingly controversial. Companies may find it hard to retain agents' loyalty as the competition for experienced agents becomes more and more intense.

Critics argue that if the practice of moving freely between companies becomes widespread and a sizeable number of experienced agents is spirited away from career companies, those companies may have to reassess their own willingness to continue to invest in agent training. To date, agents' loyalty to their primary companies has continued to run deep enough to contain this competition.

Continuity of service is difficult to preserve when a PPGA terminates because there is no field office to maintain policyowner contact. Unless a replacement can be found quickly, the company may find itself out of business in that particular territory.

In addition, the PPGA structure makes vertical growth for the PPGA difficult, because the direction and motivation for that growth springs essentially from the home office. The one-on-one contact available in the agency system is lost. There is also a certain hazard in relying too heavily on a system whose supply of trained agents comes from competitors. Because of these problems, some companies may resist using a PPGA system.

From the agents' perspective, the presently identifiable disadvantages tend to be fewer than for companies. The agents' principal loss is the support and training provided by the company's field office. However, if they do not sever their relationships with the primary company, and use their PPGA arrangements only for so-called "surplus" business, they have nothing to lose. However, to the extent that the PPGA contract requires the building of an agency, PPGAs are exposed to the same personal financial risks as general agents.

It is again obvious that the career ordinary agency system is quite varied. The personal producing general agent is another of the many marketing strategies that are constantly evolving in the competition for the most efficient delivery system of life and health insurance.

Summary

According to recent studies completed by the Life Insurance Marketing and Research Association (LIMRA), their member companies—consisting of virtually all companies employing a field force—have approximately 248,000 full-time agents under contract.[2] Another of their recent studies indicated that of this number, 135,000 or 54% are career ordinary agents, with the number growing slightly from past totals.[3] Also shown by the studies is a slight drop in the number of field offices, confirming the trend to larger field offices noted in this chapter. This information attests to the importance of the career ordinary system which, according to LIMRA, produces the "lion's share" of the ordinary business.[4]

[2] *Ibid.*

[3] V. Stanley Benfell, Jr., CLU, Seth C. Macon, CLU, Dennis Tamcsin, *Life Insurance Distribution Systems: The Career Ordinary Distribution System,* (Unpublished report by LIMRA, 1977).

[4] *Ibid.*

Career ordinary agents sell and service life and health insurance products within the framework of a multi-structured agency system. Agents are recruited and trained in field offices that vary considerably in size, structure and degree of support. The work of the individual agent progresses along a career path from basic training on simple package sales to the most sophisticated of operations dealing with such esoteric subjects as pensions and estate planning. After the basic training period, which is fairly standard, the progress of agents along the various career paths is greatly varied, and influenced by the talent and personal objectives of the agent and also the market being served.

Agents are compensated by commissions, which consist of cash and non-cash benefits. Compensation is designed for sales and service activities, with the primary emphasis on sales. Career agents place most or all of their business with a primary company, but a considerable amount of business is brokered with outside companies because of specialty products, more favorable underwriting, or attractive contractual arrangements for the agent, such as PPGA contracts.

Chapter 11

The Brokerage Distribution System

Richard E. Johnson, Ph.D.

Historically, life and health insurance has been marketed predominantly by agents with a close, and in many cases an exclusive, affiliation with one primary company. In recent years, however, brokerage as a means of distribution has become an important factor in life and health insurance marketing.

The percentage of companies presently participating in brokerage is significant. Of the 354 North American companies that are members of the Life Insurance Marketing and Research Association (LIMRA), two-thirds now accept or actively solicit brokerage business. Clearly a study of life and health insurance distribution would not be complete without a discussion of brokers and brokerage.

The Concept of Brokers and Brokerage

The terms broker or brokerage mean different things to different people. A frame of reference must be established before one can determine what the terms encompass. Webster defines the term "broker" as "an agent who negotiates contracts of purchase and sale." Webster also defines the term "agent" as "one who acts for or in the place of another by authority from him." The party from whom this authority flows is known as the principal.

From a legal point of view, it is generally held that an agent represents a principal and owes allegiance to that principal. Thus, in the life and health insurance industry, an agent represents an insurer, and the agent's actions are controlled by contract with that insurer. A broker, however, represents the applicant or the insured. The broker serves the applicant for insurance by assisting in placing risks with an insurer, yet generally receives compensation for the sale directly from the insurer, rather than the applicant. Legally, the insured is bound by the acts of the broker since the broker is the insured's agent in securing the life insurance coverage. Any misrepresentation, mistake, breach of warranty, or fraud perpetrated by the broker on the insured's behalf makes the insured as responsible as if the insured had committed the acts.[1] If this interpretation of the insured/broker relationship were consistently enforced by the courts, it would impose a severe legal responsibility upon the insured and in so doing might reduce the use of this form of marketing.

The practical definitions of broker or brokerage differ greatly within the insurance industry and especially so within the life insurance industry. A simple definition of broker used within the life insurance industry is "an agent who places business with more than one company." This chapter will use this practical definition when referring to brokers. Thus, we typically refer to a career life insurance agent as "brokering" business if a particular application is placed with a company other than that agent's primary life insurance company. In many cases an agent is a licensed agent for the companies involved, and there is no change required in the agent's legal responsibility to either the principal or to the client. The consumer generally is unaware of the legal distinction between agent and broker and usually is unaware of the agent's status.

Licensing of Brokers

The legal status of insurer representatives is complicated by the inconsistent licensing requirements of various states. Virtually all states have similar licensing requirements for life insurance agents' eligibility to sell insurance. Agents must pass a prescribed test, usually be sponsored by a given life insurance company, and may even have to take a course to prepare for the state examination. The applicant for a license must qualify from the standpoint of character and minimum age.

Typical Licensing Requirements

From these basic areas of agreement, all requirements or responsibilities for brokering business diverge. For example, in Georgia, no agent can place business with any insurer unless licensed with that insurer. An insurer who wishes to appoint an already-licensed agent to act as its agent, need only file

---

[1] David L. Bickelhaupt, *General Insurance*, 10th ed. (Homewood, Ill.: Richard D. Irwin, 1979), p. 123.

a request for a "certificate of authority" with the Georgia Department of Insurance and pay a small fee. The agent is now able to "broker" business with this new insurer. Although there are no life insurance brokers in the state of Georgia, there are agents who represent several different life insurance companies, and brokerage shops" exist that represent twenty-five or more different life insurance companies.

Wisconsin, on the other hand, presents a completely different approach to licensing. When licensed agents are unable to place business with any company with which they have a license because of capacity problems, rejection by their carrier, or unacceptable terms, they are permitted to contact an agent of some other insurer and attempt placement with the second agent's insurer. An "exchange of business" form must be completed and filed with the insurance department. Unless formally approved by the insurance department, only five such placements per agent per year may occur with any specific insurer and only twenty-five such transfers with all insurers. Wisconsin agents seem satisfied with this approach to brokerage.

In addition to this marketing technique, Wisconsin also permits brokers to exist using the "classical definition" and imposes the "classical legal requirements" upon that broker. Wisconsin started offering a broker's license to highly qualified applicants on March 1, 1979. Under this legislation, a broker cannot simultaneously act as an agent and as a broker for the same insurer. The broker's responsibility is to the applicant, and authorization exists to seek placement of contracts with any insurer doing business in the state of Wisconsin. A "pre-agreement form" is completed with each prospective insured certifying the legal relationship between the two parties. The broker cannot charge a broker's fee to the applicant and also receive a commission from the insurer. It must be made known to the client that the broker is unable to bind either the insurer or the client. This broker arrangement most closely parallels the legal definitions and distinctions between agency and brokerage responsibility. Although licensed brokers are new in the marketing of insurance in Wisconsin, there has been no great rush to seek the brokerage license. While there are 32,000 licensed life insurance agents in the state, only seven secured a brokerage license during the first year of enabling legislation.

A third example of agent/broker licensing is found in Colorado, which permits the licensing of agents and brokers. The revised statutes for the state prescribe the legal requirements of both positions as follows: "Every insurance agent . . . shall be regarded as representing the insurer and not the insured or his beneficiary in any controversy between the insured or his beneficiary and the insurer." "Every insurance broker . . . shall be regarded as representing the insured or his beneficiary and not the insurer . . . ."

This approach seems to duplicate that utilized under Wisconsin law. In Colorado, however, an agent who qualifies can also secure a broker's license, or a broker can secure an agent's license. The primary reason given for the broker to seek an agent's license is that some companies either do not recognize brokers *per se*, or that the broker without an agent's license encounters difficulty in placing certain types of business.

Although Colorado, Wisconsin, and Georgia do not use all of the combinations available to broker licensing within the United States, they do provide a representative group illustrating the great differences in approach to the problem. In addition to the difference in treatment of agents and brokers, a great difference exists in the difficulty of the test used as the license examination. Some are so easy that virtually no study is required to pass, while others may require a formal study program or mastery of a license manual which guarantees knowledge of the life insurance business. An additional group of states still permits the issuance of temporary licenses good for three to six months without the passage of any examination. Most states require an applicant for a license to be a resident of the state or defend the reasons for securing same. Many states now waive licensing examination requirements if the applicant has completed certain educational requirements or holds the professional designation of CLU (Chartered Life Underwriter).

Although some insurance representatives are looked upon as "professional" or "career" brokers, most are legally deemed agents or temporary agents of the insurer. Further complicating the problem, an agent who places business with a second insurer becomes a broker and it is said that the application was "brokered." But, the general agent representing the company which accepted that business is also called a broker. Members of the insurance industry seldom have problems in knowing what each is talking about, but it appears to the uninformed that everyone is known as a broker. In the following section many terms to be used in this chapter will be defined in an attempt to simplify a very confusing area of insurance terminology.

Classifications of Brokers

Most brokers qualify for the title "broker" under the definition of "an agent who can sell insurance for more than one company." While this definition is broad in its scope, it is the one best understood within the life insurance industry. Throughout this chapter, unless specifically stated otherwise, *any agent who represents more than one company will be classed as a broker.* Using this definition, an attempt to categorize brokers who sell life insurance follows.

In classifying brokers, an initial step is to separate those brokers who sell only life and health insurance from those who sell property/casualty coverages and life insurance. Even with these two major classifications, a problem still exists in the attempt to define the subgroups. The problem occurs because life insurance brokers do not legally exist in some states, while in others, anyone can be both an agent and a broker. In few instances is there an individual who qualifies as a broker using the classical definition, and performs no other function.

Perhaps the person who most resembles a broker from the legal point of view would be the individual who holds licenses with no life insurance company but functions as an expert in the field of substandard or impaired risk coverages. When approached by an applicant for this type of coverage, this "pure broker" would attempt to secure coverage from the company which offered the best rate for the impairment under consideration. Inasmuch as there are few individuals who are "pure brokers," they will be excluded from our categories. Thus, the major classifications of brokers in this chapter will be (1) substandard brokers, (2) brokers who sell only life insurance, and (3) brokers who sell property/casualty insurance and life insurance. Personal producing general agents will also be discussed in this section.

Substandard Brokers

An individual who places business with more than one company, especially substandard risks, but who does not warrant the title of pure broker is referred to as a substandard broker (or intermediary). A substandard broker generally runs a "brokerage shop," the term commonly used to refer to the field operation of the substandard broker. This individual holds general agent (GA) licenses with many different insurers, in some cases with as many as fifty different life insurance companies. Substandard brokers may appoint agents to the brokerage shop or may secure a "certificate of authority," which is similar to a temporary license, for agents who utilize the services only infrequently. In most states the certificate of authority is only used when the agent is already licensed. The unique characteristic of the substandard form of brokerage is that the "shop" GA (substandard broker) will know the best company with which to attempt placement of most substandard applications. To maintain objectivity and also the trust of the agents, most substandard brokers do not sell coverage directly to the consumer, but instead restrict themselves to serving only those agents who request help. Substandard brokers do not have the same legal responsibility to the applicant as do independent brokers since the substandard brokers are already licensed by the companies with which they place business. Although people holding this position carry out the usual functions of brokerage, they are not usually referred to as pure brokers.

Brokers Who Sell Only Life Insurance

Although some life insurance personnel refer to four or five different classifications of life insurance brokers, there are really only two classifications (in addition to substandard brokers). The two general types of brokers who sell only life insurance are the surplus broker, or agent of another company (including the occasional broker), and the independent broker or life broker.

The **surplus broker** or **agent of another company** is usually either a general agent or a career life insurance agent who works for a general agent or manager in a career agency. Although they are licensed agents with at least one life insurance company (the primary company), they *assume* the role of broker in their attempts to insure clients with insurers other than their primary company (hence the term surplus broker). Surplus brokers (1) may deal directly with the brokerage department of a secondary insurer, (2) may contact a general agent of a secondary insurer, or (3) may already hold a valid broker's license with the company in question. They are generally successful, educated, and trained in their field, and conduct their business in a professional manner. Many surplus brokers' clients are company executives and part of the business or corporate market. Surplus brokers normally place their business with their primary company; however, in certain cases, brokers place business with other companies due to the impaired risk of the applicant, the lack of competitive rates for a particular contract or a special need for a particular product that the broker's primary company does not have. Surplus brokers are generally not interested in using the brokerage market as a primary market for clients, but instead, only as a supplemental source of available coverage.

The "occasional broker" is not distinctly different from the surplus broker, but might be distinguished by the number of times the services of another insurance company are required. Occasional brokers simply do not seek coverage for their clients from other companies as often as surplus brokers. The reasons for this may be that the primary carrier provides for all applicants by issuing rated or substandard contracts, or the company's offering of contracts may be broad enough so that little need exists to seek the aid of other insurers. It is sometimes the case that the agent in question does not sell a sufficiently large number of cases to cause a frequent use of other than the primary company. Occasional brokers are treated as different from surplus brokers because their infrequent use of brokerage lowers their expertise in the use of other carriers. The total life insurance sales from occasional brokers is large but the amount from any specific broker is generally very small.

Typically the **independent brokers,** or **life brokers,** were previously a successful career life insurance agent, and now specializes in a particular market which may consist of professional persons such as medical doctors or attorneys. The independent broker may be characterized as dealing with a particular product such as pensions or health insurance, or working with a special product for a given group such as business coverages or tax shelters and doing estate planning for highly paid executives or the wealthy. Independent brokers usually make their sales calls on a very professional basis and are financially successful. They occupy their own office space which may or may not be subsidized by one or more of their primary companies. They represent the interests of their clients rather than a particular insurer and do not wish to be identified with any given life insurance company.

Brokers Who Sell Property/Casualty Insurance

Another major group of brokers is the group that sells property/casualty insurance coverages in addition to life and health insurance coverages. Independent all-lines brokers and national or regional brokers are the two subdivisions of this category. They will be introduced here and discussed in more detail in Chapter 12, All-lines Agents.

The **American Agency System** is the name given to the marketing system using middlemen who operate independent agencies. This classification encompasses the large group of general agents who market much of the property/casualty lines of insurance for those companies that do not use captive or exclusive agents.

Independent agents in the property/casualty field would qualify as brokers since it is common for independent agents to be licensed by fifteen or more different insurance companies. Some life insurance companies or their property/casualty subsidiaries report that 95% of their brokerage sales (as measured by premium income) each year come from independent property/casualty brokers. Chapter 12 contains an in-depth discussion of all-lines independent agents.

The terms **national** or **regional broker** refer to the nationwide brokerage houses that tend to specialize in industrial or large commercial accounts. Examples of this type broker are Marsh & McLennon or the Fred S. James Company. They offer their accounts an all-risk approach by providing risk management advice (fringe benefits, group insurance, etc.) and a continuing review of all problems involving loss or pure risk. Although the number of insurers with which they do business might be rather small, national brokers have access to virtually all companies that offer competitive rates. They are usually responsible for the entire package of property/casualty coverages of their accounts and also place the group life and health contracts. Frequently, they sell business life coverages, including the key person, buy-sell, and deferred compensation packages. Because of the large size and the national scope of these brokerage offices, they usually provide their consulting services to the home office location as well as all company branches. They can provide specialists in all subject areas required by the customer.

The Personal Producing General Agent

The increased use of brokerage of life insurance has been responsible in part for the development of the personal producing general agent (PPGA). As described in Chapter 10, PPGAs differ from general agents in that they are not particularly interested in either hiring or training new agents. They seek their success largely in personal production. PPGAs are career agents who prefer not to have the responsibilities of agency management but want the advantages secured in being named general agents for particular companies. They enjoy the contractual rights of being a GA, earn overrides on their own commissions, and may gain some prestige or other advantages that GAs may have over other agents. This differentiation is necessary to understand the attitudes of various general agents toward brokerage. Because of the PPGAs' high volume of individual sales, it is likely that a substantial amount of their business will be brokered, and thus, their mention in this chapter.

It is the feeling of the General Agents and Managers Association (GAMA) that PPGAs and the brokerage shop owners are not doing their share in promoting the well-being of the life insurance industry. The attitude of GAMA is that the traditional general agent or manager carries the burden of both the hiring and the training of agents for the life insurance industry. If this work is not continuously carried on, GAMA claims, the industry will ultimately suffer. They state that the PPGAs and the brokerage shop owners get their initial training from career GAs and then do nothing to repay the industry for their training. Although many of the PPGAs and the brokerage shop GAs agree with this appraisal, they do not anticipate taking any action to change the situation. It is their attitude that the industry offers different marketing strategies, and if the career GAs cannot hold their agents, it is their compensation system or their management ability that is lacking. PPGAs suggest career GAs and managers look to their own operation for faults and not to their competitors for help.

While all of the classifications of agents and brokers mentioned in this section form the group that uses life insurance brokerage, the large majority of all life insurance brokerage comes from only three of these categories: the property/casualty agents, the career life insurance agents, and the PPGAs.

Reasons an Agent Would Submit Brokerage Business

There are four major reasons why brokerage might be utilized by agents in the placing of life insurance business. Agents may be seeking favorable underwriting practices, unique products, and/or favorable premium rates for the clients, or they may want a ready source of companies that are available to meet the clients' every need. When an applicant for life insurance is rejected or rated other than standard by a life insurance company, the agent may attempt to secure better terms for the client. Many companies specialize in writing insurance for medically impaired risks or in issuing life insurance on people employed in hazardous occupations. Thus, an agent with a rejected or rated applicant seeks the insurance carrier with the most liberal underwriting for the applicant's particular needs. Some of the companies that have specialized in substandard risks have developed great expertise and in some cases offer substandard coverage at lower rates than normal standard coverage. Substandard brokers make it their job to be aware of these companies and the rates and products they offer.

Whether the applicant is rated standard or not, the agent may use the brokerage approach to place business with insurers offering the best rates. Some companies which were formerly deemed substandard risk companies have attempted to diversify their sales portfolio and have become competitive not only from the standpoint of underwriting, but also for the products they offer and the rates at which they will sell them. The inventiveness of these insurers has increased demand for their particular insurance products. (The products will be discussed in greater detail later in this chapter.)

Finally, it appears that some agencies take great pride in being able to provide any coverage sought by their clientele. Brokerage is thus utilized by agents to secure any coverage not readily available from primary companies, be it property/casualty or life and health insurance. Although four reasons for using brokerage are cited above, each is closely linked and the ultimate reason may be any single one or all.

Benefits of Brokered Business

The basic appeal of the brokering company to agents is "Give us your business which your own insurer will not accept." Usually the reason for the first case brokered by an agent is that the primary company has either rejected or rated an applicant too high to permit easy placement. To solve the customer's problem the agent seeks another insurer specializing in the substandard markets. It is possible that the new insurer may be willing to issue the contract to the client at standard rates and even issue it at a price lower than the primary company had published as the standard rate. In some cases the substandard company will provide a more advantageous product based on the interest adjusted index price and still pay a higher commission rate to the agent. One of the reasons for this apparent inequity is that the substandard insurer has lower overhead and fewer expenses since it does not hire and train large sales forces nor does it subsidize large general agencies. Substandard writers tend to sell a small product line and become highly knowledgeable in the items that they do sell.

The average brokered contract is larger in amount and has better persistency than that of the average life insurance company's contract due primarily to the type of clientele and their income brackets.[2] Whether this is true for all companies seeking brokerage is unknown, but the fact remains that many agents feel that they benefit from brokering business. After having been treated to good service, favorable underwriting, above-average commissions, and the issuance of a contract on an "uninsurable client," a concerned agent is even more interested in a brokerage company. Individual brokers with one primary company, seeking to continue a profitable business by extending their offerings, today frequently broker certain types of business before offering it to their primary insurer. The agent rationalizes this action by stating that the primary company would not have wanted this business or that the client would not have accepted the coverage at the price quoted by the primary company.

In addition to agents' placing their rejected or rated case with the substandard insurance carrier, agents may also seek out a carrier for brokerage because certain products are only available through brokerage. As indicated earlier, many new products start with the brokering companies, which are more flexible than the older and larger companies. Contracts such as term-to-100, retired lives reserve, flexible life insurance, and, most recently, pure options to buy life insurance at some time in the future, were initiated by companies specializing in brokerage.

Contracts Usually Handled by Brokers

Career brokers or brokerage shops offer the entire spectrum of life and health insurance products. Many brokers entered the business with the idea of selling substandard coverages to those who were uninsurable or not insurable at standard rates by the larger life insurance companies; many companies specializing in brokerage are still concentrating heavily on writing

[2] Roger R. Kolker, CLU, "Brokerage Distribution Systems," *Report on Distribution Systems*, (LIMRA, unpublished), 1977.

substandard risks. In fact, prior to 1970, almost all life insurance business that was brokered in the classical sense was substandard. Many of these insurers maintain large medical staffs not only to provide adequate underwriting expertise, but also to continue medical research on the effects of various impairments upon mortality. This research has permitted the substandard insurers to offer lower rates for various medical impairments than usually are available in many traditional life insurance companies. Some of these impairments include hypertension, epilepsy, mental handicaps, diabetes, overweight, and factors such as alcoholism, sexual deviation, and drug addiction.

New Products and Innovations

Brokerage companies have also begun handling term coverage for large amounts at very competitive rates. Several companies advertise contracts with face amounts of $250,000 to $500,000 without the requirement of a medical examination. Others offer amounts of $1,000,000 and more to applicants in "reasonably good health." The rates, usually from stock insurers, vary but are usually 10 to 25% less than the "large New York mutuals." In recent years, brokerage insurers have been offering special coverages in an attempt to appeal to an even larger group of agents. These contracts have generally been referred to as "business risks," or "jumbo accounts."

One such plan which has received wide acceptance for group pension use is the retired lives reserve product. The plan offers group term life insurance and a separate account for funds to be used ultimately for payment of premiums after termination of work. The plan in essence offers permanent life insurance coverage while the employee is working without the tax implications of permanent insurance. While working, the employee secures up to $50,000 of term life insurance without being deemed to receive any economic benefit on which to pay income tax. After retirement the reserve fund will pay the premium for the insurance. Even after retirement, there is still no taxable income to the retired employee. This product shows great promise.

The brokerage companies have also been greatly involved in the development of special contracts to fit the needs of firms utilizing H.R. 10 or Section 79 products. HR 10 refers to pension plans or retirement programs for either the self-employed or the small business with only a few employees. The Section 79 products offer group permanent insurance programs which provide favorable income tax treatment both to the employer and to the employee.

In addition, brokerage companies have utilized a "batch" approach to underwriting partnership and corporate buy-sell agreements. A major roadblock to the funding of many such agreements is the uninsurability of one or more owners, and many brokerage companies have resolved the problem with batch underwriting or issuance. This technique permits the use of credits on good risks to offset the debits on poor risks and may permit the entire case to be written as standard. As new ideas or new needs confront the applicant, the small brokerage companies tend to react more quickly with solutions than do large insurers. The competitive advantage is seldom longer than two years, because if a new product is successful, other companies will follow with similar products of their own.

Function of the Broker

The basic function of the broker today is the same as that of an agent: to serve the needs of the insurance consumer. Inasmuch as many consumers are unaware of their needs, the total function takes on a broader array of duties. These duties involve (1) identifying potential clients, (2) identifying their needs, (3) structuring the best coverage to satisfy the needs and cost constraints, (4) closing the sale, and (5) continued servicing of the account. The only difference between brokers and agents in the functions they perform is the degree of sophistication in the interview and awareness of possible solutions. The broker has a need to collect sufficient information to permit proper placement of the client's applications for life insurance. It is important for the broker to know all the companies solicit substandard coverage applications and which of these companies will offer the most reasonable underwriting from the applicant's point of view. If the broker specializes in some of the new innovative approaches to financial security, it is necessary that he or she keep informed about all legal and tax considerations affecting these products.

Compensation of Brokers

Since most brokers are agents, the commissions offered to these brokers vary as greatly as they do for agents. If the agent in question is not a general agent or is not entitled to override commissions, compensation will be paid as provided in the agency contract. Typically, life insurance companies that are licensed to do business in New York State pay agents' compensation equal to 100% of an annual premium, which is divided into a first-year commission of 50 to 55% and a group of renewal commissions totaling the balance. The renewals may be equal in amount or concentrated into three or four unequal installments. If the company does not do business in New York State, there is a tendency for the total agents' compensation to be even larger. If the agent is also a GA, overrides equal to an additional 30 or 40% will be paid. These overrides may also apply to all renewal commissions. In addition to these commissions, renewals, and overrides, GAs also may be eligible for office and expense subsidies and production bonuses. All or some of the benefits, designated as agency compensation, apply equally to brokers since brokers are licensed as either agents or general agents in most states.

Rewards for Brokers' Production

There is also a large range of employee benefits and rewards for production paid to brokers. Again we must look at the form of contract with which the brokering agent works. A general agent who acts as a broker for any given company will receive the same fringe benefits and bonus arrangements available to general agents of that other company. If the amount of business placed with a given company is large, the broker will participate in all bonuses offered by the insurer. If some of the GA's agents provide a large volume to this particular insurer, those particular agents will usually receive extra bonuses and be invited to special "sales conferences" as reward.

A rather common practice in the life insurance industry is the annualizing of commission payments. This usually serves the agent in that regardless of the mode of payment chosen by the applicant, the insurer assumes that all of the year's premium is received at the time of placement of coverage. If the commission rate on a contract is 50%, then 50% of the full year's premium will be given the agent in the next paycheck. Some brokerage companies have a tendency not to annualize commissions as they do not have the close relationship that normally exists with exclusive agents. They sometimes have difficulty in retrieving unearned commissions when contracts lapse. Thus, there tends to be a dichotomy of treatment of agents using brokerage insurers. While occasional brokers usually get or receive few extra benefits or bonuses, large producers tend to be treated as well as exclusive agents, and this treatment might include a full range of employee benefits including a pension program.

Service Fees

Normal life insurance agency contracts include a service fee allowance. The service fee usually begins at the termination of all renewal commission payments. This allowance varies from 2 to 5% and, although seldom vested, continues for the lifetime of the contract. Although the pattern is varied, many agents receive no service fee allowance on brokered business. During recent years the noticeable trends in the compensation paid to agents by brokerage companies include:

1. Increasing the total commission paid for securing brokered business where legally permissible.

2. Stressing employee benefits such as deferred compensation and group life and health benefits to secure the favorable federal income tax treatment of compensation for the agent.
3. Reducing the value of fringe benefits or bonuses to agents who only infrequently place business with the insurer, thereby encouraging these occasional brokers to increase placing business with a brokering company to take advantage of the bonuses. Thus, there is an appeal to the "top producer" to continue or increase placement of business.

Solicitation of Brokerage Business by Life Companies

Economic reasons usually force life insurance companies to decide to solicit brokerage business. They feel that the business will generate an increased flow of new business at reduced cost, or they feel that the increased flow of business will permit the company to benefit from economies of scale. After the fixed cost of the enterprise is covered, increased sales tend to produce greater profits. In addition to this, studies conducted by LIMRA indicate that far less is paid in the acquisition of brokered business than for business secured from exclusive agents.

If an insurer already has a marketing system in use, consideration must be given to the impact on existing agents of the use of brokers. It is possible that a company that has depended upon exclusive agents to market its products may alienate these agents if it seeks to increase sales by permitting brokers to sell their wares. The past relationship between the agents and the home office will be an important consideration.

All types and sizes of companies today are involved in brokerage as a means of increasing the sale of their products. A recent study conducted by LIMRA revealed that of 347 different member insurers in North America, 97 indicated that at least 40% of their business came from brokers, and 25 of these companies indicated that 100% of their business was secured from brokers. Twenty-five of the 97 companies were mutuals, and 72 were stock. Twelve of the 97 companies had assets in excess of $1 billion, while 48 had assets of less than $100 million. It can readily be seen that no particular type or size company monopolizes the business of brokerage. There is an increasing tendency for some relatively small companies to improve their growth situation by resorting to, or concentrating on, brokers as their source of business; in fact, six of the smallest ten companies in the study cited above used brokers as the exclusive source of business. Almost 70% of the companies providing any information admitted that they brokered part of their business.

The Home Office Sales Approach

A life insurance company seeking to increase its brokerage sales and seeking new outlets would want to secure contacts with agents of other companies. Few applicants for insurance seek out an insurer on the basis of its liberal underwriting or offering of special low-rate term insurance policies. Frequently, an agent will attempt to broker business for a client only if a special circumstance creates a need on the part of the client. Most companies seeking to increase their share of the market through brokerage business advertise in magazines and journals that agents are likely to read. Their advertising usually features products that will attract the type of agent whose business they want. For example, a company might advertise that it will insure up to $250,000 or more without a medical examination if certain requirements are met. These requirements might be that the applicant has had a recent medical examination or some such evidence of good health. Another insurer may advertise that its rates for a particular product are lower than any other company's. Still other companies advertise the availability of batch issuance for corporate insurance. Although many companies offer similar contracts, advertising creates an interest and an awareness in agents of the availability of such plans.

Confusing terminology again tends to make the discussion of home office brokerage efforts difficult. While the following discussion distinguishes between a brokerage manager and a brokerage supervisor, many in the insurance industry use the two terms interchangeably. The reader is cautioned to be aware that terms and job descriptions will differ within different companies.

Brokerage Managers

The insurer's home-office production department uses various avenues of contact with the field force. One such avenue is the employment of a brokerage manager. The brokerage manager is an insurance company employee whose only responsibility is to sell or market the company's products through brokers. While many brokerage managers are located in their own offices completely apart from either the home office or its brokerage outlets, some brokerage managers are located in large career agencies and report directly to the agency manager. These brokerage managers, while still deemed insurance company employees, have dual responsibilities to attract brokerage business by being available to help with difficult-to-place cases and to produce personal business. They are compensated by salary and overrides.

Brokerage Supervisors

One source of brokerage business is the brokerage supervisor, an agent in a career agency who spends part-time or full-time on solicitation of brokerage business. The agency's GA may only be licensed by one life insurance company, and that company's product is offered through the agency's agents and by the use of brokerage to other agents' clients. Usually, the GA's life insurance company offers either competitively priced products or liberal underwriting in certain substandard areas and produces an attractive product to agents representing other insurers. Brokerage supervisors are compensated by overrides only.

Training of the Sales Force

For all practical purposes, brokerage companies do not train their sales force. Inasmuch as most of their business comes from agents who are already trained, they see little need to improve on what has been accepted as a successful system. The use of agents who are already trained is one of the reasons brokerage companies are profitable and also one of the reasons they can usually offer agents higher compensation for production. When a new product is developed, brokerage companies usually circulate literature to interested agencies with some tips on how to sell the product, information on legal interpretations, or tax information which will make the product more desirable to their customers. They may also inform the brokers of how best to present proposals that have been prepared. Occasionally they organize home office seminars to provide technical training for brokers.

Service to Broker/Agents by a Brokerage Company

A life insurance company seeks to provide its brokers with good service. Brokers are likely to recommend a company to other brokers if they receive good service. It is important for an agent to receive fast and efficient service in the treatment of applicants. In many cases, the applicant has already been disappointed by having been rejected or rated and the agent has quickly sought out an alternative source of coverage. A brokering company giving good service will usually provide information, underwriting requirements, and preliminary proposals on all inquiries. Sometimes a brokerage shop prepares proposals and quotes tentative rates; at other times the brokering company prepares these.

Service to Brokerage Shops

An agent in a brokerage shop seeking coverage for a client will usually prepare an inquiry form, virtually always used for previously rejected business. The brokerage shop personnel will collect all information required for proper underwriting, including medical examination reports, medical history and medical records from doctors and hospitals, and necessary credit reports. After the underwriting file is completed, it is forwarded to the brokering insurer. The brokerage shop manager usually knows well in advance the ultimate decision of company underwriting, since underwriting is fairly predictable if all facts are known.

Generally the procedure of using the brokerage shop is efficient. The "shop" is usually located in a major metropolitan area and is available to promptly serve the local needs for brokerage. The amount of substandard business processed may be substantial, thus giving great expertise in the process to the brokerage shop manager. The brokerage insurer, using the inquiry form and all underwriting data provided by the brokerage shop, will issue a contract subject to the acceptance of the original applicant. Some life companies have reputations established on the high percentage of contracts issued at standard rates on applicants who have been either rated or rejected by other insurers.

Service to Other Brokers

In jurisdictions where the brokerage shop is not widely used, brokering companies use field offices, direct phone service, or data-phone service. With these aids, the brokering agent can seek information and secure prompt feedback on proposals. Companies using brokerage managers in the home office often have back-up personnel to provide locally all of the services required for underwriting, preparation of proposals, and rating.

The underwriting procedure for life insurance is similar regardless of which personnel carry out the function. Brokerage shop personnel perform many underwriting functions usually handled by the life insurance company home office, while some offices use field personnel to carry out the underwriting function for local brokerage managers. Even though the channel may differ depending on the wishes of the company involved, there is little data to indicate which technique is more efficient or least costly.

Service to the Policyowner

Service to the policyowner by brokering insurers is somewhat complicated due to the writing agent's close affiliation with a primary insurer. A brokering insurer must do an outstanding job in servicing a policyowner in order to gain the repeat business that might accrue from the present insurance. The original loyalty that a writing agent feels for a primary company is hard to erode. Where a primary company might contact an insured directly with mailings and informational data, a brokerage company is reluctant to do this because its contact is the broker, the conduit in the sale. Brokerage companies would like to communicate with policyowners through their brokers. This "roundabout" method creates a longer line of communication between company and consumer. Thus, the brokering insurer must take precautions to expedite all policyowner service requirements to maintain an image of efficiency. A primary company will usually notify its agents when premiums have not been paid promptly, and agents have an opportunity to jog their clients' memories regarding payment prior to lapse. On the other hand, a brokering company will perhaps inform the broker (GA) of tardy payment. The broker (GA) will, in turn, pass this information on to the brokering writing agent. This delay could permit the contract to lapse, but any attempt to bypass the writing agent might break the existing goodwill between the broker and the brokering (writing) agent.

Some companies have attempted to speed up the process of information flow by sending duplicate notices to both broker and client. This reduces the necessary time of message transmission to the writing agent, but it may break down some of the control which the broker has previously enjoyed. However, both this method and the previously mentioned "roundabout" method for contacting policyowners seem to be working with reasonable effectiveness.

When changes of beneficiary, name, and ownership endorsements are necessary on brokerage contracts, the insured, with some assistance from an agent, will typically transmit them directly to the insurer. The completed endorsements are generally returned to the insurer's GA, who in turn gives them to the broker for final delivery. Although this again is a round-about way, it permits the GA to keep abreast of all changes in the contracts under the agency's purview.

Some brokering insurers have a compensation system which bunches or stacks the renewal commissions into a small number of relatively large payments. The availability of the renewals early in a policy's life is attractive to most agents, but many agents tend to lose interest in the persistency of contracts after the renewals have terminated. The same pattern of renewals is used by some companies with their primary agents. Although research has shown that persistency problems are dramatically reduced after the fourth or fifth contract year, research has not revealed any major difference in the way agents treat their clients, whether the insurer is a primary or brokering company.

Changes in attitudes on the part of the policyowners may cause them to become unhappy with their broker. They may wish that the commissions being paid to that broker be terminated, or may wish service from a different broker. It is difficult to terminate commissions or renewals earned by an existing agent or broker, especially if the renewals are vested. Where these renewals are not vested, it is sometimes possible either to lift the renewals due to lack of service or to transfer part of the earned renewal to a servicing broker. This is not a major consideration since the number of such cases is minimal based on the number of insurance contracts existing in the brokerage market.

A problem does exist for orphan policyowners, those whose broker has left the business and who have no broker of record. Some primary companies assign nonvested renewals to another agent, usually after a 50% reduction in their size. These renewals or service fees pay for the continued service required of the new agent. Under brokerage, seldom does this occur. The policyowner is listed as a miscellaneous account, and the in-force business is handled directly by the company.

Trends and the Future

As stated previously, almost all life insurance brokers are also life insurance agents. A substantial share of all brokerage business comes from career life insurance agents affiliated with a primary insurer with whom most of their life insurance business is placed. Thus, few trends or changes within the life insurance industry will affect the brokerage segment of the industry differently from the way they do any other segment. There are, however, a few developments which may influence brokerage in the future, and they deserve mention.

The Commission or the Fee System

Most life insurance agents are compensated on a commission basis. Where large agencies or brokers conduct risk management for an entire insurance account, and coordinate the fringe benefits of the account's employees, there has been a tendency for some of the large national brokerage firms to offer to discontinue the commission basis and switch to a "service-for-fee" approach. The risk management approach involves advising the firm as to what risks to assume, self-insure, or insure with commercial carriers. Advice to a firm to increase the amount of risk it assumes reduces the amount of risk insured by a commercial insurer, thereby reducing the earned commissions for the advisor. Some agencies have offered total risk management for a fee, usually a function of the present commissions being earned on the account. By charging a fee, a risk advisor can recommend whatever is best for the client without risk of losing compensation. This trend has not evolved far within the life insurance industry, but where the entire package is administered by one brokerage agency, compensation to the agent by use of a fee is becoming more common.

Tendency of More Companies to Expand Brokerage Business

The number of companies accepting brokerage business is increasing, and today almost all companies will accept brokerage when offered. An increasingly large group of companies solicit brokerage business, and a surprisingly large group of companies sell only through brokers. The type of company that is actively seeking brokerage is not well-defined. Both mutual and stock companies are now seeking brokerage business. The companies vary in size from very small to the giants. During the ten-year period from 1968 to 1978, the assets of all the 354 LIMRA member-companies increased 108%. During this same time, the companies which admitted to accepting brokerage business increased their assets 173% and the companies using brokers exclusively increased their assets 196%.[3] Although measuring growth by change in total assets may not be the best technique, it may indicate a change of emphasis in the marketing of life insurance.

The Impact of Brokerage on the General Agency

A general agent is subsidized by a primary company, and future compensation is based on the subsidy and overrides on the agency's production. The continued subsidy by the primary company is contingent upon a successful sales record on the part of the total agency. If an individual agent is unable to place business with a GA's primary company, the agent may contact a GA with a competing company and insure the client elsewhere. This action naturally upsets the primary GA, but in the absence of a contract which prohibits this, the available responses are few. Most general agents will seek a GA contract with some other insurers so that they may offer a complete line of products. If this is not possible, the agency may wish to implement an arrangement with either a brokerage shop or with another GA whose company offers competitive specialty contracts. Sales volume is important because most companies pay bonsues based on volume. Giving a brokerage manager office space in the general agency is also an option of the GA. As previously stated, the brokerage manager may be paid by an insurance company to help out in an agency and help solicit new business. The general agent will earn overrides on all business secured by this brokerage manager housed in the agency. Although this procedure may give an individual GA adequate personal income, the total sales submitted to the primary insurance company may be less than satisfactory. A GA must constantly direct an

---

[3] All statistics compiled from *Best's Insurance Reports*, 1969 and 1979 editions (Oldwick, New Jersey: A. M. Best Company).

adequate share of the agency's business to the primary insurer to continue receiving an agency subsidy. Many general agencies are struggling with this problem today.

New Products

There have been very few completely new products, but there have been many which combined parts of existing policies and gave old coverages a new emphasis. In most cases these policies emphasize taking advantage of tax considerations. It is important for a consumer to take legal advantage of any possible tax advantage. It therefore behooves the industry to study conscientiously the tax laws and their legal interpretations in an attempt to uncover areas where insurance offers a better solution to either estate conservation or estate creation.

New companies, always in a competitive struggle to survive, have been dominant in the introduction of new products. Not all products are innovative, but they do offer the consumer a choice. Some new products, however, may hurt the long-range success of the life insurance industry. For example, one major complaint is that the present-day trend of large group term contracts which are renewable to age 100 can and will someday hurt the industry by reducing reliance of consumers on individual life insurance purchases. This argument assumes that the general public is not aware of the pitfalls of total reliance on group term insurance and that career life insurance agents will be unable to inform the general public of the inherent problems.

The interesting development is the apparent ability of the new brokerage-oriented companies to underwrite large amounts of coverage on a large group of people. If the underwriting is sound, the future will belong to those who have prepared themselves for competition, whether they are brokers, agents, insurers with broker orientation, or exclusive agent companies. Improper coverage leads to dissatisfaction with those offering the coverage, not with the insurance mechanism. One great advantage of the low-priced/yearly renewable term policy is that it gets people to "thinking big." After having bought a million dollar policy, policyowners usually feel that they need that much or they would not have bought it. The brokers feel that a trained agent will immediately start the conversion process by increasing the proportion of permanent coverage to term coverage as time passes. The yearly increase in premium will continue to remind the insured that nothing stays the same forever.

In a similar vein, the brokerage approach to life and health insurance marketing has also probably given the career agent a shot of competition. Competition tends to be good for all involved since it interferes with complacency.

Summary

Although arriving at a definition of brokerage that is acceptable to all parties is a difficult process in itself, it is not difficult to understand and be aware of the impact that brokerage of life insurance has made upon the industry during the past ten years. The commonly accepted definition of a broker today is "any agent who sells insurance for more than one insurance company." This definition tends to make brokers out of all property and casualty independent agents as well as most life insurance agents who frequently or occasionally place business with a company other than their primary insurers.

Prior to 1970, brokerage in the life insurance industry usually referred to coverages for impaired risks which had been rejected or rated by the traditional life insurance companies. Today it includes all of that and more; many life insurance companies are using brokers exclusively to market their products. Many other companies are deriving a large, if not major, share of their business through brokers. Although many agents still resort to brokerage only after a rejection from their primary insurer, some agents are now placing their business with the broker on a first-call basis.

The brokerage life insurance companies now offer "jumbo term" contracts, special contracts for business risks, special contracts for the wealthy, and their most recent success, the retired lives reserve approach to group permanent life insurance. These companies have developed unique products and have marketed them in a most competitive fashion. Many of these brokerage companies are small, and they are able to innovate and implement new products very quickly. Utilization of other companies' agents has reduced the cost of securing business for brokerage companies. They have posed a new challenge for the life and health insurance industry, and the industry is just starting to react to the new competition. It can probably be deemed a healthy competition inasmuch as both groups are selling life insurance instead of diverting insurance dollars to other uses.

Chapter 12

All-Lines Agents

Bruce A. Palmer, Ph.D., CLU

This chapter focuses on the all-lines distribution system in which an agent is responsible for the sale and servicing of both life and nonlife insurance products. All-lines distribution allows consumers to have all of their insurance needs served by one agent—in effect one-stop shopping. Thus, the products in the agent's portfolio include automobile and homeowners coverages and the various life insurance, accident and health, and annuity coverages.[1] Two major approaches to marketing all forms of insurance products exist. The two systems, exclusive agency and independent agency, will be discussed separately in the chapter.

The importance of marketing all lines of insurance through one agent has increased dramatically over the past several decades. The substantial recent insurer activity and interest shown in marketing all forms of insurance coverages have increased the relative importance of this distribution method when compared with other methods.

Insurer activities involving the sale of both life and nonlife insurance products have evidenced themselves in two ways: (1) established life insurance companies have acquired new property/liability affiliates, and (2) established property/liability companies have created new life company affiliates. The diversification into additional insurance markets has been accomplished through the formation of new subsidiary companies or through the acquisition of existing companies.

A considerable amount of the more recent formation/acquisition activity has been by large mutual life insurance companies who previously had restricted their activities, almost exclusively, to the life insurance business.

---

[1] Additional property/liability coverages may also be included.

The trend of property/liability companies' expansion of their operations into the life insurance field predates the trend of life insurance companies' expansion.

During the 1950s and 1960s, numerous all-lines "groups" were formed by property/liability insurers. These groups are affiliations of insurers having separate corporate identities but collectively possessing the authority to sell property/liability coverages in addition to life insurance. Today, there are in excess of 100 all-lines groups.[2] This original all-lines trend was followed by a development of equal importance involving the entry of large life insurance companies into the property/liability industry. The latest trend began in 1971 when Prudential established a property/liability subsidiary. Prudential's entry was quickly followed by the entry of other large mutuals, including Metropolitan, Equitable,[3] and John Hancock, into the property/liability business. Today, approximately two-thirds of the thirty largest life insurance companies have property/liability affiliates, including three of the five largest mutual life insurance companies in the industry. Although the interest and publicity surrounding the entrance of life companies into the property/liability marketplace has surfaced primarily since the early 1970s, other major life insurance companies, including Connecticut General, Occidental, and Lincoln National, have had property/liability affiliates for several decades.

Terminology

Throughout insurance literature the description of insurance marketing is characterized by varying terminology. As a result, it is both necessary and beneficial to define all-lines, as contrasted to multiple-lines, exclusive agents, and independent agents.

All-Lines versus Multiple-Lines

The term all-lines marketing refers to the distribution of life insurance (and related) products in combination with property and liability insurance coverages. Multiple-line or multi-line is a term that has been used primarily in the property/liability industry when referring to an insurer's capacity to underwrite the various property, as well as liability, coverages. In a number of instances, the term multiple-line has been applied to the combined marketing of life and nonlife insurance products. However, this is not the preferred terminology.

---

[2] See pp. 228–241 of the 1980 edition of *The Insurance Almanac* (Englewood, N.J.: The Underwriter Printing and Publishing Company) for a listing of these groups.

[3] The Equitable Life Assurance Society of the United States recently divested ownership of its property/liability affiliate, Equitable General.

State insurance regulation today prohibits the underwriting of both life and nonlife products under the same corporate entity. However, with today's holding company structures, parent-subsidiary relationships, groups, and other intercorporate forms of operation, the insurance industry circumvents this limitation on underwriting powers. All-lines marketing is accomplished through the distribution of all types of insurance products by salespersons who represent either a family of insurers or several unrelated insurance entities. Even though in many instances, it may outwardly appear that the all-lines agent (or agency) is representing only one insurer, in actuality this agent is representing two or more companies that are either financially interrelated or under common management control.

Exclusive Agents versus Independent Agents

A second set of terms that must be defined concerns a contrast between two types of all-line agents: exclusive agents and independent agents. "All-lines exclusive agents" represent only companies belonging to a single group of financially interrelated or commonly managed insurance companies. The relationship existing between the exclusive agent and the company(ies) is most similar to that existing under the traditional career agency (or career ordinary) system. Insurers who operate through exclusive agents are referred to as exclusive agent companies or direct writers.[4]

In contrast to the single insurer group representation of the all-lines exclusive agent, the "all-lines independent agent" represents a number of insurance companies (or groups of companies) that are neither financially nor managerially related. In this system, the agent apportions his or her business among the companies represented according to his or her choice. Insurers operating through the independent agent system are often referred to as agency companies. Both the exclusive agent and independent agent marketing systems will be discussed in this chapter.

Advantages and Disadvantages of All-Lines Marketing

The reasons affecting an insurer's decision to venture into new and previously untested insurance markets are varied. Some reasons are peculiar to the entry of property/liability insurance companies (or groups) into life insurance markets, some are peculiar to the penetration of life insurers into property/liability markets, and still others are common to both modes of

[4] Technically speaking, direct writers are companies operating through salaried representatives. In practice, however, the term is often used to include companies marketing products through exclusive agents in addition to those marketing through salaried representatives.

diversification within the insurance business. Both the positive aspects and the potential negative aspects of all-lines marketing are discussed below.

Objectives and Benefits

A number of objectives of diversification into new markets are common to all business, such as a desire for growth and greater cash flow. In addition, insurers have a number of objectives in mind when making a decision whether to enter the all high lines market place. Among these objectives are attempts to stabilize company earnings and profits, capitalize on the "natural" market in order to increase agent income, reduce prospecting problems, enhance recruitment and retention of agents, and provide a total product portfolio. Benefits which may accrue from diversification include the opportunity to achieve economies of scale, meet competitive pressures, and increase market share.

Stabilize Insurer Profitability

The desire for greater stability in earnings and profits through a more balanced earnings power has played a crucial role in the decision of many property/liability insurers who have adopted an all-lines marketing approach. Property/liability markets and the underwriting profits (losses) resulting from these markets are cyclical in nature. In contrast, the life insurance business is less cyclical, with insurance company earnings patterns that are more stable and predictable. Thus, many property/liability insurers have entered the life insurance marketplace intending to smooth out fluctuations in their earnings and to moderate sharp cyclical downturns in property/liability underwriting and profit cycles.

Increase Agent Income by Capitalizing on the "Natural" Market

A most important objective of all-lines marketing is to capitalize on the existing "natural" market that an agent's current prospect file represents. A wealth of potential life (property/liability) prospects exists in the property/liability (life) client files. These files form a prime contact list since the best prospect for future sales is a satisfied customer with whom the agent is already doing business. Substantial additional sales opportunities and consequently an increased earnings potential for the agent, are provided through an all-lines approach to the marketing of insurance products.

As an illustration, consider the environment surrounding the property/liability agent. Typically, a property/liability agent has more frequent client contact than does a life-only agent. This frequent contact with clients results from repetitive claims and periodic servicing, among other things. Thus, there is a greater pool of prospects and an opportunity for life insurance sales. For example, discussion with a client of the purchase of a homeowner's policy in turn may lead to a discussion of mortgage life insurance. In addition, commercial property/liability accounts offer agents an opportunity to increase their incomes through business and group life insurance sales. These may be through funding buy-sell agreements, key person insurance, stock purchase plans, split dollar arrangements, and group insurance and pension plans. Since it is likely that the client already has confidence in the property/liability agent, it may be a relatively easy matter to obtain the needed financial information necessary to present a plan to the client for business or group insurance coverages. The objective of providing agents with an opportunity for increased earnings, together with the desire for improved agent retention (discussed below), have constituted the primary reasons for the adoption of an all-lines approach by several insurer groups operating through exclusive agents.

Reduce Prospecting Problems

From the standpoint of a life insurance agent, the addition of property/liability products facilitates the making of appointments for life sales. Personal lines property/liability coverages act as door-openers for sales calls, thereby reducing prospecting problems facing the life agent. Prospecting and the accompanying fear of rejection are widely recognized as obstacles to a life agent's success. In addition, more sales are consummated when property/liability products are offered in conjunction with life and health products, thus building an agent's morale and self-image—an important factor in an individual's chance of long-term success.

Enhance Agent Recruitment and Retention

A potential benefit that may be derived from all-lines marketing is the enhancement of agent recruitment and retention of those agents. An insurer hopes that an all-lines distribution system will attract better qualified individuals and, in addition, reduce the costs associated with recruiting these agents. The traditional life agent distribution system, the career agency system, has been the subject of considerable criticism in recent years because of the high recruitment costs. Estimates cited in 1978 have placed the cost of recruiting and training one surviving agent under the career agency (career ordinary) system somewhere between \$65,000 and \$145,000.[5] Since

[5] George G. Joseph, "Agency System—Sacred Cow or Holy Crusade?" *Life Association News*, December 1978, p. 101. These estimates relate to the total costs associated with recruiting, training, and developing one successful agent who is still with the company three

these estimates are based on 1978 dollars and have not been updated for inflation, today's costs are undoubtedly higher. A major reason for these high costs is that the turnover rate for these agents is extremely high. For the industry as a whole, turnover rates for life-only agents under the career ordinary system are several times higher than turnover rates for agents selling in an all-line marketing environment.[6] In order to earn an adequate income, today's life-only agent must write several million dollars of face amount each year or find other sources of income from activities that are compatible with current life insurance sales. The selling of property/liability lines of insurance provides one such source. Strengthening and increasing the earnings potential of agents should lead to the further improvement in retention rates. Thus, it is also hoped that an all-lines marketing approach will increase the probability of agent survival in the insurance business, thereby improving agent retention rates.

Provide Total Product Portfolio

An additional objective of agents and insurers in all-lines operation is the desire to provide total service and a complete insurance product portfolio to clients. In many instances, this is the main reason stated by insurers for entry into the all-lines marketplace. In essence, consumers may benefit from "one-stop insurance shopping" as a result of convenience, total service, and confidence formed in dealing with one agent to handle all insurance needs. Further, agents or agencies that can provide total account service are in a better position than their competitors.

Achieve Economies of Scale

A potential financial benefit in moving to all-lines distribution concerns achievement of market efficiencies or other forms of economies of scale. Broadening the market base allows the utilization of the talent of a single marketing and management team in the operations of all lines of insurance. This is possible even though all-lines marketing has to be accomplished

---

years after the hire date. Included in these estimates are costs attributed to agency management time, home office personnel time, agent financing expenses, among others, in addition to the losses associated with those agent recruits whose contracts were terminated, for one reason or another, during this initial three-year period. The wide range of estimates, i.e., \$65,000–\$145,000, is explained primarily by differences in agent retention rates. The \$65,000 figure was calculated assuming a three-year retention rate of 30% while the \$145,000 amount was determined assuming a three-year retention rate of 10%.

[6] See *The Manpower and Production Survey of Multiple-Line Exclusive Agent Companies—Calendar Year 1977,* (Hartford: Life Insurance Marketing and Research Association, Inc.), p. 1.

through several clearly distinct corporate entities. The potential is present for major reductions in marginal costs through more intensive use of established home office and regional production and marketing facilities (including sharing of the same physical facilities), and, most importantly, substantial economies can be accomplished by spreading fixed company and agent expenses (including agent development costs) over additional product lines. Excess capacities in certain functions (e.g., data processing, accounting, and investments) may by transferable to other insurance lines, resulting in lower unit overhead expenses. Additionally, cost savings may result from the integration or coordination of certain other functions. For example, it is quite possible to operate an all-lines operation successfully with a unified personnel division, a single purchasing department, and one department to handle all the public relations efforts of the entire insurer group.

However, certain types of functions may not integrate well into a single department or division (e.g., claims and underwriting). In addition, it is likely that, upon initial entry into the all-lines marketplace, the home office staff will be both inadequately trained and of insufficient size to handle their new responsibilities. For example, the differing nature of the underwriting problems associated with life and non-life products and the needed experience required of home office personnel are radically different. The lack of sufficient home and regional office staff required to undertake a major all-lines marketing effort, coupled with similar field force deficiencies, could lead to potentially disastrous results. The lack of adequate professional talent has deterred more than one insurance company from entering into insurance markets which are new to that company.

Meet Competitive Pressures

A number of insurers have adopted an all-lines marketing philosophy simply in reaction to competitive pressures. Some insurers believe that in order to retain their current market positions and enjoy continued growth and survival in the insurance industry, an all-lines marketing approach must be adopted. These companies have a preconceived notion that those insurers or groups failing to offer coverages or products on an all-lines basis will be unable to retain their present market share in the lines in which they currently specialize. Some observers of the all-lines trend question whether this perceived competitive threat is real or only theorized. In any event, a number of companies have conformed to the all-lines marketing trend because they felt pressure from the entry of their competitors into the all-lines market. This desire for self-preservation may apply to the field force as well as the companies themselves.

Increase Market Share

As noted above, while some companies have entered the all-lines marketplace simply to meet the forces of competition directly, other insurers have adopted an all-lines distribution system in order to expand and increase their writings in their present product lines. In other words, these companies were seeking to increase their market share. There seems to be some correlation between increasing property/liability sales and increasing life sales. Thus, from the viewpoint of a life (property/liability) insurer, the addition of property/liability (life) lines not only broadens the marketplace but increases the sales of life (property/liability) products as well.

In summary, the potential benefits associated with all-lines distribution of insurance products are both complex and somewhat interrelated. But without question, when an all-lines marketing approach meets with success through proper planning, organization, administration, and communication, the rewards are substantial in nature.

Potential Problems and Drawbacks

While benefits and advantages to be gleaned from an all-lines marketing approach are many and varied, the combined marketing of life and property/liability products is not without its attendant drawbacks and problem areas. Certainly, an amount of general skepticism will be shown by many individuals toward the promised benefits accruing from all-lines marketing. In addition, more specific and serious potential consequences should be reviewed.

Agent Resistance

One potential drawback is the resistance or reluctance on the part of agents to assume a new task of selling unfamiliar insurance products in an unfamiliar market environment. In many instances, there may be no real demand from the field force for additional products or new coverages. The agents' earnings already may be sufficient to meet the income needs required by their chosen life-style. Further, the agent may actually fear that selling unfamiliar products will be a difficult undertaking.

Property/liability agents may feel uneasy about the sale of life products because many of them probably possess only superficial knowledge of life insurance and the accompanying sales techniques and methods. Many of these agents perceive life insurance sales as difficult and time-consuming and requiring more aggressive selling than that typically necessary in the marketing of property/liability products. Some perceptions commonly held by property/liability agents include, among other things, that (1) life insurance sales take place mostly at night and on weekends, (2) life sales activity keeps agents out of the office a great deal of the time, and (3) life insurance commissions do not provide a good income for the necessary effort involved. These perceptions create a significant deterrent to those property/liability agents considering the addition of life products to their portfolios. Such perceptions must be overcome in order for all-lines marketing to be successful. In addition to the perceived requirements of the life insurance sales process itself, many of the independent property/liability agents may fear that certain practices normally associated with the life sales environment (most importantly, the exclusive representation of a single insurer or group) will lead insurers to exercise greater control over these agents, thereby diminishing their independence.

Doubts and fears of a comparable nature exist in the minds of many life insurance agents when contemplating the sale of non-life insurance products. The marketing of property/liability coverages by agents who previously were involved only in life and related insurance sales is a totally new experience. The sale of non-life products may be perceived to require additional client contact, more attention to service (including claims handling) and updating of policy information, and result in less time available for sales efforts. Life-only agents may be reluctant to engage in the time-consuming service activities required by property/liability insurance coverages, and they may hesitate to undertake the additional state-imposed examination and training requirements necessary for obtaining a license to sell property/liability products.

Additional Agent Training and Education Expenses

Even if an agency force does not object to selling all lines of insurance, their inexperience with a new selling environment must be considered and appropriately addressed. Considerably greater breadth of insurance knowledge is required if an agent is going to handle all lines of insurance. Without a doubt, substantial additional funds must be committed to agent training, education, and licensing when marketing all lines of insurance.

Problems Particular to Life Insurer Entry into All-Lines

Established life insurance companies face particularly bothersome problems when entering the property/liability field. First, they face direct regulation and approval of property/liability rates in many states. This is a new and frustrating experience since life companies historically have not been subject to premium rate regulation. A second obstacle to life insurer entry into the all-lines marketplace is that there is no consensus on the proper method of determining the rate of return for property/liability companies.[7] Hence, it may be difficult to assess whether the entry into property/liability operations constitutes a sound financial decision for the life insurer. In addition, variability from year to year of underwriting profits (or losses) in the property/liability business may result in large loss ratios in the first few years of property/liability operations and, in turn, require substantial transfer of amounts of capital and surplus from the life insurance company.

Incompatibility of Products and Consumer Markets

Additional drawbacks include the possible incompatibility of the products and consumer markets, and the possible existence of a fundamental difference between the psychological makeup and character of agents who effectively sell life insurance and those who effectively sell property/liability insurance. Further, there are substantial differences in the very nature of the life insurance and property/liability insurance businesses:

1. The long-term nature of the life risk is totally different from the short-term nature of the property/liability risk.
2. The variation and the legal complexity of the contracts themselves are considerably different between the two fields of insurance.
3. There is one-time underwriting and, at most, one-time claims servicing in the life business versus periodic underwriting and the likelihood of substantial repetitive claims service activities in the property/liability business.

Other Resistance Stemming From Change

Finally, a certain level of resistance to any significant change(s) will always be encountered in an organization or industry due to a perceived threat to an individual's security. Change creates uncertainty about an individual's future role in the company. It leads to the scrapping of plans or courses of action already in the process of being implemented. To many people change is unwelcome, creating additional time pressures and further taxing their abilities. Even after the decision has been made to proceed with an all-lines marketing approach, significant resistance may persist from a few key executives. If so, the project may be doomed to failure; at a minimum, the effectiveness of the all-lines effort will be seriously impeded.

In summary, even with a substantial infusion of funds into a new all-lines marketing operation, it is still likely to take a minimum of five or ten years, or

---

[7] Steven W. Forbes, "Rates of Return in the Nonlife Insurance Industry," *Journal of Risk and Insurance,* September 1971, pp. 409–422.

even longer, to achieve the desired level of success in the marketplace (whether success is defined in terms of market share, profit level, or some other measure). Taking this into account in conjunction with the weighing of the relative benefits and disadvantages of an all-lines marketing approach, considerable care should be exercised in the decision-making process concerning the entry into previously untapped insurance markets. Although all-lines marketing may be the most desirable approach for one company, the diversification into new insurance markets certainly does not have to be the most appropriate direction for another.

All-Lines Exclusive Agents

The exclusive agent system—the form of all-lines marketing that is the most similar to the career agency system—has been used successfully for several decades in the marketing of life and health insurance products. Further, while large mutual companies such as Prudential, Metropolitan, and John Hancock traditionally have employed the career agency (or career ordinary) distribution system to sell life and related insurance products, their relatively recent entry into property and liability markets via existing field forces would place their all-lines marketing approach into the exclusive agency category. However, since the major features of the distribution system(s) used by these large mutuals have been described in other chapters, this discussion is limited to the characteristics of the all-lines exclusive agent systems employed by those companies (or groups) operating in the all-lines marketplace prior to the entry of the large mutual life insurance companies. It is important to note that, in a number of respects, there are substantial similarities in the all-lines marketing approaches of the exclusive agent companies and the large mutual life insurers with property/liability affiliates.

In the discussion below, generalizations, common tendencies, and averages are used in describing the all-lines exclusive agent distribution system to keep the discussion concise. However, because of some differences in the target markets, products sold, agent contract provisions, and operating procedures among the various exclusive agency companies, certain generalized statements may not be applicable to every insurer and its distribution system.

General Description of Exclusive Agents

The early history of the all-lines agent distribution system centered on the recognition by property/liability companies of a "natural" market for life insurance among their existing policyowners. This natural market consisted of insureds who had purchased either automobile and/or homeowners coverage from the company. The marketing strategy during these initial efforts was to provide all lines of personal and family insurance coverages by one company (group) and one agent, thereby increasing the likelihood that the policyowner would come back to that agent when ready to purchase additional insurance.

Two other important factors leading to the development of all-lines exclusive agents are worthy of mention. First, insurers wanted to provide agents with an additional source of income from the sale of other insurance products. Second, insurers wanted to obtain a steady source of income from new lines of insurance to assist in stabilizing the cyclical profit and loss operations inherent in the property/liability industry.

Early efforts in all-lines marketing were concentrated in small towns and rural communities since this market had received relatively little attention for life insurance sales. A substantial portion of the life insurance marketing efforts by the career ordinary agent system had been directed to the more heavily populated urban areas. Today, the all-lines exclusive agent system has matured far beyond its relatively meager beginnings in rural markets. Its impact now is substantial in the large metropolitan and suburban areas as well.

Exclusive Agents' Relationship with the Insurer

Under the traditional exclusive agency concept, insurance business is placed by the agency exclusively with the sponsoring company (group). In fact, under many exclusive agent contracts, the agent is prohibited from selling the products of an unrelated insurer.[8] In honoring the exclusivity of this contractual relationship, the company, in turn, seldom markets its products through brokers or agents of other companies and usually does not circumvent the agent through direct mail campaigns or any other device.[9] Rather, the company's products are marketed through its own agency force. The exclusive agents can feel secure in the knowledge that the company's resources are focused entirely on them. Under this arrangement, the exclusive agents and the company are totally dependent on each other; the agents and company stand or fall together, depending on product quality, service, and price.

---

[8] Certain insurers employing an exclusive agency distribution system allow their agents to broker business with other companies under specified conditions; typically, where the risk has been declined by the exclusive agency company or where the company lacks the necessary product(s) to meet the client's needs.

[9] At least one insurer is now employing a dual marketing distribution system. This company is marketing its products through its exclusive agency force in communities of medium-to-large size and appointing independent agents in the smaller communities where it does not feel there is sufficient business to justify the expenses associated with a full-time exclusive agent.

Insurers distributing their products through an exclusive agency force generally engage in substantial national (or regional) advertising and promotion campaigns directed to the insurance consumer. These campaigns emphasize both company and agent image and the relationship between the two (agent and company).

Other Characteristics of the Exclusive Agent System

Several other general characteristics pertain to the exclusive agent system. First, the agents are considered by most insurers to be independent contractors rather than employees of the insurer. As a result, the agents may determine their hours of operation, the location of the "shop," the particular business methods used, and so forth. Further, as an independent contractor, the agent may hire clerical support, but usually at his or her expense.

However, the exclusivity of this relationship requires additional company responsibilities that may not otherwise exist under an independent contractor status. Since the agent's ability to place coverage is limited to one company (group), it is quite possible that any liability arising out of the acts of the agent will be transferred to the company and the company must be aware of the possibility. Also, since the agent is permitted to sell only the insurance products of this one company (group), it is imperative that the company offer a broad spectrum of such products.

A second generally accepted principle in the exclusive agency system is that the insurance company "owns the renewals." This means that the insurer owns the property/liability business written by the agent, thereby permitting the company, upon termination of an agent, to transfer the business and the commissions payable to a new agent of the insurer's choice. Under the agent's contract, the agent is unable to transfer the business to another insurer. Due in part to this overall concept, the insurance company (rather than the agent) generally provides direct premium billing to the insured, handles routine account maintenance and policy changes, and handles claims from either regional or home office facilities. In general, company-provided assistance to the sales force and greater insurer control over customer accounts is more prevalent in the exclusive agent system than in the independent agent system. Since the company shoulders considerable administrative and service burdens, this marketing system is often characterized by highly successful one-person operations, possibly supplemented by limited clerical support.

Finally, the exclusivity of the relationship between the insurer and the agent allows sales management to emphasize motivation and training of the agent in insurance-selling techniques together with building the agent's image in the community. This can be done because a company need not spend as much of it resources to convince agents of the merits of its products and/or services—a necessary task for an insurer marketing its products/services through the independent agent system.

Profile of the Exclusive Agent Marketplace

Important features of the all-lines exclusive agent distribution system can be described in terms of a comprehensive profile of the marketplace in which the exclusive agent operates. This profile is constructed in terms of the following items: market share, description of the exclusive agent, target market, products sold, and the scales process.

Market Share

All-lines exclusive agent companies have been capturing an increasing share of the total United States ordinary life insurance market. As of December 31, 1979, these companies had approximately $111.0 billion of in-force ordinary business, or 7.0% of the aggregate $1,585.9 billion ordinary in-force for the entire life insurance industry.[10] However, during 1979 the exclusive agent companies sold over $29 billion of ordinary life insurance, representing 9.0% of the total $323.6 billion written.[11] The percentage for the new business written is higher than the corresponding percentage for the in-force business, which is indicative of an increasing market share for the all-lines exclusive agent companies.

Description of All-Lines Exclusive Agents

Nearly 35,000 licensed agents market life insurance through the all-lines exclusive agent distribution system. These agents account for approximately 14% of the full-time sales force in the United States life insurance industry. For many of these exclusive agents, 10% or less of their total earnings comes from the sale of life and health insurance.[12] Although this figure is of rela-

---

[10] *1980 Life Insurance Fact Book* (Washington: American Council of Life Insurance).

[11] *Ibid.* It should be pointed out that these amounts and percentages for the all-lines exclusive agent companies do not include the totals for the large life mutuals who now are operating in the all-lines marketplace. Obviously, if amounts for these companies had been included, the market share figures for the exclusive agent companies would have been of much greater magnitude.

[12] Although there is a relatively small number of companies marketing insurance products through all-lines exclusive agents, there is substantial variation in the life/property earnings mix among the agency forces of these companies. For example, a number of companies have exclusive agent forces (with 5 or more years of service) whose earnings from life and health insurance sales account for between 20 and 50% of total earnings, and several companies have field forces whose life and health related commission income accounts for more than 50% of total earnings. See *The Manpower and Production Survey, op. cit.*, p. 276.

tively small magnitude, its importance should not be minimized in that a large share of an all-lines agent's total expense of operation is created by and financially sustained through the agent's property/liability insurance base. Thus, to a large extent, any commission income earned by the exclusive agent from the sale of life insurance represents "clear profit" with few additional expenses directly associated with the production of that income.

Typical Commission Arrangements

Agent income from life sales is based on the commission structure. First-year commission percentages payable on life insurance sales typically are lower under the all-lines exclusive agent system than under many of the other agent-oriented distribution systems. Under the exclusive agent system, the typical first-year commission applicable to permanent insurance is 50% compared with a range of 55% to in excess of 100% under other traditional marketing systems.

As is the case under the career ordinary distribution system, the commission structure in the exclusive agent system favors the sale of permanent life insurance products. In contrast to the 50% first-year commission payable on most permanent products, term insurance policies traditionally have carried at most a 30% first-year commission, with some term commission rates as low as 10%.[13] This difference in commission rates becomes even more important when the differences in the premium rates between permanent and term policies are taken into consideration.

One other important aspect of the exclusive agent's commission structure pertains to the relationship between life commissions and property/liability commissions. First-year life commission percentages are higher than first-year property/liability commission rates (e.g., 15% on homeowners insurance). Renewal commission rates, however, favor property/liability products. While both renewal property/liability and renewal life commission rates are lower than first-year rates, the reduction in renewal commission rates for property/liability coverages is not as substantial as the reduction in renewal commission rates on life insurance products. Further, long-run aggregate commissions payable on life insurance are less than those payable on property/liability insurance primarily because of the payment of lifetime renewals (contingent on the individual remaining an agent of the company

[13] The commission structure pertaining to term policies compared to permanent policies is currently under review by both all-lines exclusive agent companies and career ordinary companies. At least one major exclusive agent company currently is in the process of leveling their term and whole life commission rates (probably at 50%) to become effective in 1982. In regard to the future, one might anticipate a greater equality between term and whole life commission rates.

and the business staying on the books) on the property/liability policies. As a result, commission income from life products may not be an effective incentive to increase life sales, and the company therefore may have to provide additional incentives to the agent in order to make life sales attractive. Incentives such as company-paid trips and special awards or recognition are often used with success.

Background and Training of Exclusive Agents

Exclusive agents generally have similar backgrounds. Prior work experience is the norm for all-lines exclusive agent recruits, who tend to be slightly older than the typical new agent in the life insurance business. Also, the majority have had some college education, with a reasonably high percentage possessing a college degree.

Training is an additional factor that characterizes exclusive agents. In a number of ways, the training of exclusive agents is similar to that provided career ordinary agents. Once recruited into the business, the exclusive agent typically receives pre-contract training of a general nature relating to the company and the insurance industry. Some limited attention is devoted to sales techniques. After the agent is contracted, substantial additional training is provided. The initial phase in this training program may last for one to two years. Subsequently, all-lines exclusive agents typically receive advanced and/or refresher course training throughout a major portion of their career. Because of the all-lines approach, emphasis must be placed on teaching product knowledge in both the initial and continuing training programs for the exclusive agent.

Target Market

Presently, there is a massive overlapping of distribution systems in the life insurance marketplace. Almost any of the agent-oriented distribution systems—including the career ordinary, combination agent, all-lines exclusive agent, all-lines independent agent, PPGA, and brokerage distribution systems—serve in multiple-market segments that are delineated primarily on the basis of consumers' income. However, because of general economic conditions (inflation and cost pressures) and the recognition of the value of segmenting markets, companies have begun to concentrate their efforts in more narrowly defined segments of the total life insurance marketplace. Companies using all-lines exclusive agents are no exception in this respect.

The majority of the marketing efforts of all-lines exclusive agent companies (groups) are becoming concentrated in what would be described as the middle-income market.[14] The sale of products to meet basic personal and family insurance needs has been predominant in this market. This is not to imply, however, that the companies employing this distribution system totally ignore the business insurance and estate planning markets. Rather, a number of the exclusive agent companies offer, at a minimum, limited agent training, product design, and services directed toward estate planning and other advanced underwriting markets. It is evident, though, that the major thrust of all-lines exclusive agent companies is centered on the individual consumer with personal insurance needs rather than more complex business and estate planning needs.

Without a doubt, the majority of the life insurance sales made by all-lines exclusive agents is to individuals who already own property/liability policies with the company or affiliate. While, traditionally, many of these sales have taken place in the smaller and/or rural communities, market penetration in larger communities by exclusive agents has increased significantly during recent years.[15] The typical client of the all-lines exclusive agent is an adult male, probably under age 40. A larger percentage of life insurance sales by exclusive agents is concentrated in the skilled labor and farm markets than is the case for the career ordinary life agent.

The middle-income market, consisting of relatively young single adults and families, is expected to grow substantially in the decade of the 1980s. Thus, it is anticipated that all-lines exclusive agents will have a strong market for their products and services for the years to come.

Products Sold by Exclusive Agents

The products sold by the exclusive agent system relate to the typical structure connecting the property/liability insurer with the life insurer. The life insurance company normally has been organized on a stock basis with the

[14] Inflation and an ever-increasing tax burden (arising from a progressive income tax) will influence substantially the types of life insurance products sold in this market. Low levels of discretionary income, coupled with needs for large amounts of life insurance protection, likely will dictate the purchase of low-premium forms of life insurance, e.g., term insurance. Therefore, it is probable that the commission income from life products alone will be insufficient to support full-time agents in the middle-income market. Rather, it is likely that the sale of life insurance products in the middle-income market will have to be made by agents who receive part of their income from the sale of other insurance products, e.g., property/liability.

[15] Because of the additional marketing of property/liability products, it has been possible for all-lines exclusive agent companies to market life insurance successfully in these less populated areas while life-only distribution systems require more heavily populated areas in order to achieve the necessary level of market penetration to support financially their agency systems.

outstanding stock owned wholly or principally by the parent mutual property/liability company. As such, the stock life insurer, in many ways, may act like a mutual company. The life insurance products marketed under this distribution system are primarily participating in that dividends may be payable to policyowners in addition to the payment of any stockholder dividends. Certainly, there are notable exceptions to this statement in that one or two of the major insurers sell only nonparticipating life insurance.

In the marketing of property/liability coverages, the exclusive agency approach is primarily a system of distributing personal lines of insurance (e.g., automobile and homeowners) to the individual and family markets. To complement the property/liability lines, packaged life insurance plans are developed which are geared toward an average consumer with personal needs rather than tailored to a specific client with business needs. These packaged life insurance plans normally consist of both permanent and term coverages (for example, family policies that provide permanent life insurance on the breadwinner and term coverage on the spouse and children). A major advantage of the packaged sales approach is its simplicity of presentation. This is extremely beneficial to an agent whose orientation is primarily property/liability lines and who has less familiarity with the life insurance product.

While the overall term/permanent product mix for the entire collection of exclusive agent companies is comparable to the product mix for the life insurance industry as a whole, it appears that the term/permanent mix for individual companies within this distribution system is related to company size. Term insurance for the larger exclusive agent companies typically accounts for about 65% of the total new volume of ordinary life insurance written as contrasted with approximately 50 to 55% for the entire industry.[16]

---

[16] Possible reasons for this relatively high percentage of term insurance include:

a. The short duration of term insurance makes it more similar to property/liability coverages than is permanent life insurance.

b. The property/liability agent is more oriented toward the sale of "pure risk" insurance. The general absence of cash values in term insurance places the term product in the "pure risk" category.

c. In addition to family policies, mortgage life insurance (a decreasing term product) traditionally has been a widely sold product in this market. The sale of this product can be tied in to the sale of the homeowners policy (a property/liability product). It is important to note that in today's inflationary economy, more and more companies are selling level-term to cover mortages.

d. Inflation may have a greater erosive effect on the capacity of consumers in the middle-income markets, i.e., those served by exclusive agents, to pay the higher unit premiums associated with permanent insurance.

In regard to the smaller companies employing this distribution system, their product mix generally is slanted more toward permanent insurance.

In spite of the significance of term insurance in the exclusive agent marketplace, substantial emphasis is also placed on the sale of permanent life insurance products. Reasons for this emphasis may include the desire for better persistency associated with permanent products and the potential that the buyer of permanent insurance will become a lifelong client of the agent.

While the major product emphasis under this marketing system is on personal lines of insurance, most exclusive agent companies do offer group life insurance products to small-sized groups. Further, these insurers offer tax-qualified individual life insurance and annuity contracts to the small corporate pension, H.R. 10, and IRA markets. Large groups constitute a relatively untapped employee benefits market for these insurers since the insurers and their agents, for the most part, are not selling commercial property/liability insurance to large business firms. In addition to group life insurance and tax-qualified individual life insurance and annuities, some exclusive agent companies sell credit life insurance through affiliated financial institutions.

The Sales Process

The sales process in the all-lines exclusive agent distribution system centers on the agent's ability to sell and service insurance coverages that collectively meet all of the prospect's personal and family needs. Life and non-life insurance products are marketed in conjunction with each other, in a complementary fashion, to construct a total insurance program for the client. Further, under this system, usual prospecting problems faced by life-only agents are reduced or eliminated in that the life sales presentation simply becomes an extension of the property/liability interview. The periodic servicing contacts relating to property/liability insurance coverages provide the all-lines exclusive agent with opportunities for additional sales of life and health insurance; and, in addition, the sale of a life insurance policy to a new prospect may open the door for collateral sales of property/liability products.

Comparison with Life-Only Agents

It is interesting and informative to compare certain observed traits of the all-lines exclusive agent system with those of the traditional career ordinary life insurance distribution system. Such items as agent retention rates, average policy size, lapse rates, production volume, and agent income are all worthy of examination.

Agent Retention

In general, the survival rate for all-lines exclusive agents is vastly superior to that of life-only agents. The four-year retention rate for all-lines exclusive agents is three times the approximate 15% retention rate for career ordinary agents.[17] As expected, there are widespread differences in the retention rates among individual exclusive agent companies just as there are substantial differences in these rates among individual career ordinary companies.

Average Policy Size

Because of the personal lines emphasis and the lesser penetration of business life insurance and estate planning markets, the resultant average policy size for the all-lines exclusive agent marketing system is smaller than the average face amount policy sold by career ordinary life agents.

Lapse Rates

All-lines exclusive agents typically market life insurance to lower income segments than do career ordinary agents. Because of a less affluent clientele and possibly other reasons (such as differing mix of business including a higher proportion of term insurance, agent's selling all product lines, and agent's writing the life coverage just for trips/awards), the average lapse ratios for all-lines exclusive agent companies generally are slightly higher than the overall industry lapse ratio.[18] However, several exclusive agent companies have lapse ratios that are quite low when compared to the industry average.

Production Volume

Data on the dollar volume and the number of new sales suggest that all-lines exclusive agents have a higher "level of activity" than do life-only agents. For example, according to LIMRA statistics, in 1977 the average life insurance production of second-year all-lines agents was over $700,000 from an average of 40 life sales.[19] This is in contrast to a slightly higher average of $912,000 of production volume from an average of 53 sales for second-year life-only agents. However, the typical second-year all-lines exclusive agent,

---

[17] *The Manpower and Production Survey, op. cit.,* p. 1. See also *The Manpower and Production Survey, Ordinary and Combination Companies—Calendar Year 1978* (Hartford: Life Insurance Marketing and Research Association, Inc.).

[18] For 1979, the median lapse ratio on ordinary business for the 150 largest life insurance companies was 9.3%. The median lapse ratio computed for a subset of seven exclusive agent companies was 9.7%. See "Lapse Ratios on Individual Business," *Best's Review, (Life and Health)* (Oldwick, New Jersey: A.M. Best Co., Inc.), September 1980, pp. 42–43.

[19] *The Manpower and Production Survey, op. cit.,* pp. 1–2.

in addition to his or her life sales, sold approximately 260 new property/liability policies. For all exclusive agents in 1977, the average number of total new sales was 350, with 30 of these representing sales of life insurance. In contrast, all career ordinary agents, on average, produced 52 new life sales during 1977.

Agent Income

All-lines exclusive agents, on average, earn larger amounts of gross commissions than do life-only agents. Further, renewal commissions constitute a greater share of total commission income for all-lines agents than is the case of career ordinary agents.[20]

All-Lines Independent Agents

The independent agent distribution system, also known as the American Agency System, is primarily a system for marketing property/liability coverages, accounting for approximately 65% of property/liability premiums written in the United States.[21] As such, many of its characteristics relate to its activities in the property/liability insurance business. Although the independent agent system has made a significant contribution to the life insurance business in the past, and it continues to do so, its main orientation is to the property/liability industry. Thus, in addition to addressing the subject of life insurance sales and the independent agent, the following discussion also will relate, to a great extent, to the independent agent's role in the property/liability insurance arena.

General Description of Independent Agents

The beginnings of the independent agent system in the United States go back at least 150 years. A number of changes have occurred in the system over the years, but it has enjoyed strong growth for much of this period. More recently, however, a significant challenge to the future of the independent agent system has been presented by all-lines exclusive agent companies, the entry of major life insurers into traditional property/liability insurance markets, and companies marketing property/liability coverages on a direct basis. Independent agents find themselves in an increasingly competitive environment with these other distribution systems.

Two factors have contributed to independent agents' increasing awareness of the need to make additional life insurance sales. First, as inroads

---

[20] *1980 Survey of Agency Opinion* (Hartford: Life Insurance Marketing and Research Association, Inc.).

[21] William B. Lusk and Douglas T. Hibbard, "The Independent Property-Casualty Agent Distribution System," *CLU Journal*, January 1981, p. 11. See also "Insurance Premium Distribution 1979," *Best's Review (Property/Casualty)*, July 1980, pp. 12–14.

have been made into their income from sales of personal lines property/liability coverages (and to a lesser extent, their commercial lines), and independent agents have turned to life sales as an additional source of income.[22] Second, in order to compete more effectively with direct writers on a cost basis, many agency companies have reduced their commission rates in recent years. Life insurance sales can provide for increased revenues without significantly increasing the agency's costs. Today, most life insurers recognize the important role that the independent agent can play in the marketing of life insurance. As a result, life sales by independent property/liability agents account for some production in most life companies. Further, sales of life insurance through this distribution system account for the major source of production in several life insurers.

A major objective of the marketing strategy employed in the all-lines independent agency system is to offer a full range of insurance products—both personal and commercial property/liability coverages as well as life insurance and related products—although the offering of life insurance products must be considered secondary at this time. Because of the wide variety of products offered, independent agent shops are often referred to as **general insurance agencies** (not to be confused with general agencies).

Representation of Several Companies

A significant feature of this marketing system relates to the concept of independence resulting from agent (agency) representation of several unrelated insurance companies (as opposed to representation of only one company or a group of related companies). The objective of multi-insurer representation is to enable the agent to choose the "best" coverage at the "best" price for the client. Thus, through multiple-company representation, the independent agent offers competing insurance products of various companies. It is typical, however, for the independent agency to have a strong relationship with one primary property/liability carrier with which it places a substantial volume of business.

The independent agent is considered to be an independent contractor. The agency is responsible for its own operating expenses that are paid from commissions earned. In addition, independent agents often have their local own advertising programs directed toward the consumer. These advertising campaigns are separate from any insurer advertising and promotional activities. Further, they usually emphasize individual agent image and recognition rather than insurer identification.

---

[22] Some experts believe that selling life insurance products has become a matter of survival for the independent agent.

Advertising

There is a noteworthy difference in the orientation or direction of the advertising and promotion campaigns of exclusive agent companies and that of independent agency companies. The close tie between the agent and company in the exclusive agent system is not present in the independent agency distribution system. In the majority of instances, an individual purchasing insurance through an independent agent perceives himself or herself to be a customer of the independent agency rather than the insurance company. This significantly affects insurer advertising efforts. If an insurer wants its products to be sold by independent agents, it must have an advertising program that persuades independent agents to market that insurer's products/services. Therefore, the advertising message of agency companies must be directed toward the independent agent rather than the ultimate consumer of the insurance product. As a result, much of the advertising by agency insurers appears in the insurance trade press. It is important to note, however, that in recent years several agency companies have been devoting a significantly greater portion of their advertising budgets to promotional campaigns aimed directly at the consumer.

Service Responsibilities

Because of the direct relationship between the insured and the independent agent, the insured generally looks to the agent for performance of all service needs. This has a great impact on the continuing service responsibilities of the independent agent. The office staff of the agency must be trained and prepared to handle a significant volume of service-related activities and procedures. The service role of the independent agent sometimes includes financing the client's premium payments that have gone unpaid. The availability of these premium financing arrangements, however, is likely to be limited to the more important clientele of the agency (as measured by premium volume and/or other criteria). The underlying rationale for agency premium financing relates to the traditional insurer practice of billing the agency for the property/liability premiums due. The independent agency, in turn, would bill and collect the premiums from the policyowner. If the client was late in remitting the premiums, the agency might temporarily finance the premium in order to avoid a gap in the client's insurance protection. Today, in order to relieve the agency of some of its administrative and service burdens, and, in addition, to develop a more competitive rate, a number of insurers have devised direct premium billing systems applicable to automobile and homeowners insurance.

Ownership of Renewals

Possibly the most important characteristic of the independent agent system in comparison with the exclusive agent system is the independent agent's "ownership of renewals or expirations" on property/liability business. Ownership of renewals by the independent agency means that the agency owns the business written, owns the customer files, and controls the renewal of the policies through selection of the particular insurance company where the business will be placed. The insurer has no right to provide renewal data and information on an insured to another agent. Probably the most significant implication of agency ownership of renewals is the pressure on the insurer to pay renewal commissions at the same level as first-year commissions. If the insurer should attempt to pay lower commissions on renewal, the independent agent may decide to place the policy with another carrier in order to receive a commission at a first-year level. In direct contrast, since the exclusive agent cannot transfer client accounts to another insurer, the company is able to pay a reduced commission on renewals.[23] This difference in commission rate structure between the exclusive agent and independent agent distribution systems produces differing levels of emphasis on new business production versus retention of existing business. Under the exclusive agent system, the production of new property/liability volume is crucial to maintaining the agent's present earnings level, since a significantly reduced commission rate may be payable on renewals. On the other hand, with a level first-year and renewal commission scale, the independent agent places greater emphasis on the retention of existing accounts.

Profile of the Independent Agent Marketplace

In describing the all-lines independent agent system, it is beneficial to examine the profile and structure of the independent agent marketplace. In this context, such features as market share, description of the independent agent, target market, products sold, and the sales process will be explored in constructing the overall profile.

Market Share

Most independent agencies have a large number of personal and commercial lines clients, possibly numbering in the thousands. These clients are contacted by the agent on a relatively frequent basis to determine general service needs, handle claims, and so forth. These regular contacts provide great

[23] Not all exclusive agent companies pay lower commissions on renewal. State Farm, for example, currently pays level first-year and renewal commissions on homeowners and automobile policies.

opportunities for the sale of life insurance. In spite of the nearly unlimited potential for life sales through this distribution system, the best estimates indicate that the amount of life insurance directly written by independent property/liability agents accounts for only 9% to 12% of all life insurance sales.[24] Thus, it must be concluded that the life sales potential in the independent agent distribution system remains substantially untapped.

Description of the All-Lines Independent Agent

Dramatic changes have taken place in the profile of independent agents (and agencies) over the last ten to fifteen years. The number of general insurance agencies today is approximately 62,000–65,000.[25] This number is well below those in operation a decade or so earlier.[26] However, in terms of the aggregate premium volume written, today's agency, on average, is larger than the independent agency of ten years ago. The smaller number of agencies and larger average agency size can be partly explained by the relatively high number of agency mergers during this time period. Other observed trends relating to the operations of independent agencies include a larger percentage of total premium volume accounted for by commercial lines business (approximately 50% today), as well as a smaller number of clients per agency. Further, a significantly increased percentage of the independent agent's personal lines property/liability insurance is now directly billed from the insurer (as opposed to agency billing of the premiums).

The independent agent profile can be generalized with reference to the typical or average (median) independent agency. Of course, no single independent agent or agency fits exactly the composite profile presented here.

The independent agency consists of two major types of producers: principals (those with an ownership in the agency) and solicitors (salespersons employed by the agency who possess no ownership interest). The typical agency has a total of three producers made up of principals and solicitors.[27]

---

[24] *Life Insurance and the Independent Property and Casualty Agent,* Research Report 1978-5 (Hartford: Life Insurance Marketing and Research Association, Inc.), p. 2. As this report points out, this range of percentages most likely underestimates the volume of life business originated by independent agents in that many of these agents have referral arrangements with full-time life insurance agents.

[25] F. Chandler Coddington, Jr., "Membership Development—IIAA Committee Reports," *Independent Agent,* October 1979, p. 91.

[26] As an illustration, in 1973 it was estimated that there were 75,000 independent agencies in operation in the United States. See "Profile of the Independent Agent," *Independent Agent,* January 1973, pp. 19–23.

[27] *Independent Agent* conducts biennial surveys of independent agents and agencies. The major results of the latest of these studies is reported in "Portrait of the Independent Agent," *Independent Agent,* January 1981, pp. 32–38. This article is the source of much of the statistical information that is presented in this section.

In addition, this agency has an office staff of three employees. Over the past several years, there has been a trend toward having the office staff perform certain in-office sales functions (e.g., selling personal automobile and homeowners coverages over the phone).

The agency may be organized as a sole proprietorship, partnership, or corporation. Approximately three-fourths of the independent agencies are incorporated. Under any of these arrangements, the independent insurance agency and its block of property/liability business (including the right to service, renew, and receive compensation on the business) can be sold to another agency. In contrast, under the exclusive agent system such sales cannot take place since the exclusive agent does not "own the business written."

The median independent agency had a total premium volume in 1979 of $650,000. More than 60% of the agencies had a premium volume between $300,000 and $2.5 million; 30% of the agencies had a premium volume of over $1 million.[28]

Approximately 80% of the independent agencies are marketing ordinary life insurance products.[29] Slightly fewer than one-half of the agencies are selling group life insurance, and about one-fifth are marketing group pension products. The agencies not selling life insurance products tend to be smaller (in terms of both premium volume and number of producers) on average than those marketing life insurance. In 1979, for those independent agencies writing life insurance, the median annual face amount written was about $300,000.

Representation of Insurers

Another salient feature of the independent agent profile pertains to the number of property/liability insurers and life insurers represented by the general insurance agency. The best estimates place the typical number of property/liability companies represented by an agency at six.[30] In spite of the several insurers represented, approximately 50 to 55% of the typical agency's personal and commercial lines business is placed with a primary carrier (although this insurer is not necessarily the same for both personal and commercial lines business). The percentage of business placed with a primary carrier appears to be a function of the size of the agency, with somewhat smaller percentages going to the primary carrier in larger agencies. The average general insurance agency also represents two to four life companies,

---

[28] *Ibid.*, pp. 36, 38.
[29] *Ibid.*, p. 38.
[30] *Ibid.*

with probably at least one of these affiliated with a property/liability insurer represented by the agency. Independent agents also typically have a primary carrier with which a majority of the agency's life business is placed. Many times, especially in the smaller-to-medium-sized agencies, this primary life carrier is the affiliate of one of the property/liability insurers represented.

In regard to an independent agent's choice of which property/liability insurers to represent, the most important selection criteria include prompt service, stable markets, fast claim service, and complete underwriting. In choosing life insurance carriers, the three most important criteria named by independent agencies are competitive rates, insurer-provided technical sales assistance, and a broad life product portfolio.[31]

Compensation of Independent Agents

The final element of the independent agent profile concerns the structure of the compensation system applicable to the sale of life products. As a result of the intense competition for the life production of independent agents, the overall compensation structure offered by the dominant life brokerage companies is liberal. In fact, although the relative importance of the individual components may differ, the total compensation package typically made available to independent agents is analogous to that granted career ordinary agents. Comparable commission rates and expense allowances generally are included in the total package. Further, as inducements to increase life production, the independent agent normally is provided the opportunity to qualify for sales contests, trips, awards, and other special prizes. In addition, the agreement between the insurer and the agent (agency) may provide for (a) persistency and/or production bonuses; (b) fully vested renewal commissions; (c) service fees payable after expiration of renewal commissions (possibly on the condition that the agent meets a minimum production requirement and actively provides policyowner service); and (d) commission overrides if the agency possesses a general agent (usually PPGA) contract and meets certain minimum production requirements. A major difference between the contracts offered to independent agents and those offered to career ordinary life agents pertains to agent financing plans: the brokerage life companies do not make available financing plans to independent agents.

In spite of the seemingly favorable contracts offered independent agents for selling life products, the total amount of commission income resulting from life sales is small due to the relatively low volume of life production. For

[31] Stuart V. D'Adolf, "Who is the Independent Agent?", *Independent Agent*, January 1979, p. 26. See *Life Insurance and the Independent Property and Casualty Agent, op. cit.* for a more extensive discussion of the selection criteria used by independent agents in choosing life insurance carriers to represent.

the typical independent agency in 1977, life insurance-related income amounted only to about $4,000.[32]

Target Market

The typical independent agency, or general insurance agency, is located in a medium-sized community of around 50,000 in population but with a total relevant market area (including the surrounding smaller communities and rural areas) of close to three times that number. About one-fourth of the agencies serve communities of fewer than 10,000 residents, with another one-fourth serving communities with a population of 150,000 or more.[33]

The client contacts and relationships established through commercial property/liability sales encourage life insurance sales by independent agents to individuals who are older and wealthier, on average, than the clients of either life-only agents or all-lines exclusive agents. As a result, the life insurance purchases made through the independent agent system are generally large, in response to the client's business insurance and estate planning needs. Even though the independent agent distribution system, like the exclusive agent system, seems to concentrate much of its life sales efforts in the middle-income market, independent agents, to a greater extent, tend to make their sales to individuals in the higher-income strata of this market.

Products Sold

In the independent agent distribution system, property/liability coverages comprise the bulk of the insurance products marketed. The independent agent system distributes a substantial volume of both personal and commercial forms of property/liability insurance.

Because independent agents have access to many companies and their products, the life and related insurance products that they sell are generally the same or similar to the products sold through other systems of distributing life insurance. Certainly, though, the life insurance product mix, (for example, term/permanent mix) in the independent agent system may vary somewhat from the mix sold in other life insurance distribution systems. Limited available data make it difficult to ascertain the overall term/permanent product mix for life insurance sales made through the independent agent system. Further, the term/permanent product mix varies widely with each specific independent agency and its clientele.[34] Presumably, the greater the percent-

---

[32] Stuart V. D'Adolf, *ibid.*, p. 25.

[33] *Ibid.*

[34] To some extent, it is possible for the life insurer to control product mix through campaigns and other special incentives and through differing commission scales.

age of the agency's life insurance clients who are owners of small to medium-sized businesses, the greater the percentage of permanent life insurance sold, since permanent products are better suited for business insurance, estate planning, and retirement needs.

The independent agent's contacts with numerous small business firms established through the handling of their commercial property/liability accounts create great opportunities for the marketing of group life insurance products. A number of independent agencies have taken advantage of this opportunity and, today, sell significant amounts of group life insurance.

Some individuals believe that an independent agent can respond more quickly to product changes in the life insurance marketplace than an exclusive agent. This belief is due to an independent agent's wider choice of companies and products. When a new and/or competitive life product comes out, an independent agent has the opportunity to market it almost immediately, regardless of the issuing company, as long as that company accepts brokerage business.[35] However, an exclusive agent is not permitted to place business with other competing insurers and must wait until such time as his or her own company may develop and market the product.

The Sales Process

The majority of the independent agent's new property/liability business comes from referrals and social contacts. Naturally, most of the prospects for life sales result from the agent's review of current client files.

There are primarily three approaches to the marketing of life insurance in a general insurance agency. These include (1) one or more (or all) of the agents in the agency producing life business on a part-time basis to complement the sale of property/liability products; (2) a full-time professional life insurance producer housed in the agency; and (3) an arrangement with an outside life insurance agent or brokerage representative who personally sells the client the needed life insurance coverage(s). Full-time life insurance producers are found primarily in the larger independent agencies. Smaller agencies generally use either of the two other approaches.

Advantages to Insurer of Marketing Through Independent Agents

A number of important advantages accrue to an insurer that distributes its life insurance products through independent agents. This distribution system requires only minimal entry costs and, overall, is a cost-effective way to market life insurance. Life business generated under this system generally

---

[35] In order to "protect" their own career agency forces, some life companies do not accept brokerage business from other agents.

has relatively low acquisition costs when compared with other marketing systems, primarily because the sales agency is already formed and in place. Additionally, in the independent agent system the responsibility for noncommission expenses is placed on the agent (agency) rather than the insurer. Under this distribution system, there are no "new business" acquisition costs (for example, financing, clerical and office support) prior to the placement of such business.

A second major advantage inherent in this distribution system relates to market penetration. The presence of 60,000-plus independent agencies (with approximately 200,000 producers) already in operation allows for more immediate and substantially greater penetration of life markets by those insurers opting for this distribution system. It would take a life insurer many years, at substantial development costs, to expand a captive agency force that would achieve the desired higher levels of life market penetration that can be attained relatively quickly through the existing independent agent system.

Third, the life production of independent agents has reasonably good persistency. In fact, the persistency of the life business written by these agents possibly is better, at least during the most important early years of the policy, than the persistency of the business written by life-only agents.

A final advantage, related somewhat to the first one discussed, is the potential lower unit costs associated with the sale of life products under this system when compared with certain other distribution systems. Lower costs per $1,000 of face amount are made possible because of the larger face amount sales typically produced in this system. The greater orientation toward commercial property/liability accounts provides significant opportunities for large business insurance, pension, and estate planning sales.

Perceptions Concerning the Future

It is anticipated that in the future, all-lines agents will become an increasingly significant force in the marketing of life and related insurance products, especially in the middle-income markets. Great potential certainly exists for the further entry of life insurers into traditional property/liability insurance markets. Inflation alone, and its effects on increased marketing and distribution costs, may provide sufficient incentive for life companies to lower unit production costs by spreading these costs over a larger base.

Additional challenges to the independent agent system and a continuation of the overall trend of increased competition in property/liability agents' traditional markets will likely increase these agents' needs for new income sources. Finding additional related sources of income may be a matter of necessity in order for many of these agents to survive in the insurance business.[36]

The aforementioned reasons, together with aggressive insurer marketing strategies and additional company emphasis and financial incentives placed on life production, are likely to lead to substantial increases in the volume of life insurance produced by all-lines agents. As the overall success of the all-lines agent climbs to higher plateaus, this will tend to compress the intrinsic separation that exists today between the property/liability industry and the life and health insurance industry.

Summary

The development of all-lines marketing has expanded the traditional realm of agency distribution. This system, in which an agent is responsible for the sale and servicing of both life and nonlife insurance products, allows consumers to have all of their insurance needs served by one agent. This chapter described the characteristics of the two categories of all-lines agents—exclusive agents and independent agents. The various reasons an insurance company (either life and health or property/casualty) would be interested in diversifying to all-lines marketing were discussed, as well as the advantages and disadvantages of such diversification. The specific target markets of and products sold by all-line agents were presented.

---

[36] The continued viability of the independent agent system has been challenged on many fronts over the past several decades. Many agency companies continue to believe that the independent agent distribution system is a good one. With this belief, these insurers should be willing to provide additional means of support to the independent agencies. One example of additional support would be company financing (partially or totally) of the non-sales staff in the offices of such agencies.

Note: The section of this chapter dealing with exclusive agents is based partly on "Multiple Line Exclusive Agent Distribution Systems," Earle B. Johnson, William H. Convoy, R. J. Davis, Charles R. Right, an unpublished study sponsored by LIMRA.

Chapter 13

Fraternal and Savings Bank Life Insurance

John E. Stinton, D.B.A., CLU

Life insurance in the United States and Canada is issued by several types of insurers and marketed through various distribution systems. Although most life insurance is issued by commercial companies using distribution systems described elsewhere in Part III, a substantial amount is sold by fraternal benefit societies and savings banks. This chapter discusses the marketing systems used by these two types of insurers.

Fraternal Life Insurance

Life insurance provided by fraternal benefit societies to their members is known as fraternal life insurance (FLI). FLI includes various types of term and permanent policies and riders that are similar in many ways to commercial insurers' contracts. The characteristics that distinguish FLI result from the distinctive features of fraternal benefit societies.

Fraternals are nonprofit social organizations, organized and carried on solely for the benefit of members and their beneficiaries, and having a lodge system and a representative form of government. As social organizations, they provide through local lodges a variety of educational, recreational, and benevolent activities for members, such as scholarships, orphans' programs, senior members' residences, and cancer grants. The members of local lodges elect members to represent them and their interests in meetings at the state and supreme lodge levels. As insurers, fraternals assume risks of premature death and disability of their members, and are regulated as insurance carriers under state insurance statutes. Thus, the lodge system and the social benefits for members distinguish fraternals from commercial insurers.

The first fraternal in the United States was established in 1868 when the Ancient Order of United Workmen was organized in Meadville, Pennsylvania.[1] FLI grew rapidly during the next several decades for three main reasons. First, the fraternal approach was one way to make life insurance more readily available to lower-income people who often were not attracted to or solicited by the commercial companies. Second, the panic of 1873 and the subsequent depression resulted in a number of failures of commercial life insurance companies. Third, level-premium life insurance and the associated reserve concept were under attack in several respects. Premium rates were thought to be excessive and, in view of the failures, there was widespread misunderstanding and suspicion concerning the function of the reserve. The fraternals claimed that reserves were unnecessary and that FLI was safer and more reasonable. Under these circumstances, FLI flourished, and by 1895 the amount in force approached the amount of ordinary insurance in force in commercial companies.[2]

The amount of FLI in force continued to grow through 1919 to a peak of $9.3 billion, then steadily declined to $5.5 billion in 1941. Since 1941 the volume of FLI in force in the United States and Canadian fraternals increased gradually to $58.3 billion at the end of 1980; however, this amount represented only about 3.3% of the individual life insurance in force in the United States and Canada. In terms of individual life insurance purchases in 1980, FLI amounted to 2.4% of the total.[3] Although FLI no longer represents a significant portion of individual life insurance sold annually and in force, students of life insurance marketing should understand the characteristics of FLI and the fraternal system of distribution.

Characteristics of Fraternal Life Insurance

During their early development, fraternals operated on an assessment basis; however, as the inherent problems associated with assessment insurance became evident, fraternals gradually shifted to a system of level premiums and reserves of the type used by commercial companies.[4] Today the major

---

[1] Richard deR. Kip, *Fraternal Life Insurance in America* (Philadelphia: College Offset Press, 1953), p. 32.

[2] Ibid., p. 11.

[3] *1981 Life Insurance Fact Book* (Washington, D.C.: American Council of Life Insurance), pp. 12, 18, and 102.

[4] Initially fraternals levied the same assessment on all members, regardless of age; however, as the average age of the membership increased, increasing assessments were required. And even though fraternals then began to grade assessments according to age at entry or increased each member's assessment as he grew older, adverse selection occurred as young

portion of FLI written and in force is on a level-premium, legal reserve basis and regulated under state insurance laws based upon the Uniform Fraternal Code developed by the National Fraternal Congress of America (NFCA) and adopted by the National Association of Insurance Commissioners (NAIC). The NFCA is a federation of fraternal benefit societies writing life or disability insurance or both; all members of the NFCA operate on a legal reserve basis. Of the approximately 100 member societies, the six largest fraternals account for more than 80% of all FLI, and the other member societies account for most of the balance.

In many respects the insurance sold by fraternals resembles insurance written by commercial insurers. The leading fraternals offer a variety of permanent and term policies, as well as the typical waiver of premium, accidental death, guaranteed insurability, and term riders. Many also offer individual annuities; however, group insurance is not sold, and variable life and variable annuities are rarely provided. All contracts are participating with the typical dividend provisions. Many other provisions are similar to those found in commercial policies, but because fraternals provide both social and insurance benefits, a "certificate of membership and insurance" also includes the rights and privileges of membership in the society.

Open Contract

One unique feature of FLI is its use of an open contract. This means that the fraternal's constitution and bylaws are included by reference in the contract between the fraternal and the member. Although the constitution and bylaws refer mainly to the structure and administration of local lodges and the duties of various officers, any amendments or changes, including improvements in benefits, in effect, alter the provisions of the insurance certificate. This feature, together with the mandatory "maintenance-of-solvency" clause, permits the board of directors, in the event of insolvency or pending insolvency, to assess the certificate holders. In contrast, commercial insurers use a "closed contract," and in case of insolvency or significant reserve deficiency, the company must reinsure, merge with another company, or be forced into receivership. In effect, the closed contract must be "opened" by agreement between the parties or by the court so that appropriate liens may be levied, because the policyowners cannot be assessed.

Both commercial companies and fraternals operating on a legal reserve basis may encounter financial difficulties due to higher than expected mortal-

healthy members withdrew in response to premium increases. For a discussion of the assessment system and the transition of fraternals to the legal reserve system, see Richard deR. Kip, Chapter V, and S. S. Huebner and Kenneth Black, Jr., *Life Insurance,* 9th ed. (Englewood Cliffs, New Jersey: Prentice-Hall, Inc., 1976) pp. 476–77.

ity, failure of investments, or for any other reason. A basic difference, however, is the manner of restoring solvency. Fraternals contend that the open contract/assessment procedure is quick, simple, and inexpensive and permits fraternals to guarantee benefits because an assessment can be levied if it is essential to solvency, whereas commercial companies with their closed contracts can guarantee premiums but cannot really guarantee benefits.

Tax Exemption

Exemption from federal income tax and state premium tax is another distinctive characteristic of fraternals. This favorable tax treatment is justified on the grounds that fraternals are nonprofit social organizations that perform a variety of charitable and benevolent activities through the lodge system. That such activities are a primary purpose is supported by the fact that some fraternals permit social memberships without insurance benefits, while others require members to be both social and "beneficial" members. Invariably those fraternals that consider the insurance benefits an integral part of total benefits have a rather well-developed field staff that aggressively solicits insurance sales. While the statutes require that all members belong to a local lodge and that only lodge members may be insured, almost anyone can become a member of some fraternals by purchasing insurance. In these cases, some people question whether favorable tax treatment is justified.

Today the distribution system of some fraternals is quite similar to that of commercial companies. The more aggressive fraternals develop new business through an agency system, but some still solicit new members and insurance through local lodge officials or salespersons rather than through agents.

Distribution of Fraternal Life Insurance[5]

As noted earlier, the amount of FLI in force in United States and Canadian fraternals at the end of 1980 was $58.3 billion, of which $9 billion was purchased in 1980. These amounts represent approximately 3% of all individual life insurance in force in the United States and Canada and 2.4% of individual life insurance purchased in 1980.[5] These and comparable figures for 1955, 1960, 1965, 1970, 1975, and 1978 are shown in Table I. FLI in force increased fivefold from 1955 through 1979 and the amount purchased in 1979 was three and one-half times that in 1965. However, FLI represents about 3% of all individual life insurance, and its market share is gradually declining.

[5] Much of the information in this section was obtained from a report dated April 13, 1977, prepared for LIMRA by Edward A. Merten, Senior Vice President-Marketing Operations, Aid Association for Lutherans.

TABLE I

Comparison of Fraternal Life Insurance with Ordinary and Industrial Insurance in the U.S. and Canada

Selected Years	Fraternal Life Insurance (billions $)	Total Ordinary and Industrial Insurance (billions $)	FLI as % of Total Ordinary and Industrial
1980			
Insurance Purchased	8.916	374.38	2.38
Insurance in Force	58.306	1,796.46	3.24
1978			
Insurance Purchased	7.548	311.70	2.42
Insurance in Force	49.084	1,603.18	3.06
1975			
Insurace Purchased	5.495	214.30	2.56
Insurance in Force	37.319	1,221.30	3.06
1970			
Insurance Purchased	3.562	138.65	2.57
Insurance in Force	24.377	833.00	2.93
1965			
Insurance Purchased	2.257	97.40	2.32
Insurance in Force	16.316	582.69	2.80
1960			
Insurance in Force	14.235	411.93	3.46
1955			
Insurance in Force	10.507	276.52	3.80

Source: *Life Insurance Fact Book* (Washington, D.C.: American Council of Life Insurance, annual).

This loss of market share has been attributed to the aggressiveness of commercial insurers and to a decline in the relative importance of the lodge system as a social institution.

Since only members of the fraternal society can buy FLI, the market potential for FLI is limited by any self-imposed membership requirements. Some fraternals restrict membership to certain ethnic, religious, or occupational groups; others cater to the general public. Where Lutheran Church membership, for example, is a requirement, the market potential in the United States is about nine million people. On the other hand, the potential market of the "general" fraternals is the entire population of the areas in which they operate. However, the NFCA reports that fewer than 4% of all insured people in the United States are covered by FLI, and fewer than 3% of individual life policies issued each year are sold by fraternals.[6]

Marketing Strategy

The marketing strategy of the typical fraternal has been solicitation of new members and package selling of family-type protection and juvenile policies to the middle- and lower-income groups. In more recent years, there has been increasing emphasis, especially by several of the larger fraternals, on programming, capital needs analysis, estate planning, and the pension and business insurance markets. These larger fraternals have developed field organizations of career agents whose promotional methods and sales efforts parallel those of agents of commercial insurers. However, for many of the smaller fraternals, officers or other employees of local lodges solicit memberships and sell insurance, usually on a part-time basis. Because fraternals attract members from all walks of life with widely varying ages and levels of income, they are not likely to concentrate their marketing efforts on any particular market segment although they often insure classes of people who are not called upon by agents of commercial companies.

FLI is marketed through a variety of distribution systems, including several forms of agency systems, lodge officers secretaries, and direct selling by home office personnel. The more aggressive fraternals, twenty to twenty-five of the members of NFCA, have field forces of full-time career agents and field management personnel similar to the agency systems of commercial companies. Variations among fraternal agency systems include use of general agents, managers, personal producing general agents, full-time and part-time agents, and brokers. Because of the membership requirement, brokerage business is limited to fraternals that cater to the general public. It is estimated that the fraternal agency system includes some 11,500 career agents and field management people, plus approximately 2,500 part-time agents. Nonagency fraternals rely upon an estimated 3,500 local lodge officers to solicit and service insurance in addition to their other responsibilities.[7] According to Merten, "an increasing number of fraternals are viewing the distribution of their insurance products and services as being best accomplished through the agency system rather than through . . . [the

[6] Merten, pp. 3–4.

[7] *Ibid.*, p. 7.

nonagency system].''[8] Merten also says, ''Any gain in the penetration of the total market will likely be dependent upon the extent those 70 to 75 societies who now do not have a career sales staff will aggressively develop one, and the extent the 20 to 25 societies who now operate in this manner continue to grow.''[9]

Invariably, fraternals require their sales personnel to be members of the society they represent. Aside from this requirement, the qualifications are much the same as those required by commercial companies. In the selection of career agents, agency fraternals often use such tools as aptitude and psychological tests, interviews, and evaluation of educational credentials and work experience. Selection standards of nonagency fraternals normally are somewhat lower, because these people often solicit and service insurance only on a part-time basis. In most states individuals involved in the sale of FLI must be licensed and meet the same requirements as anyone else licensed to sell insurance in that state. The training and education of career agents in fraternals and commercial companies is also very similar. Many fraternals have formal training programs in which home office schools supplement training provided by the general agent or manager. Career agents and field management personnel also are encouraged to complete the formal courses leading to the Fraternal Insurance Counselor (FIC) designation, and to participate in CLU study in order to increase their skills and professional competence. It is estimated that in 1980 more than 250 CLUs and 500 CLU candidates represent the five largest United States fraternals.

Compensation of Agents

In order for fraternals to attract and retain sales personnel with the desired qualifications, compensation must be competitive. Thus, it is not surprising that the methods of compensating career agents of agency fraternals are quite comparable to those used by commercial companies. Commissions are by far the most common. The following commission schedule, as a percentage of the annual premium for an ordinary life certificate, is typical: 65% the first year, 20% the second and third years, 10% the fourth year, and 2% thereafter. It is also fairly typical for fraternals to make additional payments based upon such factors as production, persistency, and length of service. For new agents, some have financing plans, such as a monthly advance or level income plan, while others merely annualize commissions. It should be noted that fraternals sometimes have considerable flexibility concerning compensation because, as nonprofit societies, frequently they are exempt from the expenses limitations of state insurance laws (New York's Section 213, for

[8] *Ibid.*, p. 13.

[9] *Ibid.*, p. 5.

example). The compensation package of many fraternals also includes such fringe benefits as pension plans and group life and health insurance, as well as participation in local advertising and other sales support activities. Incentive or recognition programs such as sales conferences, contests, and "clubs" are also common.

A variety of compensation methods are used by nonagency fraternals, including commission, salary, a flat fee per new member, a premium collection fees, and combinations of these methods. Commission schedules similar to the one above are common, as are fees up to $10 for each new member or 5% of all premiums collected. The method of compensation tends to reflect the extent of the lodge officers' responsibilities in the insurance and in the fraternal areas.

All of the usual methods of prospecting are used in selling FLI—cold canvass, centers of influence, referred leads, direct mailings, and radio and newspaper advertising. In addition, fraternal agents and representatives have the opportunity to contact members at local lodge meetings and other fraternal functions, and to advertise and solicit inquiries in lodge magazines and other mailings to members. Thus, mutual membership in the lodge provides many natural sales or service contacts. Because of these contacts, continuing service and "orphan policyowner" problems are not as common as they are among commercial companies. The extent to which policyowner service is provided by local agents and representatives varies considerably, especially between agency and nonagency fraternals.

Trends in Fraternal Life Insurance

In 1953 Richard deR. Kip wrote, "[Fraternalism] started with the assumptions that insurance need not cost much and that the fraternal ties would be priceless. Both assumptions have had to be altered."[10] FLI adopted the level-premium legal reserve system, and although the local lodge has not been eliminated, it is no longer the important social institution it once was.[11] Nevertheless, FLI in force increased fivefold over the next twenty-five years, with most of the increase attributable to changes that caused much of FLI and its distribution to resemble life insurance sold by commercial companies. Despite this absolute growth, the FLI share of the individual life insurance market is relatively insignificant and gradually declining, as Kip implied. Any slowing or reversal of this trend is likely to depend upon the extent to which other members of the NFCA develop agency systems built around career agents and agency managers similar to those of the larger fraternals and commercial companies. And there is evidence of growing

[10] Kip, pp. 182–83.

[11] *Ibid.*, p. 182.

interest among quite a number of NFCA members in development of career-type agents in contrast to part-time nonagency personnel, expansion of education and training programs, and emphasis upon needs selling rather than package selling. On the other hand, the role of nonagency fraternals undoubtedly will continue to diminish.

Savings Bank Life Insurance

Although over-the-counter sale of low cost life insurance by savings banks was suggested by Elizur Wright as early as 1874, savings bank life insurance (SBLI) did not become a reality until 1907 when Massachusetts passed the first law authorizing the establishment of a system of SBLI. Similar legislation was enacted in New York in 1938 and in Connecticut in 1941; however, none of the other states that have mutual savings banks has enacted similar proposals. Thus, for persons who reside in or are regularly employed in Massachusetts, New York, or Connecticut, SBLI is an alternative to life insurance that is sold and serviced through the other distribution systems described in Part III.

Origin and Purpose

The original purpose of SBLI was to make available through savings banks moderate amounts of life insurance protection at a considerably lower cost than weekly premium industrial insurance. Louis D. Brandeis, who led the battle for SBLI in Massachusetts, believed that prudent people, on their own initiative, would go to the nonprofit savings banks and buy low cost life insurance protection. And he thought the banks could offer lower prices because they would pay no agents' commissions and because of lower lapse rates among policyowners who would buy voluntarily instead of under sales pressures.

Despite strong opposition from life insurance agents and companies, laws authorizing SBLI eventually were passed in Massachusetts, New York and Connecticut. However, many of the issues in those early debates remain unresolved and are still being argued by proponents of various competing methods of marketing life insurance. By the end of 1980, there was about $13.3 billion of SBLI in force in the three states combined. Although this figure represents only 6.7% of the total ordinary life insurance in force in these three states, SBLI has been growing rapidly and consistently increasing its market share in terms of both insurance purchased and in force. Furthermore, only five or six companies have more ordinary in force in New York and Massachusetts than the savings banks.[12] Thus, in today's environ-

---

[12] Market share data are shown in Table II and are discussed in a later section of the chapter.

ment of consumerism and regulation, the record of this nonagency method of distribution has considerable social and economic significance for students of life insurance marketing. It is from this background and perspective that the marketing of SBLI is examined.

Characteristics of SBLI

The three SBLI systems offer various term, whole life and endowment contracts, as well as family and juvenile policies. The policies are issued by savings banks that have established life insurance departments. The laws permit banks to participate either as issuing banks or as agency banks. In Massachusetts there are now 53 issuing banks and approximately 150 other banks that act as agencies for the issuing banks. In New York there are 67 issuing banks and about 65 agency banks; in Connecticut the numbers are 12 and 45. In Massachusetts the maximum amount of SBLI on one life is $1,000 times the number of issuing banks, and the maximum allowable in one bank is $15,000. However, an individual wanting to buy more than $15,000 need not go to more than one bank, because the originating bank, acting as agent for the other banks in the system, can handle the entire application. In New York the amount on any one life is limited to $30,000; the entire amount may be written by one bank in a single policy. The maximum amount on an individual in Connecticut was raised from $5,000 to $10,000 on January 1, 1978 and again was increased to $15,000 on January 1, 1981—whether in one or more policies.[13]

In each state, overall administration of the system is in the hands of a central organization that provides actuarial, underwriting, and other services. Thus, all issuing banks in a given system use the same rates and policy forms. In a sense, then, each system is similar to a single life insurance company; however, each issuing bank is an independent unit that issues its own policies. Insurance may be written only on persons who reside in the state or are regularly employed there. This approach restricts the operation of each system to one state, although policyowners who leave the state may continue their insurance.

Over-the-Counter or Direct Mail Sales

SBLI is sold only over-the-counter or by mail. This restriction prohibiting use of soliciting agents was intended to minimize acquisition costs. As a practical matter, however, some of the functions of agents are performed by

[13] Over the years, statutory limits have been increased. In 1977 the constitutionality of the New York law was upheld in a suit by Consumers Union challenging the $30,000 maximum and the provision restricting sales to persons living or working in the state.

bank employees and by the banks and central organizations through their promotional efforts. And, although issuing banks may not use soliciting agents, each system has a sizeable number of agency banks throughout the state that accept applications for insurance and provide policyowner service. Thus, in the words of one authority, "The savings bank life insurance program, although it is referred to as an over-the-counter or nonagency movement, does not, in the true sense of the word, function without the use of agents. In reality, it has substituted the brick and mortar of an immobile bank building for the flesh and blood vitality of a salesman, hoping through mass outlets and continuous use of advertising media to offset the mobility, persistency, and persuasiveness of the life insurance company agent."[14] The marketing and administrative activities of both issuing and agency banks are described later in this chapter.

Types of Policies

The three SBLI systems offer the types of policies with terms and provisions that are typically offered by commercial life insurance companies. A brochure promoting SBLI in New York lists the following contracts: straight life; 5-year renewable term; 20-payment life; 20-year endowment; life paid-up at 65; endowment at 65; 20-, 25-, and 30-year decreasing term policies; family plan; and children's policies.[15] Group insurance is available in all three states, and in Massachusetts and New York annuities are also available. The same legal reserves are required of SBLI as those required of other legal reserve insurers. All policies are participating with the usual dividend options. In contrast to most policies of commercial insurers, "all SBLI plans pay dividends, as earned, starting the very first year . . . [and] except term insurance . . . have guaranteed cash and loan values at the end of the first year."[16] According to a senior executive with the New York Savings Banks Life Insurance Fund, " . . . 65% of SBLI sales [in New York] are term policies."[17]

Policy Issue

SBLI policies are issued by savings banks that are authorized by the state to conduct the business of life insurance. As noted earlier, each issuing bank is an independent unit that issues its own policies; however, in each state a

[14] Donald R. Johnson, *Savings Bank Life Insurance* (Homewood, Ill.: Richard D. Irwin, Inc., 1963), p. 134.

[15] "A New Consumer's Guide to Low Cost Life Insurance," The New York SBLI Fund, No. 34, 4/76.

[16] *Ibid.*, p. 14.

[17] "New York's SBLI Fund Rebuts Critical Study," *The National Underwriter,* Life and Health Insurance Edition, April 17, 1976, p. 20.

central organization provides for all participating banks most of the home office functions of an insurance company with the possible exception of the investment function. Applications received by issuing and agency banks are forwarded to the underwriting department of the central system. When an application is approved, the issuing bank issues the policy and forwards it to the agency bank for delivery to the policyowner. Premium notices and dividend checks are sent by the issuing bank to agency banks to be delivered to policyowners. The agency banks collect premiums; a popular premium payment plan authorizes the bank to deduct premiums regularly from savings accounts. Agency banks also provide all policyowner services, including policy loans and policy changes. For these services agency banks are paid a small percentage of premiums collected.

Rapid Growth

In its early days, SBLI was subsidized, directly or indirectly, by the states and by the banking departments of participating banks. However, according to McGill, "these . . . subsidies are no longer in effect, and the three systems . . . are self-supporting."[18] Even without subsidies, SBLI "prices generally have been lower than those of other legal reserve insurers."[19] Advocates of SBLI contend that savings banks can charge lower prices because they pay no soliciting agents' commissions and they have lower lapse rates. It is claimed that SBLI policyowners buy on their own initiative and, therefore, are less likely to lapse their policies. There is considerable evidence that lapse rates for SBLI are substantially lower than those for the industry; however, according to an actuary for the New York Savings Banks Life Insurance Fund, banks that place considerable emphasis on life insurance sales tend to have higher lapse rates than the other banks, and New York metropolitan area banks generally have higher lapse rates than upstate banks. Another factor contributing to lower prices is lower overhead charges, even though insurance departments of savings banks bear proportionate amounts of the banks' housing, clerical, and other overhead expenses.

Claims that SBLI prices and costs are low are confirmed by recent studies based upon the interest adjusted method (IANC) of comparing the costs of similar policies. Although the rankings vary somewhat with type and amount of policy, age of issue, and sex, Massachusetts SBLI and New York SBLI consistently ranked among the four or five lowest-cost $25,000 policies in the

[18] Dan M. McGill, *Life Insurance*, rev. ed. (Homewood, Ill.: Richard D. Irwin, Inc., 1967), p. 803.

[19] Robert I. Mehr, *Life Insurance: Theory and Practice*, rev. ed. (Dallas: Business Publications, Inc., 1977), p. 690.

Consumer Reports study.[20] In the New York State Insurance Department's 1977 study of companies licensed in New York, the New York SBLI's interest adjusted indexes generally ranked among the two or three lowest cost policies.[21] Similar evidence of the low cost of SBLI can be found in *Best's Flitcraft Compend* and *Interest-Adjusted Index* published annually by A. M. Best Company and The National Underwriter Company, respectively.

The Market for SBLI

At the end of 1980, the amount of SBLI in force was about $13.3 billion. In Massachusetts and New York, it represented more than 7% of the total ordinary life insurance, while in Connecticut it accounted for 4.4%. In terms of sales in 1980, SBLI's share of the market was 6.1% in Massachusetts, 2.5% in New York, and 2.1% in Connecticut. These figures, as well as data for 1965, 1970, 1975, and 1978 are shown in Table II. Table III compares average annual compound rates of growth from 1970 through 1979 in SBLI purchases and amounts in force with growth rates in ordinary business in each state. These data show that SBLI represents a small but rapidly growing share of the market. No doubt the rapid growth in New York is due to extensive advertising and promotion campaigns, and the rates of growth in Connecticut are distorted by the increased limit on coverage that became effective on January 1, 1978. Some people also attribute this rapid growth to increasing cost-consciousness among insurance buyers.

Advertising and Promotion Efforts

From the very beginning the strategy for selling life insurance over-the-counter has been to have large numbers of outlets and low prices. In more recent years the strategy has also included advertising and promotion efforts by the individual banks and central organizations. As the statutory limits have increased, the SBLI market has expanded to include all types of customers. Today, according to recent surveys, "Buyers of SBLI do not differ from other life insurance buyers in terms of their personal and background characteristics. The only difference appears to be that the buyer of

---

[20] *Consumer Reports,* February 1980, pp. 94–96, 105; and March 1980, pp. 176–178, 184–85. Connecticut SBLI was not included because the smallest face amount in the study, $25,000, exceeded the $10,000 maximum in Connecticut. Also the next larger face amount, $100,000, exceeded the maximums in Massachusetts and New York.

[21] *Consumers Shopping Guide for Life Insurance,* 1977. Again the rankings varied somewhat with age of issue, sex, type and amount of policy, between 10-year and 20-year indexes, and between payment and cost indexes.

TABLE II
Savings Bank Life Insurance and Ordinary Life Insurance in Connecticut, Massachusetts, and New York (millions)

	Connecticut			Massachusetts			New York			3-State Total		
Selected Years	SBLI	Ord.	SBLI as % of Ord.	SBLI	Ord.	SBLI as % of Ord.	SBLI	Ord.	SBLI as % of Ord.	SBLI	Ord.	SBLI as % of Ord.
1980												
Ins. Purchased	$ 118	5,641	2.1	$ 496	8,161	6.1	$ 615	24,080	2.5	$ 1,229	37,882	3.2
Ins. in Force	1,275	28,662	4.4	3,128	41,756	7.5	8,941	126,788	7.1	13,344	197,206	6.7
1978												
Ins. Purchased	248	4,055	6.1	172	5,883	2.9	607	17,845	3.4	1,027	27,783	3.7
Ins. in Force	1,005	23,794	4.2	2,552	35,214	7.2	7,713	108,304	7.1	11,270	167,312	6.7
1975												
Ins. Purchased	84	2,486	3.0	142	4,528	3.1	557	14,323	3.9	783	21,697	3.6
Ins. in Force	617	18,835	3.2	2,156	29,015	7.4	5,441	92,458	5.9	8,214	140,308	5.9
1970												
Ins. Purchased	13	2,009	0.6	119	3,365	3.5	118	11,116	1.7	320	16,490	1.9
Ins. in Force	127	13,990	0.9	1,512	21,325	7.1	2,477	72,806	3.4	4,116	108,121	3.8
1965												
Ins. Purchased	6	1,311	0.5	90	2,179	4.1	148	7,395	2.0	244	10,885	2.2
Ins. in Force	84	9,641	0.9	1,072	14,973	7.2	954	54,860	1.7	2,110	79,474	2.7

Source: *Life Insurance Fact Book* (Washington, D.C.: American Council of Life Insurance, annual).

TABLE III
Average Annual Compound Rates of Growth of SBLI and Ordinary Life Insurance Connecticut, Massachusetts, and New YORK 1970 through 1979

	Connecticut	Massachusetts	New York
Savings Bank Life Insurance			
Purchases	44.5%	4.7%	15.8%
In Force	29.5	6.8	15.3
Ordinary Life Insurance			
Purchases	9.2	7.2	6.1
In Force	6.9	6.5	5.1

Source: Computed from data in *Life Insurance Fact Book* (Washington, D.C.: American Council of Life Insurance, annual).

SBLI somehow recognizes the need for life insurance and acts to fill this need.''[22]

It was reported at a LIMRA Research Planning Conference in 1979 that, in spite of media advertising, about 25% of SBLI buyers said they first heard of SBLI from family or friends. Another 25% stated that they were first exposed to SBLI through pamphlets available in the banks. Low cost was cited most frequently as the reason for buying SBLI, convenience ranked second, and freedom from having to deal with a life insurance agent ranked third. Nearly half stated that they had never seen a life insurance agent prior to their SBLI purchase, and another 25% said they had not seen an agent during the two years prior to purchase. Also it was noted that many SBLI sales are made to individuals whose perceived need for life insurance was stimulated by an agent through programming, but the agent failed to keep in touch with them following the sale of a portion of the programmed amount. Information about age, sex, and ''previous ownership'' of recent SBLI purchasers shows that about one of every three policies is written on an adult female and that the proportion has been increasing, the proportion of policies

---

[22] Walter H. Zultowski, ''Who Buys Savings Bank Life Insurance (SBLI)?'' *Managers Magazine,* September 1979, p. 12.

covering juveniles has been declining rather steadily, and a substantial portion of adults owned no life insurance at the time of SBLI purchase.[23]

The actual sales of SBLI are made over-the-counter by personnel of the insurance department of issuing and agency banks. The size and qualifications of the staff of the department tend to vary with the size of the bank and the relative importance assigned to the insurance operation by the bank's top management. In a small agency bank that offers insurance primarily as a convenience for its banking customers, the life insurance business may be handled as a collateral duty by a single employee, whereas a large issuing bank no doubt will have a staff of personnel trained to assist prospective buyers in the selection of the amount and type of policy and to provide continuing service to policyowners. In New York, but not in Connecticut or Massachusetts, individuals involved in the sale of SBLI must be licensed. As stated in promotional brochures, "The personnel who serve you in New York State have taken the same State-sponsored examination as anyone else licensed to sell insurance in this state. Our SBLI specialists are at the bank every banking day to provide continuing service to policyholders."[24] The New York Savings Banks Life Insurance Fund conducts training programs to help these individuals prepare for the licensing examination. Also both New York and Connecticut offer seminars and classes for personnel of the insurance departments of participating banks. These and other advanced training programs are designed to increase the level of competence of SBLI sales and service personnel that in 1980 included thirty-two CLUs and thirty-eight CLU candidates in the three states.

Employees of savings banks are salaried; however, a variety of incentives are used to get regular bank employees, as well as employees in the insurance department, to submit names of people who might be interested in SBLI and to encourage them to buy. In addition to salaries, contests and trips are offered as incentives to stimulate the sale of life insurance. Thus, even though no commissions are paid, the compensation system encourages and rewards production. The rapid growth of SBLI during the 1970s probably was due to such other factors as extensive advertising, inflation, and increased limits, not to the methods used to compensate the sales force. Although the large number of employees of savings banks in the three states represents a sales force with great potential for continued growth, the prob-

---

[23] The information in this paragraph was obtained from Zultowski, p. 12, and from an unpublished LIMRA report on SBLI prepared by Paul W. Thayer. Also see Johnson, Chapter 10 and Appendix A for data for the 1950s and early 1960s.

[24] "A New Consumer's Guide," p. 14.

lem is "to overcome the lethargy and lack of enthusiasm of many savings bankers and bank employees . . . especially in the many agency banks in which little SBLI activity is created."[25]

Cooperative promotional programs in the name of SBLI system include newspaper advertising and radio and television commercials. Much of the growth during the 1970s in SBLI, especially in New York, is attributed to the increased use of television.[26] The advertising and promotion programs of the banks themselves include distribution of promotional literature at bank counters; pamphlet inserts in regular mailings to bank customers; direct-mail campaigns targeted at such specific groups as depositors, new parents, and recent graduates; promotion among existing policyowners, including requests for names of others who might be interested in SBLI; and use of the telephone for new sales and for follow-up work. In short, all of the usual advertising and promotional media are employed in an effort to reach potential buyers of SBLI. The record to date suggests that extensive and continuous promotion is essential in order to market life insurance over-the-counter.

Problems of SBLI

Critics of SBLI argue that any savings to policyowners resulting from elimination of agents are more than offset by the loss of such vitally important services as analysis of needs, programming, and estate planning. It is true that services provided by many agency banks are quite limited and may amount to little more than processing applications and policy change forms; however, the larger issuing banks that account for a large percentage of total business typically have trained personnel who provide assistance and recommendations in the areas of needs analysis and the amount and types of policies. To the extent that SBLI is bought in limited amounts, sophisticated estate and tax planning and capital needs analysis probably are unnecessary.[27] And to the extent that buyers are acting upon recommendations of agents who failed, for whatever reasons, to make initial or follow-up sales, limited services may be entirely adequate. Also the mere fact that soliciting agents are paid sales commissions is no guarantee that their clients need or receive better advice and service than that provided by bank personnel. Thus, there appears to be a place for this system of marketing life insurance

[25] Johnson, p. 142.

[26] See "SBLI's View of the Advertising Picture," *The National Underwriter*, Life and Health Insurance Edition, April 9, 1977, p. 2.

[27] According to Ray E. Mauger, Jr., "the average amounts of SBLI straight life policies [purchased in 1975 in New York] were $6,308 for women and $11,378 for men." These figures suggest that sophisticated planning probably is not necessary. See "New York SBLI Fund," footnote 17.

just as there are different channels for the distribution of many other goods and services.

Continuing service can be a problem for policyowners who move out of state. However, this geographic problem is common to policyowners of any regional company. Such services as beneficiary changes, policy loans, and death claims are generally handled by mail or telephone, although agents of commercial companies undoubtedly provide assistance to SBLI policyowners as well as to policyowners of other companies.

The difficulties and the challenge involved in marketing life insurance over-the-counter are implicit in the following quotation taken from a sales brochure: "To take advantage of this low-cost protection, you must make the next move. If you are interested, you have to ask about it as we do not employ outside sales personnel."[28] In an effort to create interest and motivate potential buyers to "make the next move," extensive and continuous advertising and promotion programs are used by the central organizations in all three states as well as by the individual banks.

The Future of SBLI

In 1962 Donald Johnson wrote, ". . . there does not [now] or in the immediate future, appear to be any real possibility of expansion of the savings bank movement."[29] Fourteen years later, Theodore Fuller, president of the New York Savings Banks Life Insurance Fund, said, "SBLI is in a strategic position to directly benefit from all of these trends. You might even say, SBLI is an idea whose time has come."[30] As the basis for his optimism, Fuller cited such general developments as "consumerism, inflation, the emergence of new customer groups, and the retail approach to selling." In the opinion of the author of this chapter, these changes, in conjunction with a number of specific trends of the late 1970s and early 1980s, will result in a continuation of the rapid growth of SBLI in the three states during the 1980s.

Continuing pressure can be expected from consumer groups for further increases in limits, despite opposition from agents and companies and despite the 1977 court decision in New York upholding the constitutionality of the $30,000 maximum. Pressure can also be expected for a change in the provision of the law that restricts sales to persons living or working in New York State.[31] Proponents will argue that higher limits are necessary because

---

[28] "A New Consumer's Guide," p. 14.

[29] Johnson, p. 229.

[30] Theodore Fuller, from a speech made at an SBLI executive meeting in New York, June 1976.

[31] See footnote 13.

of rapid inflation and that agents are interested only in protecting their market share. Consumerists also can be expected to push for cost disclosure, which undoubtedly will encourage savings banks to expand their television advertising with emphasis on "low-cost protection." And the increasing cost-consciousness among insurance buyers, attributable to publicity concerning improved methods of cost comparisons and recent reports on life insurance costs and rates of returns, would seem to favor the SBLI system. There appears to be some increase in the number of issuing and agency banks and the number of people involved in the distribution and promotion of SBLI. There is also some evidence of increasing concern about the quality of training of these people and development of programs to upgrade their competence.

On the other hand, there is little evidence to refute Johnson's observation of "general apathy of savings bankers toward the program, [and] there has been no mid-twentieth century disciple to champion the Brandeis cause."[32] Apparently there is also little interest in legislation to authorize establishment of SBLI systems in the other states that have mutual savings banks. The small amount of SBLI in force occasionally is cited as evidence of the difficulties involved in nonagency marketing of life insurance—an intangible that typically is "sold, not bought." The question is whether SBLI has been unable to achieve a substantial share of the market because the savings banks do not employ soliciting agents or whether they have been prevented from doing so by the opposition of agents and companies to legislative changes that would permit expansion.

Summary

Fraternal and savings bank life insurance offer consumers alternative means of purchasing life insurance. While their respective market shares for individual insurance are small, both systems constitute important topics in a discussion of life insurance distribution systems. This chapter has presented the characteristics of the market for and the typical products sold in connection with these two systems.

---

[32] Johnson, pp. 229–30.

Chapter 14

Home Service Marketing

Robert A. Marshall, Ph.D., CLU

As this text shows, a variety of life and health insurance products exist, and a variety of marketing methods are used to make these products available to the public. Some products are sold by agents to people at their homes or places of business. Others are sold as a result of advertisements in newspapers or direct mail solicitations. Some are sold in conjunction with employment, and some in connection with loans or other credit transactions.

In addition to product and marketing variety, insurers employ various premium payment systems designed to maintain insurance coverage in force. Some premium payments are mailed to the insurance company; others are made in person by the policyowner at a local office. Still other policyowners authorize premium payments through their own bank accounts or through salary deduction plans authorized at their place of employment. Premiums for some insurance are paid directly to an insurer's agent who comes periodically to an insured's home. Each premium payment system is designed to serve the needs of differing groups of customers.

Debit, combination, industrial, and home service are terms which have been used (erroneously in some cases) to describe the marketing system in which the insurance sale, premium collection function, and other servicing of life insurance products take place in the home of the insured. Home service, the most recently used term, most aptly describes this distribution system.

The home service method of marketing, which encompases the products and the premium payment system associated with it, is an example of a life insurance marketing strategy designed to provide insurance coverage and maintain that coverage for a defined segment of the insurance buying market. This chapter will analyze the characteristics of the home service marketing system and the products and services which are provided to the public through the system.

Background of Home Service

The Industrial Revolution in eighteenth century England was the environment into which industrial insurance, a traditional home service product, was introduced to provide for the individual life insurance needs of the growing working class of wage earners. Similarly, the post-Civil War industrialization in the United States produced the opportunity for introduction of the industrial insurance product and the home service marketing system for its distribution in the United States. John F. Dryden, the father of industrial insurance in the United States, saw in the Industrial Revolution an ideal opportunity for development of the mechanism to provide individual insurance protection for working class Americans. By late 1875, the Prudential Friendly Society (later to become the Prudential Insurance Company of America) was established and operational as the first home service organization in this country.

The traditional rudiments of a successful marketing strategy have always stressed product, price, presentation, and place. Without doubt, the introduction of the home service marketing system and industrial insurance at this point in America's economic development utilized this marketing strategy. Existing life insurers of the day were not providing insurance protection for wage earners. Industrial insurance contracts were small in size and consistent with the needs of the wage-earning insured. The pattern of weekly premium payments was tailored to the wage patterns of workers. The sales presentation was made in person by agents who lived and worked in the same areas as their clients, and the products and services (including weekly collection of premiums at the insured's home) were delivered to the home of the buyer.

The marketing strategy first implemented in 1875 filled a need. In 1876, the Prudential was the only company offering industrial insurance and had 4,800 contracts in force with a total face value of $443,000. Ten years later, there were three insurers in the marketplace with 1.7 million contracts in force representing $197 million of face value. By the turn of the century, 18 companies had 11 million industrial contracts in force for almost $1.5 billion of insurance in force.[1]

The home service system has provided an increasing variety of insurance products to lower- and middle-income families for over one hundred years in the United States. By 1978, 135 companies offered industrial life insurance; one of every four life insurance agents worked under the home service system, and the companies they represented had assets totalling more than

---

[1] *Home Service Marketing of Life Insurance,* (Washington, D.C.: The American Council of Life Insurance, February 1980), p. 7.

$90 billion, or 23% of the total assets of life insurance companies in the United States.[2]

In the course of the century it has been in existence, the home service system as a whole has undergone numerous changes. New products have been added to the portfolio marketed through the system, and new procedures have been instituted to develop more operational efficiency. However, the degree to which specific insurers have participated in adopting these changes varies markedly. At one extreme some insurers, operating principally in the southeastern United States, still confine their operations exclusively to industrial insurance with few, if any, operational modifications. At the other extreme, some insurers have not only adopted many new products, but have entirely deleted from their product portfolios some or all of the products once specifically identified with the home service system. Many of these have developed significant modifications in their operations.

Characteristics of the System

The variation in rate of participation in change in the home service system by individual insurers has been noted. Thus, it is doubtful that identification of any one set of descriptive characteristics of the system will be acceptable to all insurers.

The products sold through the home service system and the procedures followed in the system are designed primarily to serve the individual insurance needs of the lower- to middle-income segment of the market. Specifically, many of these insureds do not have checking accounts and thus may need the weekly or monthly visit of a life insurance agent to assist in cash remittance of premiums and a review of insurance needs. As levels of family income increase and checking accounts become more common, many home service agents have begun to sell more than just the traditional debit (or industrial) products.

Within this marketing system, **debit** refers to a home service agent's assigned geographic territory or assigned block of policyowners. The term "debit" originated in the agent's role in the premium accounting function. In the traditional home service accounting system, the agent is debited with all premiums due on the territory and is credited for those premiums when they are collected and remitted to the home office. While a number of home service companies have automated the field accounting system, the prime responsibility for premium accounting on debit products still remains with the agent, and the use of the term "debit" persists.

---

[2] *Ibid.*

In the traditional sense, the home service system incorporates the following features:

1. Assignment of every contract to an agent for service;
2. Territorial grouping of policyowners for assignment to the agent (i.e., specified territorial alignment);
3. Home service to the policyowners, including premium collection and policy services such as policy loans, claims payment, policy changes, and sales services;
4. Agent compensation for home services rendered through collection commissions, service commissions, debit expense allowances, and conservation commissions;
5. Mass field accounting for premium payments by the agent in the field;
6. Close and personal supervision of the agent who has the status of a company employee.[3]

It has been suggested that many of these features are more reflective of the products traditionally sold through the debit system than of the system itself. These distinctions will become clear with further elaboration about home service products.

Home Service Products

Insurance products distributed through the home service system include life insurance, accident and health insurance, auto insurance, homeowners insurance, and fire insurance. Some of the specific product lines are unique to the home service system; others are not. Two categories of insurance products, industrial life and health insurance and monthly debit ordinary life and health insurance, are distributed solely by the home service system because of their sales and service requirements. Interestingly, however, a number of home service companies sell one, but not both, of these products.

Regular ordinary life and health insurance, as well as some small group cases, are marketed through the home service system. According to LIMRA, for the year 1976, 43.6% of total home service agents' volume sold was regular ordinary business as opposed to the more traditional debit products.[4] This is indicative of the recent trend toward more ordinary life and health insurance sales through the home service marketing system.

The trend toward the sale of more ordinary products as opposed to

---

[3] Robert A. Marshall and Eli A. Zukay, *The Debit System of Marketing Life and Health Insurance* (Englewood Cliffs, New Jersey, Prentice-Hall, Inc., 1975), p. 9.

[4] C. A. Craig, II, "Remarks on Behalf of the Life Insurers Conference, Before the Senate Judiciary Antitrust Subcommittee," March 16, 1979, p. 1.

industrial products in the home service system is further emphasized by the mix of traditional home service products in force in United States companies. Table I indicates a noticeable trend toward the increase in monthly debit ordinary in force as compared to a decline in industrial insurance in force. Thus, in the aggregate, home service companies are producing more ordinary business—both regular ordinary and monthly debit ordinary—and less industrial business.

Industrial Life and Health Insurance

The first class of insurance that is uniquely associated with the home service system is industrial insurance. Industrial insurance is typically defined by state laws as that form of life and health insurance for which premiums are payable weekly—or for which premiums are payable monthly or more frequently—and for which the amount of insurance is $1,000 ($2,000) or less.

TABLE I
Home Service Life Insurance in Force
U.S. Life Insurance Companies
(000,000 omitted)

	Monthly Debit Ordinary		Industrial	
Year	No. of Policies	Amount	No. of Policies	Amount
1970	33	$73,569	79	$39,179
1971	33	77,974	77	39,708
1972	33	81,867	77	40,455
1973	34	84,760	76	41,087
1974	34	87,785	72	39,877
1975	34	91,985	71	39,825
1976	34	98,135	68	39,574
1977	34	102,307	67	39,418
1978	34	106,461	65	38,444
1979	35	111,537	63	38,211

Note: Totals represent all life insurance in force with U.S. companies (including both direct business and reinsurance acquired, and without deducting reinsurance ceded), whether the policyholders are residents of the U.S. or of some other country. Data for monthly debit ordinary are included in the aggregate data for ordinary on pages 17–28 of the source.

Source: *1980 Insurance Fact Book,* American Council of Life Insurance, Washington, D.C. 20006, p. 33.

In some states the policies are required to bear the words "industrial policy" or "weekly premium policy" on the contract itself. Thus, industrial insurance is legally recognized as a separate class of business, and information relative to this business is reported separately from that relative to ordinary insurance.

Industrial Insurance Premiums

The assumptions for mortality and expense factors for the premiums of weekly payment industrial policies show some difference from the assumptions used in ordinary insurance. Interest assumptions, the third factor in premiums, are basically the same for industrial and ordinary. Industrial insurance is purchased in large measure to provide dollars for burial expenses of low-income families. Historically, mortality experience among industrial life policyowners has been higher than for ordinary insureds because of the poor socioeconomic conditions of persons purchasing industrial coverage and, also, due to the less rigorous underwriting standards applied to industrial applicants. Table II shows a comparison of industrial with ordinary mortality experience. The higher mortality associated with industrial insurance contributes to higher premium rates for industrial insurance compared to ordinary insurance. Some narrowing of the mortality differences between the two classes of insureds has been noted in recent years, but systematic

TABLE II
Mortality Rate (qx) per 1,000 Persons

Age Last Birthday	× 18*	1954–58 Basic Industrial	Excess of 1954–58 Basic Industrial Over × 18	
			Death Per 1,000	As % of × 18
5	0.50	0.54	0.04	8.0
20	0.86	1.05	0.19	22.1
35	1.47	1.94	0.47	32.0
50	7.08	8.25	1.17	16.5
65	22.91	29.45	0.54	1.9
80	99.71	99.37	−0.34	−0.3

*The × 18 Table reflects ultimate experience on ordinary observed during a period from 1950 to 1954.

review of factual data has not been undertaken to verify the degree of narrowing.

Premiums for various classes of life insurance are also affected by interest assumptions of the writing company, but a significant difference in interest assumptions is not noticeable between industrial and ordinary insurance.

Expenses, the third major element affecting premium rates, are higher for industrial insurance when measured as a percentage of premium income. These differences in expense levels in industrial and regular ordinary insurance stem largely from the characteristics of the two lines of business and include (1) differences in their markets as reflected in average policy size and underwriting procedures, (2) differences in premium collection and accounting procedures, and (3) differences in policy benefit structures.

The smaller average policy size of industrial insurance results in higher unit expenses per $1,000 of insurance sold where a particular expense item is not a function of policy size, as is the case to some extent in underwriting and claims handling procedures. Additionally, part of the home service agent's compensation is a direct function of the amount of premiums collected, ranging from 10% to 20% of premiums on industrial business. As a result, the unit costs of premium collection as a percentage of premiums are higher on industrial than on ordinary business.

The industrial policy line of most insurers is less complex than the ordinary insurance line. The benefit structure is simpler and more standardized than in the case of ordinary insurance. Few policy riders are available, no loan feature is required in most states, and nonforfeiture and settlement options are simplified. These simplifications, the large number of contracts sold, and simplified underwriting procedures tend to reduce unit expenses relative to ordinary. However, overall expenses still remain comparatively high on industrial.

For practically all companies, the trend of expenses on industrial business has been upward as has been the case in ordinary business. Factors contributing to increasing expenses include inflation, reduction in the amount of new business written on an industrial basis, and little increase in average policy size or amount of premium income generated per sale. The trend has been more marked in industrial than in ordinary, because much of the industrial expense is incurred in the field rather than in the home office. While home offices have been able to offset some pressure on expenses by the use of computers and automation, field offices have not been able to enjoy the same benefits due to inflationary factors and the manpower-intensive nature of the field. However, a number of home service insurers are now attempting to expand cost-saving capabilities to the field through computerization of field accounting and premium collection functions.

Industrial Insurance Contract Provisions

In general, the provisions of industrial life contracts are similar to those of ordinary life contracts. The small amounts of coverage, the simplified underwriting procedures, and the specific need for which this type of coverage is purchased, however, have prompted some modifications and the inclusion of unique features in industrial plans. Only the distinctive contract features will be reviewed here.

Since most industrial policies are written with an abbreviated application and no medical examination, the application usually is not attached to the policy, and as such does not become part of the policy. Therefore, the entire contract provision might read as follows:

> *The contract.* This contract is made in consideration of the application and the payment of premiums as provided. This policy constitutes the entire contract.[5]

Facility of Payment Clause

Early industrial life insurance policies made no provisions for naming a specific person as beneficiary, but used what is called the facility of payment clause. This provides for payment of the benefits to anyone who appears equitably entitled to the proceeds—someone who had assumed the expenses of the insured's last illness or burial, for example. Current policies, however, permit the naming and changing of beneficiaries on much the same basis as ordinary life insurance policies. The continued use of the clause today is to permit the companies in prescribed instances to pay insurance benefits without delay and expense. Delays and expenses might be encountered upon the appointment of a guardian or other action requiring a court order (if, for example, the named beneficiary is a minor, incompetent, or otherwise not qualified to effect a valid release). If the beneficiary is the estate of the insured, payment is possible without awaiting delay caused by probate and appointment of a personal representative of the estate. Although the facility of payment clause is still used, most states require a provision for the designation of a beneficiary, and also, require that the policy provide a period of time after a loss during which the named beneficiary may submit a claim before the insurer makes any payments under the facility of payment provision.

The law requires good faith and sound judgment by the company in the exercise of authority under the facility of payment clause. An insurance

[5] In a contest of the claim for the benefits of the policy within the contestable period, however, the application may be admitted into evidence to support a plea of fraud and deceit in the procurement of the policy.

company cannot be compelled to make payment under such a clause but "may" make such payment if the conditions of the clause have been met.

Assignment of Industrial Policies

A distinctive aspect of industrial insurance is the fact that these policies provide for small amounts of protection. The expense of maintaining records of assignment and the desire of the company to make payment of benefits as quickly as practical are among the reasons a number of companies prohibit by contract the assignment of the industrial policy or its benefits. New York requires a limited assignment provision in industrial policies permitting assignments to national banks, state banks, and trust companies, but most of the states permit a clause making the policy nonassignable. In California, however, court decisions have permitted assignment of the policy.

The Incontestable Clause

The incontestable clause in industrial policies that limits the time within which the contract's validity can be contested is much the same as in ordinary policies in wording, but normally provides for a one-year contestable period as opposed to the two years that is typical of ordinary policies.

Participating Industrial Policies

If industrial policies are participating (i.e., dividend-paying), they are required by law to have provisions regarding dividend payments just like ordinary policies. However, since the amounts of dividends on weekly premium industrial policies are small, permitting a choice as to form of the dividend would increase expenses without commensurate benefit to the policyowner. Therefore, weekly premium industrial contracts usually contain a provision only for the purchase of paid-up additions to the basic amount of insurance. Some insurers, however, apply the dividends as premium credits.

Direct Payment of Premiums

Another provision that is unique to the weekly premium industrial policy involves the direct payment of premiums. Initially, it is assumed that premiums for weekly premium policies will be collected by an agent of the company at the home of the premium payor. The expenses of collection are taken into account by the company in fixing the premium rates on the policy. However, if the premium payor pays the premium directly to the company or at one of its offices over a period of time, such as six months or one year, most weekly premium policies provide a method of refunding an amount (or reducing the premium amount) equivalent to the estimated cost of collection.

The standard industrial policy provision laws in some states make such a policy provision permissible, while other states make the provision mandatory. A 10% figure is most commonly used in computing the amount of refund, or reduction, due the insured for premiums paid directly for a full year.

Loan Provisions and Settlement Options

Unlike ordinary contracts, weekly premium policies typically contain no loan provision. The small amount of insurance involved and the high rate of administrative expense to process policy loans serve to make a loan provision on industrial policies impractical. Although the majority of insurers today follow the common practice of not providing loan privileges for their weekly premium policyowners, a few have introduced contracts of five hundred dollars or more with a provision allowing for limited policy loan availability.

The variety of settlement and nonforfeiture options is much more restricted than is typical of ordinary policies. In some cases limited installment payment options are made available for policies above a set minimum size.

Supplemental Benefits

A unique feature of weekly premium industrial insurance is the common practice of providing, as an integral part of the benefit structure, certain supplemental benefits in addition to the basic life insurance benefits. The most common supplementary benefit associated with industrial insurance is the provision for payment of a supplementary amount equal to the face amount upon the accidental death of the insured—the so-called "double indemnity." The policies may provide for a greater amount to be paid if the insured dies from an automobile accident, and still another benefit may be payable if the death of the insured occurs as a result of travel accidents while a fare-paying passenger on a licensed common carrier.

In addition to benefits for accidental death, industrial policies frequently provide specific loss benefits. These benefits are a special coverage intended for disabilities that are objectively apparent (presumptive disabilities such as severance of hands or blindness). Some of the clauses provide benefits if the insurer suffers loss of eyesight or loss of limb and survives such loss for a period of at least thirty days. The amount of such benefit varies, but usually is fixed at a specified percentage of the face amount of the policy for the defined loss. Customarily, no such payment is made if the loss is caused or contributed to by disease, injury intentionally inflicted, or by an act of war while the insured is in military service of any country.

While industrial policies are similar in contractual characteristics to ordinary policies, the differences noted in this section are important to an understanding of the industrial contract. Most of the variations in benefit structure between ordinary and industrial policies result from the limited size of weekly premium industrial policies.

Industrial Insurance Underwriting

The basic underwriting factors and philosophy of weekly premium industrial insurance are the same as that for other forms of life insurance, but certain efficiencies are incorporated into the issuance of industrial insurance as expense considerations. The entire concept of industrial underwriting hinges on a single basic requirement—simplicity. This is essential when dealing with industrial insurance contracts, where processing large numbers of contracts with small face amounts makes the more complex underwriting procedures characteristic of larger ordinary sales, virtually impossible. Thus, the applications are simply constructed, to be completed with ease by the agent, and processed rapidly in the home office.

Simplicity, however, must not be confused with laxity or incompleteness. Simply constructed applications are designed to obtain the necessary underwriting information with as few questions as possible. Such questions are geared to be understood by the layman and are couched in "everyday language." These questions are restricted to the most basic and essential underwriting requirements, such as age, sex, height, and weight. Medical history questions are lumped together in general terms, and are less searching than those found in ordinary insurance applications involving larger insurance amounts. Debit agents are expected to write a relatively large number of industrial applications per week and must be able to complete them in a minimum amount of time. At the same time, the application process should inconvenience the applicant as little as possible.

When the applications are received at the home office, they must be processed simply and rapidly. The fact that some large home service companies may receive twenty thousand or more industrial applications a week demands that home office procedures be designed to handle such applications on a volume basis with simplified processing techniques. Essentially, processing is done at the clerical level because the rate structure makes little allowance for underwriting costs. The home office clerical underwriter, or approver, is part of a screening process whereby the "clean" applications are promptly approved and forwarded to the issue department for preparation of a policy. Usually the approver is trained to review applications along clearly established guidelines provided by underwriting manuals and checklists. These procedures enable the approver to recognize and pass along applications containing irregularities to a more skilled home office underwriter.

Broad Definition of Standard Risk

Home office industrial underwriting procedures necessarily, then, involve the process of sorting out substandard, uninsurable, and other irregular underwriting situations from those that are considered to be standard and in the acceptable range of the premium rate structure applicable to that class of business. In weekly premium industrial insurance, considerations regarding the definition of "standard risk" may be significantly different from those employed in connection with underwriting ordinary contracts. For example, mortality assumptions for ordinary insurance may provide for a standard acceptance range of mortality between 80% and 120% percent of normal (100%), whereas the standard industrial insurance acceptance range may be defined as between 80% and 150% of normal mortality. Industrial underwriting can be less detailed, because the standard classification of risk is broader than in ordinary contracts.

The broader definition of standard risk in industrial insurance reflects two factors. First, the mortality experience of applicants for smaller amounts of insurance is not as favorable as that for ordinary applicants for larger policies. This experience reflects, in part, the fact that the typical applicant for a large policy lives in better home surroundings, often in suburban neighborhoods. The applicant is also most frequently a white-collar or professional worker. Because of social and economic circumstances, the typical industrial applicant is a laborer, unskilled or semi-skilled, who lives in rural surroundings, industrial complexes, or urban settings. The industrial applicant is subject to greater accident risk, higher crime rates, increased instances of sickness, and less health care than an applicant for ordinary insurance. The applicant for industrial insurance usually has a lower level of attained education. The second factor necessitating broader standard classification in industrial business is the fact that the economies of handling large numbers of small unit applications will not allow the refined underwriting process necessary for detailed distinction. In other words, the requirement for simplicity in this type of businesss does not allow for as careful a delineation among risks as is possible with larger ordinary purchases.

In summary, then, the industrial underwriter usually does not develop a finely pinpointed appraisal of the expected mortality of each risk, as does an ordinary underwriter. Instead, the attempt is made to place the risk in a broad mortality group on the basis of the current application, additional questionnaires completed by the agent, and any previous experience the company may have had with the applicant.

Monthly Debit Ordinary

The collection of premiums at the home of the premium payor, a distinctive feature of industrial insurance from its beginning, has been extended increasingly since the end of World War II to ordinary insurance with monthly premiums collected by home service agents. Ordinary insurance with monthly premiums collected at the home of the insured is called monthly debit ordinary (MDO). The whole range of ordinary life insurance contracts, including whole life, endowment, and term insurance is now issued by home service companies on a monthly debit ordinary plan.

Monthly Debit Ordinary Premiums

The premium characteristics of MDO, as one would expect, are somewhat different from those for weekly premium industrial policies. The mortality base of MDO contracts is ordinary mortality, which, as Table II shows, is lower than the assumed industrial mortality. Also, the expense-loading factors are adjusted to contemplate a less costly monthly premium collection function as opposed to the more frequent weekly collection function in industrial insurance.

Monthly Debit Ordinary Contract Provisions

Although the distinctive aspects of the provisions of the weekly premium industrial policies and MDO contracts are becoming less discernible, substantial differences still exist:

1. Beneficiary provisions in monthly debit ordinary policies possess some variation, but the facility of payment clause, characteristic of weekly premium industrial policies, may or may not be used in monthly debit ordinary policies.
2. Monthly debit ordinary policies contain the standard ordinary provisions regarding assignment of the policy.
3. Monthly debit ordinary policies provide more extensive options regarding nonforfeiture values and settlement provisions than industrial contracts. Their provisions are typical of non-debit ordinary policies in this regard.
4. Monthly debit ordinary policies contain the loan provisions which are characteristic of regular ordinary policies with one exception: the automatic premium loan provision is not available.
5. In monthly debit ordinary policies, the application is attached to the policy and made part of the contract.
6. The incontestable and suicide periods for most monthly debit ordinary policies are of two years duration as opposed to the one-year

period which is more common in weekly premium industrial policies.

7. Monthly policies have more extensive options available for use of dividends if the policy is participating. Typical options in monthly debit ordinary policies are that dividends may be taken in cash, applied toward future premium payments, left on deposit at interest with the company, and used to buy paid-up additional insurance.
8. Accidental death and dismemberment benefit provisions are not an integral part of the benefit structure of the contract as they are in weekly industrial policies. These benefits can be added by rider for a specific additional premium.

Monthly Debit Ordinary Underwriting

While simplicity is also the key objective in underwriting large numbers of relatively small monthly debit ordinary policies, as the size of these policies increases, underwriting specificity becomes more pronounced. For larger monthly debit ordinary policies, where circumstances indicate it to be desirable, it is more common to require a medical examination than for weekly premium industrial policies. Also, greater flexibility exists in substandard classifications in monthly debit ordinary contracts than in weekly premium industrial policies. This is because the underwriting class for industrial insurance is broad—but with no substandard classification—whereas the underwriting class for monthly debit ordinary insurance is narrow, with up to three levels of substandard ratings.

As will be recalled, a statutory limitation exists on the amount of insurance which may be provided under most industrial policies. No such statutory limit exists relative to monthly debit ordinary. Although company practice is not uniform, monthly debit ordinary insurance minimums usually begin at $1,000 face amount. The minimum issue amount for monthly debit ordinary contracts, however, may be established in terms of minimum monthly premium amounts, for example, $10, rather than in terms of policy face amount. Normally the companies also establish an internal maximum issue amount on a monthly debit ordinary basis with reference to premium payments.

Intermediate Home Service Products

Between the extremes of definitive characteristics of weekly premium industrial insurance and larger monthly debit ordinary policies, a class of home service products called intermediate policies has developed. These contracts began appearing around the turn of the century and generally are written in amounts of $500 or more with premiums payable annually, semi-annually, quarterly, or monthly. The term "intermediate" is indefinite and may not have the same meaning among different companies. Some companies classify the intermediate policies as industrial with premiums payable monthly, while others classify them as ordinary products with integrated supplemental benefits added to the basic life benefits of the policy. Therefore, it is difficult to make specific statements regarding intermediate products.

Other Products Marketed Through Home Service

Other products marketed through the home service system include regular ordinary life and health insurance, property and liability coverages, and small group insurance cases. As previously noted, premium-notice-ordinary life insurance has increased in prevalence in the home service system. This increase represents the sale of larger amounts of insurance not encompassing the premium collection function. The policyowner instead is notified by mail of the premium due, and premium payments are made directly to the agent or mailed to the company home office. Premium-notice-ordinary policies at present constitute almost 44% of the business sold by agents using the home service system of marketing.[6]

Additionally, a significant number of home service companies have supplemented their product line with the inclusion of weekly premium homeowners insurance, weekly premium fire insurance, and in some cases, weekly premium automobile insurance. The availability of property and liability coverages through the home service system is compatible with the provision of life insurance on a frequently serviced basis and has provided an attractive marketing package to home service agents and their clients.

Some home service agents have also begun to write small group life insurance cases and salary savings (payroll deduction) plans as part of their normal activities. To a large extent, the activity in the group and salary savings markets depends upon whether the agent as an individual has the aptitude, territory, and orientation for more complex sales activities. Thus, the home service system of marketing does not restrict the home service agent to providing personal insurance coverages only.

Home Service Field Operations

The home service system of marketing is distinguished by its field-intensive system of operation. This operation requires that concentrated managerial support for the marketing function be provided at the field level. The organi-

[6] LIMRA memorandum, February 15, 1979, from Ann Luther to LIMRA Consultants of Combination Companies, entitled, "Combinations Companies' New Business Breakdowns."

FIGURE I
Typical Field Organization Chart

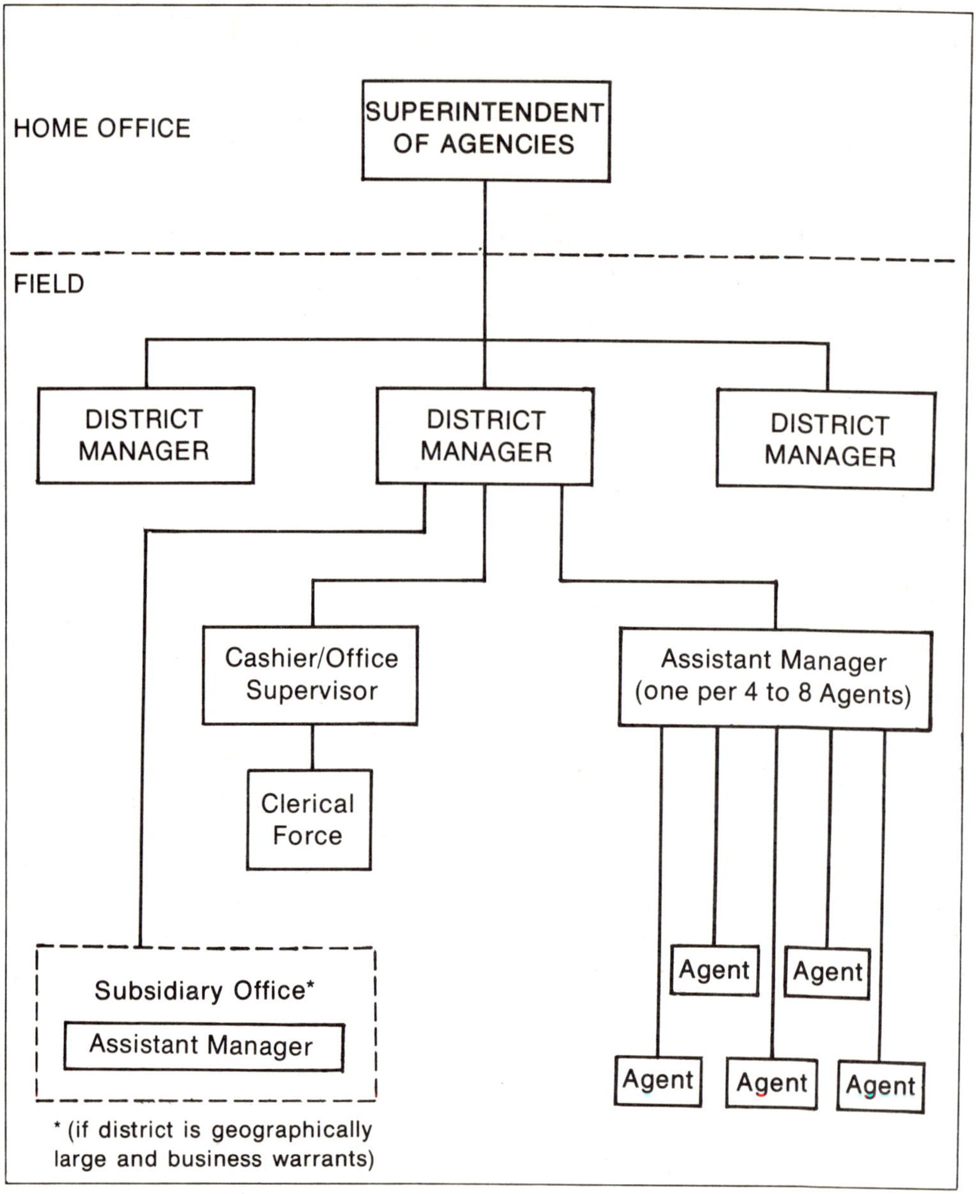

zational structure of home service organization at the field level is similar from one company to another. Figure I provides a view of the typical organizational structure for the field force of a home service company. Both home service and non-home service insurance are sold by home service agents through this type of organization. The structure is simple and has clear lines of authority. Many of the nation's leading life insurance companies use marketing structures similar to this in order to provide better field support and to maintain efficient control of the agency organization.

At the 66th annual meeting of the Life Insurers Conference (LIC) in 1976, a report was delivered that stated the total number of persons concerned with home service activities in the United States was more than 150,000.[7] Of these, there are 105,000 agents, 15,000 assistant field managers, 4,800 district managers, and 2,600 home office personnel. This report further stated that the number of companies in the home service field was estimated at 172, of which 83 were combination companies offering both industrial and debit ordinary products, an additional 78 offering only industrial products, and 11 more offering only debit ordinary.[8]

Duties and Compensation of District Managers

The district manager in the home service field organization is responsible for all of the functions of the district. This includes the training and supervision of agents, office personnel, and assistant managers and covers the sale of products, debit collections, and other managerial functions as may be necessary to assure proper functioning of the district agency.

The district manager is compensated in line with the wide responsibility and authority possessed.[9] Several basic elements are normally included in the compensation program; each element can be handled very simply or can be used in complex formulas: a periodic salary base, a longevity of service factor, a personal production factor, and a performance factor (or factors) related to the district as a whole. They represent career security, a factor for

---

[7] Many companies using the home service system are represented by their own insurance association, the Life Insurers Conference (LIC). This conference was organized in AIO as the National Insurance Trade Association. Today it represents 93 companies, of which 86 sell insurance through the home service method of marketing. These companies have offices in 21 states, the District of Columbia, Puerto Rico, the Bahamas, and the Philippines. The Life Insurers Conference maintains a staff in Richmond, Virginia.

[8] Ivan J. Houston, "The Debit Distribution System of Life Insurance," *Life Insurance Distribution Systems*, 1977 (unpublished monograph), LIMRA, p. 17.

[9] The LIC published a survey entitled "Earnings" in 1980 which found the following: in approximately 3% of the companies the district manager had an average weekly compensation rate of under $300.00; in approximately 19% of the companies weekly compensation was between $300.00 and $400.00; in approximately 37% of the companies the weekly compensation ranged between $400.00 and $500.00; in approximately 24% of the companies the average weekly compensation ranged between $500.00 and $600.00; and in approximately 17% of the companies the weekly compensation was in excess of $600.00.

dedication to the company, and factors to encourage hard work on the production of new business and the servicing of old business.

Duties and Compensation of Assistant Managers

The assistant manager reports directly to the district manager and, in turn, is responsible for the supervision of a number of agents. The function of the assistant manager is to recruit and train agents and carefully supervise their activities. This includes introducing new agents to the policyowners on their debits, aiding them in their work when necessary, and substituting for them in their work if and when necessary. Also, the assistant manager is responsible for periodic audits of agents' accounts and, in general, assists the district manager as needed.

The compensation of the assistant manager is based on the same factors as that of the district manager, except that an element for the number of agents the assistant manager oversees is also included.[10] Again, there is a wide variety of combinations of these basic elements into sub-factors for actual calculation of an assistant manager's compensation. If the assistant manager services a personal debit, additional compensation is paid for personal sales and service activities.

Duties of Office Supervisors

The responsibility of the office supervisor, or cashier, is to oversee the work of the clerical force in the district office and to report to the home office. The clerical force acts as the intermediary between the district agencies and the company's home office, reviewing and correcting all correspondence sent to the home office, forwarding home office replies to the proper agent, and, most importantly, checking premium accounting and deposit reports. The compensation basis for the cashier, or office supervisor, is most often straight salary.

Duties and Compensation of Debit Agents

The agent is, of course, the key person in a debit operation. The agent is the one who meets the policyowners and who represents the company to them. It is the agent's duty to collect premiums on in-force business in assigned

[10] The LIC study, "Earnings," (1980), also provides information on the total average weekly compensation of assistant managers: approximately 22% of the companies reported assistant managers' average weekly compensation to be below $300.00; about 55% reported weekly compensation for assistant managers to be between $300.00 and $400.00; 17% of the companies reported average weekly compensation for assistant managers ranging between $400.00 and $500.00; and 6% of the companies reported that assistant managers' average weekly compensation exceeded $500.00.

debits, to receipt the collections to the policyowner and record them properly, to deposit collections (usually twice each week) with the district office, to sell new policies, to make regular accounts of all transactions, and to render any and all services the policyowners legitimately might require.

In view of the fact that the debit agent has two major functions—(1) the production of good new business and, (2) the preservation and servicing of existing clients—the compensation plans are critical and geared to promote these activities. Specific compensation plans for home service agents vary, but they are usually based on a combination of the following elements: a service commission for premium collections, a sales commission based on new sales, and a series of bonuses or commissions based on the lapse and premium collection experience on the debit.[11]

The Times Method

For many years, a so-called times method (or increase method) of compensation was used extensively by combination and debit companies. The times system of compensation generally consisted of a collection commission based on the dollar amount of premiums actually collected on the agent's debit plus a new business commission based on the net dollar increase in the weekly premium business on the agent's debit. The compensation for net increase on the debit was based on the increase in premiums from revivals and new business written, net of decreases in premium volume on the debit resulting from causes other than death claims or maturities of policies. The debit agent's commission on this weekly premium increase was composed of payment of a stated multiple of the net increase. For example, if the net increase was 50 cents, and the agent received compensation at the rate of 12 times the net increase, then this new business commission for the week was $6 based on the net increase for the week in question.

Because the times method based compensation on net increase, it implicitly emphasized conservation. Even if an agent sold substantial amounts of new business, the effect could be nullified by heavy lapses of in-force business. Therefore, although not a direct factor in the times system of compensation, conservation of business was an important element in the compensation system.

New Compensation Methods

The times system served adequately during periods of economic prosperity, but during periods of severe economic recession or depression, excessive

[11] The LIC reported average weekly compensation amounts for home service agents as follows: approximately 31% of the companies reported the average weekly agent's compensation at less than $250.00; 42% between $250.00 and $300.00; 16% between $300.00 and $350.00; 4% between $350.00 and $400.00; and 7% over $400.00 per week.

lapses nullified the commission from new business written. The result was to make agent income inadequate and to produce agent pressure for relief from excessive lapses resulting from economic hardship.

The undesirable effects of economic fluctuations on agents using the times method prompted many home service insurers to seek new methods of agent compensation. Today, most home service companies, except some writing only weekly premium industrial insurance, base compensation for the home service agent on systems that separate the new business production and the conservation elements. One such system, variations of which are in use widely today, bases agent compensation primarily on three factors rather than two. Under this system, the agent receives (1) a collection or service, fee based on the volume of business being serviced, (2) a commission for new sales, and (3) compensation for conservation based on the persistency of business in the debit. Thus, new business compensation is more similar to that employed in connection with the sales of regular ordinary business. Where business generated by an agent on a debit territory is regular ordinary business, the compensation systems for ordinary insurance are used.

Agent Development

The constant attention required of agents on a debit to maintain premium collection services takes up a good deal of their time. Therefore, recruiting and training activities in the home service system take place largely on the job. A debit without a servicing agent, an **open debit**, will tend to generate excessive lapses if a new agent is not quickly trained to service policyowner needs.

Because of the need for constant attention to the policyowners on an existing debit, a number of states have provisions which specifically allow combination companies temporary licensing privileges relative to their home service operations. This enables home service agencies to install a new agent quickly on a debit territory. Beyond the temporary licensing provision, home service agents must be licensed by the various states just as other non-home service agents.

Much of the recruiting and training responsibility falls on the assistant manager who is directly responsible for several debit territories. If a debit is open without a replacement agent, the assistant manager may have to service the open debit personally. Thus, with many companies, when an appropriate recruit is found to replace a former agent on a debit, the training begins immediately on the job. The assistant manager accompanies the new agent into the territory providing introductions to the policyowners, and the procedures, on the job. Additional training takes place through company training programs and materials as the agent becomes familiar with the duties.

On-the-job training is made possible by the close supervision provided by the home service field organization. Most new agents have viewed the close managerial supervision characteristic of the system with approval, because it provides for their development under experienced observation and guidance. The close supervision of home service agents is not without its drawbacks. The intensive organization of field management creates a unique employer-employee relationship in the home service system which contributes materially to the company's control of its agency force. This also requires that home service companies provide employee benefit programs for their agents as well as contribute employment taxes to governmental insurance programs. Additionally, unionization efforts aimed at organizing debit agents have been successful to a modest extent, largely owing to the employee status of the agents. Where unionization efforts have been successful, the result is less company control of the agents than would otherwise be possible and, in some instances, unionization has contributed materially to the expense elements of home service company operations.

The debit organization with the specific assignment of territories to each agent for sales and service does provide blocks of business representing clients and referral possibilities. This is a significant attraction to prospective home service agents and aids in recruiting for home service operations because under other life insurance marketing systems, a new agent must generate clients and prospects from scratch, normally through some form of cold-canvassing technique.

Another feature of the home service system is the service commissions payable on the in-force block of business assigned to a new debit agent. This provides for an immediate and stable base income to the agent. No generation of new business is necessary in order to begin realizing income. This feature has a twofold advantage for the company. It is a strong recruiting feature, and the base income from service commissions coupled with the employee benefit plans provided by the insurer produce a degree of financial security for the new agent from the inception of employment.

Agent Functions—Field Accounting

A unique aspect of home service agents' duties is the mass field accounting conducted by the agent for premiums collected on home service products. In most companies, the premium accounting is done in bulk, and the records of premium payments by individual policyowners are maintained by the agent. Thus, the premium payment status of any given policy is maintained by the agent in the local office rather than at the home office. These records must be checked against records kept by the policyowner.

In the traditional home service accounting procedure, the agent, as part of his or her job, receives premiums directly from policyowners of debit products on the assigned territory. These premiums are accounted for by the home service agent, and any policy changes, lapses, death claims, and other circumstances that change the status of the policy are originated by the agent.

Two tools form the basic accounting equipment for the debit agent—the debit book and the premium receipt book. The **debit book** is a record of all weekly and monthly premium debit business charged to an agent (in force on the debit territory). The debit book contains records of the status of each policy and is arranged in family groups so that all policies in force on the members of a single family are recorded together. The agent notes receipt of premiums in the debit book. The book is looseleaf because of the numerous changes that must be made in the records.

The second major field accounting tool is the policyowner's record of premium payments, usually called the **premium receipt book**. This book is retained by the policyowner, and, like the agent's debit book, serves as a record of premium payments on all policies covering a family group with a given company.

Other forms are also used in the debit accounting process for balancing accounts and remitting cash, reporting various policy status changes, and applying for new contracts to be issued. However, these forms are no more than supportive of the basic accounting tools. Their purpose is to update the records in the debit book, the policyowner's premium receipt book, and, ultimately, the home office register.

The Cash System of Accounting

The major accounting tools traditionally have been applied under the so-called cash system of accounting. Under this system, home service companies depend on the agent to control the business on the debit as to its "date last paid" (DLP), which refers to the end of the period for which the last premium was paid. This system implies agent control of lapses as well as cash collection and remittance to the home office. Several potential problems are inherent in the cash system of accounting. First, the DLPs on the agent's collection book may not agree with the receipt books in the hands of the policyowners. Second, money collected on the debit may not be remitted to the company in the week collected. Third, it is difficult for the company to determine the DLP on individual contracts of insurance. These potential problems stem from the company's dependence on the agent's reporting DLPs.

Keeping the home office registers and the agent's debit book in balance has always been a problem for the home service companies using the cash system. Manual inspection of the agent's collection book is periodically required. Under ideal circumstances the assistant manager accompanies the agent for a week to perform this task. The assistant manager checks the policyowners' receipt books against the agent's collection book. After verifying that the two agree, the agent's book is marked accordingly. The number of weeks included within the assistant manager's verification marks is compared with the collections turned in to the district office on the summary sheets representing the period between verifications. The agent's record is either above, below, or even with the amount recorded in the district office. This method of checking is difficult and time-consuming. It is necessary, however, because the accuracy of the system depends largely on the efficiency of the personnel and the ability of the company to get inspections.

The Advance and Arrears System of Accounting

Because of the difficulties cited above, another home service accounting system, the advance and arrears system, is used by most home service companies. Under this system a weekly summary sheet is supplied to the agent by the home office. This summary sheet charges the agent for the total collections due on all business in force in his or her debit. When the summary sheet is turned in to the district office with premiums collected, the agent is given credit for current collections and advances and is noted to have arrears on business not collected. A policy in arrears must be lapsed in the fifth week. If not, the agent is called for excess arrears and may have to pay for collections that have not been made. This system tends to keep the records on the debit up to date with a minimum of lapsable business in it. However, it is a tedious technical process that may be financially demanding on careless, new, or inexperienced agents.

Use of Computers

In recent years, many companies have computerized their premium accounting systems. In companies employing computer capacity in their accounting function, the home office records include the name, address, and premium payment status of various policyowners. Thus, with increasing frequency, control of policyowner records is being centralized in the home office.

The development of computers and electronic data processing systems has introduced numerous modifications in debit accounting procedures. These systems have been employed by increasing numbers of companies to develop ways to account for premiums and to control DLPs. In most cases these systems take the control of DLP records from the agent and put it in the home office where accounts five weeks in arrears are lapsed automatically.

Under the computerized systems, collection books, as such, are virtually eliminated. Instead, the agent is given an electronically printed record book, showing name, date of issue, age, plan, premium, and amount of insurance for each account. Thus, the figures in the record books agree with the home office registers.

Additionally, the agent is furnished with a composite route list showing family accounts by total premium only, controlling each account by page number. Collections on the agent's debit are divided into three days, and a route list is prepared for each day. The route lists are marked "first day," "second day," and "third day," and collections and premium totals are balanced for each day's route list. Under this system, accounts on Monday's route list, the first day, are collected and records are forwarded to the home office Monday evening. The Monday route list is processed in the home office on Tuesday or Wednesday, and a new updated Monday route list for the following week is mailed back to the agent on Wednesday. Tuesday's route list is collected on Tuesday, and the procedure for Monday is followed here and throughout the week. Route lists are made in triplicate so that after all collections are entered, one copy is returned to the home office, one copy is kept in the district office, and one copy is kept for the agent's own records. This system provides for closer control of the DLPs by the home office and district offices.

Inspection of policyowner premium receipt books to see that they are in agreement with the route list record is still an important feature of this type of field accounting system. However, the route listing system provides weekly information on advances and arrears, and management can tell at a glance the condition of the accounts on each debit. Additionally, debits can be rerouted and new record books printed at any time. The agent is no longer required to write lapse requests. Instead, the company sends a register of lapses and new business issued to the agent showing the new debit total with net debit increase or decrease.

Needless to say, numerous variations of computerized field accounting systems exist. These systems have been developed only after years of strenuous effort. They appear to hold valuable promise for the future as accounting control devices, thereby allowing agents to spend more time on new business production.

Agent Responsibilities

The home service system of marketing is also distinguished from other life insurance marketing systems by the fact that a specific territorial system is employed: all of an insurer's individual in-force contracts within a defined geographic territory are assigned to a specific agent. That agent's responsibilities are to render whatever services may be required by and/or contractually guaranteed to assigned policyowners. In addition, new business *must* be solicited—both from new prospects and from the existing policyowners within a specific territory. In most instances, the agent is allowed to solicit new policyowners from outside the assigned territory, but owing to the built-in referred lead base provided by existing assigned blocks of policyowners, the majority of the typical debit agent's business is written within the assigned territory.

An agent assigned to a debit account is essentially given a built-in market for the sale of future policies. First, changes in policyowners' status and the migration of new people into the debit territory create situations that often lead to the sale of additional policies. The very fact that most home service life insurance policyowners tend to improve their economic status over time creates the need for additional life insurance coverage. The fact that the agent is in the policyowner's home weekly or monthly permits close observation of the types of changes that generate insurance sales opportunities.

Services in addition to premium collection are provided by the agent or initiated by the agent on frequent visits to the homes of the policyowners. Keeping up to date with policyowner needs is one of the main service functions of the agent. Typically, the agent will report to the district office twice a week and will settle debit accounts (turn in an account for premiums due and collected) weekly or monthly, depending upon company practices. Other services include the completion of claim forms and claim check delivery, beneficiary designation changes, policy ownership changes, policy surrenders, policy loans and other policy changes which must be attended to personally and directly with the policyowner in the home. Personal attention of a home service agent to such policy services is particularly important for policyowners who have little education and limited ability to transact business through correspondence.

The Home Service Market

The market for home service insurance products and distribution can be discussed in terms of the insurance needs served and demographic features of home service insurance buyers. It is difficult to isolate all of the specific insurance needs of the market that the home service system attempts to meet. It is clear, however, that the increase in ordinary life insurance product sales through the home service system indicates a broader array of needs being met by home service agents than in the past.

Insurance Needs

One of the key reasons for which industrial insurance has always been purchased is to provide for burial expenses of the insured. The small size of these contracts dictates that few dollars, if any, over the cost of burial would be available to meet the income needs of survivors. It should be noted, however, that ownership of multiple industrial policies on an insured life is not uncommon. Thus, to some extent industrial products may contribute some dollars to the survivor's income needs beyond the cost of burial of the insured.

The increase in sales of regular and monthly debit ordinary products through the home service system is an indication of an expansion of the role of the home service system in meeting survivors' income needs in addition to death-related expenses of the insured. Thus, today the complete array of family and personal insurance needs of the public are being addressed by the home service system and home service products.

Demographic Features

The market to which the home service system is targeted is the low– to middle-income wage earner and dependents. The home service system and products meet the circumstances of these families. The financial activities of many lower-income wage earners revolve around their weekly or monthly paycheck. They buy most goods and services weekly, at the grocery or department store, and must set aside funds regularly to meet monthly obligations such as rent and utilities. A study made by the Federal Reserve Bank of Atlanta in the Atlanta metropolitan area found that over 54% of the labor force were paid weekly, another 40% were paid twice a month, and only 5.5% were paid on a monthly basis.[12] For many of these policyowners, home collection of premiums is not only a convenience, but a necessary means of self-discipline, which allows them to budget their premium payments.

A Louis Harris poll revealed that 22% of all Americans 18 years of age or older lack any kind of checking account, and among minority and low income groups this percentage is as much as 50%.[13] For many of these families who do not have checking accounts, weekly or monthly collection of life insurance premiums best fits their lifestyles. If given the choice of paying on a semi-annual or annual basis, most of these families would still opt for the more frequent weekly or monthly alternatives.

The home service system concentrates on providing insurance not only on the breadwinner in the family, but on all family members. As a result, several policies may be in force within a given household covering individuals residing in that household.

Studies of life insurance buyers document the fact that families headed by

[12] Jack Blicksilver, "Market Prospects and Potential for Home Service Insurance," Federal Reserve Bank of Atlanta.

[13] *Ibid.*

women purchase a disproportionately high share of home service policies. A similar observation would be appropriate for families headed by nonwhite breadwinners. Another factor that should be considered is that a larger percentage of contracts sold by home service agents are sold on the lives of juveniles in comparison with the percentage on juveniles sold regular ordinary policies. In 1973, 21% of the policies sold by home service agents were on the lives of juveniles.[14]

Data from the United States Census Bureau clearly shows that income levels are lower in the southern part of the United States than in the North or West. This factor produces a disproportionate popularity of industrial insurance in the South. This is verified by data from the ACLI's *Life Insurance Fact Book* which shows that in many of the southern states more than 50% of the number of life insurance policies in force are industrial life insurance policies, whereas the ratio of industrial policies to total policies in the United States overall is close to 33%.[15]

Another factor which explains the concentration in recent years of home service business in the South is the income level of the population. According to a 1973 United States Department of Commerce Report, 46.7% of the southern families earned less than $10,000. This same class for the Northeast was 34.3% and for the West 37.6%.[16]

The home service system today serves primarily the south-central, southeastern, eastern, north-eastern, and north-central regions of the United States. Few home service insurers operate on a significant level anywhere in the western part of the United States.

Trends Affecting Home Service Marketing

The home service marketing system is changing as its environment changes. Certain demographic trends and public attitudes are likely to have an impact on home service marketing of life and health insurance of which insurers must be aware. In addition, the actions of state regulators will affect many aspects of the home service system.

Demographic Trends

Several demographic trends are important to those companies that market through the home service system. Statistics from the United States Department of Commerce show that the number of people living below the poverty level has fallen sharply since 1960 and that the largest proportion of people

[14] *Ibid.*

[15] "The Debit Distribution System of Life Insurance," LIMRA, p. 3.

[16] *Ibid.*, p. 7.

and families in this group tend to have female and nonwhite heads of households. In addition, the United States Department of Commerce indicates that the largest percentage of low-income families live in the metropolitan areas of the United States.[17]

Lower-income people perceive a need for modest amounts of life insurance for themselves and for the rest of their families in order to cover the contingency of an early death. Even though the total market for industrial life insurance is diminishing as the income level of the population is raised, significant numbers of potential industrial policyowners still reside in major cities; consequently, a market for this product still exists.

The need for life insurance of low- and lower-middle income groups will clash with rising sales costs brought about by inflationary pressures. Higher sales costs will put pressure on insurers to increase premiums on these smaller policies at a time when premium rates in general are decreasing. In the long run, these opposing tendencies may cause companies to develop innovative methods of distributing life insurance products to low- to middle-income groups.

The effects of inflationary pressure are already evidenced by the fact that most companies, while maintaining their home service operations for existing business, have encouraged their agents to write more regular ordinary business on a premium billed or bank draft basis. Other companies have de-emphasized the home collection concept: even though they retain agents as home service agents, they acknowledge that the greatest portion of their premiums are mailed to the company's offices.

To complicate the issue further, home service marketing in many cities in the United States has become dangerous because of high crime rates in urban areas. This problem has led many home service companies to move their marketing efforts more toward the suburbs; however, in the suburbs most of the premiums will be paid by mail and most of the service will be done by mail or through the field offices. Also, servicing suburban debit territories requires greater use of the automobile, and with the current increases in gasoline prices other problems are created.

Adverse Publicity

Traditional home service products, in particular industrial insurance, have been the subject of critical reviews by numerous public and regulatory groups. The key criticisms have been the high administrative costs and high lapse rates associated with this coverage. For example, the report of the Armstrong Committee of the New York State legislature, made public in 1906, criticized the higher costs of industrial contracts (compared to ordinary contracts), the smaller benefits, the high lapse rates, and the low earnings of

[17] *Ibid.*, p. 24.

agents. In the late 1930s, industrial insurance was closely scrutinized by the Temporary National Economic Committee (TNEC). The tone of the TNEC hearings was harsh, and the summary recommendation was severe—that a fundamental change in the conduct of the industrial insurance business should occur. Otherwise, its eventual elimination may be necessary.

In more recent times a number of states have investigated and attempted or passed legislation relative to this type of insurance. Even more recently, an extensive investigation by the Federal Trade Commission was heavily critical of industrial insurance and the home service system of marketing.

Throughout history, the criticisms have been basically the same as those that are currently being faced by home service insurers. Some of the criticisms outlined below are valid (based on fact), while others are better viewed as charges that are as yet unproven. Among these criticisms are:

1. The cost per $1,000 unit of insurance coverage for industrial insurance is greater than for ordinary insurance sold in equal amounts.
2. Industrial insurance policies have a higher lapse rate than ordinary policies.
3. The cash value build-up of industrial policies is minimal, and most do not have a cash value until the fifth year in force. The industrial policyowner is normally not permitted to borrow against the cash value. The policy loan feature is required for ordinary insurance policies.
4. Industrial agents, upon whom consumers rely for insurance advice, often are not adequately trained or qualified.
5. A high turnover rate exists within the agency force, resulting in less expertise among agents and confusion and lack of continuity in the policyowner-agent relationship.
6. Some industrial agents are accused of encouraging inappropriate and unnecessary changes in policies. Such "churning" can contribute to the already high lapse rate to the detriment of the policyowner.
7. Insurers and agents tend to sell a number of small policies covering various members of the family, rather than one family coverage policy or one larger policy covering the families' major wage earner.
8. Insurance companies tend to duplicate efforts. This results in overloading policyowners with many small policies, in place of fewer, less expensive policies.
9. There is no longer a justification for using mortality tables different from those used for ordinary insurance.

10. The higher premiums for industrial insurance are computed to reflect the higher cost of frequent home collection. However, many policyowners pay premiums in advance, thus obviating the need for frequent home collection, yet receive no compensatory discount on premiums.
11. Many policyowners and beneficiaries fail to claim nonforfeiture and death benefits due to ignorance of their existence.

In summary, it appears that the principal charge against the home service life insurance industry and the products it distributes is that it is relatively high in cost compared to other forms of life insurance. Also, companies which employ the home service system are alleged to allow their agents to engage in various improper, deceptive, and/or uninformed marketing practices. Finally, it is suggested that the companies engaged in this type of business make excessive profit on industrial and other forms of home service business.

The home service industry has been actively at work refuting these criticisms and substantiating their rebuttals. Position papers which address the criticisms of industrial insurance and the home service method of marketing have been developed by major home service companies and the LIC. Most often, justifications of cost differentials between home service products and other non-home service products are based upon the additional services rendered. Marketing tactics that are undesirable are pointed out to be exceptions rather than the rule. Studies of the profitability of home service companies compared to that of companies not using the home service system have been developed to refute the arguments that home service insurers earn excessive profits.

The future of the home service system rests not only with the changing demographic features of the population, but also with the state regulators (and perhaps with the federal government), the insurers utilizing this system, and the public to whom these products are presented. The home service system and the products marketed through it have weathered many attacks in the past. At the same time, it should be noted that, since the late 1960s and early 1970s, a number of the major insurance carriers, who in the 1800s fostered the development of this system, have withdrawn from home service product areas and in some cases from the home service method of marketing. Other companies that have retained the home service system have moved dramatically toward monthly debit ordinary and increasing amounts of regular premium notice business through the home service system. Still other companies continue to give strong support to marketing weekly premium industrial insurance in the low- to lower-middle income markets. It does appear, however, that many large companies are totally withdrawing, or are withdrawing by reorientation of products, from the weekly premium market emphasizing instead ordinary insurance marketing techniques and products. Meanwhile, smaller, more regionalized companies are assuming major roles in the weekly premium industrial markets because of the opportunity created when the giants withdrew. In an industry marked by rather slow change, the future of the home service system of marketing and its products is most likely to be revealed by evolution rather than revolution.

Summary

This chapter presented the home service system of marketing insurance as it is known today. The subject of home service was approached from two perspectives: as a distribution system and as a category of life and health insurance products. The characteristics of the system are generally in-person interviews between an agent and a prospect, and weekly or monthly premium collections by an agent. Home service products (industrial insurance, monthly debit ordinary, and others) generally have smaller face amounts and special underwriting characteristics.

Home service field operations were presented in this chapter, including compensation and field accounting. The market for home service distribution and products was described in terms of needs and demographic characteristics. Finally, the trends in demographics and public attitudes toward home service—and their possible effects—were discussed.

Chapter 15

Direct Response Marketing

Kenneth C. Otis, II
William J. Ruth, Jr., FLMI

The method of distribution or sales that permits the supplier and consumer to make transactions directly with each other is known as direct response marketing. In direct response marketing, consumers have direct access to the supplier through the mail, by telephone or other media. Direct response marketing is a broad term for the practice of contacting potential customers without the use of a salesperson. Direct response, which represents a breakthrough in merchandising, makes use of print and broadcast media as well as mail.[1] Commonly used synonyms for direct response marketing are "mail order" and "direct mail," however there is more to direct response than the use of mail. A later section in this chapter addresses the various direct response techniques and how they are used in the sale of life and health insurance products.

The marketer, after choosing its market segment, targets advertising to elicit an immediate response. The response may be an actual sale or a sales lead. The immediacy of direct response marketing makes it different from general advertising. The general advertiser is trying to build positive *awareness* of a product in support of a delivery system. The direct response marketer's objective is action-oriented. The message is designed to motivate consumers to take immediate action, that is, make a purchase on the basis of the message.

---

[1] Kenneth C. Otis, II, *Introduction to Direct Marketing,* Direct Mail/Marketing Association, Inc., Release 100.1, April 1979.

Direct Response in Life and Health Insurance

The use of direct response methods to market life and health insurance products is widespread throughout the insurance industry. Several companies use direct response marketing methods exclusively. Many companies supplement their agency system with direct response advertising. In many cases, agents use direct response techniques to locate sales leads.

Several life and health insurance products lend themselves to direct response marketing, especially those that are easily explained or demonstrated. Buyers must be able to make a purchase decision on their own without the aid of a salesperson. Most products marketed are meant to be supplementary in nature. A hospital indemnity plan, for example, which provides a clearly defined dollar amount for each day of covered hospital confinement, may be used to meet expenses left unpaid by primary medical expense coverage.

Selling insurance through direct response differs from the traditional use of agents to sell life and health insurance products. An insurance agent makes the products of one or more insurance companies available for sale to his or her clients and handles a variety of administrative functions including sales and service. The agent receives a commission from the insurer at the time of the initial sale, during a specified number of renewal periods and generally, a continuing service fee for the remaining time the insurance is in force. In many cases, the insureds may have no direct contact with the home office of the insurer, and it is the agent who recommends coverages suited to the buyer's needs.

On the other hand, life and health insurance products offered through direct response are designed to be selected without the help of an agent and so must be easily understood by the prospective purchaser. The advertising copy carries the burden of explaining everything to the purchaser. The uncomplicated design of direct response life and health insurance products reduces or eliminates administrative costs traditionally associated with insurance sales. Large volumes of basically identical products are sold, and systematic processing procedures for applications and claims are used. Because the applications contain few questions, and policies are generally for small face amounts, little need exists for any extensive underwriting function or review of each application. The large volume allows the development of routine, mechanized handling.

Increasingly, direct response life insurance products are reaching purchasers not contacted by the traditional agency system. Agents' sales efforts are often influenced by insurance companies' marketing plans. For example, if a company wishes to increase sales of a specific product, they will often provide sales support or an attractive commission structure for that product. Because of these incentive systems, many prospective insureds may be overlooked (persons who have limited insurance needs, individuals who have needs for products not currently being marketed, or persons who are geographically remote or hard to reach). Additionally, the economics of supplementary insurance product sales may preclude agency marketing. Not enough commission potential is available in low-priced life and health products to make them attractive for direct sales (agent sales). It is estimated that two-thirds of all United States households are not contacted by an agent every year.[2] Direct response marketers are able to effectively service many of these households. In this way, direct response and agency systems have worked towards increasing availability of insurance products to the public and, therefore, reaching a larger potential market.

Companies Using Direct Response Marketing

An estimated $2.75 billion in premium revenue in all-lines insurance product sales was made via direct response marketing in 1978.[3] In 1977, the life and health insurance direct response sales figure was $1.8 billion in premium revenues.[4] The size of these figures testifies to the acceptance by consumers of direct response insurance products. Reasons for continued growth and acceptance are tied to customer satisfaction with products, competitive pricing, and refinements in the areas of customer service and claim processing. As direct response companies have grown, they have become increasingly dependent on data processing. Policyowners' questions concerning coverage, premiums and claims payments can be answered quickly and easily. In turn, as more people find customer service and claims to be of high quality in direct response companies, they purchase additional products. Increased revenue and volume continually spur research and development into ways to improve direct response distribution of life and health insurance.

Those companies using direct response exclusively have no agency system and generally rely on direct mail campaigns, often in combination with other media, to market their life and health products. These insurers usually offer supplemental coverage suited to direct response distribution.

Some large, all-lines insurers, as well as smaller agency-based companies, employ direct response techniques for both sales leads and solicitation. Several companies who are not primarily direct marketers have developed products suited to direct marketing. The products are made available to

---

[2] "The Opportunity to Buy," LIMRA 1975-76 Research Report.

[3] *1980 Fact Book on Direct Response Marketing*, (New York: Direct Mail/Marketing Association, Inc.), p. 6.

[4] *1979 Fact Book on Direct Response Marketing*, (New York: Direct Mail/Marketing Association, Inc.), p. 6.

current policyowners through a variety of media. The products may also be used to broaden the customer base by attracting buyers not reached through the agency system.

Group Accounts

One situation where an agency company may employ direct response techniques is in conjunction with the underwriting of group accounts. In group accounts, both individual and group insurance are offered. The individual insurance is generally life insurance and the group insurance is generally health coverage. Group accounts lend themselves to direct marketing because of the degree of homogeneity among members of each group. Insurers may underwrite several hundred group accounts, thereby greatly increasing their policyowner base. Qualifying groups may be offered a number of voluntary supplementary insurance products including life, health, dental, or disability insurance. Advertising of the products is usually done through direct mail solicitations to group members with support through the groups' publications. In many cases, the group must meet minimum membership requirements. The membership requirement ensures a potential consumer base large enough to support specialized direct response marketing.

Direct Response Insurance Products

Direct response insurance products are subject to the same limitation as all products sold through direct marketing: they must be easily explained to enable the purchaser to make a decision without the aid of a salesperson. Various life and health insurance products have been tested and found to lend themselves successfully to direct response sales. An important point is that direct response products do not differ in content from traditionally offered products. The products are of a simplified form, having been designed to supplement basic coverage rather than to serve as a primary form of insurance.

Direct response life insurance companies, in the majority of cases, have liberal underwriting requirements. For example, applicants need not give extensive evidence of insurability. Medical examinations or detailed medical histories are not usually required of the purchaser, even though several basic medical history questions may be asked.[5] The "nonmedical" application influences the types of coverage offered through direct response. Whereas in traditionally underwritten products, the medical application mitigates the

[5] Davis W. Gregg and Vane B. Lucas, *Life and Health Insurance Handbook*, (Homewood, Ill.: Richard D. Irwin, Inc., 1973), p. 974.

degree of risk assumed by the insurer, the direct response insurer assumes a different type of risk by offering guaranteed acceptance. Under guaranteed acceptance, or guaranteed issue, no individual underwriting takes place and each applicant is automatically issued a policy. Coverages have been developed which reflect this risk. They are discussed in the following section.

Life Insurance Products

Life insurance products offered through direct response may be tailored versions of standard types of life insurance coverage or may be specially designed. Life insurance products can be divided into two types: whole and term life products. The two most frequently marketed direct response life products are graded benefit whole life and level term life.

The graded benefit, or modified, whole life product has several variations, but basically offers only limited death benefits (such as the return of premiums paid) during the graded benefit period, the first two or three policy years, to avoid antiselection. If death occurs due to accident rather than illness, the full face amount is payable. Following the graded benefit period, full face values, which may vary according to sex and age of the insured at issue, are payable. This type of coverage is usually sold in relatively low face value amounts in the $1,000 to $5,000 range. Typically, this product has been targeted at 40-, 50-, or 55-years and older age groups. The coverage is positioned as a supplement to existing coverage or as ''final expense'' insurance.

A variety of term life insurance products have also been offered through direct response marketing. Generally, face amounts fall in the $10,000 to $50,000 range. However, face amounts as low as $1,000 and as high as $100,000 are offered as well.

One popular direct response term plan is an annually renewable term plan. This type of life plan pays a constant face amount. Each year, as the contract is renewed, the policyowner pays a higher premium. Many of the plans are renewable to a specific upper age limit, typically 65 or 70. Similarly, five-year renewable term plans which break protection periods into five-year bands are also commonly offered through direct response. At the end of five years, a new premium rate based on current age goes into effect for the next five-year coverage period.

Another type of direct response term product is a level, then reducing, term policy. Here, the face amount remains constant and premiums increase, either yearly or in age bands, to a certain age. After the policyowner attains a predetermined age, the face amount decreases yearly, while premiums remain constant. This allows the younger insured to carry a needed level of protection at a premium which is affordable. In later years, as responsibilities of the policyowner decline, finances become more limited, and insurance costs rise, the insured's premium remains level.

Although annuities have been offered on a limited basis by some direct response insurers, they are generally best suited for direct response when an agent can follow up an initial inquiry from a consumer because they are a more complicated product. In these instances, the solicitations describe the available product and the final sale is made by an agent.

Health Insurance Products

Direct response health products have been developed to cover a range of health insurance needs. Hospitalization, disability, and accident coverages, as well as out-of-hospital nursing home expense and specified disease plans for cancer or heart attack are frequently marketed.

A health product which has received widespread distribution is the hospital indemnity plan. Sold on either a group or an individual basis, a typical hospital indemnity plan offers a fixed dollar amount of benefit for each day of covered hospital confinement. A clearly stated maximum, either in benefit dollars or days of confinement, describes the extent of coverage. By varying the indemnity amounts and deductible periods (for example, benefits may not be payable until an elimination period of hospital confinement has been satisfied), the insurer allows the purchaser a choice in benefit level and price.

As direct marketing of the hospital indemnity product has flourished, insurers have attempted to differentiate their products from those offered by other companies by adding extra-benefit features. Those commonly observed are double indemnity benefits for specified diseases and accidental death and dismemberment (AD&D) benefits.

In addition to hospital indemnity products, Medicare supplement health products have been widely offered to an older market through direct response. These Medicare supplements provide for payments that cover the Medicare deductible and co-insurance amounts for which the beneficiary is responsible.

Coverages for loss of income and medical care costs associated with accidents are offered by several direct response insurers. Accident insurance benefits may be offered in a lump sum according to a schedule or as indemnity similar to hospital indemnity coverage. In the case of scheduled benefits, the insured chooses a level of coverage for certain bodily injuries (for example, a broken hip, arm, or leg). A specified benefit is payable if such injury is incurred. Accident-only indemnity coverages provide a specified benefit per day for confinements as the result of an accident. Accident coverages tend to be low in premium outlay with high benefit limits.

Target Marketing in Direct Response

A target market is a specifically defined segment of the population with similar needs. The number of people in the target market may be fairly large. For example, women aged 18 to 60 form a target market for many household cleaning products. At other times the target is relatively small. Women aged 18 to 30 form a target market for bridal products. Product and distribution methods influence target market choices.

A direct response marketer uses target marketing to better define likely buyers. Once a market is defined, methods are employed to key in on a prospective purchaser. Refinement of the target market entails market segmentation using various criteria. Segmentation may be accomplished by using demographics such as age, sex, level of education or income, as well as attitudinal factors such as "responsibility," as measured by home ownership and size of family. Direct response insurers measure consumers' purchasing frequency, time of last direct response purchase, and the monetary value of such purchases. Use of such segmentation has proven advantageous to direct marketers by aiding in increasing response rates and controlling the risks involved in offering insurance to large market segments. In addition, documentation of segmentation techniques has permitted the accumulation of trend information to be used for sales analysis and marketing planning.

Well-targeted campaigns can be expected to improve the effectiveness of marketing dollars. A direct mail life insurance product developed for the young and married market results in a wasted solicitation, for example, when mailed to a resident of a retirement community.

Target Groups for Direct Response Insurers

Research and ongoing sales analysis further define population characteristics. In some instances, societal trends interact with demographics to create target markets. One of the most obvious examples is the changing role of women in the work force. With increased responsibility, more financial resources and less free time, working women have emerged as a target market for life insurance products. A number of direct response insurers offer products designed for executive women. Some companies contact working women through professional associations to which they may belong.

Credit Cardholders

Credit cardholders are another natural target market for direct response life insurance products. Several companies have become specialists in the field of direct mail marketing to both department store and bank credit cardholders. There are several advantages to marketing insurance to a target group of credit cardholders. An up-to-date mailing list is available, and, in most instances, the department store or bank provides its endorsement of the product. Also, in many cases there is billing of insurance premiums to the credit account. This billing is an added convenience to the insured, reduces the insurer's administrative costs, and perhaps improves persistency.

Senior Citizens

Senior citizens are an important target market for direct response life insurance products. As people grow older, their responsibilities and insurance needs change. Direct response life insurance products have been developed to meet the particular financial situations of this age group. Senior citizens may receive solicitations on an individual basis through a variety of associations to which they belong. Many plans developed for this target market carry low face values and premiums that are affordable by people with very limited financial resources or those on a fixed income, as senior citizens frequently are.

Research and Testing for Direct Response Companies

Successful life and health insurance companies are willing to invest in consumer research to learn about consumers' insurance purchase decisions. Performing marketing research through mail and telephone surveys is important for a direct response marketing company. Whereas agency companies can talk to agents in order to identify consumer needs, a direct response company does not have the advantage of face-to-face contact with the insured.

Direct response companies conduct four types of research and testing: (1) identification of consumer wants and needs, (2) studies of product buyers/non-buyers, (3) customer service satisfaction studies, and (4) copy testing.

Focus groups, which are moderated consumer panel discussions, can be used in conducting the first type of research, identification of consumer wants and needs. The use of focus groups is a qualitative approach in that their small sample size is ideal for studying consumer attitudes. A more quantitative approach is an insurance inventory survey, where consumers are asked to detail their current insurance coverage, gaps in coverage, and their insurance requirements. Insurance inventory surveys, conducted by insurance companies, private research institutions and the federal government are primarily used for new product development.

Buyer/non-buyer studies review customers' perceptions about a specific product offered. This type of analysis is used to follow up a direct marketing

[6] The Health Care Financing Administration annually publishes the "Annual Health Insurance Inventory," as part of its publication, *Vital and Health Statistics*.

campaign. Buyer/non-buyer studies attempt to discern reasons why people did or did not buy the product. Findings can be used to redesign the product, generate ideas for advertising copy, or suggest new product opportunities.

After a policy is sold, it is incumbent on the life insurance company to continue to measure its customer's satisfaction with both product and service. Customer service satisfaction studies can identify reasons for policies being allowed to lapse and help prevent or reduce lapsing.

Research may be performed in-house, by external marketing research professionals, on a syndicated basis by companies which conduct studies and sell the results to a large number of subscribers, or by professional organizations such as the Life Insurance Marketing and Research Association (LIMRA) and the American Council of Life Insurance (ACLI).

Once a company determines which product to offer to a specific market, advertising copy must be designed and then tested. In copy testing, the marketer wants to identify segments which respond well to solicitations contained in the copy. Additionally, depending on the sophistication of the testing, the marketer may be able to gauge the profitability of a specific advertising medium or geographic area.

The nature of direct response marketing allows greater accuracy in testing than other marketing methods because responses are so easily measured. Direct mail, in particular, allows for accurate validation of test results. The direct mailer is able to apply systematic coding techniques to solicitation pieces and thereby carefully keep track of responses received (by state, zip code, or even markets within a metropolitan area). Newspaper stuffers are also coded for measurement. Print and television ads frequently direct interested consumers to a toll-free telephone number, and operators who take calls are able to ask for information that can be classified for later analysis.

Testing may be conducted to determine if a change in copy strategy is warranted. In some instances, copy may be altered, solicitation mode (envelope size, paper stock, and style of print) may be changed, or an advertising medium, such as television, may be used for the first time. Rather than applying full financial and operational resources to a potentially unsuccessful change, the direct marketer tests on a small but statistically significant scale. Results may lead to recommendations of implementation, alteration, or termination of the ad program.

A direct response marketer is always developing new copy, and testing of the new copy is frequently conducted. Measurement of such aspects as number of responses, number of conversions, and the cost of solicitation per policy sold are important. The most successful copy is generally the one that generates the most sales at the lowest cost. In print media, two different executions, or solicitations, can be prepared, each split coded (coded differently). As responses are received, the advertisement which has the most responses is considered the "winner" of the split. Tests of responses always involve measurement against a control advertisement, currently the most productive. Test ads are run at the same time as the control. Responses are compared to the control to see if a particular advertisement execution did better or worse in response than the ad currently in use. Test ads performing significantly better may supersede the control ad and, in turn, become the control advertisement in future ad campaigns.

Direct Response Media

The direct response media used by life and health insurers take many forms. Direct mail, print media, broadcast media, and telemarketing are all important media for direct response life and health insurers. A description of each medium follows, including some principles for soliciting insurance to consumers through these channels.

Direct Mail

Direct mail uses printed mailing pieces that are mailed to potential policyowners. The printed material solicits a particular product and contains an application or inquiry form. Direct mail allows for greater specification of target marketing than other direct response media. The degree of specification is attained through the use of a direct mailer's most important tool: the mailing list. Lists of names are available for rental from list brokerage houses or directly from other direct marketers. A list is compiled according to selected criteria and may be segmented in many ways. The segmentation may result in a list of people who have responded to ads in the past; lists of people with common characteristics, such as those who currently subscribe to a particular service; business lists; and lists of professionals. In addition, a company builds its own "house list" of customers, ex-customers, and customer leads. The house list is generally the largest and most productive list used.

In many cases, lists of names are rented from other direct marketers (for example, magazine subscribers, sweepstakes participants) or from a list brokerage company. In fact, on the average, half of the general solicitations mailed in a campaign come from house lists; half are rented.[7] The names are usually rented at a fee of $30 to $50 per thousand.[8]

The mailing list industry has its own hierarchy that consists of list owners,

---

[7] *1980 Fact Book on Direct Response Marketing,* (New York: Direct Mail/Marketing Association, Inc.), p. 43.

[8] *Ibid.,* p. 46.

compilers, brokers, list managers, and computer specialists, each interacting to keep the list current and in demand. The source book for data concerning list prices, number of names, and list demographics is *Direct Mail List Rates and Data,* published by the Standard Rate and Data Service.

Direct Mail Costs

Insurance products offered through direct mail have revenue streams which differ from other products offered through direct mail. An insurance purchase is an ongoing rather than a static, one-time purchase; insurance premium payments may be made by the insured over many years; the insurer incurs administrative costs over the life of the policy. Therefore, concern with the time value of money is an important consideration when viewing direct mail insurance products. In this respect, direct mail insurance products do not differ from those insurance products sold by agents.

There are two basic types of costs incurred in the development of a solicitation piece: (1) production costs, which include printing, postage, data processing (for addressing labels), and list rentals; and (2) creative costs associated with the creation and development of copy and art work. Mailing lists, whether purchased or rented, represent a cost to the direct mailer. In addition, maintenance of house lists of policyowners, lapsers and inquirers requires extensive technical support. Analysts study response rates and decide which lists or list segments would prove most productive.

A close examination of each product's margin for marketing expenses (relative to the company's profit or return on investment goal) results in identifying what is termed an "allowable" cost for a sale and, therefore, a minimum acceptable response rate. If a sale is made with costs below the allowable amount, the direct mailer will improve on its profit objective. However, sales costs in excess of the allowable cost indicates unsatisfactory profit performance. Of course, marketing expenses are only one component in determining an allowable cost. An estimate of response rates to campaigns and number of policies sold—the conversion rate—is a consideration in determining an allowable cost. A conversion rate represents the number of people solicited who eventually purchase a product, in essence they "convert" from prospect to purchaser. In some cases, one may respond to solicitation only by purchasing the product. In this case, response and conversion rates are the same. However, in other direct mail campaigns, a person has the option of responding but need not make a purchase. The number of initial responses are used to calculate the response rate. Once a purchase is made, the conversion rate can be calculated. In addition, persistency (lapse experience), loss experience, and responsiveness to further offers, or upgrades, can influence the setting of the allowable cost.

Group–Sponsored Plans

In addition to mailing lists of general market segments, many special interest groups are likely targets for direct mail efforts. Club/association members, veterans, professional/managerial organizations, and credit cardholders are each target groups and have their own well-maintained mailing lists. Direct mail has been the predominant medium used to reach members of such groups. As indicated earlier, several companies with large agency forces have implemented direct mail methods when underwriting group accounts.

There are obvious advantages of direct response offerings to a group rather than the "general market." For example, since many groups provide access to age, sex, and income data of the membership, the direct response marketer is able to make better estimates of insurance needs of a specific group than it can for the more diverse general market. Additionally, voluntary groups often have values or attitudes in common, which may affect their buying habits and their loss experience. (A company may decide to offer better rates to an association of joggers or nonsmokers, for example.) A key advantage in group marketing is the group mailing list which enables a pre-established listing of possible buyers. Naturally, the endorsement of a product by the leadership of the group aids acceptance of the offering by individual group members.

The Mail Kit

Of equal importance with choosing a profitable market segment is the development of effective sales literature. Direct mail sales literature is referred to as a mail "kit" since it contains informative brochures, an application/order blank and a return envelope. The pieces needed by the prospective buyer to make a purchase decision and place an order are included in the kit.

The allowable sales cost determines how much may be spent in producing a mail kit. Various components such as paper stock, quantities, color process, weight, and envelope size result in "kit costing." The finished kit must have a look and tone which appeals to the targeted market.

In most cases, an insurer will mail an initial solicitation and several follow-up efforts to a prospective policyowner. The number of efforts mailed depends on historical results regarding the profitability of mailing efforts to a particular market segment.

Two basic features of life and health insurance that a company promotes are price of coverage and benefit (face amount). The specific policy feature which is highlighted in the copy may differ according to the market segment. The relative importance to the purchaser of each of these must be weighed. For example, graded benefit whole life coverage is designed to be low premium, low face amount, supplementary coverage. Premiums may be as low as $7 to $10 per month depending on the level of coverage. In the case of graded benefit life, affordability could be a key point in the copy. Likewise, copy for health insurance may emphasize the expense of medical care and the monetary benefits afforded by the coverage offered, while price is less often mentioned.

Besides the price and benefits, direct mail life insurance offers several unique selling points which are notable. One point is the availability of guaranteed issue in many direct response products. The prospective insured cannot be refused coverage if basic qualifications are met. Also, direct response sales are low pressure, since the recipient need only discard a solicitation that is not of interest. Both of these points are strong selling points and receive attention in direct mail life and health insurance copy.

Print Media

Placing advertisements for life and health insurance in print media is another effective type of direct response marketing. Advertising of insurance products in newspapers and magazines has characteristics which distinguish it from the highly specialized medium of direct mail.

With newspapers and magazines, the advertiser (the insurer) buys space. The size of the space (page, half-page, column), the frequency of the ads (daily, weekly, monthly), and the reach of the ads (local, regional, national), each has different cost and sales implications. As in direct mail, the advertiser of direct response life products who uses print media is tied to a consideration of an allowable cost. The advertiser attempts to maximize the number of sales for the ad dollars spent.

Regardless of the size of an advertising budget, the advertiser using print media purchases space (full-, half-, or quarter-page) in a publication. Essentials of the product must be explained succinctly. Because the reader's attention is divided among all the ads in the publication, a mediocre ad may appear worse in a field of good ads or better in comparison to poor ads. The ad competes not only with those in its product class, but with all ads in the issue or edition.

There are a number of advantages to advertising direct response life and health products through print media. One advantage is the relatively low cost to reach consumers as compared with direct mail. The cost-per-thousand-readers for this medium is usually dramatically less than that for direct mail. Therefore, a lower response rate is acceptable for print media than for direct mail.

The trade-off, when print media is compared to direct mail, is the degree of specification and impact of the message. Direct mail market segmentation is more refined because mail is targeted to individuals with specific characteristics. Print media reaches a broader general market. However, the availability of special interest publications, local and regional editions of national magazines, and magazine reader profiles permit marketers to choose publications best suited to their target market. For example, life and health products developed for a women's market could be placed in those publications reaching women. Also, many organizations have their own publications and may accept and even endorse advertisements for direct response insurance to their members.

The growing use of free-fall ads, preprinted ads stuffed into a magazine or newspaper that are removable without ripping or tearing, has allowed print media users to develop creative techniques similar to direct mail kits. The free-falls are not under many of the size and color restrictions that affect magazine or newspaper page ads. Creative uses of ad copy, shape of ads and envelope design have broadened the bounds of direct response advertising.

Fulfillment Kit

As with direct mail, life and health insurance products offered through print media are guaranteed issue or limited underwriting offers. The purchaser will clip a coupon or fill out an application which is sent to the insurer. Once the application is approved, a fulfillment kit is mailed to the purchaser. This kit "fulfills" the application. Though fulfillment kits differ, many include the policy, insurance identification material, and premium billing. Fulfillment kits must also include a disclosure statement in many states. Rapid response to fulfillment requests is crucial in direct response since the prospects' commitment to buying the product lessens with time. Multiple-effort fulfillment offerings are not uncommon if the prospect does not respond to the first fulfillment kit.

Broadcast Media

Direct response television advertising is used to sell many products, the most familiar being record albums and kitchen aids. (For example, sales exceeding five million dollars were reported for the "Ginsu Knife" after only one year of television selling.[9]) Direct response marketing of life and health insurance products through radio or television is used to generate leads for subsequent sales and to support other media, primarily newspaper supplements such as free–falls. Radio and television are increasingly being used to solicit sales as well as supplement other direct response methods.

The basic components of direct response television and radio marketing include the commercial itself, purchase of broadcast time, and fulfillment. Commercials range from 30 to 120 seconds. An ad generally begins with an

[9] "Dial Media: King of Television Mail Order," *Direct Marketing*, 1979.

introduction of the product. This is followed by a specific "call to action" or call for immediate response to the commercial. The last 15 to 20 seconds are then spent in specifying how the viewer (listener) can respond. Often, this includes the choice of using a toll-free number, a mailing address, or both. In insurance advertising, most ads are delivered by a company spokesperson who could be a celebrity, a company president, or a professional announcer. The spokesperson, or "talking head," is supported by graphics explaining product benefits.

To air the commercial, advertisers can buy network, spot, or spot per inquiry television time. Network and spot television time requires prepayment for purchase of air time. There are over 200 spot or local television markets in the United States. Per inquiry (P.I.) is a novel approach to television direct response marketing. With spot P.I., marketers cannot specify times when an ad will run. Instead local television stations run the ad at their own discretion. The television stations are paid by the number of responses they receive from the ad. Some advertising agencies are P.I. specialists. Their business is buying spot television time for clients. These specialists receive a commission of a flat fee per inquiry.

Telemarketing

The more prevalent direct response media in use today are direct mail, print, and broadcast media. Each of these direct response methods have begun to make greater use of the emerging medium of telemarketing, or the use of the telephone to improve life and health insurance sales. The importance of this medium has grown, as is evidenced by the proliferation of toll-free numbers. The telephone can be used for customer service, claims, and any inquiries a policyowner or prospective policyowner may have. In addition to in-bound calls from prospective purchasers, out-bound calls initiated by the insurer have become an important tool in developing and following up on leads. Still used mainly as support for direct mail, print, and broadcast media, telephone marketing is expected to play a more important role in marketing life and health insurance in the future.

Spot P.I. television, which has been successfully used in generating life and health insurance leads, can make use of telemarketing techniques. Interested consumers are urged to call a toll-free number. Telephone marketing services provide answering services with in-bound toll-free telephone lines to answer consumers' inquiries. Telephone operators first ask the caller what they are calling about since many other businesses use the same service. Operators then key into a cathode-ray tube (CRT) terminal to obtain a set of questions to ask the inquirer. The information requested generally includes name and address, but could cover other items such as phone number, age, and beneficiary. In life insurance telemarketing, unlike most consumer products, there is no order taking since only licensed agents can make a sale. Typically, once the operator has obtained the necessary information, a customized fulfillment kit will be sent to the requestor. The requestors will complete the necessary applications, forward the forms to the insurer and, thus, enroll themselves in the insurance plan.

While many who request information by phone decide to purchase and become insured, some do not follow through with a purchase. Regardless of whether a purchase is made, both buyers and non-buyers alike will be added to the company's house list for future solicitations and other product line offerings.

Telemarketing is a high-unit cost medium. However, justification for this higher cost is found in high response rates. Telemarketing is also very personal once a consumer makes the initial phone call. Personalization and mass marketing are combined in telemarketing to achieve efficiency.[10]

Two-way communication is a key advantage of telemarketing. The purchaser has the advantage of direct access to the company. The insurer may contact the insured to ask about service problems and to conduct studies, or the insurer may provide a telephone number for prospects to call for sales assistance. In any event, the direct response marketer is brought closer to the buyer. The sale of life and health insurance products initiates an ongoing relationship between insured and insurer, whether through an agency system or a direct response system. Two-way telephone access helps insureds in making their needs known, thus allowing the insurer to better serve its policyowners.

Other Direct Response Methods

Several media have long been associated with direct marketing of life and health insurance. These "old standbys" of direct response include inserts in monthly statements or bills, vending machine sales, matchbook covers, and "take one" brochures.

Vending machine sales (especially at airports) have been a profitable source of direct response travel accident insurance for decades. Matchbook cover offerings and "take one" brochures in supermarkets or other stores continue to provide low-cost opportunities for direct response insurance marketers to make sales. While these methods are not the latest direct response methods, the experience gained with these methods of "direct-to-the-consumer" marketing laid the groundwork for current direct response techniques. As with most methods, these original techniques have been

[10] *1980 Fact Book on Direct Response Marketing*, (New York: Direct Mail/Marketing Association, Inc.), p. 49.

improved upon by diversification of creative strategy and the use of better targeting methods, thereby increasing market and profit potential.

Organization in Direct Response Companies

A typical company organizational structure for life and health insurance direct response marketing includes the following functions: product management, promotion management, sales analysis, support, actuarial, and underwriting. Of course, several alternate organizational structures exist which combine these functions or assign them to different areas.

The product manager has responsibility for product line profitability. He or she considers a number of areas and gauges their potential impact on profits. Job responsibilities include setting solicitation budgets, revenue goals, pricing strategy, expense ratio guidelines, allowable acquisition costs, product research and development direction, and overseeing communication and coordination of all product activities. The product manager should have an insurance background because this person works closely with actuarial, data processing, policyowner administration, legal, marketing, and government affairs departments.

Promotion managers have responsibility for generating new revenue and usually have a marketing background. A promotion manager uses research findings, test results and insight to create a copy platform—the objectives of a particular solicitation piece (such as the message to be conveyed to consumers). If an advertising agency is used, the promotion manager coordinates the agency's efforts to deliver the finished advertising copy. Promotion managers also work with the company's media buying department to develop a guideline budget and goals, then insures execution according to plan. Finally, the promotion manager implements and coordinates direct response marketing campaigns.

Sales analysis is the heart of the direct response business. The sales analyst is responsible for analyzing and reporting sales results and tests on kits, determining profitable media/market segments, and forecasting sales. This person often has a background in computer sciences or statistics.

Support units may include an advertising agency, media buying department, fulfillment department and mail house. The mail house is becoming a highly mechanized organization where direct mail kits are assembled according to a number of specifications and are mailed. (These can be in-house or not.) The advertising agency employs experienced direct response copywriters; the media department buys direct mail lists, space and broadcast time; fulfillment receives inquiries from interested consumers and provides them with answers to their inquiries, including the policy and insurance identification material.

As in other forms of direct response, policy administration of life and health insurance offered through print media involves application processing services, policy issuance, premium billing and collection, policyowner or customer services, and claims administration. All are services that are common to traditionally offered products. Each of these functions supports the marketing effort and is put into action in response to the media. However, since there is no agent to answer policyowner questions, each administrative step must operate under the same restrictions as the initial direct response advertising, that is, each step must be easily explained to allow the insured to act autonomously.

Receipt by the company of a completed application usually allows enrollment in a plan. The policy is issued to the insured along with premium billing and payment instructions. In many cases, the insured is given a "free-look" period during which time the policy may be returned if found unsatisfactory. A toll-free number to contact customer service representatives is frequently given. Claim forms and claim filing instructions are also provided. Various means of communication including the telephone, form letters, computer letters and individualized correspondence are employed over the life of the policy to deal with claims, questions, policy changes or premium adjustments.

Issues and Concerns Related to Direct Response

Today, there are several issues facing direct marketing in general, and direct response insurance products in particular. These issues include privacy, costs, and concerns about specific direct response products.

One of the largest issues facing direct response marketing is privacy. This issue was raised at the federal level through the Privacy Protection Study Commission (PPSC). The PPSC made recommendations concerning the use of mailing lists. These lists form the backbone of direct response marketing, and any threat to the use of mailing lists affects the direct response industry. The PPSC urged direct response mailers to disclose voluntarily their list rental practices and to give people the choice of having their names removed from mailing lists. To alleviate concern about this issue, the Mail Preference Service has been instituted. This service gives people the choice of having their names removed from mailing lists. While many people enjoy receiving direct mail solicitations, there has been some objection raised to mailing list rental practices. People who prefer not to have their names available for rental through list exchange are given the opportunity to exercise this option. Usually small cards or questionnaires are included with correspondence from a direct response marketer. The cards may indicate that the marketer makes its lists available to other direct response advertisers. The recipients can then indicate that they prefer not to have their names made available.

In addition, the right of a direct response insurer to request information on applicants for underwriting purposes and to disclose that information has come under question. Restricting the ability of insurers to collect and use this information would affect the insurance industry as a whole, not only the direct response industry.

Rising postage and production costs are also of major concern to direct response marketers. The direct response industry spent $7.5 billion on postage and production in 1978. This represents a 150% increase over 1970 costs.[11] These rising costs, coupled with declining buying power of the general public, have forced a reevaluation of product offerings.

At the state insurance commissioner level and at the federal level through the Federal Trade Commission, direct marketing of insurance products has come under scrutiny. Specific types of direct marketed insurance coverage (for example, dread disease and Medicare supplements) have been subjected to minimum standards regulations. Recent federal legislation has given each state a time frame to develop minimum standards for Medicare supplement coverage sold in that state. For any state not developing minimum standards by a set time, the federal government will impose its own standard. While not directed specifically at direct response marketed products, direct response companies offering the coverage are affected by such legislation.

Direct marketers have attempted to keep abreast of issues and concerns which may threaten their continued growth. The Direct Mail/Marketing Association (DMMA) represents the interests of some 1,700 direct marketers nationwide, including direct response insurers. Its activities include programs of self-regulation, the promotion of ethical business practices, and monitoring of legislation relevant to direct marketing.

Payroll Deduction

Voluntary payroll deduction plans have recently become an important source of insurance coverage for members of employee groups in the United States. These plans are not direct response techniques in the strict sense because agents are frequently involved. However, payroll deduction, or salary savings, plans are considered to be a form of mass distribution of insurance coverage, and, therefore, are discussed in this chapter.

Payroll deduction is a means of making individual (and sometimes group) insurance available to members of certain groups, usually employee groups. Typically it involves solicitation by an agent and special arrangements for premium payments. The products offered through payroll deduction plans have identifiable characteristics. Each of these aspects of payroll deduction will be discussed below.

[11] *Ibid.*, p. 2.

Payroll Deduction as a Billing System

The term "payroll deduction" generally refers to a premium billing system that is designed to facilitate the distribution of life and health insurance. It is an arrangement where employees agree to purchase insurance coverage and arrange to have the premiums paid through deductions from their salaries. The employer, in turn, remits the amount deducted to the insurance company. The service is usually offered to all employees of an organization, and in the case of a large employer, several different insurance companies and different plans of insurance may be involved. The most pronounced example of a payroll deduction service of this type is the government allotment system in effect for military personnel and government employees. In this case, the federal government withholds a portion of the salary of service personnel to pay their insurance premiums.

The Market for Payroll Deduction

In most instances, payroll deduction plans are marketed to groups of employees at their place of employment with the permission of the employer. Insurance is offered on the lives of employees, their spouses, and their children. It should be emphasized that generally the insurance offered is individual insurance that is owned and paid for entirely by the employees themselves. Group voluntary accidental death and dismemberment (AD&D) are also sold through payroll deduction plans. The insurance can be retained by the employee even after he or she terminates employment. Thus the sale of payroll deduction insurance is not the same as the sale of group life or health insurance. Instead, the insurance owned through payroll deduction is supplemental to an employee's group insurance, and is entirely the property and responsibility of the employee.

In the case of blue-collar workers, often referred to as America's neglected market, this opportunity may be the first time such employees are offered the chance to acquire individual insurance of any form. Therefore, this system offers many people the initial opportunity to begin a life insurance estate and provides a basic portfolio of essential insurance coverage for themselves and for their families.

The Development of a Sale

The nature of payroll deduction plans can be better understood by tracing the development of a "typical" sale. The key to effective marketing is the ability of the agent to gain the permission of the employer to establish a payroll deduction system for insurance and provide adequate time for the employees to hear a presentation about the availability of insurance. Agents usually emphasize such points as (1) the ability of the employer to expand the employee benefits plan at minimal cost, (2) the need for employees to supplement their group life insurance with permanent life insurance, and (3) the likelihood that their employees are infrequently, if at all, contacted by insurance agents to update their insurance coverage.[12]

In many cases a single agent develops the prospect (here the prospect is the employer), makes a presentation to employees, and sets up the plan. In other instances, an agent who specializes in selling this type of product collaborates with an agent who has the contacts with employers, and the commission on the sale is shared. An example of the type of agent with proper contacts would be an agent who writes group insurance, pension plans, and other employee benefit products.

Once a payroll deduction plan is agreed upon, its presentation to the employees becomes part of the company's benefit communications program. Through these programs the employees are advised of all of the benefits which they may receive and their value. During these presentations, the agent(s) usually point out, when applicable, that the group life insurance benefit is on the life of the employee only, and that the coverage terminates either at retirement or when the employee changes jobs, or it must be converted to individual insurance. The payroll deduction product, most likely a permanent product, is then offered as one of the ways to fill the voids and supplement the group life program.

"Underwriting" of the Employer and Employee

After an employer consents to establishment of a payroll deduction program, but before individual presentations are made to employees, the writing company "underwrites" the employer for the guaranteed issue aspects of the risk. Life and health insurance companies that have been in the payroll deduction market for a number of years have learned that industries with high turnover are unsuitable for payroll deduction plans. In addition, certain industries have higher employee mortality or business failure rates. Industries with these characteristics generally exhibit low persistency with payroll deduction plans, thus creating little or no profitability. Among these industries are taxicab companies, parking lots, barber shops, religious organizations, fast food chains, health clubs, taverns and lounges, amusement parks, theaters and moviehouses, and convenience stores.

Once an employer has been approved, the definition of employee eligibility must be developed. The question of eligibility is an important one, since the program is offered on a guaranteed issue basis. Life and health insurance

---

[12] David M. Wynn, CLU, "Mass Marketing Small Policies by Payroll Deduction," *Life Association News,* January 1981, p. 86.

products can be sold on an underwritten basis, or they can be sold on a guaranteed issue basis. In the first case, risks are underwritten based on information contained in the applications received, and company rules and guidelines are normally followed. With guaranteed issue, no individual underwriting takes place, and all who apply are automatically issued a policy. In these cases, the assumption of the writing company is that a sufficiently large number of applicants will be secured from both healthy and unhealthy applicants without deliberate antiselection, permitting them to offer products on a guaranteed issue basis. In many cases, however, the guaranteed issue privilege is conditioned upon a minimum number of enrollees in the plan. If the writing company receives less than its set minimum (for example, 100), the plan reverts to a medically underwritten basis.

Life and health insurance companies have learned that they must exercise certain safeguards to protect against two main hazards, poor persistency and antiselection. Poor persistency is protected against by carefully selecting the type of employers solicited and by requiring a one-year waiting period, that is, the employee must be employed for at least one year before being eligible for coverage. This eliminates much of the risk of high employee turnover that harms such programs. Antiselection is minimized by requiring (1) that eligible employees be actively at work on the date coverage becomes effective, (2) that spouses and children are, at least, not currently in a hospital or being treated for a major disease, (3) that the enrollment period be limited, and (4) that limited amounts of coverage be offered.

Presentations to Employees

Once the criteria for eligibility has been determined, a formal presentation of the plans available and the procedure for enrolling is made to employees. The presentation is generally made to groups of approximately twenty employees. Brochures describing the insurance plan, premiums, paid-up values at age 65, and the cash values at age 65 are distributed. Other media may be used in the group presentation, including flip-charts and slide presentations. The points generally emphasized in these presentations are the affordability of such insurance and the advantage of owning permanent insurance to supplement their group insurance coverage.[13]

After the initial presentations to groups of employees, arrangements are established for enrolling those who desire to participate. This is usually done on a one-on-one basis, giving each employee an opportunity to ask questions and seek advice as to the employee's circumstances. Since enrollment periods are limited (three days to a week), the agent usually revisits each

[13] *Ibid.*, p. 86.

employer at least annually to re-offer the plan to newly eligible employees, and to allow those already enrolled to increase their coverage.

Products Offered Through Payroll Deduction Plans

Various types of insurance products are offered through payroll deduction plans. Most insurance companies offer ordinary life insurance with premiums payable for life, since that form of insurance can produce lower premiums than limited-pay life plans. However, life paid-up at age 65, 35-pay life, and other limited payment whole life plans are sometimes offered, as are some forms of health and disability income insurance. Still other forms of insurance may be purchased through various optional riders, usually sold as part of a "package."

Advantages and Disadvantages to Employees

From the employee's point of view, payroll deduction plans offer a convenient and simple way to purchase life insurance. Having premiums automatically deducted from one's paycheck ensures that the insurance will stay in force without the policyowner's writing a check for the premium.

The second principal advantage to the employee is that the insurance is normally offered on a guaranteed issue basis. This technique allows use of simplified forms and easy enrollment, and it provides assurance to the employees that the protection they seek is provided without the need to expose them to the rigors of physical examinations and other underwriting requirements.

The elimination of the expense of underwriting and the simplification of the expense of billing usually results in another advantage: lower premiums for the employee. This creates a trade-off for the insurer, since the elimination of underwriting invites antiselection. However, the higher mortality costs are more than offset by the expense reductions, and premium savings can usually be obtained.

Under certain payroll deduction plans, it is possible for employees to obtain life insurance on the lives of their spouses at the time they acquire insurance on their own lives. Payroll deduction plans offer similar opportunities to acquire amounts of insurance for the children of employees. Thus, the convenience of being able to provide basic insurance protection on all individual members of the family is a decided advantage to an employee.

The disadvantages of payroll deduction plans to employees center on the portability of the coverage and the amount of coverage available. When an employee changes jobs, the convenience of the payroll deduction method of paying premiums will not likely be transferable. In most cases, a job change necessitates finding another mode of premium payment, and, frequently, the result is that the insured employee allows the insurance coverage to terminate.

Most payroll deduction plans offer only small amounts of insurance. In addition, the small amounts of insurance offered cannot be offered at as low a premium rate per thousand as they could be if the amounts of insurance were larger. The normal economies of scale associated with larger policies are not present under these circumstances. In most instances, the savings attributable to the elimination of underwriting expenses and the establishment of the payroll deduction form of billing offset the greater costs that are attributable to writing smaller amounts of insurance. Thus, in the aggregate a very attractive and competitive pricing structure results.

Advantages and Disadvantages to Employers

From an employer's point of view, there are both advantages and disadvantages to offering payroll deduction plans to employees. Certainly, the employer can enjoy the additional goodwill derived from making a product available under a payroll deduction form of billing. In addition, many agents sell these products as an adjunct to an employee benefits communications program, which also results in an improvement of goodwill toward the employer and a better appreciation by employees of the company and its group benefit program.

A definite disadvantage, however, is the fact that an employer must either already have, or must establish, a payroll deduction capability within the normal payroll system to allow the deduction of premiums and their payment to the insurance company. In some cases, this can require that the employer make a commitment of a considerable amount of effort and expense to modify the payroll procedures. In addition, the employer must give the employees time to attend the sales presentation, thereby temporarily reducing their productivity. The employer must also spend some time with the soliciting agent on final working arrangements. In most instances, however, employers view this type of program as a meaningful addition to the employee benefits already offered. Since some group insurance plans do not cover spouses and children, the opportunities afforded by payroll deduction plans fill that void effectively.

Advantages and Disadvantages to the Writing Company

Utilization of direct response marketing techniques provides the writing company with much greater exposure to large numbers of potential policyowners, but significant cost may be incurred to gain this exposure. When insurance is offered on a guaranteed issue basis, the risk of antiselection always exists. People who know they are sick and suspect that they may not be able to obtain life or health insurance through other means (on an underwritten basis) are likely to enroll in plans offered through payroll deduction. The writing companies must be willing to take this risk.

The success and profitability of writing these products depends to a large degree on the persistency of the business written. Experience has shown that writing business through employers produces a high incidence of policy lapsation when an employee terminates employment. When an employee terminates, it is necessary for the insurance company to attempt to retain that business by making available other modes of premium payment. Since the payroll deduction arrangement terminates immediately upon the termination of employment, it sometimes takes several premium payment periods before the writing company can contact the employee, change the mode of payment, and institute a direct billing mode. By then, the company must bill the policyowner for several payments to make the account current, and, as a result, many policyowners lapse their protection. Since the payroll billing method is arranged between the insurer and the employer directly, the former employee's address is not updated in the insurer's records as changes occur. Hence, many employees are never found after termination of employment. To deal with these potential problems, writing companies must screen the types of businesses that are offered payroll deduction plans.

Summary

Direct response marketing of life and health insurance is an important means of insuring a segment of society. Specific products and underwriting principles are associated with direct response insurance marketing, which makes effective use of target marketing. The media of direct mail, print, broadcast and the telephone were discussed as tools of direct response marketers.

As the trend toward direct response marketing of life and health insurance grows significantly stronger, so, too, will the trend toward employer-sponsored payroll deduction plans. As larger industrial and ordinary insurance companies strive to find ways to reduce marketing expenses and lower acquisition costs, selling insurance to groups of employees at their places of employment through payroll deduction will become increasingly attractive.

Most insurers will probably approach the payroll deduction market as supplemental to its other markets, for there are risks attendant to this market. In a volatile economy, the possibility of periods of major unemployment, plant shutdowns, and strikes substantially increase the risk of losing major blocks of business sold on a payroll deduction basis. Even so, the attractiveness of payroll deduction plans seems to be growing, and the insurance industry looks for major expansion of such distribution in the years to come.

PART IV

FIELD AGENCY ACTIVITIES

Chapter 16

Recruiting, Contracting, and Training Agents

Frank E. Sullivan, CLU

Practically all of the individual life insurance sold in North America is distributed through the agency system. Control of the agency system is focused in the home office in the United States, called the head office in Canada. Distribution outlets exist in at least all major cities in which the company operates. These outlets, either general agencies or branch offices, are headed by a general agent or a branch manager, who is responsible for the office staff, and as many salespeople (agents) as the marketplace will justify. The people located in these outlets are referred to in the industry as the field force or the field, and represent the life and health insurance industry's contact with the consumer. The recruiting, contracting and training of agents will be addressed in this chapter.

It is necessary to recognize the importance of the agent's role in the insurance marketing scheme. As a representative of the insurer to the public, the agent provides the link through which products may be presented to an individual or group in order to resolve concerns and answer needs. Without an agent, there would be no family protection, no business protection, no premiums to invest, no home office to maintain, and no industry organizations.

The result of any management effort is directly related to the care given in the planning of a project. This certainly applies to the important activities of recruiting, contracting, and training new agents. With this in mind, it is imperative that a manager ask three basic questions before starting the necessary steps in recruiting, contracting and training new agents.

The first question is what is the type of company represented in the industry. There are now, and will continue to be, many different types of companies, but the key is that the person responsible for recruiting and training must know what kind of a company he or she is representing. A Stanford Research Institute (SRI) study predicts that in the 1980s there will be three major categories of companies selling life insurance:

1. The traditional life company selling only through its own full-time career field force, and selling basically the same products as sold in the 1960s and 1970s—individual ordinary life insurance, annuities and disability income insurance. This category could include fraternals and home service companies.
2. Career-type companies with expanded product lines to serve their clientele more completely and enhance the income potential of their field force. These include all-lines companies.
3. "Manufacturers" that market Section 79, retired lives reserves, and revertible term policies principally through the field forces of brokerage houses and the major mutual insurance companies because they do not have distribution systems of their own.[1]

A second question is what kind of person should go into field agency activity. It is surprising that in life insurance marketing, which is so oriented towards people, there has been little attention on the relationship of the person being recruited with the manager with whom he or she must work so intimately in order to succeed. There are ways to compensate for this problem. For example, LIMRA's Aptitude Index Battery (AIB) is a test for candidates for life insurance selling, and its credibility as a "rejection tool" is unchallenged. More will be said on this and other testing methods later.

The third question is what kind of agency the agents want to build. The beauty of the life insurance business is that a manager can determine in advance exactly what kind of an agency he or she wants to have three, five or ten years in the future, and plan for that goal. If the plan is properly laid out, it is similar to completing a puzzle because the pieces will eventually fit together.

Recruiting and Selecting New Agents

In recruiting, goal setting is important and must begin with a thorough analysis of an agency's circumstances as it moves into the fourth quarter of a calendar year. Although some companies operate on a fiscal year, the main measuring instrument of agents in the industry, qualification for the Million

[1] *Consumer Financial Decisions—Executive Summary,* SRI International, 1979.

Dollar Round Table (MDRT), is on a calendar-year basis. It takes thirty to sixty days to make projections into the following period. The agency must determine its goals for the end of the following year. Based on the history of an agency, the manager may predict how many new agents are needed fifteen months hence.

With a specific objective determined, a manager can determine from agency records how many persons must be contacted to end up with, for example, four full-time agents. If agency records are not sufficient to provide such data, LIMRA can provide information on recruiting ratios. If agency records indicate its recruiting ratios are poorer than LIMRA's, then recruiting procedures should be re-evaluated with some specific objectives in mind. Recruiting ratios are discussed in more detail in the following chapter.

Goals of Recruiting

Recruiting is such an important activity to the overall success of an agency that it is crucial to understand the basic objectives of recruiting. These objectives are (1) to select candidates as carefully as possible, that is, recruit the kind of people most likely to succeed in the insurance business, as identified by tests and profiles; and (2) to interview enough candidates to allow the law of averages to work so that the desired number of agents can be recruited.

The first goal of recruiting should be to select as carefully as possible the candidates most likely to succeeed. Obviously, this care saves time, effort, and money for the general agent, the manager, the new agent, the policyowners, and the company. The fact that this approach would also save much money is self-evident, because each hour wasted and each dollar spent on a recruit or potential recruit who does not succeed is a "non-recoverable" dollar that could have been used to increase dividends or improve products.

But, selecting the right candidate is not easy because not everyone has a personality suited to selling life and health insurance. Insurance sales is not hard work physically, but from a psychological standpoint it is an ego-shattering way of making a living, primarily because of the attitude of society towards the profession. Few students enter college in order to become life insurance agents. Reactions from family and friends to the news that someone is embarking on a life insurance sales career is frequently not enthusiastic. Candidates must be aware of the problems associated with an insurance sales career and must be selected because of their apparent ability to overcome them.

Agent turnover is high, and an important reason for the poor retention is that insurance personnel—from recruiters and top management to the trade associations and industry spokespersons—have not really prepared candidates for the realities of selling in the course of the recruiting process. Candidates must realize that a sale cannot happen until an agent is committed to helping a prospect research their family or business protection needs, and provide them with the life insurance contract that best suits their needs and capacity to pay. Thus, until potential agents are told the truth about the role a life insurance agent plays in our society, retention will not improve, nor will enough people likely to succeed be recruited.

Second, a recruiter needs to be aware of how much recruiting activity must be scheduled to recruit one agent. LIMRA makes available a formula that figures how many candidates need to be interviewed in order to recruit one agent. This formula is much more than academic, but it can vary based on the objectives of the recruiter and his or her capacity to obtain good interviews. The LIMRA formula serves as a guide, stating that, on the average, *X* candidates must be interviewed to get one good recruit and that *X* good recruits are needed to retain one agent at the end of four years.

The Steps in Recruiting

This section addresses the mechanical procedures which take a manager from getting a candidate's name to contracting him or her as an agent—these are the steps in recruiting. The steps include (1) finding sources of prospective agents, (2) determining acceptable qualifications, (3) approaching prospective agents, (4) using selection tools, and (5) interviewing the candidate. Before beginning, however, a recruit budget commensurate with objectives for the year must be developed.

Finding Sources of Agents

It is important that a recruiter establish a procedure that involves at least one action every day that is part of the recruiting process. For example, onc important task of a recruiter is to use centers of influence, or ready "pools" of people with contacts, (for example, bankers, CPAs, attorneys, or business people), to recommend names of possible candidates to the recruiter.

Probably the most reliable source of prospective agents is from referrals. Referrals may come from third persons, successful agents in the agency, and satisfied clients of the agency. Referrals from third persons, also known as nominators, may come from friends, civic leaders, religious leaders and educators. The reason that referrals are such good sources of recruits is that successful people can spot successful traits in others, and are generally willing to help recruiters.

But, even more important than the quality of the third party doing the referring is the procedure through which a manager gets a candidate's name. The right question asked of nominators will frequently result in some good candidates to interview. Nonrecruiters do not know how to respond to general questions such as, "Give me the names of three people who you think would succeed in selling life insurance." A more effective question is "Give me the name of the most impressive salesperson who has called on you in the last twelve months." Another valid question is, "Who is the most successful person you know who is always complaining about the amount of traveling his or her job requires?" A key to recruiting is to have a substantial reservoir of names of nominators and to know how to maximize the amount of time these nominators are willing to give.

It is critical that the recruiter work to develop enough knowledgeable nominators to provide the number of names necessary to staff an agency with qualified people as stated in the objectives. If the "data base" through nominators is not sufficient to provide enough candidates through the nominator process, there are other sources of recruiting, which include personal observation and visits to college campuses. Direct mail, newspaper ads, and employment agencies are also a source of recruits. Although the passing ratio on screening tests, such as the AIB, of candidates has always been the lowest among those names obtained through newspaper ads and employment agencies, these sources have always been attractive because of the volume of names generated; also, no direct involvement is required except with those candidates whose credentials are acceptable.

A new dimension has been added in the emergence of some national recruiting companies who develop an extensive data bank of people seeking a career change. These firms place ads for employment openings in the *Wall Street Journal* and other national publications. The service, not just for life insurance companies, has a data bank of people across the country who wish to consider a career change and, in some instances, a geographical change. As the responses to advertisements are received, they are analyzed and segmented by location. The information is then sent to those firms (or agencies) who contract for names in their area. Several general agents are using this vehicle with some degree of success.

Sources should be developed to keep a recruiter active for twelve months per year. No matter how few or how many names are needed, some attention must be given to recruiting every day.

Determining Acceptable Qualifications

Once a continuing source of candidates has been established, the specific characteristics wanted in a recruit must be identified. Studies indicate that successful life insurance agents have several traits in common.

The majority of people who succeed in life insurance selling enter the business between the ages of twenty-five and forty-five. Age twenty-five or above is set because it seems that, for most, insurance sales does not offer a stimulating enough opportunity to be a person's first job effort. This is understandable. Many jobs look more glamourous than life insurance selling, and starting salary to new entrants in the job market means more than earning potential. However, after three to five years in a comfortable job that offers little immediate challenge, is quite confining, and has a salary level that moves slowly, a young person is ready to accept less glamour for a job with more potential. This outlook generally holds true up through age thirty, (and in some instances up to age forty-five), but as a general rule, the majority of changes from age thirty-five to forty-five come about because the person has reached a "dead-end" in his or her present job. A candidate wanting to leave a dead-end job is a good risk. A person over age thirty-five who takes the chance of leaving a "safe harbor" to try a new challenge has character—the kind of character necessary to succeed in life insurance selling and in a commission business. For this reason, at least part of any recruiting program should be designed to pursue people over age thirty-five who are seeking a career change.

Married candidates are also more likely to succeed, especially if the spouse approves of a career in life insurance selling. Perhaps this is due to the motivation of most married people to make a good and consistent income and to try to remain with their jobs.

College graduates have better success than noncollege graduates. But there may be an interesting explanation for this. If an agency limits its attention to candidates over age twenty-five, then it means that the noncollege people have been working for seven to eight years and, if they are succeeding, they may be already beyond the income level of a starting agent. They are not likely to be eager to come in at entry level in a career of selling life insurance, whereas college graduates in the twenty-five to thirty age group may be coming from their first job where progress was too slow for their ambition.

Another very important qualification is the candidate's previous history in sales of any line. As will be seen more clearly in subsequent paragraphs, insurance is a selling career, and if the person cannot sell, he or she cannot succeed. If the ability to sell successfully has already been demonstrated in another line of work, it is a clue to the potential success the candidate may have in life and health insurance. This does not, however, mean that people without previous selling experience are automatically more likely to fail than those with experience. A candidate must be ambitious and competitive to succeed in this most competitive field; and if obvious evidence to this effect does not exist in their past performance, they should be eliminated from consideration.

A little recognized trait that is important for recruiters to consider is a candidate's capacity to absorb information and training. The AIB and other tests will help here, but recruiters must be very careful. Related to this is the reason(s) a candidate wants to change. When a candidate says he or she is bored, the recruiter should know what it is that bores the candidate. Many candidates say their jobs bore them, but to make a living selling insurance, candidates must be willing to discipline themselves to absorb information and training. Agencies place varying emphasis on such qualifications as the agent's business and professional contacts, health, and commitment to self-improvement.

Some qualifications have exceptions. Certainly some people outside the twenty-five to forty-five age range have been successful, just as many single people have become successful agents. However, the recruiter must rely on the general guidelines—at least at the beginning—and those listed do apply more often than not.

Business or professional contacts should always receive a low priority in selection criteria. If a person can sell, he or she can sell to anyone. Even if an agent has good contacts, they will be used up quickly, and then the moment of truth must be faced. While an agent may be a native of the marketplace, his or her eventual success may be due to the ability to grow out of those contacts and move into other markets—beyond the "natural" connections of any one person.

In addition, recruiters must become extremely well-versed in all rules and laws that govern equal employment opportunity in life insurance sales. The fact that some of these rules may seem inappropriate to a specific situation is irrelevant. Many suits are in the courts today because the recruiter did not know the law. Thus all recruiters must be very careful and conscientious as they make their selections.

Approaching Prospective Agents

Every step of the approach to a candidate should be taken as if a career depended upon its success. The more concentration on the procedure, the fewer interviews will be needed to achieve success. A candidate's first impression of a recruiter is an important factor in the candidate's reception to the idea of an insurance selling career.

A procedure should be established whereby the candidate is written a sincerely flattering letter indicating that the recruiter has heard some impressive things about the candidate from a nominator. The recruiter should then say that he or she is building an organization over the next several years and expects to have some exceptional growth opportunities in which the candidate might have a place. An interview is then set up with candidates who respond favorably to the apporach.

Using Selection Tools

During the initial interview, the manager may choose from several tools available to assist in the selection of agents. For more than fifty years, LIMRA has been perfecting the process of selection, and many other private companies and consultants have specialized in the area of testing potential insurance agents.

LIMRA's AIB is one of several tests designed for use in the insurance industry and has tested over one million candidates for hundreds of life insurance companies in the United States, Canada, and around the world. In Canada, the AIB is called the Inventory of Insurance Selling Potential. AIB "Form 2" has been designed for the use of combination companies. The test is a rejection tool that predicts, with remarkable accuracy, the potential of an individual and especially identifies those candidates most likely to fail in insurance selling rather than those most likely to succeed. It saves time, effort, and money for the manager, and it helps candidates learn more about themselves and their potential.

The AIB is administered by LIMRA and centrally scored by a computer, which assures objectivity and compliance with equal opportunity laws and invasion of privacy regulations. Companies can determine what score they wish to use as a minimum acceptance level. That is, a company may set a minimum score below which they will not contract a candidate.

Interviewing the Candidate

Once the AIB (or other selection test) indicates that a candidate should be pursued further, perhaps the most critical task in recruiting is the selection interview. Good agency managers devote 20% or more of their time to selection interviews.

It is helpful for the manager to conduct a structured interview. To assist the manager in this task, LIMRA produces a guide for use in the selection interview called the Selection Interview Blueprint (SIB). It is a workbook which guides the interviewer step by step through the entire process, making it much easier for the recruiter to be professional and thorough. A good interview also lessens the candidate's apprehension.

Recruiters must be willing to admit that selling life insurance is a tough way to make a living, and candidly explain this to potential recruits, in order to avoid recruiting and retention problems. If the candidate is made aware of the problems as well as the benefits of a career of selling life insurance, many long-range problems can be avoided.

Selling life insurance is an especially lonely business. The ego of a salesperson can be shattered many times a day. Thus, a major step in the selection process is the interview(s) with the spouse of the candidate. If the agent cannot come home to an understanding environment and an understanding spouse, the chances of success are substantially reduced. Meyer Friedman M.D., a noted cardiologist and author of the best-selling book *Type A Behavior and Your Heart,* said that a person can stand unbelievable stress either at work or at home, but he or she cannot stand stress at both places.

In summary, despite the fact that the process of recruiting deals almost exclusively with people, it is also a procedure. The danger is that it can become too personal and the recruiter's judgment can become clouded by subjective reactions to the candidate. Objective evaluations are crucial to the success of any recruiting activity.

Trends in Recruiting

Three key trends have potential consequences for the future of recruiting: the recruiting of minorities, the recruiting of women, and the recruiting of experienced agents. The insurance industry is continuing its concentration on the recruiting of minorities and women. It is now recognized that women and minorities make excellent salespeople. The insurance industry, through all of its segments, including home and field offices, must be committed to total involvement of these groups.

Recent studies indicate that practically every company is hiring a high percentage of experienced agents—agents from other companies. This is a very controversial subject among agency companies, yet study of some of the reasons shows that such practices may make sense for both agent and company.

Some companies have validation programs that are so restrictive that it affects agent retention. In a validation program, a company sets a minimum premium volume that a new agent must sell. If an agent does not make enough sales to justify the "salary" being paid, he or she does not "validate." The validation programs of many companies are so stringent that agents leave or are terminated just as they are beginning to reach their break-even point.

In addition, many agents "outgrow" their local agency, and rather than move to another locality to stay with the company, they change company affiliation in the same city. This occurs because some general agents or managers are not as capable as some of their competitors or may not have the same ambitions for themselves, their agency or their agents. Thus, the agent looks for a more compatible environment.

Finally, insurance sales is a restless business and the grass always looks greener in someone else's pasture. Sometimes moving to another company proves to be a right move, but often the lesson is learned that the environment seldom changes the person.

Overall, the trend of recruiting from other companies' field forces is not viewed favorably by agency companies. However, few companies can recruit another company's agent if that agent is happy, and making that person happy at work begins with the first moment he or she is contracted by an agency. Retention will improve when real effort is made to satisfy agents in their work.

Contracting a New Agent

The process of preparing a person to sell life insurance has both legal and educational components. From a legal standpoint, all states and most foreign countries require that a person be licensed to sell life and health insurance and have a contract with a specific company or general agent. In addition, many states and many companies require that certain educational requirements be met before a person may be licensed or at least before he or she is permitted to start to sell. Pre-contract training and the elements of an agent's contract are discussed in this section.

Pre-Contract Training

A program that is somewhat unique to life insurance selling is pre–contract training or pre-contract orientation. The program is not similar in all companies, but the objectives and characteristics are similar in all programs. The concept is based on the fact that, because it is so difficult to predict success for an agent, anything that can be done to narrow the margin of error is worthwhile to all parties. Thus, the more prospective agents can learn about their jobs before they leave their current employment, the fewer failures will occur. This approach is selection oriented: the better job of selection that is done, the greater is the potential of improved agent retention.

Pre-contract training works in the following manner. Once a candidate and the recruiter have agreed that there is enough mutual interest to continue discussions about a career in insurance sales, but still not enough to make a final decision, a trial program is in order. A schedule is worked out which permits the candidate to continue at his or her current job while studying the principles of life and health insurance, as well as the principles and practices of the particular life insurance company.

The great value of pre-contract training is that it introduces the candidate (trainee) to the three major subjects a salesperson must master to succeed in life and health insurance selling. These three subjects are the skills of prospecting, making the presentation, and closing the sale. None of these skills is a natural trait; however, they can be acquired by people who are committed to learning. In pre-contract training that commitment or lack of it shows itself early. A person in pre-contract training who misses one deadline, shows a lack of commitment and the agency manager must realize this at the outset.

Another very important item to be learned in pre-contract training is how to fit into an agency as a commissioned salesperson. The trainee has the opportunity to meet and observe successful life insurance agents in action. This is the time to take the state examination, and to complete all licensing procedures. It is truly a "try-out camp" for people who are seriously interested in the career of selling life insurance. The length of pre–contract training programs vary according to circumstances, but such programs seldom run more than ninety days; by that time, the manager should know how the trainee fits into the agency. Any more time leads to procrastination. If a candidate can complete the program sooner and looks promising, then the date for formal contracting can be accelerated.

The Agent is Contracted

A trainee who performs well throughout pre–contract training is ready to be contracted. The main element of the contract between an agent and the company is the definition of the plan under which the agent will be compensated. A legal contract (which is pre-approved in the state where the agent is to be contracted) is drawn between the agent and either the company or the general agent, depending upon which distribution system the company uses. As a general rule, those companies which operate through general agents have their contracts with the general agent and the agents in turn are contracted by the general agent. Almost all other companies (home service, managerial, all-lines, etc.) contract their agents directly.

Financing New Agents

Even though the sale of life insurance is basically a commission business, it becomes very evident that a plan to help the new agent meet living expenses while becoming established is needed. This is true for three reasons. First, training time required at the outset reduces the number of hours the agent can devote to actual selling. Second, because compensation is a percent of the premiums actually paid, early sales on a monthly or quarterly basis do not generate enough income to live on. Finally, in time, up to 50% of the agent's income will be derived from renewal commissions, but he or she will have none of these in the first year, and relatively few in the first three years of the career.

There may be as many forms of compensating new agents as there are companies in the life insurance business, but most come under the accepted industry term, financing. In financing, dollar assistance is provided to new agents until they are established in their careers. Financing, in its many forms, undertakes to estimate what it costs an agent to live and what that agent will be earning in three years. A three-year financing, or subsidy, period has proven to be the time needed for an agent to get fully established.

The dollar amount that an agent must sell to meet a specific financing plan can be very precise if it is determined in a vacuum. For example, if the average size premium is $20 per $1,000 of life insurance, then the average size commission is about $10 per $1,000. Thus, if financing provides $1,000 per month income, an agent must sell $100,000 per month of life insurance, or at least average that amount over the period of time that a training allowance subsidy is paid.

Of course such decisions are made in the real world, and companies lose money on training allowances because many agents fail. To hedge this loss most companies require a validation schedule whereby the agent's sales (production) must meet certain quarterly benchmarks set by the company. If sales fall short of the minimum, the compensation is reduced or terminated. A second hedge for the companies is the company's contractual right to the renewal commissions on insurance that stays on the books after the agent terminates. Neither of these hedges prevents companies from losing money in financing, but they do serve as monitors of the system.

The life insurance industry must find ways to improve financing of new agents in the 1980s and beyond. In the early 1950s, a typical financing arrangement was $250 per month. This meant that an agent had to sell $25,000 per month, a reasonable amount in that era. Now, inflation and competition are forcing companies to consider $2,000 per month financing. Thus, an agent would need to sell $2,000,000 worth of life insurance in his or her first twelve months. That is difficult and unrealistic. Means of dealing with agent financing is one of the high priority issues that must be addressed in the near future.

Commissions

Once the financing or subsidy period is over (usually thirty-six months), the agent must move on to a full commission contract. Commissions are a way of life in selling life and health insurance. A major cost to insurers is the acquisition cost, what it costs to put business on the books. Since agent compensation is the major component of acquisition cost, compensation must be a definite percentage of the premium income, which dictates that it be a commission, calculated as a percentage of premium.

Although there is some variation in the amount of commission paid by different companies, that variation is less than commonly believed. This is because it is governed by two powerful forces: competition and New York law. Since insurance companies are selling dollars for future delivery, they must be similar in their allocation of costs or they will not be competitive in terms of premiums. If one company pays out 50% of first-year premium as compensation and another pays out 100%, the latter will have difficulty in delivering a competitive product. Commission schedules must be high enough to attract good agents, but not so high as to adversely affect the cost of the policy.

As a result of the Armstrong investigations at the turn of the century, the New York Insurance Commissioner mandated the maximum commission percent that life insurance companies could pay if they wanted to do business in the state of New York. To this day, these laws are still the greatest influence on life insurance commission schedules because so many companies do at least some of their business in New York.

Traditionally, a contract approved in New York pays an agent 55% of the first-year premium as a commission. In addition, the agent receives 5% of the premium as a commission in the second through the tenth year if the business stays on the books. Were it not for inflation it would appear to make more sense to "level" the commission over the first ten years; this is a possibility for the future because a good agent is highly taxed on the 55%, and yet finds it difficult to give good annual service and make a profit on the 5% renewals. To "level" would mean to take the total of all ten years' commissions (55% + [9 × 5%] = 100%), divide it by ten years, make an adjustment for the value of the money, and pay the agent the same (level) amount for all ten years.

Renewal commissions may be either vested or nonvested. Vested commissions indicate that future renewal commissions are guaranteed to an agent should he or she leave the insurance company and/or the business. It is a controversial issue which is handled differently in many companies. Many believe that renewal commissions should go to the agent serving the policyowner, whether the original agent or not, and thus argue against vested commissions. Others believe that *all* commissions should go to the agent who sold the policy, even if the agent is no longer with the insurance company, and thus argue for vested commission. Some believe that the insurance company is entitled to the return of their dollar investment in the agent, and the balance should be the agent's.

Other Aspects of the Contract

Other benefits in the contract relate to what the company or the general agent provides the agent in the way of technical support, managerial support, and training support. In some people's opinion, these items can outweigh the dollar support many times. In the daily work of a life insurance salesperson, much is routine. If the company or the agency can undertake the routine work (computer service, equipment, illustrations, etc.), it will give an agent much more time to be innovative and thus make more sales.

Training Provided for Agents

A good life and health insurance agent gets closer to the financial problems of the family than most other professionals. In view of this, those agents must be trained to serve families in the best possible way. The subject will be divided into training for new agents and training for established agents. The techniques for training are discussed in this section.

Training New Agents

To begin the task of training, a manager must prepare new agents to constantly study and learn new concepts. A person entering life insurance selling must be committed to the fact that to succeed he or she must become a perpetual student. The day will never come when all studies will be complete because the subject of insurance and related fields are constantly changing.

Principles of Insurance

Training for new agents centers on the principles of insurance, company contracts and practices, sales techniques, and planning and personal work habits. The principles of life insurance include the description of a policy contract, how it works, and the benefits in the event of death, disability or forfeiture. Different policy plans and their important provisions are described. An understanding of the needs that life and health insurance are designed to meet are essential to an understanding of the principles of insurance.

In addition, as an agent grows in life insurance selling, the need for technical training increases. In today's complicated economy even people of modest incomes have tax problems, and everyone who owns real estate in the United States faces a potential major estate tax. Thus, the agent must be trained in income and estate taxation as it applies to life insurance, general business and accounting practices, advanced underwriting and all the complexities of pension and group insurance legislation as vital steps on the career path. The life insurance industry is strong in providing education through company programs, the Life Underwriters Training Council (LUTC) and the CLU program, and commercial programs. Attendance at MDRT and CLU meetings is equivalent to refresher course.

Company Contacts and Practices

It is important for an agent to have general information about the company right from the start of his or career. Many companies are over 100 years old and have a unique history. Even more important, the agent should learn everything about the company's product portfolio, its rules, regulations and requirements.

Sales Techniques

Obviously, learning good sales techniques is essential for a new agent. A salesperson is trained, not born naturally. He or she must learn prospecting because a minimum of twenty to thirty new names must be developed each week. A prospect is a person who has an insurance need, can afford to pay to have the need solved, and who can be seen on a favorable basis. A favorable basis is a circumstance under which the agent will have the time and the privacy to make the presentation, whether it is in the prospect's home, office, a restaurant or the agent's office. This is a skill that must be learned for survival.

Once prospecting skill is acquired, the next subjects for training are (1) the sales presentation, (2) the objections, and (3) the close. The time a prospective buyer gives to an agent is priceless. Therefore, the agent must maximize this time with a deserving sales presentation. More sales are lost because of a poor sales presentation than for any other reason. Yet, here again, the approach in a presentation is a skill that can be mastered. In training, a new agent must be convinced of the value of following a presentation as if it were a script. This leaves no room for errors in the presentation. Many believe sales presentations should take fifteen minutes. In the presentation, a salesperson articulates the reasons for insurance, what a prospect needs, what is available to meet the needs, and how best to pay for it.

Objections—reasons prospects give agents for not being interested in buying a product—are as old as the art of communication. Thus, it is essential for new agents to learn the skill of handling objections. Many believe that if someone is truly a prospect, he or she is not really objecting, but rather is saying, "You have not told me anything that is convincing about your product." For example, the objection, "It costs too much," really means "You have not convinced me that my family needs the protection to the extent that I should pay that much in premium." Another objection, "I can invest my money elsewhere and do better," is translated, "I do not relate the immediacy of the death benefit to the small premium charged." The well-trained salesperson does not argue against objections, but rather tries to determine the underlying reasons for a prospect's objections. This is a difficult thing to do, and is acquired over time. The agent emphasizes that protection of the family (or business) is a desirable objective. If a prospect's objections can be dealt with effectively, the prospect completes the application, and agrees to a medical examination and a follow-up interview.

The close consists of the effort of the agent to assist the prospect in making a decision. At this time the agent has the policy in hand (if the applicant is approved), and only the decision to buy needs to be made. If the prospect agrees to buy, he or she becomes a client or policyowner. If the prospect says "no" to a purchase, the agent must retrace each step with the prospect up to the close. If the prospect still does not purchase, the agent should thank the prospect and leave. Much emphasis is placed on "closing the sale," probably more than is warranted.

Planning and Personal Work Habits

Although planning and personal work habits are difficult to teach, they have more to do with the success of a salesperson than does any other component. It does not take a genius to sell life and health insurance. What it does take is a person who can be disciplined to do those things that are identified as the keys to success in selling. These are prospecting, the approach, the presentation, verbalization, the close, and last and most important, keeping clients satisfied after the sale. It is essential that these aspects of selling are planned as part of the salesperson's daily routine. One approach to planning and time control is to encourage the agent to operate as if he or she had the authority to plan every minute of the week exactly as if he or she were in complete control.

Life insurance sales can provide a fascinating career. If an agent exerts extra effort, the insurance business provides great opportunity for both personal and professional growth. Also, general agents and managers have the freedom to build a strong local agency, regardless of the size and stature of the company they represent.

Who Should Conduct Agent Training

Training new agents is perhaps the most important long-term function of any agency. Therefore, the basic responsibility should rest with the senior person in the office, whether a general agent, manager, or district manager. As an agency grows, the manager can, and must, delegate some training activities to subordinates. To be effective, training must be done at approximately the same time every day or every week, and delegation of training to an assistant manager facilitates this. To have the agent's training program interrupted for any reason invites trouble.

Each life and health insurance company should have a basic training program in which they run schools, provide the study materials, keep agents up-to-date, and so on. But, the day-to-day training has to be done on the local level under the overall supervision of the senior most person in the office—the general agent or manager. One question that needs to be answered is the optimum length of a training period. A formal training program may have a designated length; however, in the insurance industry, training should be continual.

Types of Training

There are two types of training, home office training and agency office training. Home office training usually runs for one week and is frequently on a specialty subject, for example, business insurance, pensions, or advanced underwriting. In addition to this, many companies have a basic training course that runs one week for people who have been in the business less than one year. This home office training usually is classroom training, lasts all day, and involves homework and role-playing. Most companies do an excellent job in this area.

Unfortunately, there is room for criticism regarding individual training in the field. First, it is difficult for a company to develop a program that will apply in agencies throughout the country. But, of even greater concern are the individual capacity and commitment of trainers at the local level. The training program for new agents and the ability of the managers doing the training are important factors for any prospective agent to consider in the decision of which agency to join. Individual training of agents needs to be conducted in a personalized manner because each agent is unique and each situation is different.

NALU produces a formal program known as "The Career Path of the Life Underwriter." It was designed by the leadership of several industry organizations and educators. It recognizes various levels of expertise of agents and permits them to grow accordingly. Training should be designated according to the levels in the career path program: basic, intermediate, advanced, and continuing. Each basic training program is set up somewhat differently, with a specific timetable that is important to follow. As agents progress in their careers, they may move to the next step in the career path.

Training Established Agents

The life insurance industry, like most other industries, has awakened to the fact that the need for continuing education is great and that some valuable resources are wasted by not keeping established agents up-to-date. The investment that companies and agencies have in established agents is so great that everything possible should be done to keep them well-trained and aware of all new developments relating to the business. This training should also focus on improving skills. A salesperson can never be at a point where improvement is impossible.

Such training of established agents must be heavily promoted by the company and general agents/managers. Years ago it was considered unnecessary for an established agent to have to be trained continually. Today it is well-recognized fact that, with the rapid changes in economic conditions and tax laws, agents and their clients benefit from continuing training.

Some attention should be paid to the changes in behavior and attitudes of agents as they grow and become more successful and set in their ways. An emphasis on behavioral learning in the advanced training of salespeople thus becomes important. The MDRT, the American College, AALU and General Agents and Managers Conference (GAMC) frequently present psychologists and psychiatrists as speakers at their meetings to help agents better understand themselves and their clientele.

Selling life insurance is a lonely job, particularly after one becomes well-established. Thus, in addition to the items mentioned above, there is a need to motivate established agents to continue to collect names, call on prospects, and make presentations on a regular basis. This motivational material is supplied through reading matter, audio cassettes, video cassettes, and meetings. The following groups have meetings that place a high emphasis on agent motivation: MDRT, CLU Forum and Institutes, AALU, national and local associations of life underwriters, in addition to company meetings.

The opportunity for continuing education and training provides the means for future success in the life insurance business. Established agents who take advantage of these learning opportunities will benefit professionally and personally from the experience.

In summarizing the training area, perhaps the most important component is the equivalent of a "report card." All salespeople have great intentions, but the distractions of the business make it easy to forget them and move on to the next sale or the next problem of the day. Therefore, a good program may require an agent to make a complete analysis of all phases of his or her career at the end of each year and make written plans in advance of the first of the calendar year. These plans should include all production plans, personal plans, and training programs, and are reviewed on a regular basis (for example, quarterly) by the manager and the agent.

The Future of the Agency Distribution System

The agency system is the somewhat generic term through which the majority of individual life insurance is sold in the United States, Canada and many other countries. It has many differing characteristics, but the most common denominator is a single agent making a single sale to a specific prospect, one-on-one. This one agent reports to a supervisor, a general agent, or a manager who works in or runs a somewhat autonomous local office for a national or regional life insurance company.

Tremendous opportunities exist for many life insurance companies in the future and most particularly to those using agency distribution systems. As mentioned earlier, the Stanford Research Institute sees three major categories of companies selling life insurance in the fourth quarter of the twentieth century: the traditional company, companies with expanded lines, and "manufacturers" using others' distribution systems. All three categories will use the agency distribution system to differing degrees. Just as there will be changes in the looks of some life and health insurance companies, and in the products sold, there will be some changes in what is traditionally called the agency distribution system, but probably not as much as some are predicting.

Consumers' wants and needs are changing, and the product mix of the business has recognized this. An ever-increasing percentage of the protection afforded consumers is coming through government plans and employer plans, with a smaller percentage coming through individually purchased programs. But, this makes the need for competent agents even more important than before. A professional is needed to dovetail the best of all programs, and the people trained in the highly professionalized programs mentioned in this chapter will be in great demand. Despite some opinions to the contrary, a person who is considering depositing a substantial sum of money to provide family and business protection wants and needs the personal services of a knowledgeable agent.

While there is some consumer criticism about the cost of the compensation programs used in the life insurance business, it does not take into consideration the fact that policies that are kept in force will require service for thirty, forty, or fifty years, long after the commission payments to the agent have ceased. In addition, field work is extremely difficult, but much needed. The field forces of the life insurance companies are responsible for bringing billions of premium dollars into the economic system each year. Life and health insurance need to be explained and sold and serviced. The insurance industry owes policyowners the best products, sales and service. Many believe the career agency system is the best system to provide this. With premiums going down and expenses going up, agents are forced to be more productive to survive.

In summary, more life insurance will be sold in each of the remaining years of this century. There will be fewer companies than there are today, and there will not be appreciably more agents or agencies. Thus, those in the field will be producing large volumes, earning more commissions (in dollars not percents) and servicing more clients.

Summary

Companies should be giving greater support to the field in order for each agent and each agency to become more productive. Companies must do this by providing the best product possible; by recruiting the highest qualified candidates; by training them in the most professional manner; by providing agents with a total support "package" for pre-approach, approach, the interview, and for creating a client. Recruiting, contracting, and training are essential field activities. Both those at the home office and in the field must be aware that these activities are effective only if they are carefully planned and executed.

Chapter 17

Field Management

Philip R. Pepper, M.B.A., CLU

This chapter is concerned with the organization that makes life and health insurance sales by agents possible. The agents who sell the policies that produce the premiums on which the industry depends have to be recruited, trained, managed and motivated as well as replaced when attrition occurs. The policyowners require service from time to time as well as additional coverage as their needs change.

All of these essential functions come together at the field agency level and the person whose job it is to orchestrate and conduct the operation is the field manager. That is why most observers consider the job of field management to be the critical link in the ongoing progress and vitality of the whole industry as it is presently organized.

While there are a number of distribution systems employed within the life and health insurance industry, the career agency system is the most widely used and accounts for the bulk of the premium income. Field management, in one form or another, is a function that is common to those systems employing an agency force.

This chapter presents to the reader the many facets of the complex job entrusted to the field manager. The specific duties and responsibilities of the field manager will be described and some of the problems that make the job difficult will be discussed. In this way, there will be a better understanding of why those who are highly successful as field managers deserve to be as well-compensated as they are.

In any company, those who are responsible for the management of individual field agencies may have one of several titles, branch manager, agency manager, or general agent, to name but a few. In this chapter, field personnel charged with managing and developing agencies will be called field managers or agency heads. Home office officials who have the responsibility for appointing and supervising field managers will be called agency vice president or director of agencies. This will help avoid confusion, despite the wide variety of titles used in the industry.

Duties of the Field Manager

In general, a field manager's duties include managing people, managing time, and managing money. More specifically, the manager must manage resources to achieve the common objectives of the agency and of the company. To achieve these objectives, a field manager works through the traditionally accepted management functions of planning, organizing, and controlling. In addition, motivation must also be added as another management function. A field manager's success will be measured in terms of agency growth in production, agency growth in manpower, the degree to which agents and staff reach their potential, the increase in profitability of the agency, and improvement in agent retention.

Planning starts with the field manager's concept of the agency. This is essential to future success because it is the manager's ability to conceptualize that determines the organizational form of the agency. Planning includes determining the size of the agency, the markets to be served, the degree of specialization (pensions, estate planning, and business insurance) to be involved in, the role of the manager and the relationship between manager and associates, and plans for ultimate succession of the field manager.

Organizing consists of manpower development and directing the agency office staff. Manpower development involves locating, selecting and contracting agents, activities which collectively are known as recruiting. It also encompasses all aspects of agent training from the neophyte to the most sophisticated sales agent. The field manager must work with the office manager and clerical staff and define their duties. Another duty in organizing is determining the role of assistant managers and sales supervisors and the stage of development of the agency at which they should be added.

The controlling function includes setting production objectives, expense ratios and profit targets, then monitoring the actual results and, where necessary, taking corrective action to achieve the objectives. Also included here is the monitoring of individual agents' activities with a view to measuring their performance.

Motivating consists of providing positive supervision for agents. It includes providing guidance and direction to both agents and staff to help them grow as individuals and as salespeople. As growth occurs, appropriate recognition will reinforce their achievements and encourage further effort. Many field managers design contests and conduct sales campaigns as part of their motivational efforts.

This chapter looks at the activities of field managers from a slightly different perspective. Instead of the traditional functional approach, this chapter will look at these activities in terms that are more commonly used in the life and health insurance industry. In other words, the duties of the field manager consist of (1) manpower development and continuing education, (2) supervision of the field force, (3) motivation of agents and staff, (4) office duties, (5) public relations activities, (6) interpreting company policy, (7) developing second-line management, (8) expense control, (9) personal production, and (10) allocation of time.

Manpower Development and Continuing Education

Manpower development is the process by which the number of full-time career agents in the individual agencies is not only maintained but expanded. Because career agents are so important to companies using an agency system, it is accurate to say that the highest priority job for a field manager is that of developing manpower resources by the activities of recruiting and training new agents, and training established agents.

Companies evaluate their field managers by the number of career agents under contract and the average production per agent. To achieve a net increase in manpower, a field manager must recruit and train new agents and keep existing agents up-to-date in their sales skills through continuing education.

Be it a large established agency or a newly opened office, virtually every field manager starts each new year faced with the need for recruiting new sales personnel. It is not enough to put an ad in the local newspaper and wait for applicants to arrive. Happily, that process usually attracts good secretarial and clerical employees; however, up to now, few managers have been able to solve their agency manpower needs by relying on advertising. Just as it takes special skills to sell life and health insurance, it takes special talent to recruit agents to a career in life and health insurance and make them successful. The subjects of recruiting and training were dealt with in Chapter 16 and will not be repeated here. However, the following sections are concerned with how these essential activities fit into the overall duties of the agency head who is charged with building a career agency.

Recruiting

Recruiting is not one activity, but a process in which the sequence is usually (1) locating, (2) testing, (3) selecting, and (4) contracting. Rather than go through the whole process with one recruit at a time, many field managers locate several prospective agents at one time and then put them through these steps as a class. Since there is some fallout in the selection process, the class technique allows some recruits to be added to the agency from each recruiting drive. For this reason, recruiting a class rather than one agent at a time is a more efficient use of a field manager's time. It is common practice for field managers to devote as much as a full month to the recruiting process in order to have a class of recruits ready to start their training together. If the recruiting objective of an agency is to have a large force, the recruiting process may have to be repeated during the year.

Agent Training

The importance of training a newly appointed life insurance agent cannot be over-emphasized because the ability to sell is a skill that must be learned. Pre-contract training is widely used and can be a very effective selection device by putting prospective candidates through specific training assignments. During pre-contract training, it is essential that the field manager make clear to the prospective candidates what will be expected of them and get from the prospective candidates an understanding of their willingness to live up to those expectations.

In pre-contract training, field managers expect their agent candidates to learn what life insurance is and how it works, learn a basic sales presentation, become familiar with the company rate book and the company's most popular policies, study the licensing notes and successfully pass the state life insurance examination, and learn prospecting techniques and compile a list of contacts. By asking prospective candidates to undertake such assignments and to devote the time necessary to accomplish them while they are still working at their former jobs, the field manager will have a good reading on the candidates' willingness to complete assignments and to make an investment in their future careers. The candidate who does not complete these assignments is unlikely to do so after he or she has been contracted, and field managers will eliminate those who do not successfully complete the precontracting phase. This also gives the prospective agent the chance to withdraw before the contracting process is complete.

If the pre-contract training has been comprehensive, then the new agent is ready to start selling as soon as he or she joins the agency. This is important for agents who are financed because it gives them the maximum time period in which to make sales and validate their financing arrangement. Waiting to train the agents until their financing has started is costly both in terms of money and the field manager's time.

Naturally, individual field managers vary the timing as well as the content of their training program for new agents. However, during the first full year, an agent will normally be expected to accomplish the following:

1. Become thoroughly familiar with all the life and health policies offered by the company and learn the situations for which each is best suited;
2. Determine the needs of a family for income if the breadwinner dies. This is done by identifying their money needs by means of a checklist, known as a fact-finder. This is a method of measuring existing life insurance and other assets against those needs and proposing life insurance to cover deficiencies. The entire process is termed the case method;
3. Master the company's selling system and make at least one sale per week using it; and,
4. Develop reliable sources of good prospect referrals.

In addition, the new agent will be expected to attend all agency meetings and training sessions scheduled for the class.

The field manager will make an assessment of each agent's aptitude, and will guide the agent into additional markets, usually starting in the second year. These markets would include those that need business life insurance, life insurance for estate conservation, pensions and other employee benefit plans, if offered by the company, as well as group insurance. For a particular agent to acquire a full range of skills, this training would need to be spread over a two- or three-year period.

Not only must the field manager arrange time to schedule the necessary study classes, but the field manager must give the agent ample opportunity to practice the principles taught in the class. This involves giving the agent direct contact with clients which, in turn, requires that the field manager allow time for making joint field sales calls with the agent. Joint field calls are both a means of training and a method of supervision which can be employed throughout an agent's career. Joint field calls permit an agent to observe the field manager in action and then, reversing roles, allows the field manager to observe while the agent conducts the sales interview. Each joint field session should be followed with a critique while the events are still fresh in the agent's mind. One of the field manager's objectives should be to structure these joint field calls so that the agent feels comfortable and looks forward to the activity as an opportunity to learn.

Field managers have access to a wealth of training materials. These are made available by the field manager's own company, as well as by industry associations and commercial publishers.

Established Agents–Training and Continuing Education

Muscles that are not exercised atrophy and become weak, and so it is with human skills that go unused. Sometimes an established agent's production levels off or reaches a production plateau. When this happens, the field manager must determine the real cause. One possibility is that the agent has stopped growing or learning. Another reason can be boredom as a result of using a single sales technique over and over until the presentation becomes stale, uninteresting, and, as a result, ineffective.

Time and effort devoted to keeping established agents informed of new products and marketing developments is well worthwhile. In the first place, they can put this information to immediate use because they have prospects to call on. Agents who feel they are well-informed will be enthusiastic and energetic. Conversely, agents who feel they are not growing become discouraged and will eventually leave the agency; this is a complete waste of the field manager's earlier efforts. In the second place, keeping established agents growing and producing will be financially rewarding because such agents have already proven that they can sell and can make a living in life insurance sales—something that is unknown about a newly recruited agent replacing an established agent who terminates. The key to reactivating and energizing an established agent is to encourage a change in attitude, thereby rekindling the enthusiasm for the business and the will to succeed that new agents frequently have.

Helping established agents to keep their selling skills up-to-date is a vital part of a field manager's job because of the important contribution established agents make to total production and to agency manpower growth. A field manager must allocate time to work with established agents because they need and want a share of the manager's time.

Conducting joint field calls is also important with established agents because it provides the opportunity for the field manager to observe and evaluate a salesperson's activities. Field managers who make joint sales calls report that the activity is much more effective when they spend a whole day with an agent rather than basing their assessment and recommendations on a single interview. Joint calls also provide the opportunity for the field manager to demonstrate techniques to the agent. This can be particularly effective when established agents are being encouraged to break into what is a new market for them.

The review of an agent's annual production projections by the field manager provides an excellent opportunity to discuss each agent's plans for personal development. Discussions would ordinarily include objectives such as earning the CLU designation, earning the National Quality Award (NQA), and qualifying for MDRT membership. Discussions can center on how the agent can be prepared to gain entry into new markets in terms of study or special skills. It is particularly important for field managers to identify prospects in new markets and give an agent feedback on entering new markets.

Supervision of the Field Force

The level of supervision provided for agents varies in its intensity depending on an agent's experience and length of service. Close supervision is particularly helpful to a new agent until he or she develops good work habits and feels comfortable in the working relationship with the supervisor. At the outset, a daily session to review the previous day's activity is mandatory. Such sessions should reveal the way in which a new agent spent the day and verify that the activities were in accordance with the work patterns that had been agreed to. This would include the number of calls made to secure prospects, the number of calls made to arrange interviews and the number and outcome of any selling interviews that were scheduled. While in the early weeks there will be a good deal of joint field work with the agent's supervisor, this should not change the pattern of a review the following day of what was accomplished and what the plans are for the coming day. This review will offer opportunities to correct any misunderstanding on the agent's part and will help the agent to most effectively plan the next day's activities. After, for example, sixty days, such sessions might be held on alternate days; this schedule can be gradually relaxed to a point where a review is conducted once a week.

Agents react positively to supervision under the following circumstances: (1) agents are told what to expect at the outset, (2) agents view the supervision as helpful in improving their performance, and (3) agents help set the objectives that are being measured.

Weekly reports of each agent's activities and sales are required in most companies. It is important that agents understand that their own sales statistics enable them to monitor their performance against agency standards and to measure improvements in their own productivity. Agents should be encouraged to calculate their own statistics every week and to take pride in their improving effectiveness as indicated by these ratios. Their so-called "batting averages" might include all or some of the following:

- number of new prospects secured per week
- number of new cases opened per week
- number of closing interviews conducted per week
- number of sales or applications per week
- ratio of sales to cases opened
- ratio of sales to closing interviews conducted
- average size sale per application
- average size sale per case opened

Such statistics should be compiled on a cumulative basis since they are more meaningful when they cover a period of six or twelve months. Comparing one quarter with a subsequent quarter should demonstrate in a tangible way trends in an agent's performance. While such activity analysis is viewed by some as useful only to a new agent, many successful agents keep statistics over a lifetime to make sure that they are maintaining their "batting average." Where a class has been recruited together, there is value in their meeting regularly, not only for instructional sessions, but informally in a way that friendly competition can develop based on comparing their day-by-day accomplishments.

Successful field managers have developed the practice of having some form of communication with each of their agents every day. This may simply be a matter of situating the office in a position where the field manager can see the agents as they arrive in the office. A field manager may "make the rounds," visiting each agent at a time when the agent is usually in the office; similar courtesy is extended to all members of the field office staff. The purpose of these visits is to demonstrate to the agent the field manager's interest and concern. Such visits also permit the field manager to give special attention to an individual who may appear to need it for one reason or another. In such cases, the field manager can find out what is troubling the agent and what the field manager can do to rectify the situation. This simple process helps to avoid misunderstandings and the resulting loss of production.

Motivation of The Field Force

Motivation is defined as a stimulus which results in action. In sales, a field manager provides the stimulus to motivate the agent to take action that results in sales and related goals. There is nothing sinister in this since it will assist both the manager and agent to achieve their mutual objectives. A field manager uses formal in-depth reviews and group meetings, encourages attendance at industry organization meetings, takes personal interest in an agent, provides special office privileges, and conducts sales contests, all in the name of motivation.

Many field managers schedule a formal in-depth review with each agent every month to identify developing activity patterns. This is done on a one-on-one basis where the field manager reviews the agent's production records and previously set personal objectives, the purpose is to discuss the agent's progress towards these objectives and possible ways to improve. It is important that the field manager is prepared for such meetings and makes certain that there are no interruptions; this will not only save time, but demonstrates to the agent his or her importance to the agency in the eyes of the field manager. This sense of value to the agency cannot be overemphasized as a motivating force.

Groups of agents who are at approximately the same stage of development can be stimulated by being in study groups, particularly if agents can set the agenda and select the subject matter to be studied and mastered. Some become enthusiastic if they are placed in the position of expert within the agency on, for example, an aspect of estate planning, business insurance, or pensions. Asking agents to lead an agency seminar on a subject or to write an article for a company publication can also be stimulating. This can be useful for those who have completed their first year and who have demonstrated an interest in getting into new markets. The field manager in many cases can be more effective in such groups if he is a resource and a guide rather than an instructor.

Most field managers share the view that insurance industry associations make a substantial contribution to the continued success of the industry and that industry organizations such as NALU and GAMC are deserving of the support of those who have chosen the field as their vocation. Field managers encourage their agents to join and to attend meetings of local chapters of these associations. Many field managers attend regularly and introduce their new agents at the earliest opportunity. Similarly, experienced agents should be encouraged to attend meetings of local CLU chapters to learn of new developments and become acquainted with sales techniques applicable to sophisticated sales situations.

Another technique used by field managers to motivate their sales force is personal attention. Field managers may make it a point to have lunch with those agents who do not get into the office as regularly as others; this is especially true of any agents in detached offices when they visit the main establishment. Some field managers plan agency dinners at least once a year. These can be timed to coincide with a visit of an agency vice president or other senior person from the home office and can demonstrate to the agents that they are an important part of the agency team. In many agencies, the field manager makes it a point to recognize birthdays, not only of the agents, but also the staff, and, in addition, service anniversaries, births, marriages, and wedding anniversaries. Some agency heads send birthday cards to members of the families of the agents and staff. This is a function of motivation in that the field manager intends to show appreciation of an agent's service and to make the agent feel that he or she is essential to the success of the whole organization.

In a number of agencies, agent motivation is affected by the allocation of private and semi-private offices. These are made annually on the basis of production so that the agents who have done the best job of producing new business are assigned the best accommodations. However, it is important that if this is the basis for allocation of office space, this basis should be well-publicized and open to all concerned; some field managers make it a point to review the rules with the agents periodically to make sure that they are fair and acceptable to the majority. It is not unusual to provide secretarial help, either full-time or part-time on a similar basis, or in some instances to give an allowance towards the cost of secretarial help based on an agent's production.

Most companies sponsor one or two sales campaigns during the year, often in the spring and the fall, and the result is that often production peaks during these periods but slumps between such events. To help level off production and the resulting flow of commissions, many field managers plan special events within their own agencies designed to keep field activity at acceptable levels. Each of these motivational activities is intended to demonstrate to agents the concern of the field manager for their welfare and thus stimulate them to higher production.

Office Duties

While the responsibility for collection of premiums has been centralized in home offices in the majority of companies, the individual field manager is still responsible for a good deal of the service to policyowners. Many of the requests for service are purely routine, such as beneficiary changes, loan requests, repayments and changes in the use of dividends, and can best be handled by the clerical staff. When complaints are received, they should be handled by the person in charge of the office staff so that the policyowner will be satisfied. However, the agency head must be prepared to take over any complaints if allegations of misrepresentation or irregular applications of funds by the agent are made.

The extent to which individual agencies are involved in bookkeeping, payroll, and related activities will vary substantially among companies. Thus, the amount of time an agency head will have to devote to these activities varies. However, in all instances the field manager must have data provided regularly on the revenue and expenses that determine the agency's profitability and provides an early warning of any negative trends. This dictates the need for an agency budget and regular statements to show actual performance compared with planned objectives.

Many agency heads set aside a specific time each week with their office manager to review routine problems, to discuss exceptions and to communicate pending developments. Most companies provide a manual of standard operating procedures for use by the person in charge of the office, and such routines should be able to be followed without involving the field manager. On the other hand, the field manager must set aside sufficient time to handle correspondence with policyowners when needed and also with home office executives if it cannot be handled by the office manager. Maintaining a good working relationship with all of the home office departments is the goal of most agency heads since this not only contributes to a smooth agency operation, but enables all concerned to do their job more effectively.

Public Relations

One of the important duties of the field manager is to present the company in a favorable light to three distinct constituencies: the personnel of the agency, the policyowners, and the public at large. The responsibility for public relations at the agency level falls to the field manager and whether the manager chooses to focus on the accomplishments of agents and staff or on the growth and prestige of the agency, the message must be well-conceived and carefully planned.

The underlying rationale for public relations activities at the agency level are (1) to instill pride in the agents by honoring them and recognizing their achievements, (2) to make agents look good to their policyowners by publicizing their achievements, and (3) to make the agency look good to the public at large and to prospective recruits.

Recognizing Agents' Achievements

In many agencies, recognition is given to agents for outstanding performance and subsequently publicized to the audiences mentioned above. Some typical types of recognition are:

- Agent-of-the-month award
- Rookie-of-the-year award
- Agent-of-the-year award
- agency lives leader
- company production club qualifiers
- persistency leaders

Similarly, recognition of the successful completion of academic courses or professional designations, such as CLU, FLMI, and LUTC, are of particular significance to the achiever and deserve publicity within the agency, in the company, and, where appropriate, to the policyowner. Industry recognition, such as National Quality Award, National Sales Achievement, and membership in MDRT, are well-deserving of publicity. Other achievements to publicize would be the election of a member of the staff to an office of an industry association, and staff service on committees of such organizations or to voluntary community organizations. The agency head should not overlook the fact that the company house publication is always looking for news and will welcome the opportunity to give publicity to individuals who deserve recognition along these lines. Recognition of agents' achievements, while a part of public relations, is an important factor in agent motivation as well.

Publicizing Agents' Achievements to Policyowners

Publicizing agents' honors and achievements may take the form of agents' pictures displayed in a prominent spot or on the agency bulletin board or reproduced in the company's agency publication. Such items are publicized so that they may be seen by the families of those given the recognition. Similar means may be used to recognize those members of the agency staff who render outstanding service.

Field managers can achieve the goal of promoting agents to the public by building up the individual agent in the eyes of clients and prospective clients. Copies of the company or agency publication can be provided to clients when a particular agent is recognized for industry accomplishment. Similarly, announcement cards are available when agents receive the CLU, NQA, or similar recognition. These are an excellent means of communicating with policyowners and enhance the perception of the agency as a good place to do business.

Every contact with one of the company's policyowners should be viewed as a public relations opportunity because, aside from premium billing, insurance companies have limited contact with policyowners. Several surveys of policyowners have indicated that the policyowners feel they do not hear from their agents frequently enough. Routine conservation notices, responses to loan requests and letters sent on policy anniversaries or at maturity should include some reference to the agent's involvement or the willingness of the agent to render service and assistance. Most agencies do not do this, and, therefore, the agency that uses these opportunities to communicate to policyowners stands out from the rest.

Many field managers write to policyowners in advance of their regular recruiting activities, telling them that the agency growth has opened up opportunities for new agents and inviting them to nominate candidates for consideration. While the primary purpose of this is to get names of possible candidates, it is an excellent opportunity to inform policyowners of the progress of the agency which serves them and their community.

Publicizing the Agency to the Public

In addition to agents' accomplishments, a field manager would like the agency to have a good reputation within the community. Achieving this is another purpose of public relations at the agency level.

Because the rates for display advertising in most metropolitan daily newspapers are now very high, it is difficult to justify such expenditures on a regular basis. Most agency heads must explore other opportunities to communicate with the public at large. Some agencies have built a favorable public image by volunteering the services of agents and/or the field manager as speakers before service clubs or for career-day programs in high schools and community colleges. In cases where an agency plans to serve a new section of its city or county, they may choose to prepare the way for their agents by portraying the agency as a successful and progressive business organization. Publicity of this kind may be directed to a specific audience by means of direct mail or by using a community newspaper. In both cases the costs are modest in comparison to advertising in a daily newspaper.

Many agencies, and some companies, have developed brochures describing the services performed by members of the agency and the specific qualifications of their members. These brochures are designed to acquaint the community with the agency's areas of expertise and specialization and, because they are specific, their use with qualified prospects can be rewarding.

Interpreting Company Policy

Proper interpretation and subsequent communication of company policy is an important facet of the field manager's job. The manner in which the field manager communicates policy to staff and agents will influence their reactions and acceptance. Therefore, the manager should schedule any announcements of change, particularly in policy, only after fully understanding the underlying rationale for the change. Follow-up may also be required to insure timely and prompt implementation.

Developing Second-Line Management

Another duty of the agency head is to develop individuals for second-line management, the level of management in an agency that works closely with agents, known as assistant managers or sales managers. This involves teaching the skills of recruiting, training, and supervising life insurance agents to those demonstrating the ability and desire to move up to second-line management.

Field managers have several reasons for wanting to develop second-line management. First, it is essential that qualified personnel train and supervise new agents as the agency grows through recruiting. Field managers need others to help them in this task. Second, there is a long-range need to find an ultimate successor to the field manager, especially in view of the time it takes to develop fully qualified field managers. Third, an agency's proven second-line management development program is a valuable aid in recruiting new agents because this can be offered as additional inducement to join that agency.

Candidates for second-line management are generally agents who volunteer their services because they wish to emulate the lifestyle and standard of living of a field manager, or in whom the field manager recognizes managerial traits that could be developed. They may come from the field manager's own agency or from agencies of other companies. Quite naturally, as agents mature and enjoy more success they wonder about management as an opportunity for them. They see a successful field manager enjoying a good standard of living and some of the privileges of a successful executive. If the opportunity for management is not available in an agent's own agency, then the agent is vulnerable to overtures from other companies. Either way, candidates can find out if they are suited to management only by trying it under actual field conditions. The program must recognize the value of learning from one's own mistakes and the importance of reinforcing those things one does well.

A few field managers have been so successful with their programs that in addition to their own needs they have provided a steady flow of trained managerial talent to other agencies within their company. However, company-sponsored second-line management development programs have generally failed to produce a regular flow of trained candidates. In part, this can be explained by the fact that many companies have not provided adequate financial incentives to agents to become field managers or, in addition, to field managers to devote the required time to a management development program. This problem is covered more specifically, however, in the section on agent and field management retention.

Expense Control

One of the field manager's jobs is managing money, including controlling expenses. It is important to distinguish between personal compensation paid to the field manager for managing the agency and the monies provided to cover the agency's expenses. The latter are often designated as expense reimbursement allowances (ERA). The expense allowances pay operating costs such as rent, clerical salaries, telephone, and stationery, and in addition, are intended to cover discretionary expenses like sales promotion and public relations, advertising, expenses associated with recruiting and other costs that will contribute to long-term growth. The agency head must be prepared to make expenditures of this kind if the agency is to prosper and grow.

In managerial companies, recurring expenses that have been authorized and are within budget are frequently paid directly from the home office, and where this occurs, the company provides periodic statements of expenses paid, how such expenses compare with previous years and the relationship between such expenses and current year's production. In contrast, in typical general agency companies, the general agent receives an amount based on production, spends it as necessary and has an individual system of expense control.

Only those agencies that operate on a profitable basis can, in the long run, be considered successful and afford to continue. Therefore, financial plans must be carefully prepared and then monitored to make sure they are adhered to.

Personal Production

Some field managers, in addition to their managerial responsibilities, conduct a substantial personal practice with their own clientele. In such cases, the field manager must set priorities to accommodate this dual role. Where agency functions have to be delegated to others, field managers frequently use part of their managerial remuneration to pay for the services of these assistants.

Allocation of Time

Field managers have many duties for which they are responsible. The question inevitably arises how to allocate the manager's time. There are a number of factors that will influence the decision, including (1) the stage of development of the agency, (whether it is a newly opened office just starting to recruit agents, or a large established agency), (2) whether the manager is working alone or has a number of assistants, and (3) the degree to which the field manager engages in personal production.

In a newly opened office, sometimes referred to as a scratch agency, the field manager and a secretary comprise the entire staff. At this stage, the manager needs to concentrate on recruiting new agents; once this is done, the manager becomes immediately involved in their training and joint field work. After this, supervising new agents will take most of the manager's time until the stage is reached when more agents need to be recruited and the process starts all over again. In newly opened offices, it is not unusual for the agency head to engage in personal production, but this may be restricted by company policy. In some companies, even a scratch agency will have an assistant manager to do the new agent training and the joint field work, thus allowing the field manager to build the agency more quickly by concentrating on the recruiting and selection processes.

In large established agencies, the field manager must allocate a considerable portion of time to dealing with office staff, policyowner service, motivation and retraining of established agents, plus regular contacts with both administrative and agency personnel in the home office. Large agencies usually have assistant managers or sales managers to recruit and supervise new agents in what are actually independent production units. Such agencies frequently employ specialists to do the initial training of the new agents. In such cases, the field manager may not even meet a prospective agent candidate until he or she has been hired.

From the outset, the field manager must be or quickly become a highly organized person because the job is so unstructured. As the agency grows, more responsibility must be delegated, otherwise the manager will be unable to give personal attention to those matters on which the success of the agency depend.

Selecting Field Management

Many industry leaders, both in home offices and in the field, have come to recognize the importance of selecting future field managers from among those candidates who demonstrate an ability to conceptualize; that is the ability to recognize and understand the duties of their job, their relationship with those with whom they work, and the relative importance of each activity, and to see themselves as successful agency heads.

To build a career agency, a field manager must have the ability to attract talented people to the agency, describing to them the reality of the opportunities and the problems that exist in the agency. A prospective field manager must be able to recognize people who have the potential for success as an agent. To be effective, a field manager must quickly build a strong sense of mutual trust with agents and project to the agent the manager's concept of the agent's responsibilities.

In addition to helping agents build a relationship with their clients, the field manager must also understand the need to help build meaningful relationships between the agent and the agency, the agent and the company, the agent and the field manager, and the agent and the agent's family.

Characteristics Sought in Field Managers

In common with good managers in all businesses, the life and health insurance field manager must have these characteristics: integrity and trustworthiness, ability to conceptualize, leadership, judgement, enthusiasm and energy, positive attitude, executive and business ability, and salesmanship. In the past, salesmanship was often used as the primary test when considering candidates for life insurance field management, but experience has demonstrated that a good salesman does not necessarily make a good agency manager. One could argue about the ranking of the other characteristics; however, none are unimportant.

Sources for Field Managers

Field managers may come to manage an agency from another company or they may come from within their own company. Table I indicates the various sources and previous positions of field managers.

In the United States, approximately three-quarters of the field managers in managerial companies come from within their own companies, while 25% had previously been with other life insurance companies. The figures are somewhat different for the general agency companies in that 39% of their appointments had previously worked for another life insurance company. A higher percentage of branch managers than general agents had been either assistant managers or management trainees before becoming field managers. In Canada, two-thirds of the field managers are appointed from within their own companies.

TABLE I
Previous Positions of Appointees by Type of Appointment

	United States		Canada
	Manager	General Agent	Manager
Same Company			
Assistant manager or GA	35%	27%	33%
Management trainee	20	7	7
Home office	8	8	6
Agent	11	16	18
	74%	58%	64%
Other Company			
Manager, GA, assistant manager or GA	19%	26%	25%
Agent, broker, management trainee, home office	6	13	9
	25%	39%	34%
Outside insurance, unknown	1%	3%	2%
	100%	100%	100%

Source: LIMRA, Research Report 1976-1

Agency heads in the life insurance business share common characteristics with managers in other industries, and yet only 1% of the managerial appointments and 3% of the general agency appointments come from outside the insurance industry. This may suggest a potential source of good management candidates that has been almost totally overlooked.

Field Management Compensation

Almost without exception, the agency head is compensated for services according to the terms and conditions of a written compensation contract. In general agency companies, the typical arrangement is a contract that provides for a scale of commissions (sometimes called first-year override) based on the first-year premiums for new business and a separate scale or scales to be applied to premiums paid in the second and subsequent policy years (a renewal override). In addition, the general agent receives expense reimbursement allowances based on first-year premiums and in many cases a renewal expense allowance.

In managerial companies, the compensation is typically an annual salary based on a formula applied to the previous year's agency production. A substantial number of companies design their formula to induce some desired action. For instance, some companies pay extra compensation to the manager based on the production of each new career agent for that agent's first two or three years, some pay a bonus for net gains in manpower, others base the bonus on number of recruits. Another variation is paying a bonus when annual production exceeds that of the previous year. Others offer bonuses based on persistency targets or improvements in agency persistency. Regardless of the type of contract that any one company may offer to the agency head, the job of the manager and general agent charged with building a career shop differ only in the emphasis that is placed on individual elements of the job. The payment of expenses, which is also an aspect of managerial compensation, was discussed in an earlier part of the chapter.

Agent and Field Management Retention

In an industry that is based on mortality tables, it is not surprising that the insurance industry's preoccupation with statistics extends to include survival rates for agents and managers. Since other industries do not measure survival rates for their salespeople as closely as the insurance industry, there are few standards that may be used in determining whether agents' and managers' survival rates are "normal". Nonetheless, retention of agents and field management is a vital concern to life and health companies.

The Interaction of Agent and Field Management Retention

In the selection of a field manager, one hopes to choose a candidate who will not only succeed in building the agency but who will continue to lead the agency for an extended period of time. The retention of the agency head has a double impact because it affects the retention of the agents, as well as other activities in an agency. The agency head is the contact between agent and company and prospective agents often make their career decisions to a large extent on their perception of their ability to work with the manager as a team. Any subsequent change in agency management may cause an agent to reassess the relationship with the agency and with the company.

The life insurance business is unique in that the buyer has been encouraged to look to the person who sold the policy for continuing service. This arrangement is the basis for paying agents their renewal commissions, but it also means that the buyer may have to look elsewhere for service or additional sales if the agent leaves the business. It is evident, therefore, that any improvement in the retention of both agents and field managers can make a substantial contribution to promoting the twin aims of policyowner satisfaction and agency continuity.

Agent Retention

The statistics on agent retention maintained by LIMRA over many years show a surprising consistency for the life and health insurance industry. In 1978, statistics for all ordinary companies showed the following:

- 69% of new agents survived to enter the next calendar year
- 48% of those that enter the second year survive to enter the third calendar year
- 65% of those that enter the third year survive to enter the fourth calendar year
- 75% of those that enter the fourth year survive to enter the fifth calendar year
- 84% of those that enter the fifth year survive, and are classed as established agents.[1]

These retention ratios, when applied to a group of 100 new agents contracted, for example, in 1982, would produce the following results: 69 agents (.69 × 100) would survive 1982 and be under contract at the beginning of 1983; 33 agents (.48 × 69) would survive 1983; 21 agents (.65 × 33) would survive 1984; 16 agents (.75 × 21) would survive 1985; 14 agents (.84 × 16) would survive 1986 and then be classed as established agents. There is a higher survival rate in the year in which an agent is recruited because new agents are recruited throughout the year, and on the average have only six months under contract. To survive the second and later years requires that an agent be under contract a full twelve months.

---

[1] LIMRA, *The Manpower and Production Survey, Ordinary and Combination Companies, Calendar Year 1978.*

When survival data is presented in this form, it leads some critics to state that a five-year loss ratio of 86% is high. A more positive statement would be to recognize that after five years, fourteen agents have become established producers for each 100 hired. As mentioned above, there are no such figures in other industries to which insurance agent retention ratios can be compared; however, it is important to recognize that improvements in retention rates would improve agency operations and policyowner satisfaction.

Turnover Among Mature Agents

Experienced agents, who by definition are those under contract for six or more calendar years, do experience turnover, but the rate is relatively low and includes mortality and morbidity losses as well as lack of success in the business. The retention rate for all experienced agents as a group is taken as 91%, but where detailed records are available, the survival rate for those in their fifth to ninth year is 83%, tenth to fourteenth year 92%, fifteenth to nineteenth year 94%, and twenty years over 95%.[2]

This means that as an agency matures and if an agency's retention rates match those of the industry, each twenty new agents recruited may add two or three to the total, bringing the number of agents in the agency to thirty-three or thirty-four at the end of the sixth year and thirty-five to thirty-seven at the end of the seventh year.

Factors Influencing Agent Retention

There are many factors that affect the agent and influence his or her chances of success or even survival in the life insurance business. These include (1) the selection criteria used at time of hiring, (2) training methods and the atmosphere of the agency, (3) the type of feedback and supervision an agent receives, (4) the agent's ability to build a relationship with clients for repeat sales, and (5) external factors, such as the economy and competition. In general, the more a field manager adheres to accepted selection criteria, training methods, and supervision techniques as described earlier, the better agent retention will be.

Some new agents desire to complete their training before attempting the first sale. This can lead to problems if the agent is being financed because most validation requirements assume that sales will be made in the first two or three weeks under contract. Because of the need to validate by making sales, the field manager must take into account the sales potential of a new agent in determining the level of financing.

In supervising, the field manager must give the new agent an accurate

---

[2] LIMRA, *Manpower and Production Survey,* 1979.

assessment of the agent's progress. This allows the agent to correct any practices before financing is terminated and before they become bad habits.

Some agents will be able to validate their financing by making many sales even though the unit size is small, but the real success in life and health insurance sales comes when agents can make repeat sales and can grow with their clients. This is a function of the agent's sincerity, belief in life and health insurance, and ability as a salesperson.

While economic conditions, including inflation, and competition from other agents are sometimes cited as reasons for high agent turnover, it can be argued that these are poor excuses for failure. Inflation has actually increased the need for life insurance, not diminished it. By the same token, real competition for insurance does not come from other agents but from other financial instruments as well as tangible consumer products that give the buyer immediate gratification.

How Agent Turnover Affects Profitability

There are several ways in which agent turnover affects profitability, both at the agency and the company level. At the agency level, high turnover means that the field manager must spend additional time and money on recruiting, training and supervising additional new agents to replace those who did not survive. This means there are fewer resources to train and supervise the rest of the agents, thereby increasing their chances of leaving the agency. It is a vicious circle unless the field manager can make sure that the time spent in recruiting, training and supervision is effective and productive.

The cost to the company and to the agency in financing a stream of new agents is not limited only to the dollars advanced to them in anticipation of future commissions. The cost includes rent for office space, cost of clerical and secretarial help, office furniture, extra staff used in training and early supervision, plus the cost of life and disability benefits and Social Security contributions. In addition, there is a hidden cost because the policies sold by a terminated agent are prone to lapse, which means that the share of agency and company new business expenses are not recovered.

The cost of policyowner dissatisfaction cannot be readily quantified, but it is a real cost. Even policyowners who do not lapse their policies can be unhappy because they no longer have an agent in the company unless another agent can be persuaded to "adopt" them. Thus, agent turnover is costly to all concerned: the company, the agency and the policyowner.

Responsibility to Improve Retention

Companies cannot improve agent retention by edict or resolution. It can begin with adding a dimension to the job descriptions of the directors of agencies and the agency vice president. Up to now, few agency officers have been charged with and measured by improvement in retention ratios of those agencies they supervise. If retention is to be improved, agency officers will need specialized training so they may be in a position to assist their field managers. Also, retention may be linked to the compensation plan, thus demonstrating that company management is willing to pay for improved agent retention.

In addition, those who hire field managers must commit themselves to hire only those who meet specific criteria. Field managers will be able to improve retention if they receive training in the selection and training of agents, conduct more joint field work with new as well as established agents, and provide regular feedback as part of agent supervision. Field managers must be committed to (1) contracting only agents who meet predetermined criteria, (2) terminating those agents who are not successful, (3) providing feedback to agents on their progress, (4) training agents to assess the needs of their clients so that in making a sale they are also laying a foundation for repeat sales, and (5) giving recognition only to those agents who are measuring up to their potential.

Turnover Among Field Managers

Unfortunately, turnover is not confined to agents. Field management turnover is a problem as well. This is demonstrated by a LIMRA survey which shows that the heaviest turnover among field managers occurs in the third through fifth year under contract.[3] As a result, on the average the typical agency head has held that position for 5.3 years. Typically, an agency head is appointed and it is assumed that one or two years will be needed to either get the agency started if it is a scratch agency, or to give the agency direction if it is an established one. By the beginning of the third year, however, most companies want to start seeing some results in the form of increased productivity. This may account for field management turnover's being heaviest in the third through the fifth year. Those field managers who survive five years are likely to be achieving growth and progress in their agencies and are then likely to remain in the job for a number of years.

Other Factors Affecting Agency Growth

Retention ratios are not the only factor in agency growth. In predicting the success of any agency, the productivity of the individual agents and the survival rate are equally critical. The production level achieved by a new agent in the first year is important for two reasons. First, there may be more new agents than established agents in an agency, the higher their individual

[3] LIMRA, Research Report 1976-1.

productivity, the greater total production they represent in absolute terms. Second, production levels achieved by new agents in their first year have a strong influence on their success patterns in later years and thus influence the prospective production level of the agency.

Not all agents continue to increase their productivity each year and obviously this is a limiting factor as far as agency growth is concerned. The tendency of agents to reach a plateau in their activity level can best be seen by looking at the number of sales that they make. Studies indicate that an agent sells an average of twenty policies in the first year, forty-nine policies during the second year, fifty during the third year, fifty-six during the fourth year, and forty-six during the fifth and later years.[4] Agents may increase their production even if the number of policies sold is relatively level by increasing sales skills and knowledge of sophisticated techniques that lead to the sale of larger policies with a correspondingly higher annualized premium. Annualized premiums are the annual premium for a policy regardless of the frequency with which premiums are paid.

During inflationary times, any agent who is not at least increasing annualized premium by an amount equal to the rate of inflation is, in fact, falling behind. Obviously, those who are succeeding in growing are expanding their annualized premium at a rate higher than the rate of inflation.

Developing Future Field Managers

Proper development of future field managers is essential for continued progress in agency operations. Many companies have what they call a second-line management development program in which agents who express some interest are given the opportunity to "try their hand" at management. Unless adequate selection and training efforts are made, the success rate will be low, and in the process, many good agents will give up a career in the life insurance business after a disappointing managerial experience.

As discussed earlier, proper selection of field managers is vital in reducing turnover or, more positively, in improving retention. To this end, some companies are beginning to introduce programs to evaluate agents who are thought to have management potential and to apply very precise selection standards. This may involve a psychological evaluation and apprenticeship under present field managers where all aspects of the management job will be taught.

The statistics on turnover among field managers suggest that insurance companies have not done a good job of providing training for second-line management candidates who aspire to a job as field manager. And yet there is

[4] LIMRA, *Manpower and Production Survey,* 1979.

no lack of training materials. In addition to training material developed by individual companies, organizations such as GAMA, the American College, and LIMRA have developed some excellent materials. The difficulty is that the available material is not used well enough or, in many cases, not used at all. Some companies have considered putting candidates for field management through formal training in management at the college level.

Field Training for Second-Line Management

Because there is so much pressure on a new field manager it is essential that any training take place before the appointment. Once the management candidate has been selected, a joint training program between the agency and the home office should establish clear guidelines and time schedules. The candidate will benefit from working with and observing established field managers, conducting actual recruiting and training sessions, and getting close supervision throughout the program. One or more experienced agents should eventually be assigned to the management candidate's unit so that the candidate can gain experience in supervising agents who operate in a sophisticated market. When the annual review of the agency plans are scheduled by the field manager, the candidate should have the opportunity to observe, in detail, preparation for and the actual planning sessions.

Unless managerial candidates are scheduled to continue indefinitely in a subordinate capacity within their agency, they must be made aware that getting their own agency will involve relocation. Advance notice is important so they and their families are psychologically prepared for a move.

A field management training program undertaken before the appointment of a candidate to an agency would necessitate a compensation package that gives field managers the financial incentive to develop and train potential second-line managers. Further, field managers will be losing an established agent when the candidate assumes a managerial position in another agency and must be compensated for this loss. It is also essential that those who do not succeed in field management be assisted financially so they may re-establish themselves in personal production. This aspect is important because despite careful selection, many agents will find that they either do not like management or do not have the aptitude for management. The compensation package must also provide financial incentives for interested agents to make the transition from personal production to field management without reducing their standard of living.

It is important that each agent be aware of the managerial training program. Agents should be encouraged to enter such a program only if an unbiased assessment indicates that they have the personality and temperament to succeed as field managers.

Continuing Training for Established Field Managers

A program designed to prepare management trainees for their role as future field managers does not address the needs of those field managers already established. This is not to say that they need different skills, but rather that two additional factors are at work. First, many managers will not admit that they need additional training since they have demonstrated some success. Second, most managers will not feel that they can devote time to retraining on the assumption that their agencies will lose momentum which could jeopardize their position and affect their income.

These objections are more psychological than real, but nonetheless must be considered if a company is committed to a retraining effort. In such cases, a number of companies have refrained from starting any general retraining program until they are ready to introduce a totally new procedure in order to ensure that all field managers would participate. Once the need is established for a special training session, it is relatively simple to use this as a springboard and plan a refresher course on the complementary skills.

When the highly successful field managers are involved in the special training session, the training should be assigned to the most senior person in home office involved in the training, which would be enhanced by the personal attendance and involvement of the agency vice president. Involvement of the directors of agencies in these seminars provides the basis for close support to reinforce the newly acquired skills until they are fully ingrained in the field managers. Just as with management trainees, these retraining seminars for established field managers should be followed closely by a visit to the agency by the seminar leader (trainer) in order to make available on-the-job technical assistance. Many companies conduct periodic refresher courses to follow the basic training as an integral part of any new training program for established managers.

Most field managers recognize the necessity of being aware of and familiar with the many technical aspects of life and health insurance selling. In this way, they respond to their most knowledgeable agents and challenge the others.

Many insurance organizations provide educational material and continuing development programs designed for field managers. In addition to the programs offered by LIMRA, the American College offers certificate courses in management conducted through correspondence. Annual CLU seminars are an excellent source of information. The Association of Advanced Life

Underwriters (AALU) conducts meetings each spring and produces a steady flow of technical bulletins. The Annual LAMP Meeting sponsored by GAMC provides information on trends in agency management and features outstanding field managers. Recognition throughout the company of the efforts of their established field managers does a great deal to create an atmosphere in which they and their agencies can grow.

Summary

For the foreseeable future there will be unlimited opportunity for those who can successfully manage life insurance agencies. The trend to larger agencies is likely to continue because unit costs can be maintained or reduced by the economies of scale in large agencies.

As the current class of field managers retire, there will be ample opportunity for those in second-line jobs to move up to succeed them. There will continue to be opportunities for agents with aptitude to enter second-line management programs. However, the complicated job of the field manager will remain critical to the continued prosperity of the life and health insurance industry and the agency system of distribution. Both agents and companies depend on their field managers to undertake a wide variety of tasks. It is becoming increasingly evident that companies have a responsibility to prepare individuals for field management as best as they can for the welfare of its agents, agencies, and policyowners. Therefore, it is imperative that high standards are maintained.

PART V

LIFE AND HEALTH INSURANCE MARKETING IN THE FUTURE

Chapter 18

Trends in Insurance Marketing

Darrell D. Eichhoff, CLU

In the preceding chapters, this text discussed the markets, products and distribution systems that make up the marketing activities of life and health insurance companies today. From these discussions one might indeed conclude that even in the "certainty" of today, insurance marketing is a complex activity. Looking to the future, which is inherently uncertain, can appear futile were it not for the fact that it is in the future that the industry will find its challenges and must find its opportunities. By trying to predict the future, management can position itself to react to alternatives as they unfold and, on occasion, shape the future.

This chapter will consider three main components of the possible future of life and health insurance marketing: changes in the marketplace itself, changes in the products that may be bought in the marketplace, and changes in the methods of distribution that may be effective in placing them there. These components will be as closely interrelated in the future as they have been in the past and are in the present. For instance, for many years the purchases of personal life insurance leaned heavily toward the level premium permanent whole life product sold through the career agency system. Whole life provided the compensation necessary for the maintenance of the agency system, and the agency system seems to have been the most effective method for providing coverage for the marketplace.

Changes in the Marketplace

The first factor to be considered in looking at the future of life and health insurance marketing is the marketplace. While the marketplace may be affected by products and distribution systems, successful marketers will be responsive more to the marketplace than vice versa[1]—as can be seen in the success of industrial insurance and the debit system in response to the Industrial Revolution and the success of family plans during the baby boom of the 1950s.

An overview of the marketplace shows that the population of the United States has been steadily increasing, though at a generally declining rate. At the same time, until very recently, per capita personal income has been increasing.[2] Thus, the overall marketplace has been favorable: there have been more people with more money to spend.

And spend they did for financial security. Expenditures for life, pension, and health insurance from private carriers increased as a percentage of personal income from 7.0% of aftertax income in 1960 to 9.7% in 1976. This growth occurred in spite of and at the same time as the government sector was expanding its security programs. However, expenditures for life insurance and pensions in the private sector have been a relatively constant percentage of income during this period, while such percentages for life insurance alone has decreased.[3]

Changes in the demand for insurance products will be primarily the result of changes in demographic trends, attitudes and values, technology, broad economic forces, and government activities, as discussed below.

Demographic Trends

Demography, the study of vital and social statistics such as births, deaths, and marriages, is basic to the study of the marketplace. Certain demographics, in fact, lie at the very heart of the need for insurance. They define the "who" of the market—who the purchasers are, who has bought what and who might buy what. Although many demographic results can be predicted fairly accurately, the trends must be constantly monitored, for changes in the trends can upset carefully laid marketing plans. Such changes may result in companies' aiming at a market that will eventually change dramatically.

Among the many demographic trends that can be seen today, at least six will have significance to the life insurance industry: shifts in the relative size of the various age groups, changes in family structure, the increase in the number of women in the work force, shifting ethnic patterns, changes in the geographic patterns, and increases in family incomes.

---

[1] Robert Carlson, Ph.D., "Marketing through the 80s," LIMRA, May 1979, p. 41.

[2] *A Guide to Consumer Markets 1977–1978*, The Conference Board, pp. 9, 117.

[3] "Security Expenditures in the United States," Research Report 1978-2, LIMRA.

Changes in Age Distribution

In addition to knowing the numbers of prospective clients in the marketplace, the mix by age is fundamental to insurance market planning. For instance, life insurance purchases have been shown to be correlated with events such as births, marriages, and the purchase of a home.[4] These events in turn are related to the number of people in the primary family formation age group of twenty to thirty-five. The number of people between forty to sixty is also significant, since they can be characterized as relatively affluent, in a position to spend less and save more with a decreasing perceived needs for additional insurance (based on what they've accepted as societal "norms"). The over age sixty-five group is one whose income is limited, and savings are often spent. Each group has special characteristics and needs, suggesting correspondingly unique marketing approaches.

Table I illustrates some of the changes in the relative size of age groups. These changes have implications for insurance marketing in the future. First, the high fertility rate in the 1950s (about 120 per 1000 women aged fifteen to forty-four) gave rise to a "baby boom;" the babies born during this boom reached their twenties during the 1970s. While the fertility rate has declined significantly[5] and is expected to continue to decline somewhat more (or, at the very least, level off at the current low "zero population growth" rate), the effect of the 1950s baby boom will be to create another increase in aggregate births during the 1980s and perhaps 1990s. Thus, even without looking at other factors, such as changes in family structure, the marketer should recognize that the need for "family responsibility" type insurance should continue strong over the next twenty years; only after that time may it start to decrease somewhat.

A second trend can be seen as the baby boom generation ages and changes in its insurance needs. During the 1970s, those born in the baby boom moved from their teens to their twenties, going from school to the job market, to forming families, and thus establishing the need for insurance. The effects of such movement are apparent, for instance, in the age distribution of ordinary life insurance purchases as seen in Table II. While these results are influenced by a number of factors, the force of the baby boom has undoubtedly affected the circled figures.

In the 1980s this baby boom group will continue to work, earn, and spend—which makes it a prime market for life insurance. By the 1990s,

---

[4] "Buyer-Initiated Sales and the Agency System," Research Report 1979-4, LIMRA, p. 20.

[5] "Population," Data Track V–1979, Social Research Services, American Council of Life Insurance, p. 17.

TABLE I
U.S. Population by Age Groups, 1950–2025
(numbers in millions)

Age	1950		1977		1990*		2000*		2025*	
	Number	Percent	Number	Percent	Number	Percent	Number	Percent	Number	Percent
Under 5 years	16.4	11%	15.2	7%	19.4	8%	17.9	7%	19.5	7%
5 to 19 years	35.3	23%	57.5	26%	52.5	22%	58.9	23%	61.0	21%
20 to 34 years	35.7	24%	53.2	25%	59.1	24%	51.4	20%	56.9	19%
35 to 49 years	30.8	20%	35.1	16%	50.5	21%	60.3	23%	56.4	19%
50 to 64 years	21.7	14%	32.3	15%	32.2	13%	40.1	15%	51.0	17%
65 years and over	12.4	8%	23.5	11%	29.8	12%	31.8	12%	50.9	17%
Total	152.3	100%	216.8	100%	243.5	100%	260.4	100%	295.7	100%

*Mid-range Series II projections.

Source: U.S. Bureau of the Census. *Current Population Reports,* Series P-25. Nos. 311, 704, and 721; and unpublished data, 1979.

TABLE II
Ordinary Life Insurance Purchases in the United States by Age of Insured

	% of Policies		% of Amount	
	1968	1978	1968	1978
Under 15	17	15	4	5
15–24	32	27	27	19
25–34	25	32	36	41
35–44	15	15	22	23
45 or Over	11	11	11	12
Total	100	100	100	100

Source: *1980 Life Insurance Fact Book* ACLI, p. 14.

however, this generation will have moved into their forties and will have begun to save, primarily for retirement. As a group (based on past experience) they will not become spenders again until after 2010. They thus represent a prime marketing challenge for the 1990s—one well worth researching in the 1980s.

The third effect is the growing percentage of people over sixty-five. The elderly can generally be characterized as a group which spends accumulated funds for current (as opposed to future) needs. Health and casualty insurance are of primary interest to this group. Estate conservation can also be a concern. One might also include in this category those who will be reaching this age in a few years, since they are probably already planning, and prefunding, for their retirements.

The elderly are significant because their numbers have almost doubled in the past twenty-five years. This segment of the population will continue to increase, although at a somewhat lesser pace, in the near-term future. Their numbers will then increase more radically again as the baby boom matures in the first quarter of the twenty-first century. The desires and needs of this group have also been changing as increased longevity lengthens their retirement years, as the "good life" becomes more common, and as retirement incomes are threatened by inflation and health care costs.

The proportion of people approaching retirement who own life insurance has increased somewhat over the last twenty years and is not much less than the proportion at younger ages. After age sixty-five this proportion decreases somewhat more rapidly. Health care insurance for this group has been largely provided by the government. But the health insurance need is so real that supplements to the government programs have been quite successful. This group has also been responsive to many other specialty programs. Thus, this part of the marketplace would appear to still have good market potential.[6]

Changes in Family Structure

An underlying motivation for insurance purchases, particularly life and health insurance, has been a sense of responsibility for other members of a family. This created a strong demand for the family-type life and health products which came to the marketplace with so much success towards the end of the 1950s.

However, there is much talk and demographic evidence that the family structure is not as strong as it used to be. The reaction in the marketplace has been a reduction in sales and product offerings of the family plans—these plans had represented 18% of the total ordinary life sold in 1968, but only 10% by 1978.[7] The "breakdown" of the family can be seen in many areas: the marriage rate has decreased; the divorce rate has increased; cohabitation, the single-parent household; and the childless marriage are more common. Yet, the number of households has increased by 26% since 1970 and may increase by another 20% by 1990.[8]

Products and distribution systems geared to less traditional forms of family structures will have to be given consideration: for example, life cycle coverage; the relaxation of certain insurable interest requirements; and various transfer provisions, such as those under Split Life. However, since concern for the family is such a fundamental motivation for a great many life insurance purchases, careful monitoring of this area is imperative, particularly for those companies that wish to continue operating in the family-oriented markets. Other "living" coverages, such as health, casualty, and savings, would seem secure in any case.

The Number of Women in the Work Force

Dependence on males to support the family and on females to take care of household functions has also been fundamental to the insurance marketplace, but these roles seem to be changing. Women in all categories—single, divorced, widowed, and married (both with and without children)—have been entering the work force in increasing numbers. Women's incomes also have been rising, even though they are still well below men's incomes.

In insurance, these changes have already been reflected in both sales and

[6] Ibid, p. 27.

[7] *1980 Life Insurance Fact Book,* American Council of Life Insurance, p. 14.

[8] *A Guide to Consumer Markets, 1977–1978,* The Conference Board.

manpower. In 1978, 29% of all policies sold were on women, up 32% in the preceding ten years. Only about 7% of the sales force is now women, but, of new recruits, women have increased from 9% to 16% of the total in the last five years alone.[9] Women continue to be influential in family purchasing decisions.[10] It is important that insurers make women a part of their market studies because it is becoming increasingly clear that their buying power is significant and that there are smaller markets within the general category (for example, women who are working, nonworking, single, married, and with or without dependents), each having varying needs.

Shifts in Ethnic Balance

The effect the growing proportion of nonwhites may have on insurance marketing is hard to determine. The nonwhite population has been expanding more rapidly than the white—since 1950 the white population has increased 40%, but the number of nonwhites has almost doubled (other-than-blacks, more than tripled). This has increased the proportion of nonwhites in the population to over 13%.[11] Expected increases in immigration, especially from Latin America and Asia, higher nonwhite fertility rates, and a decreasing mortality gap are expected to increase the proportion of nonwhites to perhaps 19% by the turn of the century.[12]

"Ethnic" statistics are less and less available because of antidiscrimination laws. Moreover, ethnic needs may be heavily influenced by related economic characteristics. Many feel that ethnic groups, however, have strong affinity ties, and many insurance agents from ethnic minorities have become successful by cultivating their so-called "natural" markets. Thus, analyses of these groups would seem worthwhile.

Since many nonwhites are relative newcomers, either to North America or to the modern industrial job market, their economic status may well be more determinant of their market characteristics than race. Those in middle-income brackets will have insurance needs similar to those of whites and can be reached in the same way. Those in lower-income brackets may respond to different marketing methods, such as variations of the home service approach or use of direct response small group enrollments and salary deduction plans.

---

[9] Lois Underhill, "Talking to Her About Life Insurance," and Boyd Christenberry, "Industry Should Recruit More Women Agents," *The National Underwriter*, Life and Health edition, (Dec. 29, 1979).

[10] Judy Klemesriand, "A Wife's Role in Big Decisions," *The New York Times,* (Nov. 24, 1979), p. 68.

[11] "Population," Data Track V–1979, p. 30.

[12] *Ibid.*

Changes in Geographic Patterns

Geographic demographics are of significance, both on a national and local level. On the national level, major geographical movements, such as to the Sunbelt and away from the industrial Northeast, could warrant redeployment of manpower and even different marketing approaches.

On the local level, similar actions could result from residential changes such as the movement from rural to metropolitan areas, especially to the metropolitan suburbs. This latter migration has been made predominantly by the more affluent. Some blacks, low-income whites, and blue-collar families are increasingly joining this migration.[13]

The overall expansion of the suburbs, though, has moderated of late.

FIGURE I
Regional Personal Income Per Capita as Percent of National Average

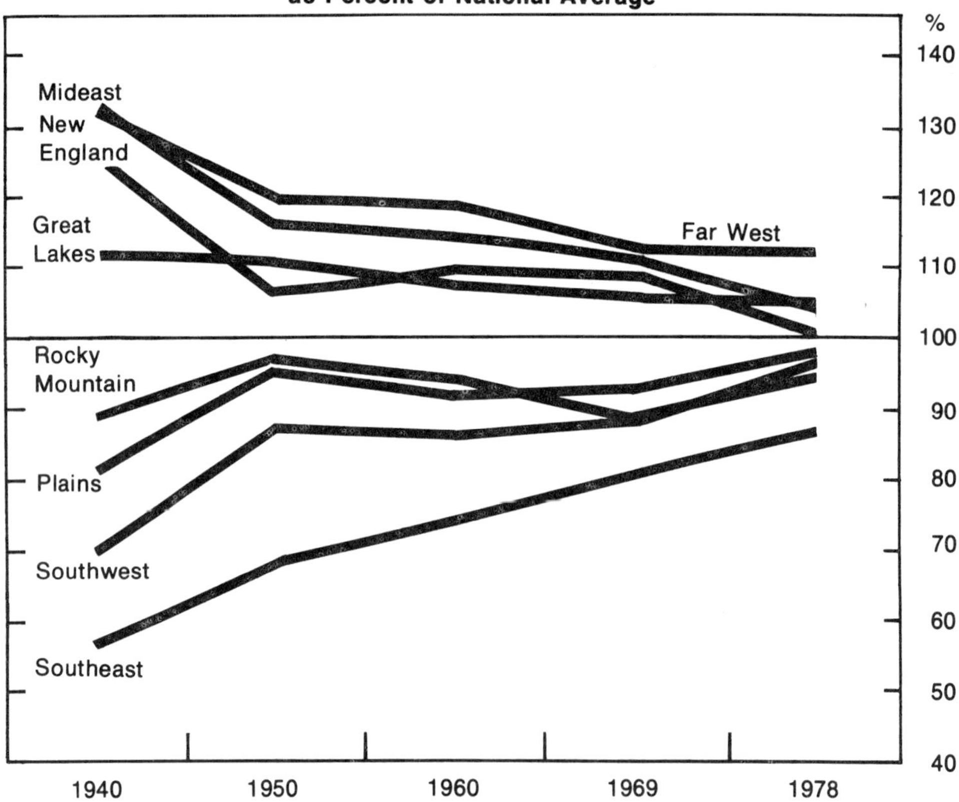

Source: "Economic Road Maps," The Conference Board, February 1980.

[13] *Ibid.*, p. 36.

Energy and housing problems are slowing the growth of the suburbs and/or causing an "urbanization" of them. Local stores are increasingly providing the means for mass selling. Population concentrations such as the elderly in Florida can also have implications on marketing and manpower strategies and may further complicate the problems of the long-time established small-town independent agents.

The apparent blending of incomes by geographic area, however, as shown in Figure I, suggests that geographic assimilation may take place over the long run, and that short-term geographical marketing diversification, particularly if too refined, might not be worth the effort.

Changes in Family Income

Perhaps the most significant demographic factor in the marketplace is the economic status of a client. Almost by definition, insurance is a product aimed at protecting individual finances. Moreover, both the need for insurance and the means to pay for it tend to increase, sometimes dramatically, as income increases. More sophisticated selling techniques are also generally needed as incomes rise. Thus, identification of market trends by income level is of utmost significance in formulating future marketing strategy. Table III demonstrates that there has been and is expected to be a continuing increase in families with higher and higher incomes:

While increasing affluence appears to be a positive trend for insurance marketing, it also raises challenges. For instance, where higher income is achieved from earnings of both spouses, will the need for insurance be equal to the sum of their earnings, or will the dual incomes provide a cushion so

TABLE III
Percent Distribution of Families Before-Tax Income Level*

Income Groups (constant dollars)	1980	1990	2000
Less than $5,000	9.5%	6.5%	4.5%
$ 5,000–10,000	19.0	13.5	11.0
10,000–15,000	20.0	16.0	13.0
15,000–20,000	19.0	18.0	16.0
20,000–30,000	19.5	23.4	22.5
30,000–50,000	10.0	14.0	17.5
50,000–over	3.0	8.5	15.5
Total	100.0%	100.0%	100.0%
Median Income	$15,400	$18,750	$24,000

*Total money income from all sources and all family members.
Source: Business Economics Department, Metropolitan Life, May 5, 1980.

that the survivor's income will be considered sufficient (or at the very least, a form of partial insurance)? Another potential problem might be that agents, particularly new, young ones, will have trouble approaching and identifying with the growing numbers of affluent people. Also, as incomes rise and agents project them to rise even further as part of the sales analysis, amounts of insurance recommended for income replacement may increasingly exceed client's preconceived notions as to what is a reasonable amount of insurance to buy.

Beyond these categories of income and associated problems, lie many other characteristics of the various income groups which will also affect marketing to any of these segments. For instance, while 46% of the total work force was employed in white-collar jobs in 1978, 88% of those earning $50,000 and over were in such jobs.[14] Such facts, coupled with a plan to move into marketing to the higher-income groups as it grows but becomes more competitive, could greatly influence a company's marketing approach.

People's Attitudes

A second major force in the marketplace involves people's attitudes and values. Attitudes influence an individual's perception of needs and decision-making; they shape, even as they are sensitive to and influenced by, other forces. Moreover, they are influenced by the myriad of experiences and feelings of their lifetimes.

While fundamental attitudes may be studied on a global or public attitude basis, it is the individual's situation to which life and health insurance sales must be sensitized. Thus, in marketing, global attitudes must be studied through surveys conducted by governments, major polling firms, and the life and health insurance industry's own research organizations, as well as on a company basis. These surveys and studies consider not only the public as a group, but all those involved in individual marketing—particularly agents, where they are a factor. Attitudes will also be studied with regard to major events such as wars and fads. These public attitude monitors may indicate which markets should be sought, how they should be sought, how the products should be designed, and the methods by which the products should be distributed.

Three basic needs have been and apparently will continue to be influential in the marketplace: the need to know (consumerism), the need for self-fulfillment (freedom of life-style), and the need to have (entitlement). The advent of these needs and attitudes can be traced in part to many of the events and environments of the past. For instance, consumerism is the

[14] Fabian Linden, "Up the Ladder," *Across the Board,* The Conference Board, October 1979, pp. 70–73.

by-product of a presumably better-educated and informed population which will demand, either directly or through government intervention, simplified products and pricing, along with the ability to choose freely from among various alternatives to satisfy their needs. This movement alone may lead to the separation of the protection, investment, marketing, and services facets of insurance products in one shape or another, so that consumers can have knowledge of what they are buying and thereby have the ability to decide what they want for themselves.

Consumerism leads to the second need—for self-fulfillment—in that not only do people want to know for the sake of knowing, but they want to know for the sake of molding things for themselves. Motivation will also be individualistic. Not only will choice be important in terms of the elements of insurance products, but all of the elements may need to be flexible in themselves to support varied individual life cycles.

The last of the three needs—the need to have—suggests that in this fast-changing world many consumers may, for instance, not want to prepay under the level premium concept, nor perhaps even provide for their heirs. The desire to have *now* could supersede providing for the future. This attitude may not only change insurance products, it could in the future (if not already) change management/employee relationships both in corporate headquarters and in the sales organization. In a few instances, groups of sales representatives have organized to present a more united and powerful front to urge management to improve both products and compensation packages.

Technological Change

As Peter Drucker theorizes in his book, *The Age of Discontinuity*, discontinuities can be and often are more significant to future trends than to past trends.[15] Perhaps this is most evident in new technology. Advances in computers, communications, and television can, in the short-run, result in more accurate, more simplified, less expensive, and speedier administrative services for many businesses—insurance in particular. This should lead to improved public relations and perhaps even help overcome some of the anti-business/anti-insurance prejudices which have increased in recent years.[16] Over the long run, advances in these areas could lead to greater assistance to salespeople. At the same time, however, it could lead to the replacement of salespeople in prospecting, programming financial needs, and

[15] Peter Drucker, *The Age of Discontinuity*, (New York: Harper and Row, 1978).

[16] MAP-1979, ACLI, pp. 31–35.

even advising and selling to clients. In the extreme, medical technological advances could seriously affect the basic needs, pricing, and market for life and health insurance products.

An example of the impact of technology on insurance products can be found in the new ability of companies to service the complicated flexible products, such as adjustable and universal life, that came on the market in the late 1970s.

Economic Conditions

Certainly insurance, as a money-centered concept, is affected by economic conditions. Even if basic decisions about buying and surrendering a policy are somewhat insulated from transitional economic changes, investments and many other facets of the insurance business (some of which can affect both sales and profitability), are seriously affected by changes in economic conditions.

For instance, the cost of doing business is profoundly affected by inflation. Certainly the expenses of insurance salespeople (e.g., for transportation) are increased, while, on the other hand, much of their earnings are sheltered from corresponding increases (e.g., a reducing premium-per-$1,000, and non-inflated renewals). The decision of a policyowner to cash in a policy when faced with unemployment, or to borrow against it when market interest rates are higher than premium loan rates, are other examples of the economy's effect on the insurance mechanism. Certain product changes, such as new money-type pricing, flexible policy loan interest rate provisions, and de-liberalized definitions of disability are also reflective of the effect of the economy on the insurance business. Inflation, or perhaps even the threat of it, may lead increasingly to the separation of the protection and savings elements of life insurance. One marketing approach that might be attempted in response to inflation will be to sell with inflation (rather than against it), by indexing all elements of the product and supporting the investments. The stability or instability of the dollar and its continued use as the basis for world currency must also be closely monitored in developing international insurance markets.

In addition, the economy affects other general market forces such as demographics, attitudes, technological changes, and government. The effect of major economic upheavals, such as the Great Depression and the inflation/stagnation scenarios of the 1970s, also have very basic and far-reaching effects. Certainly those who lived through the Depression are more conscious of security than the generations that have followed them. Perhaps the inflation of the late 1970s will have profound effects in other directions. Certainly, experience with extremely high inflation rates in other countries must be considered. For instance, in inflationary economies it would appear that indexing and term insurance are heavily relied upon for insurance coverage.

Government Actions

Government actions, as they affect the insurance marketplace, may be subdivided into three areas: regulation, taxation and intervention. It is important for marketing managers to be aware of and plan for these factors.

Regulation

In the regulatory area, the government maintains close contact with the life and health insurance industry. However, this area does not appear to be of prime significance in terms of limiting marketing over the long-term. In some cases, it could be used advantageously; for example, mandatory cost comparisons can be used advantageously by a low-cost company.

Nevertheless, many significant issues loom which will need to be dealt with thoughtfully and perhaps forcefully. Some of the prominent issues are: standardization of forms (beyond policy language simplification); elimination of risk classification distinctions (such as sex, age, and location); more privacy requirements; increased pressure for more flexibility in required policy loan and nonforfeiture provisions; possibility of universal coverage; cost and other disclosure requirements; more antitrust regulation or, in the opposite direction, allowing banks and others to enter the insurance business and vice versa; and establishing criteria (and hopefully incentives) for increased productivity. As already indicated, while regulation is often bothersome, in the right proportions and in the right areas, it can be helpful. To a large degree, a company's influence, as well as its flexibility and creativity, will be a key to how government regulation will affect its marketing strategies.

Taxation

Taxation has been and appears to be an ever-growing factor in the sale of insurance and other financial contracts. As taxes rise, they must, by sheer volume, be levied more and more against the prime insurance markets of families in the middle- or upper-income class and businesses. In such an environment there will be an ever greater demand for products which provide tax shelters. Issues of prime interest to the insurance business will include: revision of the 1959 Income Tax Act; retention of the historic treatment of cash value accumulations within the contract; extension of income tax shelters for contributions to "qualified" retirement plans; and changes in limits for taxation of life insurance proceeds, employer group life contributions, and estate taxes. As an example of the possibilities in this area, the effect of taxation on investing in people versus physical equipment may come into greater play in determining cost effective approaches to the sale of insurance; and, of course, the balance between group and personal, term and permanent, life and annuity could also be seriously affected.

Intervention

Intervention may be the greatest governmental threat to the private insurance business. The expansion of government social security programs for death, disability, and retirement income and health insurance could seriously erode the market for privately sold insurance. The government seems to "provide for the needy" (e.g., the poor, the elderly, the handicapped, the young), but is continually expanding its definition of "needy," leaving only the highly competitive higher-income groups for additional private coverage. Such governmental intervention, however, will be limited by the public's satisfaction with it, which in turn is dependent on the public's perceived need for governmental coverages, the efficiency of such programs, and the taxes imposed to provide them. A prime marketing challenge is thus not only to sell private coverage for its own profitability, but also to forestall new or expanded government programs. This is nowhere more evident than in health insurance, where adequate individual coverage may have to be a prime goal of the insurance industry, even if some of it must be sold at a marginal loss.

Changes in Products

Having viewed the possibilities for the future marketplace, it seems appropriate to consider next what products and services might be needed, offered, and purchased in that marketplace. To set the stage, a look at what has been purchased to date seems a likely starting point. Next, possible products of the future will be discussed.

Today's Products

Expenditures for ordinary life insurance have decreased markedly as a percentage of personal income over the last two decades. Some of these expenditures have shifted to personal annuities, but much has been replaced by group and governmental coverages, as well as by expenditures for products and services offered by other businesses. There may also have been a decline in the overall need (actual or perceived) for life insurance.

There has also been a shift away from the higher premium forms of ordinary life insurance. Over the last twenty-five years, the percentage of life insurance in force on policies with large cash values per $1000 decreased from 20% to 6%; those with moderate cash values decreased only slightly from about 68% to 61%; while those with no cash values increased from 12% to over 33%.[17] As a percentage of issue, more than half of all sales in the United States are now term insurance.[18] In addition, over this period the premium-per-thousand has been further decreased by mortality improvements and higher-interest earnings, which have far outpaced expense increases due to inflation. As a result, the average premium-per-thousand for life insurance has decreased by 50%, from $25 to $12.50.[19]

Changes in Product Features

At the same time, and particularly over the last ten to fifteen years, the variety of policy forms on the market has increased dramatically. As in the past, some of the new forms involve redesigns of the premium-paying, benefit, and/or cash value schedules (deposit term and graded premium are two of the most dramatic examples). However, recently, changes in even more basic elements have become the focus of product innovations. For instance, there have been changes in the persons insured (e.g., joint and last-survivor and contingent life); the investment media (e.g., variable life and "new money" pricing); the loan provision and how it is used (e.g., flexible loan rates and vanishing premiums); the taxability of the product (e.g., products for pensions and "wrap-around" annuities); and dividend options (e.g., the economatic and fifth and sixth dividend options). Unbundling, breaking benefits down, as in split and universal life, has also occurred, but not without controversy. In addition, insurance companies have begun to market related insurance and financial services. Perhaps the most significant expansion along these lines has been to property and casualty coverages, particularly auto and homeowners. Mutual funds, variable annuities, assorted tax shelters, dental, vision care, and legal care coverages are also sold.

These changes in products can be traced, at least in part, to the marketplace. For instance, the trend to lower premiums seems to be a function of many of the marketplace's changes—the more highly educated populace, the related consumer movement, and communications, together with inflation and more affluence, appear to have significantly influenced the trend to term products and brought prices down through competition.

---

[17] "*Financial Behavior and Personal Security,*" Data Track II–1975, American Council of Life Insurance, p. 34.

[18] "Buyer's Study," LIMRA, 1979.

[19] Ibid., 1955, 1979.

Similarly, the trend away from the family policy could be said to be tied to the weakening of the nuclear family unit and the related decrease in the number of children per family. Considering its fairly high premium, this policy form has also been affected by inflation. As a result, family policies have increasingly come under scrutiny not only by the public, but also by companies which in turn directed their marketing efforts away from these plans.

As a last example, the trend towards flexibility and diversification in product design, particularly forms such as adjustable or universal life, "new money" products, and variable life, can certainly be traced to inflation and changes in life-styles.

Product changes are also a function of the distribution systems employed to deliver the products and of the companies which offer them. Whole life insurance has traditionally been the main product offered and sold by life insurance companies using agents as a means of distribution. However, as will be discussed in somewhat greater detail later, competition in the marketplace, and the marketplace itself, have tempered the position of both the sales representative and the industry. As a result, both have been willing to compromise their traditional positions in the belief that a small sale is better than no sale. Therefore, in addition to developing innovative ways of selling whole life, both the agent and the industry have been more and more content to sell products such as term, graded premium whole life, and annuities, to reduce commission rates, and to enter into new types of less profitable selling arrangements.

Products of the Future—Basic Considerations

Study of trends in the marketplace and distribution systems as they may affect product offerings will be particularly necessary in the sharply competitive, inflationary, and ever-changing environment of the future. Basic market research into the needs, wants, and abilities of consumers to buy insurance products and other related financial services will need to become increasingly sophisticated. In addition to company and industry studies, outside research firms and academicians will be brought in. More elaborate surveys will be undertaken, and more scientific studies will be made through such new techniques as focus groups and psychological analyses. Moreover, direct marketing from companies to consumers will increasingly permit live controlled tests of consumers' wants and needs.

It will continue to be worthwhile to monitor the products being marketed by other companies both inside and outside of the insurance industry. Sources for following innovations of other groups include the "Who Writes What" publication; various other insurance and news publications which highlight developments; attendance at industry meetings at which product designs are discussed either formally or informally; listening to those involved in product distribution particularly if they are agents; consultants; consumers; and, of late, getting information on products and prices from computer firms that do policy illustrations.

In considering products for the future, four main areas seem paramount: (1) price and its competitive ramifications; (2) packaged versus segmented benefits; (3) flexibility of coverage; and (4) type of coverage.

Price

Price is obviously important to the sale of any product. The main question about price is "How important is it to consumers?" The answer is a subjective function of the product or service being offered and the purchaser's perspective. In life insurance, where the product and its price have for the most part been rather complex, price *per se* does not appear to have been primary in the past. This is particularly true of permanent and participating life insurance, where the cost structure of the product is complex and not even fully determined until all contracts have run their often-long courses. Variations in policy structures have further hindered cost comparisons.

In recent years, with inflation and inflationary expectations running strong, coupled with the "me" and "now" feeling, low initial outlay insurance plans such as graded premium, economatic, low cash value, minimum deposit, and term, have flourished with the consumers' perception (or misconception) that these are less expensive plans.

A related question is that of replacement of in force policies. The industry has traditionally discouraged replacements because they have generally not been in the consumers' best interests. Recently, though, widening gaps in pricing have accelerated replacement activity and may have made it justifiable in more cases (e.g., older nonparticipating permanent plans) than in the past.

Greater and continued cost disclosure and a more highly educated populace seem to have increased the importance of price to the consumer and will likely do so even more in the future.

This makes it more important than before to emphasize to consumers other incentives to purchase, for example, cash flow, tax-deferrals, and retirement fund build-up.

In any case, both the real and imagined prospect of a price-conscious consumer has seemingly led to more competitive pricing. This is particularly true for term, annuities, nonparticipating and higher-amount contracts, where the products are less complicated and/or the buyers' ability and desire to differentiate based on cost is greater. The influx of other financial institutions into the picture, especially in the savings area, seems to sharpen the competition further.

Competitive Pricing

More competitive pricing is being accomplished in various ways. Some companies seem to have cut costs by reducing sales commissions, margins, and/or profits. Others have initiated or accelerated more fundamentally sound programs, such as becoming more selective in their underwriting, managing their expenses more closely, and refining their distribution systems. Others have gone even further, introducing significantly new structures into their pricing, such as the "investment generation" or "new money" allocation of interest earnings. This has the effect of tying interest earnings more closely to the monies upon which the earnings were made. These new money products appear more equitable and competitive for new savings dollars as interest rates rise. These products have disadvantages in that they would not be competitive in a declining economy, are administratively complicated, and confuse further cost disclosure. Still other companies have been protecting themselves by diversifying their distribution system or product offerings, or by introducing non-guaranteed rates.

Pricing and Risk Classification

Before leaving the price facet of products, one other potentially revolutionary aspect of insurance pricing must be discussed—risk classification. The consumer movement has led some consumerists, government people, and perhaps others to the conclusion that risk classification should be based on an individual's personal characteristics rather than on those of some class to which he or she may be assigned. While this has more impact on casualty insurance, where there is lobbying for ratings for auto insurance based more on driving record than on age or sex, similar thoughts have been expressed with respect to life insurance. Differentiation on account of race has not been permitted in life insurance for some time, and classification on the basis of sex has recently come under scrutiny. Needless to say, the outcome of this issue will have great effect on life insurance pricing in the future.

Packaged versus Segmented Benefits

Another basic issue which must be continually monitored and considered in product design is the question of how much to "package" the various elements—risk, investment (savings), service, and marketing—that make up the insurance contract. All of these elements and their corresponding prices have been effectively packaged into the whole life product, which provides for the insurance risk for as long as it continues, even as it increases with age, with a convenient level premium. At the same time, it provides for forced tax-deferred savings accumulations, provides dollars for capital investment in the community, pays reasonable commissions, and is adaptable to many forms of market presentation. Moreover, the whole life concept has been sold both within the industry and to the general public as the proper and responsible product to buy.

These features, however, limit the extent to which some of the elements of the contract can be refined. As such, the whole life product is facing competition from products which concentrate on just one or perhaps two of these main elements. As early as the 1930s a major paper was written describing how whole life could be split into its decreasing term and increasing savings elements.[20] Companies have continually attempted to market products which concentrated on, and were more responsive to, one or more of these separate elements.

Risk and Savings Elements

The most prominent of these attempts has been directed at the two main elements of whole life—its risk and savings features—most often in the familiar form of "buy term and invest the difference." This theme itself has had many variations, ranging from straight renewable/convertible level or decreasing term combined (theoretically or practically) with savings in a bank or a traditional annuity all the way to split life, universal life, deposit term, and even minimum deposit. Each of the risk and savings elements has also been marketed with special twists, such as cost-of-living riders, accident and cancer insurance coverages, and variable, money market, and new-money annuities.

In some cases, and perhaps to an increasing degree, this strategy of featuring one or two of the various elements of the insurance contract has met with success. Quite often, however, such successes are qualified

---

[20] G. W. Fitzhugh, "Actuarial Notes: Analysis of Level-Premium Policies," *Record of the American Institute of Actuaries*, Vol. 25, 1936, p. 105–126.

ones, since carving out one feature not only means giving up or compromising in other areas, but often results in more direct competition with other financial institutions, such as with banks when savings are emphasized. By making the product less complex, consumers can make comparisons more easily than before and can thus put competitive pressures on the product. Such competition, in turn, may not allow sufficient margin for profits or the support of the applicable distribution system. Thus, there is a likelihood that whole life products will continue to flourish because of their real value and their perceived stature in the public arena, and because of their real and their perceived value to the insurance business itself. At the same time, because of an increasingly knowledgeable public and cost pressures, it is likely that separate-element type contracts will be marketed even more aggressively in the future.

Marketing and Service Elements

Attempts have also been made to improve upon the product's marketing and service elements. On the marketing side, a significant change has been the replacing of the commission with a negotiated fee. This is increasingly being used in higher-income, tax, and business planning markets. A recent LIMRA survey shows that the percentage of Million Dollar Round Table members who are charging fees has been increasing.[21] This trend may be expected to continue to increase as these purchasers become more sophisticated and competition becomes more extreme. In some respects, it can also be said that these marketing fees have been separately or specially handled for pricing purposes in sales through savings banks or other salaried representative situations, in direct response, and even in group selling.

In the service area, some companies have thought about or are already charging fees for certain special services, such as for policy changes, and service on pension plans, and in group insurance where service is the main feature of many contracts. Check-o-matic and transfer accounts are other service agreements being used increasingly.

Flexibility of Coverage

A related issue to packaged versus segmented benefits is benefit flexibility. Conceptually, because family relationships are becoming more varied and other life-styles less rigid, and because the economy is subject to more volatile changes, it would appear that flexible-type coverages would be very desirable. Flexible coverages allow policyowners to make a wide variety of choices. These

[21] *Executive Bulletin–10,* LIMRA, June 1978.

include such products as adjustable, split, and variable life; cost-of-living features; the increasing use of riders (particularly in place of the full-fledged packaged family plans); minimum deposit and other cash flow-type arrangements; and, in the most exaggerated illustration of flexibility, the advent of the cafeteria or flexible benefit approaches in employee benefit packages.

Other products allow policyowners to change their choices in the course of the life of the policy. These may allow switching the investment media for the savings accumulation portions of contracts, changing from premium-paying status to non-premium paying status and back again, and shifting the relationships between the savings and protection elements of insurance. New packages of flexible arrangements sound good on the surface, but they are often very confusing to salespeople, the public, and even those who must administer them.

Types of Coverage

As the economy and the demographics of our society change more and more rapidly, it becomes clear that certain products or coverages will be increasingly subject to their own cycles. The marketplace will not always necessarily be interested in the same types of coverages. It becomes worthwhile therefore, to consider offering related products for sale. Health insurance and savings vehicles to provide for retirement were natural by-products of the life insurance contract. Life insurance companies are now turning to property and casualty insurance and legal, dental, and vision care coverage. These coverages are particularly effective since they are high demand products that have built-in increases in inflationary times. Moreover, neither group insurance nor governmental insurance has taken hold in all of these areas as yet. Beyond these products, insurance companies are likely to branch out into other less-related fields, some of which may not be on the traditional risk-sharing basis. These might include will preparation services, cash management accounts, computer services for consumers, and money market services.

Changes in Distribution Systems

There are basically four systems of distribution prevalent in the insurance marketplace. The first, and most traditional, consists of agents selling to individuals on a one-to-one basis. The second involves groups, where an employer or other third party purchases or supports the purchase of insurance on behalf of employees or constituents. The third system, which has not yet come fully into its own but has great potential, is direct response marketing from company to individuals, either through the mail, TV, telephone, or newspaper. Lastly, though not a system used by insurance companies *per se,* is the channel provided by governments, mainly the social security systems. There are various crossovers and subdivisions within these categories (e.g., third-party sponsored direct marketing and group solicitation for individual insurance on a salary savings basis), but these four seem to capsulize the main distribution systems to date.

Expenditures attributable to these distribution systems are roughly divided 25% through salespeople, 20% through group, less than 5% through direct response, and 50% through government.[22] As will be discussed below, these proportions are likely to change in the future, as will the systems themselves and their subdivisions.

The Evolving Systems—Basic Considerations

It has been observed that people are too expensive to continue to be used as a major method of selling. This concept may lie close to the heart of the future of the distribution of life and health insurance.

In the sale of life insurance, salespeople have been the traditional means of distributing the product. For the agent, the primary problems have been prospecting and being able to endure the frustrations of rejections. So, it is not surprising that the first technological breakthroughs to aid in this process were industrial insurance and the associated debit system. This "technology" allowed for easy and simple, sales of small policies to the masses, with frequent and automatic contact through the collection of weekly premiums. The cost of production under this system, however, deteriorated relative to other distribution systems over the years—partly because the collection service could be done more economically by other means; partly because of the cost of handling small policies; partly because of market shrinkage as a result of rising incomes; and partly through the development of more amenable technology for selling such small coverages in the form of group and governmental programs.

As various approaches have been developed to help and improve upon individual salesmen selling to individual prospects, continual trade-offs have naturally occurred between productivity and unit cost.

The Evolving Systems—Government

In large part, governmental coverage began as an outgrowth of the Great Depression, with the government attempting to make sure that everyone,

[22] *1980 Life Insurance Fact Book,* ACLI.

particularly those who could not afford it, would be protected from financial disaster. Through the years the governmental programs have flourished because "perceived" needs far outweighed "felt" costs. In part, this perception might be tied to the method of financing Social Security, which has from its inception been on a "pay-as-you-go" basis, with present beneficiaries as a group always receiving more than they paid in. There seems now to be a growing reluctance against further increases in contributions to Social Security, a reluctance exacerbated by the difficulties of inflation and increases in other taxes. The effectiveness of government-provided services is also being questioned.

The Evolving Systems—Group Insurance

Group insurance is another example of a "technological" advancement that has allowed insurance to be distributed more economically than through one-on-one selling. In some cases, it might obviate the need for personal insurance. However, in most instances, it acts best as a supplement to individual insurance.

There are two reasons why group insurance will most likely remain a supplement to, rather than a replacement of, individual insurance. In the first place, employers can afford only a certain amount of dollars for fringe benefits. Secondly, all coverages are not equally desirable to all employees. Many employees do not gain full benefit of the coverage, for example, coverage above two times income may be more than needed if the insured has no spouse or dependents. Thus, employers are often reluctant to increase benefits vertically. Employers may, however, still be willing to increase expenditures horizontally, for example, to cover medical expenses and then to expand to other coverages such as dental and vision care. Depending on employee or union pressure, and on the treatment of employer contributions employers might even be willing to expand into fringe benefits such as group legal, automobile and homeowners insurance.

Alternatively, employers may move away from employer-pay plans and into salary deduction and other types of optional and contributory coverages "delivered" to employees with the employer's endorsement utilizing mass marketing techniques. In somewhat the same category, flexible or cafeteria approaches may be developed, allowing an employee to choose from a number of coverages provided by the employer. The more flexible the choices and the more complex the coverage, the more necessary personal and individualized advice becomes.

The Evolving Systems—Direct Response Marketing

As indicated earlier, direct response marketing is relatively new and has great potential for growth. The computer's ability to collate and analyze lists of mailing addresses has enabled insurers to focus their marketing efforts, improve response rates, and thereby reduce distribution costs.

Direct response technology has begun to be applied to the problem of prospecting, albeit with only mild success to date. And yet, some see direct response posing a threat to the further use of sales personnel. Nonetheless, because direct response marketing provides a direct link between companies and the consumer, it has great potential for marketing.

The Evolving Systems—Agency System

Regardless of the expense of using salespeople and the efficiencies of the distribution systems mentioned above, the individual agent still seems necessary in many instances to sell that which is not bought: life and health insurance products. A look at response rates to direct mail, the contribution levels in group where optional and dependent coverages are offered, and the average amount of life insurance in force compared to personal incomes and assets shows that the need to sell life insurance still exists. Purchasing insurance is more than an intellectual exercise; it is an emotional one, and the emotions are such that they need to be stimulated. In addition, as the amounts of insurance increase, personalized advisory services are often also needed to help determine a prospect's financial alternatives. Such advisory services can become very extensive and technical.

Therefore, since an agent still appears to be necessary, the question remains how to maximize productivity and minimize costs of selling through individuals, especially in an inflationary and increasingly competitive environment.

Consider the various functions an agent performs. First, recalling the debit example, what is happening to the role of the agent in the collection function? The mail, checking accounts, credit cards, and computers more and more have removed that task from the salesperson's responsibilities. (It is instructive to note in this respect that the independent casualty agent has, in many cases, not given up this function.

But taking the agent out of the home made a second and perhaps more important function—prospecting—more difficult. Many attempts have been made to simplify and improve results in this area. To date, however, most of the successes have revolved around the agent's working harder—obtaining referred leads, telephone or door-to-door canvassing, following up pre-approach letters and service calls. Mass solicitations for salary savings, direct response advertising or mailings, and television have also been tried; cable television may be another approach that will soon be used.

As a result of rising costs and the need for more personalized services, though, agents may need to be more selective about whom they can afford to solicit and sell. Since such selection is predominantly a factual matter, it may be a candidate for assistance by technology such as the computer. Fees for all services, rather than commissions for sales, may be another approach to improving payoffs in this regard.

Agents will also need more sophisticated tools for presentations. Again, technology may be helpful in this function. For instance, in addition to better product illustrations or numerical needs analyses, technical information such as tax, legal, and business alternatives may be made available to the agents from computer-accessible data banks. Agents may then concentrate on an area only agents can do well—creating the emotional impetus to buy.

All-lines sales might also enhance agent income and serve as prospecting tools. But other industries (property and casualty insurers, securities brokers, and banks) are also diversifying into life insurance as an aid to their own businesses, thus increasing competitive pressures. While such expansions have obvious potential synergistic benefits, each also brings at least some of the special difficulties of the new lines. The result, at least in some cases, may be to end up with the same, or perhaps new problems.

Agent selection, training, psychological and monetary motivation, guidance, and education will be more critical to company success than ever before. Thus, for instance, in the area of recruiting, long-term efforts may be necessary to incorporate a well-founded positive image of the insurance sales career into the early consciousness of youth. Attempts must also be made to retain more of the good recruits. Perhaps this can be done by easing the stress on the new agent, emphasizing service in the first year rather than attempting to provide heavy incentives and validation requirements for selling a highly technical, consumer-resistant product.[23]

Functionalized and specialized management and sales support will be more necessary as the marketplace becomes more complex, sophisticated, and service-oriented. Greater cross-experimentation between the streamlined controls of the branch managerial system and the bottom line flair of an entrepreneurial general agent setting will also be necessary. And, in many cases, companies may continue to move beyond such managerial systems into PPGA arrangements to save on management and agent develop-

[23] "Factors Relating to Salesman Turnover," Research Report 1972-11, LIMRA, The Conference Board.

ment expenses, and, even beyond that, into selling totally through brokerage arrangements. More companies may try to balance several such arrangements at the same time.

Primarily as a result of the inflationary and competitive environment, and spurred by "technological" efficiencies, the forms of outlets for the distribution of life and health insurance are likely to become even more varied, with the agent becoming increasingly vulnerable, though still at the heart of the total system. Experimentation and change, particularly in a technological sense, are likely to flourish as companies attempt to capture (or retain) the insurance market. The evolving forms, particularly on a micro level, will likely depend on markets served. Thus, the poor, the aged, and the young are likely to be served mostly by the government; working people are likely to obtain their coverages from mass outlets like group and direct response, and excess amounts should continue to be the province of the agent. Overlaps will undoubtedly persist, both between and within these groups, with technology likely to play an ever-increasing role in providing economic security.

Index

A

B

C

D

E

F

G

J

K

L

N

O

P

Q

R

S

T

XYZ